MEASURING THE EFFECTS OF RACISM

MEASURING THE EFFECTS OF RACISM

GUIDELINES FOR THE ASSESSMENT AND TREATMENT OF RACE-BASED TRAUMATIC STRESS INJURY

Robert T. Carter and Alex L. Pieterse

COLUMBIA UNIVERSITY PRESS   NEW YORK

Columbia University Press gratefully acknowledges the generous support for this book provided by Publisher's Circle member Tony Tripodi.

COLUMBIA UNIVERSITY PRESS
Publishers Since 1893
New York   Chichester, West Sussex
cup.columbia.edu

Library of Congress Cataloging-in-Publication Data
Names: Carter, Robert T., 1948– author. | Pieterse, Alex L., author.
Title: Measuring the effects of racism : guidelines for the assessment
    and treatment of race-based traumatic stress injury /
    Robert T. Carter and Alex L. Pieterse.
Description: First. | New York : Columbia University Press, 2020. |
    Includes bibliographical references and index.
Identifiers: LCCN 2019056075 (print) | LCCN 2019056076 (ebook) |
    ISBN 9780231193061 (cloth) | ISBN 9780231193078 (trade paperback) |
    ISBN 9780231550130 (ebook)
Subjects: LCSH: Cultural psychiatry. | Psychiatry, Transcultural.
Classification: LCC RC455.4.E8 C372 2020 (print) | LCC RC455.4.E8
    (ebook) | DDC 362.2—dc23
LC record available at https://lccn.loc.gov/2019056075
LC ebook record available at https://lccn.loc.gov/2019056076

CONTENTS

PART III WHAT TO DO WITH WHAT WE KNOW: PRACTICE APPLICATIONS

ACKNOWLEDGMENTS

WE ARE PLEASED AND HONORED to complete *Measuring the Effects of Racism* and describe how our work on race-based traumatic stress began. We begin by sharing the experiences that led the first author (Carter) to develop the model of race-based traumatic stress injury because we think the path that led to our work in trauma is unusual and atypical.

We suspect that many people usually begin doing trauma work through their clinical practice and training. But that was not the first author's path; instead, it was through legal and psychological assessment work (mostly as an expert witness) in cases of biracial custody, equity issues in school systems' racial desegregation plans, and racial discrimination and harassment in schools, the workplace, and in consumer racial profiling. As scholars and researchers during the early phases of our work, we were focused on racial-cultural issues. It was that research emphasis, which people thought would be beneficial in expert witness and consultation activities, that resulted in Carter being asked to engage in what ultimately resulted in a consideration of how mental health and legal professionals might deal with targets of race-based acts and how to help them seek relief.

For help in the assessment of psychological harm in some of the legal cases, we turned to the *DSM* and the mental health literature to try to account for emotional effects of racism. We learned that the literature offered little or no help, and we were left with standard disorders. As we learned, PTSD was an inappropriate diagnosis because the core criteria could not be met. With this revelation, we eventually began to think about how, or if, racial encounters were related to trauma. In collaboration with Janet E. Helms, Alex Pieterse, and others, the first author began to talk about racial trauma in a series of presentations and published articles.

For us, the evidence from these experiences was growing and that standard and traditional approaches to treating or recognizing trauma did not include racial experiences. So we wondered if it were possible that racial trauma could be identified through psychological research; if so, then maybe it could also be used in legal efforts to redress racial injuries perpetrated by individuals, organizations, and social systems. The question led to the research program described in the book and the Race-Based Traumatic Stress Symptom Scale. The path was an unusual one, as there were several different types of experiences that came together to form our current focus. The publication of our scales allows us to share our methods and procedures with colleagues. We hope those concerned with the law, will share the vision we have about race and how it impacts people psychologically and emotionally—something that had not been the case in the past.

The damage caused by racism has nuances reflected in race-based traumatic stress injury. And while all who are exposed to such stress do not develop psychological symptoms, some who are injured need avenues of redress, recognition, and healing. We hope that the publication of this book will influence future assessments, recognition, and responsiveness to individuals experiencing racial trauma.

We would like to thank Stephen Wesley of Columbia University Press for his support and patience through this process, and foremost for his responsiveness to the subject matter. Columbia University Press has proven to be an innovative proponent with a willingness to provide a platform for new and unconventional work, acknowledging the importance of new ideas in our complex world. We thank Patricia Bower and Kelly Blewster for their careful and detailed editing of the manuscript, and our graduate assistants, Ramon Garcia, Katheryn Roberson, and Lynsay Paiko, for their assistance in searching the literature.

We also thank our families for their support and patience while we were busy with this effort: Adrienne Carter, for her unswerving presence and encouragement; Portia, Themba, Luyanda, and Thandise Pieterse for their patience and understanding. To our colleagues and former research team members, many of whom are noted in the citations in the book, but also to those who are not, thank you for the years of hard work and effort on the many projects we conducted together. Finally, we thank our clients and patients who have shared their stories of racial trauma with us, and who have trusted that we would facilitate and provide the recognition and validation that they deserve.

INTRODUCTION

RACE AND RACISM ARE INTEGRAL elements of American society, structural aspects without which the United States (and its predecessor colonies) could not function well or be prosperous. Much of the country's political and social activity has been dedicated to establishing a racial caste system and maintaining it at all costs.[1] Racism in the New World colonies and, later, in the United States did not begin as a system of racial oppression, a point that is a matter of debate among scholars; rather, some contend that it evolved over time and later was justified to support its continuation. Others note that Africans and Native Americans were from the outset considered and treated as inferior people. In the early years of the colonies, people who provided labor were indentured servants, and people of all colors and religious backgrounds held the status of servant.[2] Various historians tell different stories of the history of race and racism within America, but there are some important distinctions to make for the full story to be told. Lerone Bennett Jr. states that "for two hundred years black, brown, and yellow men and women were held in bondage in America."[3] George Marsh Fredrickson argues that racism (i.e., unequal status between racial groups) as a conscious belief and an ideology should be distinguished from prejudice since prejudice is a matter of feeling but discrimination is based on action.[4] He contends that the explicit or conscious forms of racism that characterized the nineteenth and twentieth centuries differ from what he calls implicit or societal racism, which is based on actual social relations and was dominant in the eighteenth century. For Fredrickson, when one racial group treats the other as inferior, even in the absence of any conscious belief, it is still racism. And societal racism can exist long after the rationale has been discredited.

Europeans are said to have had a negative perception of Africans based on contact with Africa in the fifteenth century and on assumptions made about the difference in physical appearance and cultural practices between White Europeans and Black Africans.[5] Blackness was equated with uncivilized people, and the color black was associated with evil in the language and customs of England. Ignored in these early contacts was the rich and long history of civilization and culture that existed in Africa before these encounters.[6] Africans were not savages; they and other people (e.g., in South America and Asia) had lifestyles and cultural practices distinct from those of Europe.[7]

The arrival of Europeans in the New World resulted in the subjugation of the Native people, referred to as "Indians" by the European explorers. During the colonial period of 1492–1776, Native Americans were enslaved by explorers and colonists; however, Native American slaves succumbed to illness and escaped in large numbers; they were subsequently replaced by Africans brought to America via the slave trade.[8] Between 1619 and 1649, a small number of Africans were introduced into Virginia as "servants. Some, and perhaps most, of these early arrivals were freed after a limited term of service."[9] James Horton and Lois Horton observe that the "Africans brought to Jamestown in the early seventeenth century were bound laborers, not all were treated as slaves. . . . During the early colonial period, American concepts about race, slavery, and standards for race relations were still being formulated and were not yet as fixed as they would become in the eighteenth century."[10]

There is an ongoing debate as to the status of Africans in the colonies, specifically whether Africans in the early colonial period in North America were treated as slaves or servants, and the precise factors contributing to their eventual nonhuman status is also a matter of debate. Some contend that international law meant that Africans were slaves regardless of where they were taken; others argue that race prejudice combined with physical differences are the determining factors that sealed the fate of Africans. From another perspective, it is suggested that Africans were segregated from the colonists, and it was this that made their enslavement possible.[11]

Nevertheless, societal racism—the conviction that Africans and people of color in general were inferior because of their race and should be treated accordingly—held sway from the early seventeenth century until an ideological justification to maintain slavery and establish a system of racism was instituted in the nineteenth century.[12] That people of African descent (hereafter

referred to as Blacks) were inferior was taken for granted and required no justification in the early years of the colonies. Societal racism operated without
an explicitly stated ideological rationale for well over one hundred years, until
the late eighteenth century, when a few citizens of the new United States of
America argued that the nation should live up to its principles of equality
and abolish slavery and all it represented. In response, supporters of the status quo provided a justification that Fredrickson describes as "explicit racism, a public ideology based on the doctrinaire conception of the black man
as a natural underling developed therefore directly out of the need to defend
slavery against nineteenth-century humanitarianism."[13] This racist ideology
became ascendant toward the end of the nineteenth century, when it was
justified by scientific views of race that replaced the religious justifications
of the past.[14] During this time the emerging discipline of psychology built
on the earlier notions of the biological inferiority of Blacks (see Jefferson's
1784 *Notes on the State of Virginia*) by providing empirical support for the
apparent intellectual inferiority of Blacks, thereby bolstering the work of anthropologists who had already outlined a scientific racial hierarchy that would
in time fuel the eugenics movement.[15] This racist ideology both contributed
to and was energized by the effort in the South to establish legal segregation
and continue oppression of Blacks well after the order of emancipation was
signed by President Abraham Lincoln in 1863.

It is clear that the long and ongoing story of American racism, "first as a
way of life (societal racism) and then as a system of thought (explicit racism),"[16]
is still being enacted.[17] That racial ideas and feelings have shifted and changed
over time is clear, but many would argue that the racial arrangement of White
domination and subjection of people of color that marks the beginning of
the nation is essentially unchanged at its core.[18] It is also clear that "America . . . was not born racist; it became so gradually as the result of a series of
crimes against black humanity [and other people of color] that stemmed primarily from selfishness, greed, and the pursuit of privilege."[19]

There is evidence that, since about 2001, the United States has seen a rise
in more overt racial tensions and official support of Whites and White racial
causes. This is reflected in actions taken by the Trump administration and
his appointees and in other events that show how race continues to be a central and disturbing feature of U.S. society. Some would argue that racism
has saturated the society, though it sometimes fades from clear view and at
other times assumes a more dominant position. To illustrate, in August 2017
Sari Horwitz and Emma Brown, writing in the *Washington Post*, reported

that the Justice Department, under the new leadership of Jeff Sessions, the U.S. attorney general, was "planning a new project to investigate and sue universities over affirmative action admissions policies they determine discriminate against white applicants."[20] This plan, which has since been put into action, is just the latest in a long history of attempts to maintain White dominance in the United States. There was a notion that—with the election of a Black man, Barack Obama, as president in 2008 and 2012—race had become less salient and the issues and concerns of people regarding race and racism had diminished. Yet evidence to the contrary has emerged to show that race, racial inequality, and racism remain central factors in the social and political lives of the U.S. population and that consideration of race still divides the country.

Some cite as evidence the role of race in the election of Donald Trump as the forty-fifth president of the United States: "Our analysis . . . indicates that Donald Trump successfully leveraged existing resentment towards African Americans in combination with emerging fears of increased racial diversity in America to reshape the presidential electorate."[21] Trump was explicit about his thoughts regarding people of color and immigrants (mostly of color) and played to Whites' negative racial attitudes to build support for his candidacy. Some of the actions taken by his administration and his comments toward White nationalists (e.g., following the Charlottesville, Virginia, protests of August 2017) fuel fear that he harbors hostility toward people of color. E. J. Dionne and colleagues note that "studies suggest that to ignore or downplay the role of race and immigration in creating the Trump coalition is to be willfully blind to the obvious. . . . It also requires ignoring strong racial undercurrents on the websites of the far right, including an increasingly open embrace of white supremacy."[22] In starker terms, some suggest that the election of Donald Trump was in part a reflection of the fear that Whites hold of Blacks and other people of color, a fear that for many is not explicit or even acknowledged. Ta-Nehisi Coates states:

> I think the old fear of Good Negro Government has much explanatory power for what might seem a shocking turn—the election of Donald Trump. It has been said that the first black presidency was mostly "symbolic," a dismissal that deeply underestimates the power of symbols. Symbols don't just represent reality but can become tools to change it. The symbol of Barack Obama's presidency—that whiteness was no longer strong enough to prevent peons from taking up residency in the castle—assaulted

the most deeply rooted notions of white supremacy and instilled fear in its adherents and adversaries. And it was that fear that gave the symbols Donald Trump deployed—the symbols of racism—enough potency to make him president, and thus put him in position to injure the world.[23]

Indeed, empirical data support the role of racism within voting patterns of the 2016 election. Brian Schaffner, Matthew Macwilliams, and Tatishe Nteta find that among voters strongly affiliated with being White, being told that people of color would outnumber Whites by 2042 resulted in these individuals being more likely to support and vote for Donald Trump.[24] Some conclude that a main driving force of President Trump's election and postelection support has been racial resentment on the part of Whites. As the first year of Trump's presidency came to a close, the social commentator and journalist German Lopez wrote, "Economic anxiety isn't driving racial resentment; rather, racial resentment is driving economic anxiety. . . . Racial resentment is the biggest predictor of white vulnerability among white millennials. Economic variables like education, income and employment made a negligible difference."[25]

The evidence therefore suggests that the current political reality has its roots in the past and that race continues to be powerful in shaping American society, just as it was when the foundations of the United States were being laid many centuries ago. Unlike other countries, the United States has been unable to attend to or acknowledge the impact of its racial history. South Africa and Canada also carry shameful histories surrounding race, but they have used processes such as truth and reconciliation commissions to help address and take responsibility for their systems of racial oppression in an effort to change the present and the future. In 2017 the Canadian government settled a legal action by indigenous people whose children had been removed from them and placed in foster homes and boarding schools. The government admitted to its actions and agreed to pay damages and set up systems to remedy the harm as much as possible and to ensure that similar actions do not occur in the future. As Ian Austen reported in the *New York Times*, "For decades, Canadian social workers forcibly separated indigenous children from their families, putting them up for adoption to nonnative families in Canada and around the world. On Friday the Canadian government took the step to make amends for that adoption program, which began in the 1960s and lasted till the 1980s, by agreeing to pay 750 million in Canadian dollars in legal settlement."[26] In stark contrast, in the United States we debate the meaning of statues honoring leaders of the Confederacy. An article on the BBC website states:

> It has been 150 years since the last shots were fired in the U.S. Civil war, but a debate still rages over how history will remember the losing side. Hundreds of statues dedicated to the Confederacy exist all throughout the Unites States, and often serve as an offensive reminder of American's history of slavery and racial oppression. Recent decisions by local governments to remove those memorials have triggered a backlash from a vocal group of Americans who see their removal as an attempt to subvert U.S. history and southern culture.[27]

Although race continues to be a profound and provocative aspect of the American experience, what receives less attention are the ways in which people are racially oppressed,[28] as well as the harm that such practices bring to those unable to prevent the negative outcomes associated with segregated educational systems and housing, unequal employment opportunities, constant surveillance of non-White communities by law enforcement, and mass incarceration of Blacks and Latinos/as. Throughout 2019, leading into the presidential election of 2020, Trump has fanned the flames of racism with a series of comments, actions, and statements.[29] The *Atlantic* devoted an entire issue—titled "An Oral History of Trump's Bigotry"—to the topic.[30] Systemic racism has been a part of North American society for centuries, initially as slavery and racial segregation and today as overt and covert practices of racial discrimination. In the mid-twentieth century, traditional or old-fashioned (legally sanctioned) racism abated somewhat (for a short time) and then was reasserted in various forms disguised as focusing on something other than race—social class or cultural disadvantage.[31] Now, in the twenty-first century, issues of racism in many areas of everyday life have resurfaced, and overt expressions of racial hostility are again reflected in national and local media coverage and other sources (i.e., court decisions and litigation). Racism has recently been implicated in law enforcement, higher education, health care, housing, and employment. For example, consider the events regarding racist comments, symbols, and songs on college campuses, and protests by racial-minority college and university students occurring across the country.[32] There has been a weakening of voting rights for racial minorities;[33] many people of color continue to encounter racial discrimination in housing;[34] at least twenty-six African American men and women have received violently unequal treatment by law enforcement authorities in New York, Cleveland, Ferguson, Baltimore, Tulsa, and other cities;[35] and awareness continues to grow regarding the persistent disparities in treatment of racial minorities and immigrants in the health care, civic engagement, and criminal justice systems.[36]

It has fallen to those who contend that racial inequality is harmful to document the various ways in which injustice affects the physical and psychological well-being of individuals and groups. In the twentieth and twenty-first centuries, researchers have shown through empirical investigations how the ideology of racism and its accompanying behavioral manifestation—racial discrimination—affect psychological functioning. What has emerged from the effort, which we describe in more detail in this volume, is an approach for understanding, assessing, measuring, and treating the psychological effects of racism. We document the presence of race-based traumatic stress (RBTS) as racial trauma and show how mental health professionals can measure the harm or injuries from racism.

Empirical evidence has accumulated over several decades documenting the psychological and emotional effects of racism and racial discrimination. In general, researchers have found that people who are exposed to racism experience stress[37] and have adverse health outcomes such as depression, anxiety, and hypertension.[38] It is therefore imperative that a more complete understanding of the health effects of racism and racial discrimination be established. The purpose of this book is to examine the psychological and emotional responses to racism, which are discussed as a form of oppression.

Many scholars describe oppression as a system in which the dominant group uses its power to restrict the subordinate group's access to resources, resulting in gross systematic disparities.[39] Oppression is a process of dehumanization that creates social and physical isolation, lack of access to all types of resources, and blocked opportunities. In North America, people of color (i.e., historically disenfranchised Black, Native, Hispanic, Asian American, and other groups) have been longstanding targets of oppression,[40] with racism the most prevalent contributing factor in health disparities and social inequality between Whites and people of color.[41] Evidence from integrative reviews and meta-analyses indicate that exposure to racism and racial discrimination is negatively associated with psychological health and positively associated with psychological and physical distress.[42]

Given the presence of racism in society, valid and sound conceptual models, measures, and procedures that access the emotional outcomes specific to race and racism are needed. While various useful instruments exist to measure the stress from racism,[43] many capture only the frequency and magnitude of the stressors and do not determine whether one's reactions reflect RBTS as racial trauma.

Robert T. Carter's conceptualization of RBTS injury as racial trauma links emotional reactions to a specific encounter with racism or racial discrimination, showing the ways in which different dimensions of racism may generate different kinds of stress responses, including traumatic reactions.[44]

This volume is designed to acquaint the reader with the various aspects of the models and measures associated with RBTS as racial trauma. We guide the reader through illustrations of racial encounters that have occurred in stores, housing complexes, schools, and workplaces to show instances of racial discrimination and to highlight how the model of racial trauma evolved and is applied to these complex situations. To illustrate, consider Mark, a healthy, middle-class African American man in his late twenties. He worked as a salesman in a retail store for a few years. During his employment in the store, Mark alleges that he was denied time off, given menial assignments (e.g., mopping), and spoken to in a demeaning manner by his store manager, treatment that was not experienced by other employees. In addition, he claims he was required to ensure that Black customers did not steal anything. He was disturbed and upset by this treatment and the tasks he was asked to perform. Mark states that he followed documented and published procedures to file several complaints against his manager during his employment. Mark alleges that his store manager retaliated by threatening to fire him. He endured the mistreatment and threats of termination because he needed the job. He was fired nevertheless. We outline the psychological implications of experiences like those encountered by Mark, herein understood as RBTS, and we provide clinicians a way of assessing and responding to those experiences in a manner that is effective and therapeutic.

The book is organized into three parts. In the first, we review what we know about racism and health by addressing the use of common terms and concepts, including *race, mental health, people of color, culture,* and *racism.* We discuss and address research associated with the concepts of stress and trauma and present a selective review of the literature on discrimination and race-related stress and its mental health effects. We also define classes of racial encounters that are used to connect those encounters with mental health effects. Finally, we explore individual and contextually based variables like socioeconomic status, race-related coping, and racial identity ego statuses that account for the various ways in which individuals and groups respond to racial stress and trauma.

The second part focuses on what we need to know about racial trauma and describes the framework of RBTS, including empirical evidence to support the model. The chapters provide an assessment procedure for RBTS. We describe the Race-Based Traumatic Stress Symptom Scale, review its application and use, and show the research evidence that has been generated to support the instrument. We also discuss the utility of an interview schedule that accompanies the RBTSSS and introduce a short-form version of the RBTSSS.

The last part of the book focuses on what mental health professionals must do for clients dealing with racial trauma. We discuss the clinical utility of the RBTS, offer guidelines for treating RBTS as racial trauma, and provide recommendations for practice. We discuss forensic applications and offer strategies for testimony in legal settings and assessment. Case illustrations and vignettes are used to highlight the clinical utility of the RBTS model. We conclude by addressing the training of mental health professions for dealing with racial trauma, and discussing emerging issues for prevention and policy.

We believe that you will find this volume to be a critical and urgent addition to the developing literature on the psychological impact of experiences of racism and racial trauma.

PART ONE

WHAT WE KNOW ABOUT RACISM AND STRESS

1

TERMS AND CONCEPTS DEFINED

MANY OF THE TERMS we use to discuss racism and its impacts on individuals and society have multiple meanings and connotations, both in scholarship and in everyday language. This book joins a wide body of literature directed at a varied audience, so we want to start by defining the terms we use frequently, including *race, racism, racial discrimination, racial identity, stress, trauma, culture,* and *people of color.* Since our central theme involves racism, we will spend more time discussing how it has been and is defined. Our discussion highlights what some definitions fail to convey about racism; many do not offer a way to connect psychological and emotional effects to racial incidents.

First, though, we define terms that are not interchangeable, that have clear and distinct meanings. We define *mental health professionals* to mean people trained in the disciplines of psychology, social work, education, psychiatry, or counseling, as well as related disciplines such as nursing or public health. A key notion in the term is *mental health.* For most disciplines, it is defined as the absence of disease or psychiatric disorder.[1] Others argue that there is a continuum from healthy functioning to impairment, and diminished mental health is exemplified by a reduced ability to meet the demands of daily living, of work, or of providing for one's self and one's family. The surgeon general's 2001 report on mental health notes that it involves functioning successfully so that one is able to perform activities, maintain personal and family relationships, adapt to situations, and handle adversity effectively.[2] Failing to function well hinders the performance of life activities, and personal relationships are compromised. Racial-cultural scholars critique the traditional definition of mental health by pointing out that "traditional Western mental health models have failed to set standards that would validate the experiences of black [and other] Americans [of color] who live in a racist environment."[3]

The observation that people of color have been overlooked points to the existence of social and economic structures, laws, and customs that prefer and make White culture normative and that therefore hinder and block the presumed markers for mental health that are more representative of people of color.[4] The White-normative perspective promotes the idea that people of color have not evolved unique cultural behaviors and patterns that have aided in their resistance and adaptation to racially hostile societal structures. Moreover, the White-normative view ignores the fact that people of color have established their own organizations and institutions that reflect and support their psychological health and well-being.[5] From this perspective, surviving and adapting to a racially hostile community, extending the family system beyond biological ties, being present-oriented, and valuing group interests over those of the individual are factors that contribute to the mental health of people of color. The most inclusive definition of mental health, offered by the World Health Organization (WHO), builds on the WHO's definition of *health*—"a state of complete physical, mental and social well-being and not merely the absence of disease or infirmity"—by defining mental health as "a state of well-being in which every individual realizes his or her own potential, can cope with the normal stresses of life, can work productively and fruitfully, and is able to make a contribution to her or his community."[6]

RACE

Race is defined as a social construction in which people in the United States are identified by their skin color, language, and physical features and are grouped and ranked into distinct sociopolitical groups with different degrees of access and opportunity within the larger social structure.[7] The groups include Whites, people of color, and biracial individuals who have "at least one parent who has been classified as a racial minority."[8] *People of color* refers to historically disenfranchised Americans, Black/African, Hispanic/Latino/Latina, Asian/Pacific Islanders, Native American/Indigenous Indian, and biracial people.

Racial group rankings are used in multiracial societies to distribute social rewards, economic resources, and access and opportunity in general.[9] Racial groups in the United States and the North American colonies were socially and legally separated for centuries and therefore were able to sustain distinct cultural patterns and preferences, so race is also associated with a group's distinct culture and values. Thus, American racial-cultural groups differ not only in terms of skin color but also in their cultural practices, worldviews, and values.[10]

RACIAL AND CULTURAL DIFFERENCES

Culture is defined as a system of meaning with values, norms, behaviors, language, and history that is passed on from one generation to the next through socialization and participation in the group's organizations and institutions.[11] Culture is reflected in the existential principles endorsed or followed by a group in terms of its view of human nature (evil/good/mixed), relationships to nature (harmony/master/subjection), sense of time (past/future/present), social relationships (follow elders/group-based/individual), forms of self-expression (emotional/contemplative/actions-based), and other factors.[12]

These principles serve as guides to how societies are formed and organized and how their members' behaviors are promoted and valued, and they undergird members' beliefs and rituals. A cultural group that holds that people exist both as substance and as spirits, for example, will embrace different practices than a group that does not believe in nonmaterial existence.

Elements of American culture dictate people's belief systems, behaviors, and expectations, including, to some extent, those of people who have been held apart from the mainstream of society. American culture has evolved from White ethnic (i.e., country and culture of origin) values and beliefs,[13] and it dominates the cultural and social landscape. Some of the existential principles of White American culture, according to Robert T. Carter[14] and Edward Stewart and Milton Bennett,[15] endorse the following propositions: (a) that individualism expressed through personal preferences is the valued form of social relations; (b) that self-expression reflected in a combination of conformity to social expectations and achievement of goals based on external criteria (e.g., school grades, good job) is most valued; (c) that social structures should be grounded in authority and power that is hierarchical and communication patterns that are verbal and valued only if standard English is used; (d) that the time focus is future-oriented; (e) that values about human nature derive from Judeo-Christian religious systems; (f) that the ideal family structure includes only immediate (nuclear) members; and (g) that standards for music, beauty, and social traditions (e.g., holidays, monuments) are de-rived from European cultural traditions and values.

We understand health, both physical and mental, through the lens of our cultural worldview, and this interpretation is embedded in our professions and institutions. Researchers have shown that cultural beliefs about what mental illness is affect its course and treatment. In mental health, culture is often viewed from traditional assumptions.[16] For White Americans, a person with schizophrenia is seen as "crazy," with no hope for recovery, whereas in other countries he or she might be viewed as having a temporary condition that can be addressed.[17] People with schizophrenia often do better in devel-oping countries than in North America.[18] Cultural variation in the under-standing of mental illness exists even within the United States, as Schatell notes:

> A 2010 study conducted in inner-city Hartford, Conn., found that European-Americans tended to express beliefs about mental illness that were aligned with the biomedical perspectives on disease. In contrast, Latino and African-American study participants more commonly emphasized "non-biomedical interpretations" of mental illness symptoms—meaning that they focused more on spirituality, moral character and social explanations for mental illness.[19]

Race and culture also influence epidemiological findings, as noted by the fact that Black African Americans are more often diagnosed with schizophre-nia and are less often seen as having affective disorders.[20] Some researchers argue that this diagnostic pattern reflects cultural bias on the part of many clinicians (irrespective of racial-cultural group membership), who are social-ized and taught during their professional training to see people of color and Blacks as more disturbed than Whites.[21]

The overwhelming majority of research studies draw conclusions that are believed to apply across racial-cultural groups—that is, to be universal when participants in the studies are members of the majority group. Thus, the ex-pressions of normality and illness found in clinical and nonclinical popula-tions of the majority race and culture are assumed to be true of all people irrespective of race, culture, or ethnicity. Evidence to the contrary has been mostly ignored or de-emphasized.[22] Research evidence has made it clear that universal categories of mental illness (e.g., depression) no longer are appro-priate or valid. Rather, the patterns of onset and duration and even the nature and clustering of specific symptoms vary widely across racial and cultural groups.[23] For instance, Latino/a and Asian patients are more likely to express psychological distress in the form of physical or somatic complaints, including dizziness and tiredness. If a health provider does not probe the patient to describe his emotional state, the patient may go untreated for an underlying mental health condition.[24]

Variation can also be found in how people of color view and understand the self. Among many Asian cultures the self is interdependent,[25] whereas in dominant North American cultural practices the self is viewed as independent and located within the individual. Construals of the self have significant implications for social behavior, emotional expression, and other aspects of psychological functioning.[26] Variation exists in this pattern among different racial-cultural groups,[27] and how one constructs a personal identity is understood to be a product of cultural understandings of the self.[28] Regardless of culture, we are primarily human beings and therefore share physiological and neurochemical systems. Still, although some common expressions of emotion do seem to characterize human experience, subjective meaning influences those expressions, and they vary by race and culture.

Differences are easy to see when people speak another language and wear distinctive clothes. Variations—for instance in thinking and in interpersonal relationships—are more difficult to understand when greater similarity is perceived between groups. It is hard to discern racial and cultural variation within the United States because many groups of Americans have been in the society for centuries and have adapted to but not integrated into the mainstream culture. Nevertheless, cultural and racial differences exist. For instance, all members of racial groups vary in how they understand themselves as racial beings—that is, in their psychological orientation to their racial group membership.

RACIAL IDENTITY

Race refers to one's presumed social demographic (skin-color group) and cultural group.[29] When a person indicates that their race has meaning, this is thought to reflect their *race identity*, sometimes called *racial identity*. As the term is typically used, *race* has social implications, and people infer psychological meaning from sociodemographic group membership. When used in this way, *race* has no psychological meaning. Rather, the psychological meaning of the term is reflected in how one thinks about their racial group member-ship. The psychological meaning a person attributes to their racial group has been defined as *racial identity status*, or one's psychological orientation to their race. Racial group members' psychological orientation to their race may vary within and between racial groups.[30]

Discussion of racial identity, which has appeared in the psychological lit-erature for more than forty-five years,[31] provides a framework for under-standing psychological processes associated with racial categorization and racism and their influence on human development and behavior. To date, racial identity models and measures have been developed and used in em-pirical research for all racial groups. Whereas models created for non-Hispanic Whites are typically characterized by the abandonment of racism and the development of a nonracist identity, models for people of color capture a pro-cess characterized by the abandonment of reliance on White culture for self-definition or acceptance, and the development of a positive racial iden-tity as a member of a nondominant racial group.[32] However, patterns of reso-lution are similar across racial groups. We briefly describe models created for Whites and people of color (historically disenfranchised Americans). We summarize the statuses of racial consciousness according to theory for Whites (contact, disintegration, reintegration, pseudo-independence, immersion/em-ersion, and autonomy) and people of color (conformity/pre-encounter, dis-sonance/encounter, immersion/emersion, and internalization). The least mature and more externally derived racial identity status attitudes are con-tact (Whites), conformity (Asians, Native Americans, and Hispanics), and pre-encounter (Blacks), and are associated with the denial of racism or en-dorsement of a color-blind worldview. Disintegration (Whites), dissonance (Asians, Native Americans, and Hispanics), and encounter (Blacks) are also externally defined statuses characterized by conflict or confusion about the meaning of one's race, while reintegration and pseudo-independence (Whites) and immersion/emersion (Asians, Native Americans, Hispanics, and Blacks) status attitudes are characterized by in-racial-group idealization and immer-sion and active out-racial-group rejection. The more mature and internally derived racial identity status attitudes are internalization (Asians, Native Americans, Hispanics, and Blacks) and autonomy (Whites), which are gen-erally associated with resolution of conflict regarding racial differences, ac-ceptance of race and of self as a racial being, and development of a racial identity that is not based on notions of inferiority or supremacy.[33] We now turn to definitions of racism that have emerged over time.

RACISM

Definitions of *racism* vary widely across academic and popular literature. More recently, definitions tend to favor an ahistorical conceptualization that locates racism primarily within the attitudes, beliefs, and behaviors of an individual or of particular groups. It is important to highlight the ways in which the definitions of racism locate its focus on beliefs and attitudes or abstract ideas. A review of the various terms associated with racism is important because the terms reflect how one defines the nature of racism. To illustrate, terms such as *hate, bias,* and *prejudice* emphasize a person's individual attitudes, while *nationalism, xenophobia,* and *White nationalism* relate to political ideologies. Other definitions in the scholarly literature emphasize behavioral and rational processes that are captured by phrases such as *modern racism, symbolic racism,* and *aversive racism.* These references center on beliefs held by Whites that discrimination is a phenomenon from the past, and they focus on feelings of ambivalence between negative attitudes toward Blacks and a rational endorsement of fairness and egalitarian attitudes.[34]

From one perspective, a key notion associated with these ways of defining racism is the emphasis on personal character as opposed to systemic processes. More important is the fact that these definitions overlook how the group in power attaches meaning to its behavior by stating what is acceptable and what is not. In this way it determines if or when a group or its members fail to meet the standards of good character or appropriate behavior. Thus, the rational approach to racism "makes it easy to maintain one's superior status without opening one's self to accusations of racism."[35] Nevertheless, the definitions focus on Whites' beliefs about their social status and their view that Blacks and other people of color must earn their social status and must do so without preferential treatment. As we point out in the introduction, Whites' resentment toward people of color reflects the notion that no adjustments should be made for past racial oppression. There is little in the rational and logical definitions of racism that points to a system of oppression or to the imposition of beliefs and values. More important, there is no information in these definitions on the relationship between racism and mental health.

Several definitions of racism strive to explicate the systemic dynamics of domination and oppression embedded within the United States' sociohistorical context. For instance, prior to the 1960s, White racism was not recognized or acknowledged, even though slavery had existed and was justified and supported during the seventeenth, eighteenth, and nineteenth centuries. Joe Feagin writes, "In describing the white-on-black oppression that has persisted from the seventeenth century to the present day[,] I use . . . the term 'systemic racism,' which I consider the best overview term for the centuries-old-oppression."[36] He defines racism as a system that operates as a form of oppression. Few others have done so.

The social unrest of the 1960s led to the recognition that White racism matters and that it bears a direct effect on people of color. The belief in the inferiority of Blacks and other people of color had been taken for granted and for over three centuries was thought to be self-evident. The system of racial oppression was rationalized as "in the best interest of" the lesser or disadvantaged people. The existence of White racism was not formally accepted until the late 1960s. The term was introduced by the Kerner Commission Report on Racial Unrest,[37] which states:

> White racism is essentially responsible for the explosive mixture which has been accumulating in our cities since the end of World War II; among the ingredients . . . are pervasive discrimination and segregation in employment, education and housing . . . Black in-migration and White exodus . . . creating a crisis in deteriorating facilities and services and unmet needs in . . . the Black ghettos where segregation and poverty . . . converge to destroy opportunity and enforce failure.[38]

Nevertheless, since its introduction into our language and everyday parlance, the term *racism* has been used and defined in many different ways.

David Williams and Ruth Williams-Morris describe racism as an organized system that leads to the subjugation of some human groups relative to others.[39] They contend that such systems of subordination reflect ideas of inferiority and cultural deprivation that rank and categorize groups. The ranking of a group's worth relative to that of other groups supports and justifies the development of negative beliefs and attitudes toward the out-group. The negative beliefs generate differential treatment of out-group members (people of color) by both individuals and the social institutions of the in-group (White Americans). Williams and Williams-Morris emphasize the systemic or institutional aspects of actions and beliefs rather than individual behaviors and attitudes. Rodney Clark and colleagues view racism as "beliefs, attitudes, institutional arrangements, and acts that tend to denigrate individuals or groups because of phenotypic characteristics."[40] Hussein Abdilahi Bulhan also sees racism as a form of oppression based in racial categorization and a system of domination that designates one group superior and the others inferior.[41] Bulhan suggests, though not in specific terms, that people of color are harmed by such treatment because oppression is a form of violence that can be internalized.

This definition of racism begins to establish a possible conceptual link between racism and specific mental health effects, but the reference to the violence of oppression is so broad that it fails to provide a foundation for linking racism to particular mental health outcomes. While the definitions discussed so far capture important elements of racism, in general they do not convey a way to connect particular experiences to mental health effects, nor are the systemic aspects of racism made clear.

Michael Omi and Howard Winant assert that the meanings surrounding race and racism are reflected in social relationships determined by the historical context and the political climate at a particular time in history.[42] This perspective helps us understand the variations in meaning attributed to racism over time. For Omi and Winant, race is an organizing principle of social relations at the micro (individual) and macro (collective) levels. They coined the term *racial formation* to capture the process of how racial meaning is shaped and altered to determine social relationships. This construction is useful for comprehending the central and changing nature of racism, but it does not provide a connection between racism or racial formations and psychological functioning. Omi and Winant focus primarily on racism in a political and historical context somewhat removed from the direct reactions of individuals to encounters with racism.

Chalmer Thompson and Helen Neville[43] agree with the structural emphasis presented by Williams and Williams-Morris[44] and add a discussion of how racism affects the mental health of both people of color and Whites. For these scholars, racism is structural and ideological and operates on individual, institutional, and cultural levels. Additionally, Thompson and Neville suggest that racism has changed in its form and application over time, shifting from overt, legally sanctioned acts of violence, discrimination, harassment, and denigration to more covert, illegal, subtle, and indirect acts of aversion and hostility. It is through structural racism that a social system of racial stratification has been maintained that limits people of color's access to and participation in social, educational, economic, and political processes.

Martin Marger describes from a sociological perspective the process of racial categorization and racism.[45] Here racism is seen as denial of primary structural assimilation—that is, an absence of close personal relationships with people from groups in power and authority—and it operates as a system of impediments that limits access to opportunity and life choices for people of color. Denial of access and opportunity may produce psychological effects, but what types of effects are produced and in what way do the mental health effects manifest is unclear.

The functional utility of racism is captured by Thompson and Neville, who state that ideas of race serve to protect the social structure and allow for ongoing racial discrimination.[46] The racial ideology of out-group inferior status is maintained via negative racial stereotypes communicated through the media, science, social policy, and popular beliefs. Eduardo Bonilla-Silva concurs[47] with the ideological notion by linking the contemporary experience of racism to a color-blind belief system.[48] A number of scholars have emphasized the distinction between institutional racism and individual prejudice.[49] James Jones observes that individual racism is distinct from prejudice in that it includes the use of power by the dominant group to oppress out-group members (people of color). This theme is captured in many of the definitions discussed previously. Institutions are composed of individuals, and institutional culture is reflected through the combined will of the individuals by way of their beliefs.

Joe Feagin[50] consistently draws attention to the systemic and institutionalized nature of racism, stating, "This white-generated and white-maintained oppression is far more than a matter of individual bigotry, for it has been from the beginning a material, social, and ideological reality. For a long period now white oppression of Americans of color has been systemic—that is, it has been manifested in all major societal institutions."[51] The implementation of racism creates barriers that are individual, institutional, and cultural, and it endorses acts that compromise the dignity and well-being of people of color at all levels of social participation. Thus, individual racism involves believing in your racial group's superiority and the inferiority of out-group members and using the power of the group to assert one's beliefs.

Institutional racism is evident in unequal outcomes based on race in social systems and organizations such as those in the educational, mental health, health, occupational, and political realms. To illustrate, evidence of institutional racism can be seen in the fact that while college and university faculties are more racially diverse, people of color hold only 10 percent of tenured jobs.[52] This means that 90 percent of tenured faculty positions in the United States are held by White faculty members even though Whites account for only 62 percent of the population. In 2020 there were ten people of color in the U.S. Senate. Over the years it has been noted that Whites account for between 87 and 92 percent of the Forbes 500 executive-level positions, between 80 and 85 percent of public school superintendents, 90 percent of athletic team owners, and 98 percent of U.S. presidents.[53]

Cultural racism is defined as the belief that the characteristics and values of one's racial group are superior to those of other racial groups.[54] Regarding cultural racism, Derald Wing Sue writes:

> When, for example, White Euro-Americans use power to perpetuate their cultural heritage and impose it on people of color while diminishing the importance of or destroying another group's way of life (cultural genocide), it represents racism of the extreme kind. History is replete with governmental actions used in the United States to stamp out the language and religious practices of Native Americans. In cultural racism's contemporary form, some teachers forbid the use of a second language in their classrooms.[55]

Contemporary definitions of racism include both description and utilitarian aspects. Paula McClain and Jessica Carew state that racism "is the belief that race is the chief determinant of human characteristics and capabilities and that differences among the races provide for superiority of one race. Racism is the primary condition that leads to discrimination against one race by another."[56] Elizabeth Brondolo and colleagues identify racism as "as the processes, norms, ideologies, and behaviors that perpetuate racial inequality."[57]

We use the word *racism* to mean the "the exercise of power against a racial group defined as inferior, by individuals and institutions with the intentional and unintentional support of the entire (race or) culture."[58] We concur with David Williams and Selina Mohammed, who define racism as an "organized system premised on the categorization and ranking of social groups into races that devalues, disempowers, and differentially allocates desirable societal opportunities and resources to racial groups regarded as inferior."[59] We understand racism to be distinct from personal prejudice in that it involves the use of group power through organizations and institutions as well as the imposition of the cultural preferences of the group in power. Thus, *racism* as the term is used in this volume refers to the transformation of racial prejudice into individual racism through the use of power directed against racial groups and their members who are defined as inferior by individuals, institutional members, and leaders; furthermore, racism is reflected in policies and procedures with the intentional and unintentional support and participation of the entire dominant race and culture.[60] As such, racism as an ideology—and racial discrimination as a behavioral manifestation of that ideology—can take distinct forms that can have both direct and indirect harmful mental health effects.

Although the various definitions of racism that we have reviewed in this chapter adequately describe the elements of racism and the avenues through which it is expressed, what remains missing are definitions that allow for an analysis of the relationship between a particular type of racist experience and a person's emotional and psychological reaction. Still, even broadly defined, racism is a form of stress and as such affects the mental and physical health of its targets.

Stress is understood to be an internal biopsychosocial response to external events that can be neutral, positive, negative, or unwanted. The response can hinder functioning when it is experienced as overwhelming. How a person is affected by a stressful event and whether the event generates adverse health outcomes depends on his or her individual characteristics and on various social factors. Shelley Taylor notes that studies on psychobiological reactions (i.e., changes in heart rate and blood pressure) show that stress may produce distress and disease.[61] Thus, although a stress response can help a person adapt to a taxing event and the aftermath, it can also be associated with distress, disease, and dysfunction.[62]

In the next chapter we review the research on stress to convey an understanding of how stress operates, how it affects individuals, and how the relationship between stress and health has been investigated. This discussion is particularly relevant because studies of discrimination and race-related stress have been built on the foundation of basic stress research, and similar methods are used to examine life-event stress and race-related stress. However, historically, researchers who have studied stress and its effects have not focused on the health-related impacts of race or racism.

2

UNDERSTANDING REACTIONS TO STRESS: TRAUMA, TRAUMATIC STRESS, AND POSTTRAUMATIC STRESS DISORDER

OVER THE LAST FEW DECADES our understanding of the effects of stress has evolved. We have moved from thinking of stress in simple terms of "fight or flight" and "stimulus and response" to viewing it as a multidimensional phenomenon that has many sources and triggers a broad range of biopsychosocial reactions. We know that stress is implicated in our daily lives, overall health, and experiences of illness.[1] We also know that racism and racial discrimination are sources of stress and that health implications are associated with the stress of racism.[2] In this chapter we discuss current understandings of stress to sharpen our focus on the stress-related effects of racism.

STRESS AND HEALTH

In detailed reviews of the health and psychological research, scholars including Shelley Taylor[3] and Edward Sarafino and Timothy Smith[4] define stress, note its characteristics, outline its dimensions, and discuss how best to adapt to its presence. Stress is defined as "a negative emotional experience accompanied by predictable biochemical, physiological, cognitive, and behavioral changes that are directed either toward altering the stressful event or accommodating to its effects."[5] Sarafino and Smith note that stress is composed of two essential elements—one physical, which has to do with how the body responds, and the other psychological, which involves how an individual perceives situations. Stress can be thought of as an environmental stimulus, and the activating event as a stressor. Physiological reactions might include increased heart rate, and psychological reactions might include feeling anxious.

Sarafino and Smith refer to the combined physiological and psychological response to a stressor as "strain."[6]

A more traditional view understands stress as sets of transactions between the person and the environment. Thus, stress is a process wherein the transactions are mutually influenced. The process view of stress holds that people are active and can determine through actions, thought, and feelings how a stressor affects them. According to Richard Lazarus and Susan Folkman, people can judge whether an environmental demand is something they are equipped to handle.[7] This approach prioritizes an individual's appraisal of the environmental demand and defines stress as occurring if the demand is perceived to be beyond the individual's ability to respond effectively.[8] Several assessments can change the intensity of the stress one experiences, such as considerations of harm/loss (i.e., the degree of damage that has occurred), threat (i.e., the possibility of future harm), and challenge (i.e., a positive outcome). Our appraisal of our ability to meet the demands brought on by stressors determines the degree of stress we experience. Sarafino and Smith observe that "when we judge our resources as sufficient to meet the demands, we may experience little or no stress, but when we appraise demands as greater than our resources, we may feel a great deal of stress."[9] Higher stress levels can compromise our physical and psychological health and lead to illness. Because stressors activate physiological systems that in turn can affect our mental state, a link exists between stress and both physical and mental health.[10]

When harm or threat is perceived, our bodies react by triggering responses designed to prepare ourselves for flight or defense, such as increased heart rate and rapid breathing, designed to supply greater oxygenation to muscles and major organs, and the activation of the endocrine system, resulting in the release of cortisol, which helps the body store fuel and aids in physical recovery. Too much stimulation for too long, however, can be harmful.[11] The overproduction of these circulating hormones can be dangerous to health. It can result in the suppression of immune functions and in adverse changes in heart rate and blood pressure, and can produce changes in neurochemicals that can contribute to psychiatric disorders.[12] A reaction like increased heart rate can occur outside of awareness and last for days, weeks, or even years after the initial event,[13] exerting an abnormal demand on the heart and increasing the chances of cardiovascular dysfunction such as hypertension or cardiac failure.[14] Accordingly, evidence indicates that stress can be associated with adverse physiological effects that can result in illness.

Strong emotional responses can occur if the stressor is sudden as opposed to gradual. The nature of the reaction to stress depends on several factors, including the amount of effort the stressor requires (e.g., interest, striving) and the level of distress (e.g., anxiety, uncertainty, dissatisfaction) associated with it. For instance, effort without distress is positive and life enhancing. Distress without effort means that one is likely to feel helpless and out of control, which will trigger a stronger physiological response.[15]

How we think, feel, and behave influences the way the stress affects us. We rely on our cognitive processing to adapt to stress, but that very same cognitive processing can be disrupted by stress. Executive functioning helps us pause and plan during stressful events.[16] If our cognitive resources are interrupted, we can have difficulty with stress we encounter in the future, because cognitive functioning is impaired. Julian Thayer and colleagues observe that because our cognitive functions involve the brain's operations to slow our physiological responses to stress, impaired thinking can lead to an inability to regulate the physiological systems associated with the stress response.[17] A relationship also occurs between our emotions and our cognitive responses to a stressful incident. If we determine an event to be a challenge, we might feel excitement; if we sense a threat, we might feel fear, an emotion that has both psychological and physical elements. We may also feel sad, depressed, or angry. The emotion will affect the level of stress we experience and will influence our ability to adapt.[18] What we think and feel in turn directs our behavior; in some stressful situations (e.g., disasters), we move toward other people for support or assistance, while in other situations we may be motivated to move away from people. For instance, if stress evokes anger, we may engage in negative or aggressive social behavior. In instances where people are socially rejected, they may respond with aggression. For example, being terminated from your job might prove so stressful that your personal relationships suffer. People who are experiencing high levels of stress often have less self-control and lash out at those close to them.

How we think, feel, and behave are not the only factors that influence our stress reactions but also who we are. Our gender, racial group, sexual orientation, social position, and developmental history all contribute to how we process stressful experiences.[19] Women report more major stressors than do men. Men are more reactive than women and are slower to recover if their competence is in question, while women react more strongly when families are challenged. Being a person of color or being poor affects one's stress levels.[20] Members of nondominant racial groups are exposed to a larger number of major stressors that might be associated with disproportionate rates of illness across racial lines,[21] and stress is thought to be greater if our life goals and efforts to survive are involved.[22] The experience of being rejected or unfairly assessed can produce significant stress responses in the form of high blood pressure and increased levels of stress hormones. Sarafino and Smith describe empirical findings that "social rejection and exclusion can be so stressful that they are experienced as painful and such experiences in fact activate the same brain circuits responsible for physical pain."[23]

People of color in American society continue to experience social exclusion and rejection in ambiguous, unpredictable, and uncontrollable ways, so it is important to understand these experiences in the context of stress.[24] We contend that the conditions of strain and deprivation that racism produces for many of its targets create a range of mental and physical health consequences.[25] For people of color, these experiences take place in addition to typical stressful life events such as unemployment, poverty, discrimination, sudden death, marriage, war zone combat, assault, accidents, and natural and technological disasters.[26]

Evidence demonstrates that stress related to racial discrimination occurs over the life span, starting at birth; researchers have shown that racial differences exist for mothers and result in low birth weights of their children after exposure to racism. Tyan Parker Dominguez and colleagues examined stress and racial differences in birth weight and found that, in racial group analyses, racism was a significant predictor of birth weight for African Americans but not for Whites.[27] Shawn Utsey and colleagues[28] and David Williams[29] report that, for Black Americans, race-related stress is a stronger predictor of psychological distress than stressful life events, and that psychological resources (e.g., optimism) could reduce that distress. Michelle Sternthal and colleagues examined racial differences (among Blacks, Whites, Hispanics) in stress prevalence, exposure to different stressors, and any relation between the stressors and health outcomes.[30] They found racial differences in overall and cumulative exposure to eight stressors (life events, employment, discrimination, job discrimination, and so on). Blacks have the highest exposure and higher clustering of the stressors, Hispanics who are American-born have patterns similar to those of Blacks, and non-American-born Hispanics have profiles similar to those of American Whites. The stressors are highly correlated with poor mental and physical health. Carter et al. identified discrimination stress to be related to a range of adverse health- related outcomes while Lu et al. provide evidence to suggest that racism-related stress could be associated with longevity, when looking at aspects of an individual's DNA.[31] In a review of the literature on stress and racial health disparities, Peggy Thoits states that "the past five decades have seen a meteoric rise in the number of studies examining the physical and mental consequences of traumas, negative events, and chronic strains. Sociologists have demonstrated definitively that burdens of stress account substantially for gender, race, [and] ethnic . . . differences in bodily and emotional well-being. [These] findings point insistently to the origins of damaged health in conditions of structural disadvantage tied to individuals' positions in the stratification system."[32]

Some events and experiences are particularly severe, and the associated stress can become traumatic.[33] Interpersonal relationships and interactions at various levels of the social structure in the United States that are characterized by racial stratification both shape and determine a person's experience of self, health, and life outcomes. It is important to understand the influence of racial categorization as a type of social structure on health in terms of stress reactions and coping. Stressors can produce reactions that vary in terms of severity, duration, and frequency. Severe stressors and the resulting responses can lead to emotional and psychological behaviors that are indictors of trauma. When stress is experienced as severe, it may be traumatic and convey a great effect on health and healing.[34]

RACIAL DISCRIMINATION AND RACE-RELATED STRESS

We have introduced our discussion of racism as a type of traumatic stress by first reviewing the research on stress and health. Studies of discrimination and race-related stress were built on the foundation of basic stress research, and similar methods were used to examine both life-event and race-related stress. However, much of the early research on the physiological and psychological effects of stress lacks a focus on the health-related impacts of race or racism.[35] As discussed, stress causes health problems because its effects can be enduring and can cause chronic damage.[36] Documented physical and mental health disparities have been shown to be race-based in that people of color fare poorly regardless of economic resources. The Institute of Medicine's report *Unequal Treatment: Confronting Racial and Ethnic Disparities in Health Care;*[37] the Substance Abuse and Mental Health Services Administration's report *Racial/Ethnic Differences in Mental Health Service Use Among Adults;*[38] and the surgeon-general's report *Mental Health: Culture,*

Race and Ethnicity[39] are examples of such documented evidence. All three point to racism and discrimination as major contributing factors in health and mental health disparities; therefore, racism-related stress should be an important consideration when examining relationships between stress and health

Scholars have shown that the conditions of restricted housing, segregation, and limited economic opportunity and access to social participation produce chronic stress and poor health for many people of color.[40] The study of stressful life events and psychological health is different from the area of research that focuses on the development of more severe stress reactions such as posttraumatic stress due to exposure to life-threatening events. In part, the former is concerned with major and everyday events such as marriage, relocation, or work-related activities, while the latter focuses on events that are more extraordinary, more severe, and, as a result, less common. The two are related in that both are forms of stress, yet the critical difference is the severity of the event that produces the stress, which in turn might result in a trauma-related response.

SEVERE STRESS, TRAUMATIC STRESS, AND TRAUMA

Stress occurs as a biopsychosocial interaction wherein external events (stressors) are appraised (judged by the person) demanding or challenging or as unwanted and negative and therefore requiring some form of adaptation.[41] Trauma is a more severe form of stress in terms of both the nature of the stressor and one's reaction to it. For example, posttraumatic stress disorder (PTSD) is defined in the *Diagnostic and Statistical Manual of Mental Disorders (DSM)* as "exposure to actual or threatened death, serious injury or sexual violence in one (or more) of the following ways [including] . . . directly experiencing the traumatic event."[42]

In addition, for the reaction to be characterized as traumatic, it must result in symptoms of intrusion or reexperiencing, avoidance, and changes in thoughts or affect that are mostly negative (e.g., blocked recall, exaggerated beliefs, lack of interest in activities, an affect that is withdrawn and distant). Eve Carlson's notion of traumatic stress focuses on emotional pain as the core criterion instead of physical danger.[43] In addition to emotional pain, Carlson suggests that the experience should be perceived as sudden and out of one's control, and that the ensuing emotional distress can cause psychologi-

cal impairments in the areas of interpersonal relationships, self-esteem, identity, and depression as well as feelings of guilt and shame.[44] *Impairments*
here means actions and emotions that hinder daily functioning and alter social relationships in a way that compromises one's abilities.

BRIEF HISTORY OF POSTTRAUMATIC STRESS DISORDER AND TRAUMATIC STRESS

The recognition of psychological trauma is more constrained in the mental
health profession, and its use and meaning have evolved over a short period
of time. Race has not been explicitly studied in life-event research, nor has
it been a focus in studies of trauma, yet a number of scholars argue that race-
based experiences fall within the domain of traumatic experiences.[45]

Issues of severe stress are usually assessed with the use of the most recent
edition of the *DSM*. The definitions of various forms of stress-related disorders have been altered over successive editions of the *DSM*.[46] Therefore, it
would be helpful to review the definitions of severe or traumatic stress that
have evolved over time. Race-based experiences are not currently considered
within the domain of the *DSM* or in the context of severe stress reactions.
The *DSM* criteria for trauma are limited to experiences that are threats to
life and other physically dangerous incidents, which narrows the types of
events associated with stress-related disorders. However, some argue that emotional distress can cause PTSD.[47]

Trauma was first recognized in psychiatric and mental health diagnostic
systems in the late nineteenth and early twentieth centuries. Incidents of
stress-related trauma were first recognized as the result of combat (shell shock)
or in civilian life solely as the result of railway accidents.[48] As more social
and physical science researchers worked to understand traumatic reactions,
it became clear that the stress resulting from trauma had distinct psychological, social, and physiological components. For instance, extreme stress reactions increase adrenaline and decrease endorphin production, resulting in
heightened muscle tension and greater sensitivity to pain. These changes cor-
respond to psychological manifestations as well. M. L. Boone and colleagues indicate that traumatic events engrain or leave a lasting picture of
the events that contribute to intrusion, nightmares, and possible flashbacks.[49]

Mental health professionals recognized extreme stress reactions in the
1980s. However, concern with these types of events can also be traced to the

mid-nineteenth century in accounts of people who were injured in accidents.[50] The *DSM III* offered a definition and the first set of criteria for a diagnosis of PTSD, one type of stress-related disorder. Prior to the *DSM III*, which was released in 1980, "gross stress reactions" and other manifestations of stress were believed to result from overwhelming environmental events.[51] Racism or discrimination was not among the events considered. What made the 1980 classification of trauma noteworthy was its application to a wider range of events such as assaults, disasters, and abuse.

PTSD is usually the cornerstone used for understanding trauma in mental health practice and research, so its criteria are important. The criteria for PTSD (in the *DSM-III-R, DSM-IV, DSM-IV-TR,* and *DSM-5*)[52] have evolved, in part due to social and political shifts, to incorporate additional symptoms and criteria. For example, *DSM-5* defines PTSD as "exposure to actual or threatened death, serious injury or sexual violence . . . [and] directly experiencing the traumatic event."[53] Added to Criteria A—the first and most critical criteria, without which a diagnosis cannot be made—are witnessing the event and sexual violence. Nevertheless, the key to the criteria is possible death or serious injury—in other words, physical assault.

The *DSM-5* requires eight criteria for a diagnosis of PTSD.[54] Criteria A requires that an event be directly life threatening, reflect a serious injury, or reflect threatened or actual sexual violence. Added to this edition were learning about the trauma of a close family member or friend, and experiencing exposure to the details of a trauma but not through social media, television, or pictures. Additional Criteria C requirements draw from Criteria B and D through H, which cover such areas as reexperiencing the traumatic event; engaging in avoidant behavior and thoughts; having reactions characterized by hyperarousal or startle responses or sleeplessness; experiencing negative thoughts and feelings that either began after the event or are worsened after the event; or experiencing symptoms that last more than a month, impact functionality, and are not due to medical illness or substance abuse.

Nnamdi Pole and colleagues reviewed related disorders (e.g., adjustment, acute stress, and dissociative disorders) and observed that while changes to PTSD in the recent edition of the *DSM* do a better job of capturing "the range and intensity of symptoms seen in many individuals subjected to repeated interpersonal trauma,"[55] most experiences of trauma are more reflective of criteria associated with complex PTSD, which is not currently included in the *DSM*.

Even though the PTSD category and criteria are built on empirical support, it is our view that PTSD as a diagnostic category does not capture the stress associated with experiences of racism, even though stressful racial experiences are noted to be traumatic.[56] There are three ways in which the PTSD criteria are not a good fit for stressful racism experiences: (1) Stressful racism experiences are broader than a threat to life and do not only reflect serious injury. Racism is not an event that is primarily physical in nature or directly life threatening. (2) Emotional and psychological responses to racism are not easily captured in a symptom checklist, as is the case with the PTSD criteria. (3) There is little variation for symptoms to cluster or be based on one's subjective perception; in fact, the PTSD criteria ignore the person's subjective perception. Of critical importance for our discussion of racism-based stress as a type of trauma is the recognition that although there is some overlap in symptoms, race-based traumatic stress (RBTS) is not PTSD, and the understanding of race-based trauma should not be approached from the perspective of PTSD.

Taken together, the criteria for PTSD leave out many experiences that have the potential to produce trauma.[57] Although some scholars[58] argue that parallels exist between the experiences of physical violence and racial incidents, many of the types of incidents associated with racism are not physical in nature.[59] Racial incidents can be more subtle, are systemic, and are targeted not merely at an individual but at the individual based on their racial heritage. Here we agree with Andrea Roberts and colleagues, who state that the "DSM has been overly focused on events with intense physical as opposed to psychological impact."[60] Pole and colleagues note one concern with using a PTSD framework to understand racism-related trauma, writing that "many with PTSD find themselves incorrectly believing they are to blame for their trauma or symptoms and have other negative beliefs about themselves, other people, and the world."[61] An additional and significant limitation of the PTSD frame is that it fails to capture the psychological impact of racial events and therefore fails to capture the type of stress associated with racism-related experiences.[62] The unique differentiating aspect of racism-related experiences, in contrast to the types of trauma events required for a PTSD diagnosis, is the fact that racism-related experiences are located in a larger experience of oppression and subjugation based on racial heritage. This aspect of racism-related stress is captured by Samantha Holmes and colleagues, who state:

> The wording of Criterion A arguably best lends itself to interpersonal forms of oppression and, even so, has the potential of capturing only a narrow subset of interpersonal oppression (e.g., physically violent hate crimes) while neglecting other frequent iterations. Criterion A's failure to incorporate

oppression, broadly speaking, may be the consequence of the narrow definition of violence[;] culturally . . . the current definition of trauma conceptualizes violence within the cultural zeitgeist as primarily interpersonal and
physical, while widely discounting systemic, institutional, and psychological trauma.[63]

Furthermore, recent treatment guidelines for PTSD are also less than helpful for various reasons.[64]

TRAUMATIC STRESS: BROADER CRITERIA THAN PTSD

Mental health professionals and social scientists have had a long-standing
interest in the incidence and prevalence of recent (within one year) and lifetime exposure to severe stress and PTSD. Regarding the prevalence of
trauma, one objective of epidemiological studies of people in the general
population who have experienced traumatic life events has been to determine
whether the definition or classification of a traumatic event could go beyond
that provided by DSM criteria. Fran Norris argues that a traumatic event
could be defined as any event perceived or experienced by the individual as
shocking enough to produce symptoms of intrusion, numbing, and arousal.[65]
Thus, Norris offers a broader definition of a traumatic event as "a violent event
marked by sudden or extreme force from an external agent."[66] A way to understand how racism-based experiences are associated with stress that leads
to trauma can be found in the definition offered by Carlson, which does not
rely solely on evidence of psychopathology or a life-threatening event.[67]

Carlson, Judith Lewis Herman, and, more recently, Pole and colleagues[68]
offer alternative ways of assessing and defining traumatic stress reactions given
some of the limitations of the DSM definitions of PTSD, acute stress reactions, and other diagnoses in terms of the range of experiences that can produce such a response.[69] The goals of Carlson's model are to (a) expand the
definition to include a wider range of traumatic events and explain a wider
range of responses to trauma, thus including events and experiences that are
psychologically and emotionally but not physically threatening; (b) allow for
a life-span developmental perspective of traumatic events, which takes it beyond single events and short-term effects; (c) include a wider range of reactions; and (d) allow for research since it presents hypotheses that can be
examined. These goals are incorporated into our thinking about the emo-

tional effects of racism. Our perspective is centered on emotional and psychological harm that may not be short term or reflect a single event, and that has associated with it a wide range of reactions or a cluster of symptoms that can be tested in research.

Carlson argues that trauma is not well understood despite its prevalence and the level of distress it causes.[70] Most research has focused on single events, such as those experienced in combat and natural disasters (life-threatening physical danger) and their related short-term effects (after one to three months). Models of trauma tend to separate short-and long-term effects. Knowledge about trauma has only begun to accumulate since the late 1980s, so information is limited. Trauma is hard to study since events associated with trauma cannot be controlled. Researchers cannot pretest people or predict who will be affected. Moreover, it is impossible to manipulate elements of traumatic experiences. Treatment must be rendered prior to research activity, and research interventions can make the trauma worse. More important, people are less likely to discuss their traumatic experiences than they are other emotional or psychological reactions. Given the nature of traumatic experiences, the information provided by research subjects may be compromised due to confusion and disruption. These factors make research on trauma experiences complex and difficult at best.

Carlson's model of traumatic stress includes three essential elements. The first is the perception that the event is negative or painful. As Carlson states, "Some experiences are traumatic because they are emotionally painful . . . or because they involve the threat of emotional pain. In this case the negative valence is related to the psychological meaning of the event to the individual, not the physical consequences of the event."[71] The psychological pain produces or causes damage or threat of damage to one's sense of self. Thus, the key aspect of this element is the perception of the event. If one does not perceive an event as negative, it will not produce harm. This aspect of trauma is consistent with general models of stress as conceptualized by Lazarus and Folkman.[72] Further, to cause trauma the threat must reach a certain threshold, which may vary from person to person. Some events might be so negative that they would produce trauma in most people, and others may affect few; it remains unclear what the threshold is. For RBTS, an event could be emotionally painful such that it has negative psychological meaning.

The second element is that the event is experienced suddenly. It is more difficult to adapt to an event that occurs without warning than to one that is gradual and takes place over time. As Carlson writes, "Escaping a traumatic response is more likely if one has months or years to adjust to a negative event."[73]

The third element is that the event is experienced as uncontrollable. The belief that one has some degree of power over events serves as a form of protection. Trauma is more likely in situations in which one believes that he or she is unable to control the noxious event. Carlson notes, "The ability to control an event renders it more predictable, and the ability to predict an event may make control over it more possible . . . predictability *is not* an essential element in the trauma process". Given the various levels at which racism occurs (individual, institutional, and cultural), many of its aspects can render encounters emotionally painful, uncontrollable, and sudden or unexpected. And given the centuries-long persistence of racist practices, some elements of racism can be considered predictable and cumulative, but not in a way that permits an individual to have a sense of control. Most forms of racism constitute assaults on one's sense of self in ways that heighten tension. Therefore, RBTS is primarily associated with events that are experienced as sudden and uncontrollable.

Researchers have found that people with severe stress and PTSD share three core symptoms that may be expressed through one or several physiological, emotional, cognitive, or behavioral modalities.[74] These are (a) intrusion or reexperiencing, (b) arousal or hyperactivity, and (c) avoidance or psychic numbing. For example, a person might have thoughts or images that "intrude" on daily life, experiencing images of the encounter (reexperiencing) and loss of memory or recall of the specific elements of the event (numbing). He may be anxious or express anger through aggression or hyperactivity. He may stay away from the people involved in the event or the location where it happened. He may experience sleeplessness or startle easily (arousal) or may have difficulty with concentration (intrusion).

In addition to the core reactions of intrusion, arousal, and avoidance, other symptoms are associated with severe stress, such as depression and anxiety. A person may experience a loss of self-worth and have difficulty with intimate and interpersonal relationships. Guilt and shame may arise due to self-blame and a sense of responsibility for the experience. Some scholars refer to self-blame and feeling responsible in the context of racism as "internalized racism" or appropriated racial oppression.[75] David Williams and Harold Neighbors state:

> The normative cultural characterization of the superiority of whiteness and the devaluation of blackness [or people of color], combined with economic

marginality, . . . can lead to self-perceptions of worthlessness and powerless-ness. Several lines of evidence suggest that the internalization of cultural stereotypes by stigmatized groups can create expectations, anxieties, and reactions that can adversely affect social and psychological functioning.[76]

Other factors influence responses to trauma, including the person's phys-ical state, life stage, and developmental status; the severity of the trauma; the social context before and after the event; and the nature of life events before and after the trauma. An important factor is severity, which includes the num-ber of events, their intensity, and their duration. For instance, Carlson points out that "to the extent the person is biologically vulnerable, . . . is younger, the trauma is more severe (e.g., multiple, highly intense events of long dura-tion), the social context is unsupportive, and previous or subsequent life events are very stressful, there would be a more pronounced and long-lasting trau-matic response."[77] Since people of color are subjected to numerous forms of racism over the course of their lives, many are vulnerable to higher rates of poor physical and mental health, numerous life-event stressors, and less so-cietal support and recognition of their circumstances.[78] It is reasonable to hold that racism is a traumatic stressor. Consider further that for trauma to be se-vere, events might be frequent and intense. Intensity has to do with the number of areas of life that racism affects. Furthermore, since racism remains chronic and pervasive, it is reasonable to hold that people are frequently vul-nerable to its effects. Said another way, people of color are vulnerable to stress from racism because of their exposure to repeated events over time, the unsupportive social context, and the related negative and stressful life events associated with targeted group members' lower social status.

Herman proposes that consideration be given to what she calls "complex post-traumatic stress disorder,"[79] which refers to severe or traumatic stress re-actions that are experienced over prolonged periods or repeated over long intervals of time, and that lead to changes in personality structure. The ways that people of color have had to cope with racism may fall within the shift-ing systems of meaning such that many have held on to aspects of their cul-tures of origin and have come to be suspicious and distrusting of Whites as well as aspects of White culture and society. For instance, some groups of color assign cultural importance to forms of emotional expression that are uncommon among Whites and that place value on connections to nature (e.g., Native Americans) and ancestors or on being in harmony the spirit world. These cultural expressions, which have been documented by many scholars, may reflect how members of various disenfranchised racial groups manage the constant stress of racism or shift meaning in how they understand life or in their perceptions of themselves.[80]

The term *severe stress* or *traumatic stress* is used in this work to refer to reactions to racism in terms of mental health. The broader criteria are particularly useful in assessing the effects of racism given the fact that those effects may be expected but may nevertheless occur suddenly. Racial incidents may be repeated and may reoccur, subtly and covertly, in language (e.g., "boy" or the N-word) or symbols (e.g., the noose, certain animals, the Confederate flag). They take place within the context of a society that for centuries sanctioned and made legal various forms of racial terrorism, harassment, and denigration. So we employ the concept of traumatic stress in assessing and understanding race-based experiences both as stress and as trauma.

Although racism has not been a direct focus of the research on PTSD and stress, those studies provide indirect evidence of the possible role of racism in the lives of study participants. One of the strengths of the PTSD literature is that it includes people of color. Additionally, several important trends can be observed. One trend is that although not all people develop PTSD or traumatic reactions to potentially stressful events, people of color, both as civilians and as combat veterans, show higher levels of PTSD than Whites.[81] In studies that identify risk factors for the development of PTSD (e.g., violence), people of color are exposed to many such factors in greater proportions than Whites. Furthermore, scholars speculate in the face of these findings that racism may play a role in the racial differences they report.[82] Our review in chapter 3 of the empirical evidence associated with the psychological impact of racism provides strong (albeit indirect) evidence of the emotional and psychological impact of racism, which we believe can be understood within the framework of traumatic stress.

3

REDEFINING RACISM: DOCUMENTING RACISM'S EFFECTS

IN THE PRECEDING CHAPTER we discussed PTSD and life-event stress and suggested that the high rates of PTSD endured by people of color might be associated with racism and race-related experiences. Research focusing on traumatic life events has not considered racism as a factor in trauma reactions. However, much attention has been directed to the health and mental health effects of discrimination and race-related stress, and this research offers further evidence of the adverse health-related outcomes associated with experiences of racism.[1] In this chapter we explore the research on discrimination, racial discrimination, and race-related stress to show how these events affect mental and physical health. We also discuss the limits of this work and introduce a way to redefine racism and racial experiences to more directly connect racial encounters to emotional outcomes and stress-related reactions. We include reports of individual studies, integrative reviews, and meta-analyses (i.e., in which studies are grouped and analyzed).

Scholars call for an examination of race-related stress[2] and argue that being a member of an oppressed and stigmatized group could be a type of stress that is ignored in social science theory and research. Additionally, scholars now emphasize the need to understand racial discrimination and systems of oppression when assessing stress and trauma.[3] David Williams and colleagues summarize the empirical evidence,[4] and Williams writes that research "reveals that institutional racism shapes socioeconomic status (SES) and . . . reveals that cultural racism, with its associated, negative images, stereotypes, and prejudice, can be damaging, . . . [and] interpersonal discrimination is a potent psychosocial stressor that has pervasive negative effects on health."[5]

Researchers have investigated the prevalence and frequency of discrimination, and some have studied the psychological, physical, and emotional effects in experimental and naturalistic settings and through survey research and meta-analyses. Various studies conducted with racially diverse samples (Whites and people of color) have found that the incidence and prevalence of racial discrimination tends to be high for people of color and that exposure to such incidents of racism is associated with lower levels of health and psychological well-being. The American Psychological Association's study on discrimination reveals that about 70 percent of people, irrespective of race, report experiencing everyday discrimination (e.g., poor service, disrespect), and close to 50 percent report major discrimination (e.g., police stops, unfair treatment in health care).[6] Assari, Gibbons, and Simons conducted an eighteen-year study of racial discrimination among Black youth and found that young Black males of higher SES living in White communities report greater incidence of racial discrimination over time. People of color report greater frequency of everyday discrimination compared to Whites. The reports note that in general, experiencing discrimination is related to higher stress and poorer health, a conclusion that has been supported by meta-analytic studies that examine the relationships between discrimination and health.[7]

In our review, we use *racism* and *racial discrimination* to subsume the various terms used by researchers (e.g., *perceived racial discrimination, ethnic discrimination, self-reported discrimination, perceived racism, race-related stress*). Several instruments have been used to measure discrimination, racism, and racism-related stress.[8] In studies of racism-related stress, most investigators do not provide the results of specific encounters with racial discrimination but instead report the sum of experiences through a total scale score, even though the instruments assess for various types of racism, including individual, institutional, and cultural.

As we note in chapter 1, racism and racial discrimination may operate at interpersonal, institutional, and cultural levels, and encounters can vary across different domains, including covert as opposed to overt acts, acts that result in life stress, acts that are racial stressors, and acts that reflect conflicts and encounters resulting in racial trauma. Even though racial incidents manifest in various forms, findings have consistently indicated that racism or racial discrimination is associated with both mental and physical health outcomes.[9]

THE IMPACT OF RACIAL DISCRIMINATION
ON PHYSICAL HEALTH

Exposure to racism and racial discrimination is shown to lead to compromised physical health. For instance, "increased levels of *everyday racism* resulted in 'neuroendocrine-autonomic dysregulation' leading to the accumulation of excess body fat in a sample of 43,103 Black women."[10] Additional research[11] suggests that experiences of racial discrimination contribute to negative health outcomes as the recipients try to manage the impact by adopting "detrimental health behaviors, such as smoking, excessive alcohol use, or illicit substance use," actions often used to cope with the pervasive social stressors associated with minority group status.[12] Although the effect is small, findings also indicate a relationship between perceived racial discrimination and hypertension.

In general, the research indicates that racial discrimination is associated with health-related problems even when controlling for potential confounding variables (e.g., acculturation, sociodemographic variables, social support). Researchers report links with preterm and low-birth-weight infants of African American and Arab American mothers increased breast cancer incidence; increased abdominal obesity and greater bodily pain in African American male veterans. Emerging evidence suggests that racism and racial discrimination might have an impact on longevity. In a study examining telomeres, nucleotide sequences associated with the aging process, in a sample of ninety-two African American men, Chae and colleagues report that experiences of racism are associated with an acceleration in the aging process as measured by leukocyte telomere length. Thus, racial discrimination is associated with a range of health concerns, including attitudes toward health, many of which could also compromise emotional and psychological health. Although the research does support a connection between racial discrimination and physical health, the association is not as strong as the relationships found between racial discrimination and mental health, which we address later in this chapter.

Researchers also report a range of findings between institutional racial discrimination and health outcomes. For instance, in a study of 1,652 Filipino Americans, A. B. de Castro and colleagues report significant associations between workplace discrimination and high blood pressure, diabetes, migraine headaches, and stomach ulcers, even after controlling for sociodemographic and work-related variables.[13] Rebecca Din-Dzietham and colleagues report positive associations between race-based discrimination at work and hypertension for Black adults.[14]

Although the preponderance of studies indicate that interpersonal and institutional racial discrimination adversely affect physical health for people of color, particularly African Americans, the findings of other studies are inconclusive. Some researchers, for instance, Charlotte Brown and colleagues and Rosalind Peters,[15] find no significant associations between racial discrimination, chronic racism, and hypertension among multiethnic adults. Nevertheless, the relationships have been found, and it may be that some of the health effects are moderated by individual-level factors (e.g., racial identity, coping style), even when controlling for possible confounding variables, making the links less clear for some scholars, however, significant positive relationships continue to exist. In sum, poor physical health can compromise mental health and overall psychological and emotional well-being.

THE IMPACT OF RACIAL DISCRIMINATION ON MENTAL HEALTH

As noted previously, integrative reviews and meta-analyses show strong associations between discrimination and negative mental health outcomes.[16] In the studies we examined, researchers explored the relationships between racial discrimination and a range of mental health variables.

We organize the literature into findings related to three broad categories: indicators of general emotional and psychological well-being (i.e., well-being, self-esteem, life satisfaction, anger, quality of life, and general mental health); indicators of psychological distress (including race-related stress and trauma-related outcomes); and the presence of psychiatric criteria (depressive and anxiety symptoms, psychiatric disorders, and so forth). Some studies contain multiple findings and cut across our categories; in such instances, they may be reported in more than one category.

INDICATORS OF GENERAL EMOTIONAL AND PSYCHOLOGICAL WELL-BEING

By *well-being*, we mean emotional and psychological health as reflected in high levels of self-esteem and life satisfaction, and lower levels of mental health symptoms. Brenda Major and colleagues found a link between exposure to racial discrimination and low self-esteem in a study of 191 Latino/a American students.[17] Another study found a negative relationship between general mental health and racial discrimination in a sample of 399 middle-class African American men.[18] In a national survey, Carol Ryff and colleagues found that racial discrimination is a negative predictor of well-being for females only, and that the greater the exposure to racial discrimination, the less women felt they had a sense of life purpose, personal growth, autonomy, mastery of one's environment, and self-acceptance, and the women's relations with others were less positive.[19] Gilbert Gee and colleagues found that three indicators of racial discrimination—namely, goals discrimination (diminished ability to achieve personal goals because of race), discomfort and anger (due to interpersonal mistreatment because of one's race), and health care discrimination (perceptions of receiving suboptimal health care due to one's race)—are inversely related to psychological well-being.[20] Christopher Liang and Carin Molenaar found that racial discrimination is positively associated with belief in an unjust world, anger rumination, and negative affect.[21] Belief in an unjust world is directly and positively associated with both anger rumination and negative affect. Finally, belief in an unjust world significantly mediates the direct relationships between both race-related stressors and anger rumination and negative affect. Delida Sanchez and colleagues found in two samples that among people of color who experience racial discrimination, confrontation is associated with greater psychological well-being, and this relationship is mediated by autonomy promotion, thus providing preliminary evidence that confrontation may aid in the process of regaining autonomy after experiencing racial discrimination and may therefore promote well-being.[22] Asani Seawell and colleagues conducted a longitudinal study about the role of general and tailored social support in decreasing the impact of racial discrimination on depressive symptoms and optimism among African American women.[23] Their results show that higher levels of general and tailored social support predict optimism one year later. Although initial levels of neither measure of social support predict depressive symptoms over time, changes in tailored support predict changes in depressive symptoms. They found a buffering effect of tailored social support but not general support on depressive symptoms. Mushonga and Henneberger, in a study of protective factors for Black students' mental health, found that spirituality, social support, self-esteem, and racial identity (low centrality and high public regard) were associated with positive psychological health in Black traditional students but not nontraditional students.[24]

A meta-analytic study by Aprile Benner and colleagues of 214 articles investigated the relations between racial discrimination, emotional distress, and risky health behaviors.[25] Exposure to racial discrimination was linked to higher levels of depressive and internalizing symptoms; greater psychological distress; poorer self-esteem; lower academic achievement and engagement; less academic motivation; more externalizing behaviors; risky sexual behaviors; and substance use for the adolescent participants.

The literature on race-related experiences and psychological well-being appears to suggest that experiences of racism and racial discrimination have an adverse effect on well-being, and this finding holds true across racial groups as well as across age brackets among U.S.-based populations.

INDICATORS OF PSYCHOLOGICAL DISTRESS

Psychological distress is reflected in the elevation of a set of psychological symptoms. It includes, but is not limited to, race-related stress and trauma-related symptoms. Racism is found to be predictive of lower levels of mental health and higher levels of psychological symptoms.[26]

Naa Kwate and Melody Goodman investigated the impact of racism on the mental health of African Americans at cross-sectional time points and longitudinally over the course of one year.[27] Results varied by time point and outcome, with only some measures associated with distress and with effects being stronger for poor mental health than for depression.[28] Overall, individuals who deny thinking about their race fare the worst. Longitudinally, greater frequencies of racism predict worse mental health across outcomes. The results support theories of racism as a health-defeating stressor. In another study, Kwate and colleagues found that past-year and lifetime racism are positively related to overall psychological distress in adult Black women.[29] Bonnie Moradi and Cristina Risco, in a sample of 128 Latino/a American adults, also found that racial discrimination is indirectly associated with lower self-esteem through loss of personal control and is positively associated with psychological distress.[30] Similarly, in a study by Emma Wadsworth and colleagues, Black African Caribbean women who indicate that they experienced racial discrimination at work had higher levels of psychological distress.[31]

DEPRESSION, ANXIETY, AND TRAUMA:
FORMS OF PSYCHIATRIC SYMPTOMS AND DISTRESS

Several studies report that experiences of racism are associated with increased psychological distress. Alex Pieterse and Robert T. Carter found that past-month racist events are predictive of psychological distress over and above that accounted for by life stress.[32] Similarly, a survey by Robert Sellers and J. Nicole Shelton note that racial discrimination and psychological distress are related.[33] In their study, the most frequently reported racial hassles are "being ignored, overlooked, not given service; [being] treated rudely or disrespectfully; others reacting to you as if they were afraid or intimidated."[34] Recently, Laura Castro-Schilo, Alyson Cavanaugh, Yesenia Mejia, and Richard Robins investigated whether, for 674 Mexican youth, changes in peer discrimination at seventh and ninth grades predicted greater depressive and anxiety symptoms in twelfth grade and greater discrimination by peers.[35] Hans Oh, Andrew Stickley, Ai Koyanagi, Rebecca Yau, and Jordan Devylder, using two national probability studies, found that Blacks, Latinos, and Asians in the United States who experienced the highest levels of everyday discrimination had greater odds of reporting thoughts of suicide during their lifetime when compared with people who did not report discrimination.[36] Although suicide is not directly an outcome of anxiety or depression, it is fair to argue that depression and anxiety are aspects of having thoughts about taking one's life.

Monnica Williams and colleagues found that racial discrimination accounted for obsessive-compulsive disorder (OCD) symptoms in a sample of African American adults, and in the same sample everyday discrimination not associated with race did not predict OCD symptoms.[37] Donte Bernard and colleagues found that young African American women who have higher levels of exposure to racial discrimination and those reporting lower levels of distress from racial discrimination are most vulnerable to negative mental health outcomes.[38] Shervin Assari reported that higher levels of education protected Black women better than Black men from depression and psychological distress after exposure to racial discrimination.[39] Kathy Sanders-Phillips and colleagues report, based on a sample of 567 African American high school students, that racial discrimination is related to more depressive symptoms that, in turn, are associated with greater past-month alcohol and marijuana use.[40] Rheeda Walker and colleagues examine racism experiences in a sample of 722 African American youth (mean age = 10.56, standard deviation [SD] = 0.64) and explore whether racial discrimination contributes to symptoms of depression and anxiety as well as subsequent suicide ideation and morbid ideation.[41] Results reveal both direct and mediated effects of racism on later suicide and morbid ideation. For boys and girls, the effect of racism is mediated by symptoms of depression.

Irene Park and colleagues, in a longitudinal study, examine whether anger regulation plays a mediating role in the racial discrimination–mental health relationship among 269 Mexican-origin adolescents ranging in age from twelve to seventeen.[42] Results indicate that outward anger is a significant mediator, while anger suppression and control are not significant mediators. Within a given individual, greater racial discrimination is associated with more frequent outward anger expression, and, in turn, more frequent outward anger is related to higher levels of anxiety and depression.

RACISM AND TRAUMA SYMPTOMS

Researchers consider the psychological responses to racial experiences to be traumatic stress reactions. As noted previously, several scholars and researchers argue that racial discrimination can produce reactions associated with race-based traumatic stress (RBTS). Carter and colleagues, investigating the experiences of racism endured by people of color, asked individuals how they were affected by the experiences.[43] Of the 262 participants, 74 percent report lasting psychological effects. For all racial groups, extreme emotional distress (36 percent) is the most frequently reported emotional effect, followed by mild emotional distress (16 percent) and hypervigilance or arousal (15 percent). Lower self-worth, avoidance, and distrust are reported with nearly equal frequency, at 9 percent, 8 percent, and 8 percent, respectively. Positive outcome (3 percent), intrusion (2 percent), and other effects (3 percent) are reported much less often. Many of the emotions they found are consistent with the indicators of traumatic stress reactions discussed by Eve Carlson.[44]

Carter and colleagues grouped racial incidents into two kinds: avoidant experiences, such as being denied access or services or being stereotyped, and hostile experiences, such as verbal assaults or being profiled.[45] The two categories were used to predict two types of psychological reactions, injury and no injury, with corresponding emotional and psychological reactions. The researchers found that participants who were racially harassed were two times more likely to experience psychological and emotional effects that constitute psychological injury (e.g., extreme emotional distress, hypervigilance, avoidance, intrusion) than were the participants who experience avoidant discrimination. These reactions are also similar to the symptoms associated with the traumatic stress reactions presented by Carlson,[46] and they therefore support the notion of RBTS.

In an investigation of race-related stress, trauma symptoms, and ethnic identity, Anna Khaylis and colleagues found support for a positive relationship between race-related stress, and trauma symptoms among ninety-one undergraduate students reflecting White, Black, Asian, and Latino/a participants.[47] Elena Flores and colleagues investigated the role of ethnic discrimination among a sample of 110 Mexican American adolescents and also found a positive relationship between experiences of discrimination and trauma symptoms, suggesting that their finding lends support to the notion of RBTS.[48] Pieterse and colleagues examined interpersonal racial discrimination experiences, racial climate, and trauma symptoms among college students.[49] Data analyses indicate that Asian and Black students report more frequent experiences of interpersonal racial discrimination than do White students. Black students also perceive the campus racial climate as "not welcoming" at a higher rate than do White and Asian students. Furthermore, when controlling for generic life stress, racial discrimination contributes to the prediction of trauma-related symptoms for Black students, and negative racial climate contributes to trauma symptoms for Asians. Thus, for Asians, when the campus is, in general more hostile, this experience is more emotionally impactful; for Blacks, more direct interpersonal actions result in trauma-related reactions. The findings from the literature suggest a consistent relationship between self-reported trauma symptoms and perceived experiences of racial discrimination. Furthermore, the findings reflect studies drawing from varied racial and ethnic groups.

Recently, T. B. Loeb and colleagues examined how histories of trauma and adversity, as well as perceived discrimination, might be linked to somatic symptoms, posttraumatic stress syndrome (PTSS), and depressive symptoms.[50] In five hundred multiracial community participants (Black and Latino), the researchers found that discrimination, previous traumatic events, and adverse events were related to somatic symptom severity. More important, posttraumatic and depressive symptoms were associated with somatic symptoms. Finally, in a systematic review of twenty-seven published research reports, Katherine Kirkinis and colleagues document effect sizes ranging from .12 to .61 in studies examining the association between self-reported racism discrimination and trauma-related symptoms,[51] meaning that for the most part researchers find racism and racial discrimination to be related to trauma reactions.

Although scholars typically do not use terms such as *traumatic stress* or *trauma reactions* when examining the experience of racism, the findings noted above suggest a link between experiences of racism and a type of trauma response. Therefore, current empirical findings lend support to the model of RBTS in which racial incidents are associated with trauma-related signs and symptoms such as arousal, intrusive thoughts, avoidance, lower self-esteem, and increased emotional distress.[52] Nicholas Sibrava and colleagues examined PTSD and its relationship to discrimination in a longitudinal study that involved participants with anxiety disorders (139 Latinx and 152 African American adults), from the Harvard/Brown Anxiety Research Project—Phase II.[53] The participants were followed for five years, with a small remission rate. The investigators reported that more frequent experiences with discrimination were related to PTSD diagnostic status, but did not predict any other anxiety or mood disorder.

Robert T. Carter, Kathrine Kirkinis, and Veronica Johnson, in a study with 421 multiracial adult participants, examined patterns of relationships between RBTS and PTSD-like symptoms, using Canonical correlation analyses.[54] They found that RBTS symptoms were significantly related to PTSD-like symptoms as measured by the trauma symptom checklist–40 (TSC-40), especially when individuals indicated that they had undergone negative race-based experiences that were stressful. The results show that RBTS seems to produce PTSD-like symptoms—particularly dissociation, anxiety, and depression—as well as a mixed array of symptoms associated with trauma history, sleep disturbance, and sexual problems. That is, experiences other than exposure to or being a witness to violent or accidental death, serious injury, or sexual violence can produce traumatic stress symptomology. The findings, however, indicate that RBTS is different from PTSD; while there is overlap, the authors contend that RBTS is not PTSD. In particular, they argue that overlap between symptoms does not occur in a one-to-one fashion with PTSD criteria or its symptom checklist. For instance, while RBTS involves reactions of hypervigilance, intrusion, and avoidance, as does PTSD, the occurrence, in the study, is not identical for both. In addition, the RBTS symptoms were not uniformly associated with TSC-40 symptoms, which reflect PTSD-like symptoms. In fact, for participants in the RBTS group with scale elevations, only hypervigilance was strongly associated with TSC-40 symptoms, while the other non-PTSD-like RBTS symptoms (e.g., anger) were related to TSC-40 symptoms.

SUMMARY OF RACE-RELATED STRESS AND RACIAL TRAUMA STUDIES

The literature on race-related stress and racial trauma reveals several associations between racial discrimination and psychological distress, including racism-related stress and traumatic stress reactions for Black, Latino/a, Asian American, and biracial populations. We found that the specific racial incidents reported in the literature are primarily interpersonal. For instance, the most frequently reported encounters include being ignored, overlooked, or denied access or services; being treated unfairly, rudely, or disrespectfully by people in the service industries or while shopping; or being treated as dangerous in a public setting, resulting in humiliation. Specific types of encounters with racism, such as verbal assault, physical assault, being profiled, and nonverbal harassment, are also reported. Experiences of institutional racial/ethnic discrimination are reported with less frequency and include being treated unfairly in the workplace and perceptions of racially hostile academic climates. Even after accounting for general life stress, past-month racist events predict psychological distress for Black men[55] and Black women.[56] Even though the links between perceived discrimination and psychological distress are compelling, it is crucial to consider various individual-level factors such as racial identity.

DIAGNOSTIC AND STATISTICAL MANUAL OF MENTAL DISORDERS CRITERIA STUDIES

Many studies examine psychological reactions to exposure to racial discrimination by using psychiatric criteria as defined by the *Diagnostic and Statistical Manual of Mental Disorders*, fourth edition (*DSM-IV*),[57] and several studies explore specific symptoms of anxiety and depression. A few studies explore whether a relationship exists between racial discrimination and *DSM-IV* psychiatric disorders, resulting in mixed findings. Deidre Anglin and colleagues examined the association between racial discrimination experiences and psychotic symptoms in a sample of urban, predominantly immigrant and young adult people of color.[58] They found that racial discrimination is significantly associated with psychotic symptoms and with higher odds of reporting eight or more distressing psychotic symptoms, even after adjusting for anxiety and depression symptoms. In a related study, Anglin and colleagues sought to explore whether race-based rejection sensitivity (RS-race) for people of color correlates with intrusive thoughts associated with being a target of racial discrimination.[59] They found that RS-race and racial discrimination are significantly related to higher levels of psychotic symptom distress. The findings suggest that racial discrimination and RS-race may both be important for understanding risk of distress along the psychotic spectrum among young adults of color.

Henry Willis and Enrique Neblett looked at the role of racial discrimination as a risk factor for increased obsessive-compulsive psychiatric symptoms in African American young adults.[60] Results indicated that racial discrimination is a risk factor in the development and maintenance of OC symptoms, and specific patterns of racial identity are vulnerability factors and protective factors. Diedre Anglin and colleagues wanted to determine if strong ethnic identity protected against negative racial discrimination and adverse mental health outcomes.[61] Some 644 racial-minority adults were administered self-report inventories; participants who had high ethnic identity and were exposed to discrimination reported fewer symptoms than participants with low ethnic identity. This suggests that ethnic identity helped to protect participants from the adverse mental health effects of racism.

Li Maio, using a nationally representative sample of Asian immigrants in the United States, examined whether racial discrimination, language discrimination, and vicarious racism experiences increase the risk of psychiatric disorders for Asian immigrant groups.[62] The investigation found that both perceived racial discrimination and language discrimination have strong adverse effects on mental health only for Filipinos, while Vietnamese and Chinese immigrants are affected by vicarious racism experiences. Gee and colleagues found that everyday racial discrimination among Asian Americans is associated with increased chances of having a mood or anxiety disorder within the past twelve months.[63] Nnamdi Pole and colleagues found a positive relationship between workplace racial discrimination and PTSD symptoms in Hispanic police officers when compared to White officers.[64]

On the other hand, some studies report conflicting results regarding psychiatric disorders. Dennis Combs and colleagues examined the relationship between racism and paranoia (cultural mistrust, nonclinical paranoia, and clinical paranoia) in 128 African American college students.[65] The authors found that in this cohort racism does not predict clinical paranoia but is a significant predictor of cultural mistrust and nonclinical paranoia. Sirry Alang looked at symptoms that constitute a shared picture of depression among African Americans to see if their symptoms fit with criteria for major depressive disorder (MDD) in the fifth edition of the DSM (DSM-5).[66] Seventy-four African Americans participated. She found that the depression symptoms reported by the participants included classic symptoms listed in the DSM-5, such as sadness and lack of motivation. But other indicators that were common in the sample were inconsistent with DSM-5 symptoms of MDD, such as paranoia and rage. Some typical symptoms among African Americans are not included in the DSM-5 or in research instruments developed based on the DSM and thus are likely to be overlooked in epidemiological surveys and in clinical assessments of depression.

INTEGRATIVE REVIEWS AND META-ANALYSES

Integrative reviews and meta-analyses indicate that exposure to racism or racial discrimination is inversely associated with psychological health and positively associated with psychological and physical distress.[67] Integrative reviews of racism and health that have included various racial groups found the strongest relationships between racial discrimination, negative mental health, and unhealthy behaviors.

Researchers have also shown that people of color exposed to the stress of racial discrimination may try to manage it by adopting detrimental health behaviors, with findings showing that racial discrimination is associated with use of marijuana, tobacco, and alcohol among Black, but not White, participants.[68] Yet not many meta-analyses have fully examined the association between detrimental health behaviors (e.g., smoking, alcohol use, or illicit substance use) and exposure to racism, with substance use outcomes as an important proxy for health effects.[69]

Elizabeth Pascoe and Laura Smart Richman's meta-analysis and research synthesis includes 134 studies focusing on unfair treatment and discrimination, found effects of discrimination on mental and physical health. The covariate (social support, group identification, etc.) analyses yielded weak and nonsignificant findings. However, they did not specifically investigate direct effects of racial discrimination.[70] In a meta-analysis of 328 studies, Michael

Schmitt and colleagues examined sexism, racism, and sexual orientation with respect to mental health reactions (e.g., anxiety, depression, psychological distress); they found supporting evidence of discrimination's harmful effects on psychological well-being, with effect sizes (r) being larger for disadvantaged groups ($r=-.24$) compared to advantaged groups ($r=-.10$).[71] In the few meta-analyses that focus specifically on racial discrimination, findings reveal again that it is associated with poor health.[72] Similarly, in a meta-analysis of twelve studies conducted between 2000 and 2013 and involving Black men, Angelitta Britt-Spells and colleagues examined the effects of discrimination on depression and found a positive relationship ($r=.29$).[73]

Whereas the findings of meta-analyses that focus on racial discrimination are robust, these studies have typically not included other racial-cultural variables. A meta-analysis conducted by Debbiesiu Lee and Soyeon Ahn that analyzed fifty-one studies on American citizens' and immigrant Latinas/os' discrimination experiences with behavioral aspects of culture (e.g., language use for acculturation) left out psychological racial-cultural variables (e.g., racial identity, racial socialization).[74] Another meta-analysis by Lee and Ahn examined twenty-seven studies that focused on the association of racial identity, ethnic identity, and racial socialization with racial discrimination and stress. They found that racial discrimination and psychological distress are significantly and positively related ($r=.21$), and that this relationship varies based on racial identity and racial socialization. They also found that ethnic identity is not related to distress or racial discrimination but that racial identity is related to both.[75]

Yin Paradies and colleagues examined through meta-analysis how racism, ethnicity, and nationality determine health outcomes (physical and mental).[76] Their investigation involved 293 studies published in twelve countries with participants from various racial (including White) and age groups. In line with prior studies, they found that racism is associated with poor health, and that the association with mental health is stronger than it is with physical health. The authors found that the type of racism exposure, the research methodology, and the subject's ethnicity moderate the relationship between racial discrimination and health outcomes. Robert T. Carter and colleagues reviewed 105 studies published between 2000 and 2011 on the relationships between racial discrimination and health outcomes among racial-ethnic minority Americans.[77] They also tested for the moderator effects of measurement strategies, cultural factors, substance use, gender, and racial group differences and found a statistically significant effect size ($r=.17$) between racial discrimination and health, with the largest effect for mental health that did not differ by racial group. Results suggest that the direct relation between racial discrimination and psychological distress was strongest for studies with multi-item measures.

Carter and colleagues conducted another meta-analysis of 242 studies (1,805 effect sizes) between 1998 and 2015 and examined correlations between racial discrimination, health (physical health, mental health, and substance use), and cultural outcomes in more detail; they explored acculturation, racial identity, collective self-esteem, ethnic identity, and racial socialization as cultural outcomes among people of color.[78] They found that the direct overall relationship between racial discrimination, health, and culture is strongest for mental health ($r = .21$), then substance use ($r = .16$), cultural variables (e.g., acculturation, racial/ethnic identity, racial socialization; $r = .10$), and physical health ($r = .07$). Findings also indicate that Asian and Native American racial groups have stronger effects from racial discrimination than do Blacks, a finding that is consistent with other investigations.

Priscilla Lui and Lucia Quezada examined how microaggressions negatively affect adjustment outcomes among marginalized people.[79] An analysis of seventy-two studies shows statistically significant correlations between microaggression and adjustment outcomes ($r = .20$) (95 percent confidence interval [CI] [.16–.23]). Microaggressions were more strongly associated with internalizing problems, stress/negative affect, and positive affect/adjustment than with externalizing problems and physical symptoms.

SUMMARY OF THE DIRECT EVIDENCE

Despite the existence of some direct evidence supporting the contention that racism is experienced as a stressor, nonetheless resistance persists on the part of mental health professionals to accept the conceptualization of racism as a form of severe stress or trauma. Perhaps the idea that racism is a traumatic stressor is hard for professionals to accept because it is relatively new in the literature. Or perhaps the denial is another manifestation of racism. Kwame Mackenzie and Kamaldeep Bhui identify ways in which racism is minimized in mental health care, including a denial of racism, clinicians becoming personally offended by the idea that they are acting in racist ways, or clinicians blaming the targets of racism with accusations of oversensitivity or statements indicating that they have a "chip on their shoulder."[80] Indeed, failing to acknowledge societal racism, diminishing the impact of historical racism on current social realities, and a lack of awareness of social privileges that stem from being a member of the dominant racial group are identified as mechanisms through which racism is maintained.[81] Therefore, a hesitancy to appreciate that experiences of racism are potentially traumatic could be viewed as evidence for the ongoing impact of race and racial categorization in American society.

Although our brief review of the literature confirms that experiences of racism and racial discrimination are prevalent and harmful, the findings on the frequency and impact of racism do vary as a function of how racial discrimination is perceived, measured, or assessed. It is hard to know if specific types of racism (e.g., discrimination, harassment, physical violence) affect people differentially. Carter and colleagues' preliminary studies suggest that acts of racial hostility may have greater lasting mental health effects than acts of racial avoidance, but more research is needed.[82] The studies confirm that people are exposed to various types of discrimination, and that some types affect people more than others. Unpacking racism to account for specific categories and their mental health effects is warranted.[83]

RECONCEPTUALIZING RACISM AND MENTAL HEALTH

Carter and Janet E. Helms[84] and Carter[85] note that racism can and perhaps should be reconceptualized into distinct classes that encompass the various levels on which racism occurs (i.e., individual, institutional, cultural). The classes that Carter and Helms have proposed include avoidant racism, hostile racism, and aversive-hostile racism. The rationale for unpacking racism is to reduce the ambiguity associated with the various kinds of race-based experiences, and to help people who are targets be more specific about the nature of their experiences. Being stopped by the police because of your race (hostile), being ignored by salespeople in a store or being denied housing (avoidant), and not being promoted at work or having your abilities and professional skills constantly questioned in subtle ways (aversive-hostile) are all acts of racism. Yet each type is distinct and bears a different emotional impact. We contend that important details related to the potential stress produced by each type of experience are lost by grouping them together as general acts of racism, discrimination (disparate impact), or bias, as is typically the practice in social discourse, in organizations, and in legal proceedings.

It is possible to measure the effects of racism if more specific classes are used, as we outline below. Moreover, we think that people of color might respond differently when asked about experiences of racial discrimination or racism when using the classes of racism categories. It may matter to people to know if they are being avoided or harassed, or if they are being treated as if they are dangerous. Knowledge and recognition of the different classes of racism may aid the individual in coping with racism-related experiences, could assist clinicians who are working with psychological and emotional outcomes of racist experiences, and could be beneficial in the legal context when seeking redress for any injury sustained by acts of racism.

AVOIDANT RACISM

Avoidant racism is indicated by behaviors, thoughts, policies, and strategies that aim to maintain distance or minimize contact between the dominant racial group members and nondominant racial groups or its members.[86] Avoidant racism helps dominant racial-group members participate in racism without overtly appearing to do so. Avoidant racism may occur at the individual level (e.g., denial of opportunity or access to a person of color), at the systemic or institutional level (e.g., systematically providing substandard education or health care), and at the policy and cultural level (e.g., standards and practices that exclude people of color; ignoring or denigrating the cultural contributions of people of color). Researchers cited previously have found that racial discrimination includes, but is not limited to, exclusion from social and work networks, dismissal or denial of personal achievements, and limited or restricted opportunities for achievement (e.g., discouraging students of color from enrolling in advanced high school courses required for college admission). The research reviewed here suggests that emotional responses to being discriminated against include fear, tension, anxiety, depression, sadness, anger, aggression, resolve to overcome barriers, social cohesion, and taking strength from the experience. Many experiences of avoidant racism that people of color encounter, especially Blacks and Native Americans, have powerful historical elements that give meaning and salience to symbolic, subtle, verbal, and nonverbal messages that alone can produce race-based stress. The goal and purpose of avoidant racism, therefore, is to maintain the position of dominance and subservience across racial lines.

HOSTILE RACISM

Hostile racism entails using feelings, thoughts, actions, strategies, behaviors, and policies to communicate the target's subordinate status due to his or her membership in a nondominant racial group.[87] Acts of racial hostility can be explicit, and implicit. In fact, in the absence of explicit policies and procedures for filing and handling claims of racial harassment in most organizations, individuals can assume that the organization does not prioritize its response to acts of racism or racial discrimination. Racial hostility can occur as quid pro quo pressure to go along with organizational racial practices and policies as a condition of continued participation.

Emotional reactions to hostile treatment include anger, rage, powerlessness, shame, guilt, helplessness, low self-esteem or persistent self-doubt, suspiciousness, and distrust. Other reactions are positive and adaptive, such as resolving to prove people wrong, confronting the person or persons, or using the feelings as a source of personal or group strength.

AVERSIVE-HOSTILE RACISM

The third class of racial discrimination, aversive-hostile racism, reflects incidents of discrimination that include elements of both avoidance and hostility. Aversive-hostile racism involves thoughts, behaviors, actions, feelings, or policies and procedures that are meant to create distance between racial groups. The distancing is an act of hostility and fear (e.g., socioeconomic exclusion, White flight). The aversive behavior can be either intentional or unintentional; what matters for the actor is the outcome of creating distance between racial groups.

Aversive-hostile racism is described in the work of John Dovidio and Samuel Gaertner[88] and other scholars[89] who explain contemporary racism. They note that over time racism has changed and has become symbolic, modern, subtle, and hidden within the guise of nonprejudicial or nonracist behavior and justifications. According to these scholars, strong negative feelings toward people of color operate on the subconscious level. We do not contend that racism is subconscious. The negative perceptions are not conveyed as open hostility; rather, they manifest themselves in color-blind beliefs and practices and through expressions of discomfort and disgust. Individuals who hold such attitudes find interactions with people of color aversive. People and institutions that operate in this fashion are thought to be ambivalent, color-blind, or liberal and thus may discriminate in some instances and not in others.[90] When individuals or organizational leaders justify their actions or decisions by claiming that factors other than race were responsible, then racism can occur without challenge, and the person who claims that racial discrimination took place is made to look foolish.

The definitions of classes of racism can guide mental health professionals in their analysis and assessment of race-based experiences. Furthermore, they might serve to enhance investigations of the mental health effects of racism. Finally, they are valuable as the basis for measuring the mental health effects of racism and for identifying race-based stress and traumatic stress. We will revisit the classes of racism in more detail in part II, where we discuss a new approach to assessing racial trauma that incorporates the class of racist experience. First, we turn our attention to factors identified in the literature that influence the relationship between experiences of racism and health-related outcomes, and that might explain some of the variability in that relationship.[91]

4

VARIATIONS IN RESPONSES TO RACIAL DISCRIMINATION

IRRESPECTIVE OF THE UBIQUITOUS nature of racism within American society, not everyone who experiences a racial incident reports psychological pain at the level of traumatic stress.[1] In this chapter we review several types of variation within racial groups based on acculturation, social class, and other factors, and we discuss racism-related coping and psychological variation based on one's racial group or racial identity.[2]

WITHIN-RACIAL-GROUP VARIATION

Considerable heterogeneity exists within racial groups along many factors, including religiosity, social class status, gender, and cultural values.[3] It is important, therefore, to avoid treating members of racial groups as monolithic or psychologically similar.[4] A common error within social science research has been to infer psychological attributes from sociodemographic racial categories. At its worst, this approach informed much of the scientific racism of the twentieth century;[5] however, some evidence shows that scientists, scholars, and researchers continue to treat racial group members as monolithic demographic categories without attending to individual variation.[6] In so doing, social scientists make the false assumption that people who are presumed to be part of a particular racial group are psychologically invested in that group's culture, and that group members should be treated as if there is no difference between them. Sources of within-group variation are seldom accounted for beyond socioeconomic status and gender.[7]

The centuries-long presence of racism in the lives of many people of color has resulted in a range of coping strategies and constructive responses that have been passed on to younger generations and other group members through socialization, community, and social support. In addition, people have developed various types of psychological resolutions (e.g., racial-identity ego statuses) regarding the meaning they attach to their race, their own racial group, and out-groups. Research indicates that individuals who are more invested or psychologically connected to their racial group might be more likely to perceive racial discrimination and also to be negatively impacted by a racial event.[8] Findings suggest that racial and ethnic identity influence both how one perceives racial discrimination and the psychological outcomes associated with experiences of discrimination.[9]

COPING WITH RACISM

Attention has been directed to how people of color cope with racism, including both adaptive and maladaptive strategies. Given that there is no comprehensive theoretical model of racism-related coping,[10] scholars who have examined racial-group-specific coping behaviors have tended to use measures that were created to assess strategies for coping with general life stressors.[11] These studies, which primarily examine the influence of approach and avoidant strategies, have yielded mixed results. In some, avoidant strategies are associated with lower life satisfaction,[12] negative emotions,[13] distress,[14] and hiding one's emotions.[15] In others, avoidant strategies are associated with decreased symptoms, while approach coping is associated with increased symptoms[16] and decreased reports of psychological stress.[17] These inconsistencies could reflect differences in the measures used to assess situational coping styles compared to dispositional coping styles, and they could reflect the influence of unmeasured moderating variables. They may also reflect the use of generic coping measures in racism-related coping research[18] and the differences in racism-related coping that exist across racial groups.[19]

More recently, instruments designed to specifically assess racism-related coping have emerged in the literature.[20] The studies identify a range of behavioral and culturally informed coping responses, including actions that could be defined as active coping (resistance, education, advocacy, confrontation) and others that appear to be more consistent with avoidant coping (hypervigilance, self-preservation, detachment, use of substances). The strategies also appear to align well with the racism-related coping described by David Mellor, who suggests that coping strategies can be defined by their functionality, with some strategies designed to prevent injury and others designed to prevent or respond to racism.[21] Just as scholars argue that race-related stress is different from general stress, several scholars suggest that generic coping measures cannot adequately capture the range of specific race-related coping strategies that people of color use to deal with racism.[22]

Deborah Plummer and Steve Slane investigated coping in a sample of White and Black adults selected from various universities, churches, and work settings.[23] Respondents were asked to describe a general stressful situation and a race-related stressful situation. The researchers found that both Blacks and Whites experience race-based situations as more stressful than other experiences, and they use different strategies to deal with them. In racially stressful situations, Blacks use a greater number of coping strategies than do Whites, and they use confrontation more than other options. The authors suggest that because Blacks experience more stress, they use more ways to cope. These findings are supported in other investigations.[24]

Sharon Danoff-Burg and colleagues report gender differences for Blacks, with women using social support to cope with racism-related stress more than men.[25] Differences also occur in responses to varying levels of racism-related stress. For instance, Black women use avoidance to deal with individual racism. Self-esteem and life satisfaction are lower when avoidance coping is used. Thus, these studies suggest that coping varies for people of color as a function of the type of racism and the source of the stress.

Some coping strategies identified in the literature are directly linked to individual variation that occurs within racial groups based on cultural socialization.[26] Scholars have outlined culturally informed responses to racism that both provide protection and can heighten individual sensitivity to experiences of racism. Incorporating spirituality or religiously based coping reflective of African cultural values is linked to African American coping styles.[27] Karina Walters and Jane Simoni have shown that cultural factors associated with traditional forms of healing and culturally informed spiritual beliefs are associated with resilience and protective factors among Native American women.[28]

In the literature on coping, a disproportionate number of studies, using both quantitative and qualitative methodologies, focus on Black Americans,[29] with notable exception.[30] A smaller number of quantitative studies assess the influence of psychosocial variables such as racial identity,[31] racial socialization, and cultural orientation.[32] These studies highlight the importance of appreciating that individuals might vary within a racial group according to their psychological identification with the group. This difference in identification could explain some inconsistent findings in the racism-related coping literature as well as the fact that experiences of racism have different impacts on individuals. We now take a closer look at these variables, including racial/ethnic identity and racial socialization.

RACIAL IDENTITY

Racial groups have distinct sociopolitical histories that influence perceptions of both the individual and the group. These histories, coupled with an individual's personality and how he interacts with his family and community systems, contribute to how that individual responds to environmental stress, and that response influences the types of experiences he will encounter. For instance, Asian Americans and Native Americans are perceived and treated differently than African Americans. African Americans' history of slavery has set them apart from other groups of color, as has the Nation status of Native Americans. As is the case with other forms of stress, racism is moderated by factors such as social class, acculturation, gender, coping, and racial identity ego statuses, and scholars provide some information about how these factors affect the perception of race and racism.

Racial identity theorists conceptualize race as a psychological construct that allows for a more complex understanding of the processes involved in responding to race-based experiences.[33] Racial scholars suggest that racial identity acts as a buffer for Americans of color against the negative or harmful effects of exposure to racism and discrimination.[34]

Racial identity is now considered to be a core aspect of personality and racial socialization,[35] and in that sense should have particular relevance for understanding how individuals respond to race-based stress. Racial identity theorists explain the varied manner in which schemas, affective states, and behaviors can be classified according to the various racial identity ego statuses that individuals psychologically embrace or reject, or whether they are ambivalent about their race and racial group and about the dominant racial group.[36] Racial identity statuses, as outlined by Robert T. Carter[37] and Janet E. Helms,[38] have empirical support in the research literature and are applicable to all racial groups.[39] Other models have also been proposed in studies in the psychological literature, namely, the multidimensional theory of racial identity and the multidimensional inventory of Black identity (MIBI).

The multidimensional model includes *salience*, which is person and situation specific and refers to how relevant an individual's race is to their self-concept; *centrality*, which is a person's perception of self by race, and there are feelings of negativity or positivity in both public (i.e., how others see Blacks) and private domains (i.e., how one feels about Blacks); and *ideology*, beliefs about how Blacks should exist within and interact in society. An expanded model of Nigrescence and a corresponding measure, the Cross Racial Identity Scale (CRIS), were later developed. The CRIS outlines three Pre-Encounter subscales, Assimilation, Miseducation, and Self-Hatred as well as one Immersion-Emersion Anti-White subscale and two Internalization subscales, Afrocentric and Multiculturalist Inclusive.[40]

Helms's model of racial identity ego statuses vary from less mature (i.e., an ego status that relies on identification with the external dominant racial group) to more mature (i.e., an identification that is internal and is associated with one's own racial group). Models of racial identity exist for Whites, Blacks, and people of color. For people of color, racial identity ego statuses as defined by Helms include (a) Pre-encounter/Conformity, in which race is not salient; (b) Encounter/Dissonance, which is considered to be a transition status; (c) Immersion/Emersion, in which one idealizes one's own reference group; and (d) Internalization/Integrative awareness, in which one internalizes investment in one's own racial group.[41] Racial identity statuses have been shown to be associated with many race-related variables, including race-related stress, racism-related coping, perceptions of discrimination, psychological functioning, preferences for social change activities, and perceptions of institutional racism.[42]

RACIAL IDENTITY STATUSES AND RACE-RELATED VARIABLES

Racial identity has also been found to be associated with psychological functioning in the context of racism. David Chae and colleagues found that higher racial centrality is associated with greater reports of racial discrimination.[43] Additionally, lower reports of racial discrimination and holding anti-Black bias are associated with greatest risk for depression. These findings suggest that unconscious as well as conscious processes related to racial identity are important to consider in measuring racial discrimination. Shawn Jones and colleagues examined the association between racial identity and emotional responses to blatant and subtle racial discrimination vignettes in a sample of 129 African American college students.[44] They found that the significance and meaning that one places on race affect emotional responses. Deidre Franklin-Jackson and Carter found that racial identity and racism-related stress predict psychological distress, with Pre-encounter status attitudes related to psychological distress, and Internalization status attitudes related to psychological well-being.[45] The findings associated with these analyses suggest that racial identity status attitudes serve as complex filters for racial stimuli and psychological outcomes. Robert Sellers and J. Nicole Shelton, using the MIBI, found that individuals who express a higher endorsement of racial ideology are less impacted by experiences of racial discrimination.[46] In the same vein, Anna Khaylis and colleagues found that a strong ethnic identity is related to increases in PTSD symptoms in response to higher levels of race-related stress.[47]

A study by Helen Neville and colleagues of psychological variation in how racial stressors are perceived and how coping is used found that Immersion/Emersion status attitudes are associated with lower levels of psychological health, increased perception of general stressors, and greater use of suppressive coping styles.[48] Internalization status attitudes are associated with less awareness of race-specific stressors, and encounter status attitudes are related to greater perception of race-specific stressors.

Sellers and Shelton examined whether Black racial identity, as measured by the MIBI, is related to perceived discrimination and psychological distress, finding that those who feel being Black is important (racial centrality) report experiencing more discrimination. Nationalistic racial ideology and public regard were found to buffer the effects of perceived racial discrimination. For instance, if a person thought that Blacks are held in low public regard, it lessened the negative impact of discrimination.[49] Furthermore, Lori Hoggard and colleagues found that racial identity status attitudes are predictive of how participants interpreted racial cues, and that individuals who held a belief that others tend to view African Americans negatively had increased vulnerability to blatant racism.[50] Melissa Greene and colleagues found that individuals who reported higher levels of commitment to their ethnic identity reported lower levels of self-esteem in the face of experiences of discrimination, leading the authors to conclude that "that the effects of racial and ethnic discrimination on the psychological well-being of ethnic minority youth depend, in part, on how youth think and feel about being a member of their ethnic group."[51] Tamika C. B. Zapolski, Marcy R. Beutlich, Sycarah Fisher, and Jessica Barnes-Najor reported that collective ethnic-racial identity (i.e., believing that others viewed your group positively) was related to better health outcomes for African American youth, yet these same beliefs did not buffer the effects on health outcomes.[52]

RACIAL IDENTITY AND COPING

Researchers have found that racial identity status attitudes are associated with preferences for particular coping strategies[53] and social change strategies.[54] The research also indicates that certain aspects of racial identity influence perceptions of discrimination or the attribution of ambiguous life events and daily hassles to racism.[55] Certain types of generic coping strategies are associated with better mental health outcomes in dealing with racism, with some studies suggesting that racial and cultural variables may influence the selection of strategies used to cope with racism,[56] and preliminary evidence suggesting that the efficacy of particular strategies for coping with racism is influenced by individual differences.[57] These conclusions suggest that there could be a complex interaction between racial identity and racism-related coping that affects the psychological impact of racism and discrimination, an idea that has received little attention in the literature to date.

A study conducted by Jessica Forsyth and Robert T. Carter provides an important window into the complex relationship between racial identity, racism-related stress, and coping strategies.[58] Using a sample of 233 Black American adults with an average age of thirty-three and with higher participation by females (74.7 percent), Forsyth and Carter examined the relationship between racism-related coping strategies and racial identity status attitudes and their combined association with psychological functioning as assessed by participant scores on the mental health inventory and the symptom checklist. They identified eight racism-related coping strategies: (1) *hypervigilant* strategies, which were reflected in increased caution in interactions with others who are not Black, the use of avoidant behavior to elude any racially charged interactions, and mental concern with the incident; (2) *confrontational* strategies, characterized by direct expression of anger and/or dealing with the perpetrator in some way; (3) *empowered action*, which involved using community and/or legal resources to hold people accountable for their actions; (4) use of *social support*, which comprised a range of behaviors and thoughts including seeking advice; sharing one's experiences with friends, family, and others who could relate; providing support for others in

similar situations; and using efforts to minimize the effect of the racial incident; (5) *spiritual* actions, such as seeking guidance from religious members and leaders, and using practices such as meditation, prayer, and singing;
(6) *constrained resistance*, which included both passive (e.g., slowing work,
use of substances) and active (e.g., use of intimidation) behaviors to resist racism; (7) *bargaining*, including efforts to make sense of the experience while
maintaining a positive perspective; (8) *racial consciousness*, comprising efforts
to connect with or express one's cultural heritage and history and to take
action against racism.

Hierarchical cluster analysis of racial identity status attitudes and coping
strategies resulted in a four-cluster solution: encounter bargaining, pre-encounter
constrained resistance, immersion cultural hypervigilance (hypervigilant and
culturally focused strategies involving, e.g., spiritual and racial consciousness),
and internalization-empowered confrontation—all of which differed significantly from one another on each of the clustering variables. The results of a
multiple analysis of variance indicate that there are significant differences
between the groups in psychological symptoms but no differences in well-
being. Overall, the results suggest that the combination of racial identity
status attitudes and coping strategies reveal important information about
how participants use coping styles in the context of racial-identity status to
deal with racial discrimination. For instance, the internalization-empowered
confrontation cluster group had lower levels of psychological symptoms
when compared to the encounter bargaining and immersion cultural hypervigilance cluster groups. How racial identity is related to coping with racism
tells something about how the patterns are related to one's emotional
health. To further illustrate, we discuss findings associated with two of
the racial identity-coping style clusters, namely, encounter bargaining (EB)
versus internalization-empowered confrontation (IEC, a combination of
empowered action, spiritual, and constrained resistance coping).

The EB cluster group is more characterized by pre-encounter, encounter, and immersion racial-identity status attitudes than the IEC cluster group.
The EB group's use of racism-related coping strategies is close to the sample
mean and yet is higher than that of the IEC group. The racism-related coping pattern reveals that the EB group relies primarily on bargaining strategies, followed by confrontation and social support, to deal with racial
encounters. They use moderately and equally the racism-related coping strategies of hypervigilance, empowered action, racial consciousness, and constrained resistance, but they do not use spiritual coping strategies much or at

all. The high levels of pre-encounter, encounter, and immersion status attitudes that characterized the EB group indicate that there is considerable inconsistency regarding their racial identity resolutions. The struggle around color-blind and racially naive beliefs and attitudes as well as the growing feelings of racial pride and investment in identifying as Black reveal a clash. The presence of encounter attitudes suggests that the struggle comes about due to increased exposure to or awareness of racism.

In contrast, the IEC group's racial identity status attitude with the lowest score is encounter, and the group's scores on pre-encounter and immersion-emersion are lower than scores on internalization. This pattern of racial identity attitudes suggests that individuals in the IEC group have greater comfort and stability with their racial identity. It is also likely that the racial identity stability of the IEC group leads to better skills in managing stressful racial interactions so that they result in less interpersonal conflict. It also seems to indicate that members of this group use less effort in coping with racism and direct more energy toward direct resistant actions (i.e., confrontation, empowered action, constrained resistance, and spiritual activities). Their thoughtful use of bargaining, hypervigilance, and racial consciousness means they have the capacity to assess racially ambiguous situations and to anticipate racism so that their coping strategies are more proactive. More important, they feel confident to handle racial situations relatively well, as evidenced by their low reliance on social support. In contrast, the EB group's primary reliance on bargaining strategies to cope with racism seems to reflect their encounter and pre-encounter attitudes and reveals a potential lack of self-efficacy when dealing with racial incidents. Individuals in this group possibly doubted their capacity to discern racist incidents and might have questioned whether their own behavior played a major element in the incident they experienced. Therefore, their coping centered on efforts to manage how others perceive them. Their reliance on bargaining could also mean that they attempted to deny the psychological and emotional significance of the incident and thus to reframe it, trying to understand the actions of the perpetrator. Given that bargaining was among the racism-related coping strategies most strongly related to each of the psychological symptoms, and that research has found that coping strategies characterized by self-doubt are associated with increased anxiety and distress,[59] the EB group's primary reliance on this strategy likely contributes to the increased psychological distress they experience as compared to the IEC group.

The Forsyth and Carter study provides evidence of within-racial-group variability associated with how one responds to racism-related stress.[60] This type of variability could be one explanation for differences in psychological outcomes associated with the experience of racial incidents. But research indicates that not everyone who experiences a racial incident will report trauma-related symptoms.[61]

Delida Sanchez, Leann Smith, and Whitney Adams examined the links between racial *marianismo* gender-role (e.g., women are expected to be good) beliefs, racial socialization (preparation for bias), coping strategies (engagement versus disengagement), and mental health outcomes among 211 Latino/a college students.[62] They investigated the effects of ethnic socialization and *marianismo* in the association between racial discrimination and coping strategies. Then they tested the effects of coping strategies on racial discrimination and mental health outcomes. Findings indicate that racial discrimination was related to *familismo* (i.e., the identification with one's family) and spiritual *marianismo* pillars, preparation for bias, and engagement coping strategies. Furthermore, they established a link between racial discrimination and engagement coping strategies and preparation for bias. Finally, racial discrimination, disengagement coping strategies, and self-silencing *marianismo* attitudes are negatively related to mental health, revealing a complex pattern of relationships between gender socialization, identity, and worldview and coping with racial discrimination.

These studies indicate that coping strategies are linked with one's racial-identity status, psychological functioning, and mental health outcomes, and they influence the perception of racial discrimination.

SOCIAL CLASS, ACCULTURATION, RACIAL SOCIALIZATION

Beyond racial identity, other variables have been identified as influencing the relationship between perceived racism and psychological outcomes. Among these are structural factors such as socioeconomic status or social class[63] and psychological experiences such as acculturation[64] and racial socialization.[65] Given our focus on individual-level variables, we examine some of the literature associated with acculturation, racial socialization, and social class as they affect individual variation in psychological outcomes of racism experiences.

SOCIAL CLASS

Social class is defined as "one's position in the economic hierarchy in society that arises from a combination of annual income, educational attainment, and occupation prestige."[66] Social class is influential in psychological processes like mental health disorders and substance use/abuse.[67] Alex Pieterse and Carter report that stress associated with racist events contributes in a unique and independent fashion to both psychological distress and well-being in a sample of Black adult men.[68] Furthermore, the findings outline differences in racist incidents and psychological reactions in that middle-class men experience more racism-related stress. First, we note a further finding by Robert T. Carter and Janet E. Helms, in which they examined the relationship between social class and racial identity attitudes, even though social class was measured in several ways.[69] They did not find any association between racial identity and social class for their sample of Black Americans. In an experimental analysis examining the relationship between social class and responses to perceived ethnic and racial discrimination, Sarah Townsend and colleagues found that middle-class Latinos/as report more feelings of uncertainty and fewer adaptive responses to discrimination than their working-class counterparts.[70] Naa Kwate and Melody Goodman indicate that women of higher education or social class status report more frequent experiences of racist incidents; however, when measuring social class by self-report, this relationship is not supported.[71] Moore-Berg and Karpinski argue that it is important to consider both race and social class not as separate but as intersecting categories that together influence intergroup processes.[72]

It appears, therefore, that socioeconomic status might influence the perception of racial discrimination and might have some indirect impact on psychological outcomes associated with racial incidents; however, the findings also appear to depend on how social class or socioeconomic status is operationalized.

ACCULTURATION

Acculturation is a shift in values and behaviors toward the host culture by individuals transitioning across cultures.[73] Most research examining psychological aspects of acculturation within the United States focus on the experiences of Asians and Latinos/as. Research findings are inconclusive regarding the impact of acculturation on racism and psychological outcomes. Saul Alamilla and colleagues examined 113 Asian Americans for influences of behavioral and values acculturation and enculturation and found that acculturation to American cultural values as compared to enculturation to Asian American values is related to fewer psychological symptoms.[74] Also, in a study of 130 adult Latin American immigrants, Alamilla and colleagues found that less acculturated individuals reported higher levels of psychological distress.[75] Furthermore, Lucas Torres and colleagues discovered that greater endorsement of values associated with White society led to lower psychological distress in association with experiences of racism.[76] On the other hand, Beverly Araújo Dawson indicates that among 243 Dominican immigrants who experienced racism in the workplace, those who reported lower levels of acculturation reported higher levels of psychological distress.[77]

John Berry and Feng Hou explored the role of acculturation in the experience of racial discrimination and psychological well-being among a sample of three thousand adult second-generation immigrants to Canada.[78] Results indicate that those who are marginalized in their acculturation status report less well-being in the context of discrimination than those who identify as assimilated. Part of the inconsistent findings could be associated with the manner in which acculturation is assessed as well as the moderating effects of other characteristics, including gender. A good example of the complexity of variables like acculturation when assessing the psychological impact of racism is noted in the examination of 123 Somali adolescent refugees conducted by Heidi Ellis and colleagues. Here, acculturation is found to be protective against racial discrimination for girls but not for boys. Both boys and girls, however, do report negative psychological outcomes associated with racist incidents.[79] William Liu, Rossina Liu, and colleagues implicate acculturation in the process of racial trauma.[80]

Although the findings vary, it is important to appreciate the role that cultural orientation might play in either providing a protective buffer against experiences of racism or possibly exacerbating the effects of racism on psychological health.[81]

RACIAL SOCIALIZATION

Racial socialization is defined as the instillation of both positive messages about one's racial heritage and messages preparing one to experience bias and discrimination. Racial socialization is understood within a developmental context and reflects active parental involvement in shaping a child's understanding of himself or herself as a racial being.[82] Racial socialization is noted to have a significant impact on how individuals perceive racism as well as how individuals are impacted by racial incidents.[83] To illustrate, Enrique Neblett and colleagues examined relations between perceived racial discrimination, depressive symptoms, externalizing behaviors, and racial socialization among a sample of 369 African American adolescents.[84] Findings indicate that racial socialization moderates the relationship between discrimination and depression such that higher levels of racial socialization are associated with lower levels of depressive symptoms when encountering racial incidents. However, as in the case with acculturation, the findings do not always follow a similar direction. Mia Bynum and colleagues, in a study of 247 African American college students, found that racial socialization moderates the relationship between racial incidents and psychological stress but does not affect the relationship between racial incidents and psychological distress.[85] A weakening of the relationship between racism and stress is noted, but not for racism and psychological distress. April Harris-Britt and colleagues examined the impact of racial socialization on the relationship between perceived racism and self-esteem in a sample of 128 African American eighth graders and found that racial socialization contributes to higher levels of self-esteem in the context of racial discrimination.[86]

More recently, investigators have employed the concept of racial socialization in intervention studies, also examining whether racial socialization indeed acts as a protective psychological barrier against experiences of racism. Riana Anderson and colleagues describe the use of support groups grounded in the principle of racial socialization.[87] Findings suggest that the support group was well received by the participants and that the intervention increased a participant's ability to identify race-related stress and decreased the stress associated with racism-related experiences. In another study Riana Anderson and Howard Stevenson describe an intervention designed to help heal race-related stress and racial trauma through racial socialization.[88]

The literature on racial socialization appears to provide some evidence of its buffering effects; however, the findings seem to vary according to participants' age, and to date the bulk of research has been undertaken with African Americans. Still, it is encouraging to see that the construct of racial socialization is being extended beyond the experience of Black Americans.[89]

Linda Juang and colleagues describe the findings of twenty-two empirical examinations focused on racial socialization among Asian Americans.[90] The findings draw from both quantitative and qualitative investigations and reach conclusions that are similar to findings gleaned from studies focusing on Black Americans. Regarding the impact of racial socialization in the context of racial discrimination and negative racial experiences, Juang and colleagues state, "Promoting awareness of discrimination and preparation for bias are related to both positive and negative adjustment, with evidence that no preparation or too much emphasis on discrimination is related to poorer adjustment. Finally, highlighting mistrust and avoidance of outgroups seems to be the most consistently related to negative adjustment."[91]

Scholars have also started examining the role of racial socialization among the Latino/a population. Sanchez, Smith, and Adams describe an investigation into the role of racial socialization—operationalized as being prepared for the experience of racial bias, coping styles, and mental health outcomes—in a sample of 211 Latino/a college students.[92] Their findings suggest that racial socialization plays an important role in the types of coping strategies participants reported when perceiving racial discrimination. Specifically, engaged coping is employed as an indirect effect of racial socialization. As is the case with the other variables we describe in this chapter, findings are inconsistent. Noé Rubén Chávez and Sabine Elizabeth French report findings from a study examining the moderating role of racial socialization in a sample of 109 Latino/a college students.[93] They found no evidence of a moderating effect for racial socialization in the relationship between racial discrimination and various aspects of mental distress such as anxiety, depression, and loss of behavioral/emotional control.

The extent to which positive messages of one's racial heritage might buffer experiences of racial discrimination among other groups of color is yet to be consistently established in the literature. Furthermore, inconsistent findings might be associated with the way racial socialization is assessed, with the variation that occurs across racial and ethnic groups, and with individual-level variables such as racial identity ego status attitudes.

SUMMARY

We examined individual-level psychological variables that affect the mental health consequences of racial discrimination among various groups. We have also provided information drawn from the empirical scholarship on the psychological impact of racism experiences, and we have identified factors associated with the different psychological effects of racism and racial discrimination.

Although variables such as gender are found to affect perceptions of racism and coping strategies,[94] the evidence indicates that gender does not account for different outcomes associated with the experience of racism or racial discrimination.[95] The variables of racial identity, level of acculturation, and racial socialization, however, are found to influence how individuals react to experiences of racism.[96] Socioeconomic status or social class is another important variable.[97]

Given that people's exposure to racism and racial discrimination is prevalent, and given that the psychological impact of such exposure is adverse, it is important to consider how best to assess and treat that impact. Furthermore, these considerations might have important bearing on the extent to which racist incidents can be understood as traumatic stress.

Having provided a context in which to comprehend what racism is and how it is stressful, we turn in part II to a more specific discussion of racism as a traumatic stressor.

PART TWO

WHAT WE NEED TO KNOW ABOUT RACIAL TRAUMA

5

RACE-BASED TRAUMATIC STRESS AS RACIAL TRAUMA

FRAMEWORK FOR RACE-BASED TRAUMATIC STRESS

Despite policy statements and proclamations of the importance of racial/ethnic diversity or multicultural considerations in training and practice for mental health professionals, the reality of race and racism's effects on psychological functioning and development continues to be underrepresented in the theoretical, empirical, and practice-related literature.[1] Furthermore, little information is available in mental health theory, research, or practice about race and racism's effects, or about how race as an aspect of human personality in the United States should be understood,[2] even with the publication of the special issue on racial trauma in the *American Psychologist*[3] and the recent guidelines from the American Psychological Association (APA) on race and ethnicity provides little direct discussion or focus on race in psychotherapy or human personality.[4] We note that in the last decade, the APA put forward as policy multiple guidelines for various groups (women, LGBTQ people, older people, disabled people, etc.), yet it was not until 2019 that the guidelines on race and ethnicity were proposed; as of this writing, to our knowledge, these guidelines are still not policy.

The contemporary focus on multiculturalism in psychology has its origins in the civil rights movements of the 1950s and 1960s, which largely focused on race. Robert T. Carter describes the manner in which people of color were initially viewed as inferior in the psychological literature, a paradigm that has shifted, mostly due to scholars pushing back, arguing that people of color in the United States are culturally different, not inferior.[5] Subsequently, the notion of cultural difference shifted to employing the term *multicultural*, which includes many categories, such as gender, age, sexual orientation, religion, disability, and so on. Each category, it is argued, should be thought of as "cultural" and treated as equally valid irrespective of one's race. The multicultural perspective therefore diminishes the importance of race, with race becoming one of many factors to fall under its umbrella. Don Davis and colleagues observe that what they call the multicultural counseling competencies (MCC) movement has been around for decades, growing out of mental health disparities among people of color. They note that the competencies "are now included in accreditation requirements and guidelines for all areas of psychological science. . . . Similar emphasis on MCCs have occurred across several disciplines, including education, social work, counseling, law, and medicine."[6]

Janet E. Helms and Donelda Cook,[7] as well as Carter,[8] have observed that terms such as *culture, cultural diversity*, and *multicultural* are used as substitutes for race, and that using these terms disempowers historically disenfranchised Americans (Blacks, Native Americans, Hispanics, and Asians), just as such use diminishes the experience of race, which is a central aspect of stratification within American society.[9] Most aspects of difference referred to as *multiculturality, diversity, ethnicity, gender*, or *social class*, for instance, have few racial distinctions. These terms refer to so many social demographic groups that they become virtually useless for explaining the ways in which the therapy process (or mental health) is influenced by racial . . . factors. Moreover, the use of ambiguous language makes it easy to encourage acceptance of cultural pluralism of various types "without actually acknowledging it."[10] Helms, Cook, and Carter all suggest that the terms do not threaten most Whites, and the ambiguous language allows people to think of themselves, regardless of race, as an oppressed "minority" due to their gender, age, geography, sexual orientation, social class, and so on. Thus, race is obscured and diminished.

Although gender and social class oppression do exist and are endemic in our society and history, racial group classification is the only demographic variable that is associated with legal bondage, the status of being viewed and treated as property—like a phone or a car or a home—to which the owner could do as she wished. Property is usually an object, not a person, and enslaved people had no right to protest their treatment as nonhuman and their social exclusion. Thus, disenfranchised Americans had no way to diminish the effects of racism on their mental and emotional health.

Carrie Hemmings and Amanda Evans's study on treating race-related stress and trauma found that many counselors report having clients with race-related issues but acknowledge their lack of training to deal with such issues in therapy.[11] Of the few counselors who say they received training to treat race-related issues, most report that their training was through continuing education taken after receiving degrees in mental health.

MENTAL HEALTH TRAINING AND RACE

Historically and currently, the training received by most mental health professionals lacks any significant exploration of race or racism as a distinct aspect of the lived experience of American society.[12] Yet this does not mean that nothing about race is taught.[13]

The treatment and theoretical orientations of most mental health professionals and therapists does not allow for an explicit consideration of the psychological meaning and importance of race, in part because race has been thought of as a social or anthropological construct and therefore irrelevant to psychology. Members of racial groups have been thought to have particular personality traits, cognitive structures, and behaviors that are impediments to growth, obstacles to treatment, or permanent sources of dysfunction.[14] Therefore, race is seen as unimportant to universal notions of human development that serve as the guiding principles of most interventions and theories of human personality and development. For practitioners learning personality theory and human development, the topic of race has been virtually absent except to mention the inferiority or disadvantages of poor inner-city people, racial minorities, or people of color. José Causadias and colleagues point out that there is

> a cultural (mis)attribution bias in American psychology, [and all mental health disciplines have] the tendency to see racial/ethnic minorities as members of a group whose traits, beliefs, and behaviors are shaped primarily by culture, and to perceive the White racial/ethnic majority as autonomous and independent actors who are instead largely influenced by psychological processes. Because this bias rests on assumptions about human behavior that are not supported by evidence and may lead to differential treatment of members of specific social groups, it constrains psychologists' explanations of behavior and cognition.[15]

The misattribution works by using people of color in studies that have "culture" as the focus, while noncultural studies (the focus of mental health) have few people of color. Causadias and colleagues argue that this practice compromises the external validity of noncultural psychology because what we know about minorities remains restricted or distorted. . . . It negates [the fact] that Whites are also cultural beings and that cultural processes . . . also shape their perceptions and behavior in meaningful ways. . . . The cultural (mis)attribution bias situates White behavior as the gold standard of human experience against which all other groups should be compared. When minorities depart from this norm, they are considered deviant and deficient.[16]

Most mental health practitioners are taught that psychotherapy should be guided by one's theoretical orientation, whether psychoanalytic, psychodynamic, a variant of the classical approach, humanistic or client-centered, behavioral, or some combination of these. Since their creation, many of these theories of human personality, growth, and development have evolved, been expanded, or been altered. Each model has its ideas about personality development, psychological dysfunction, and therapies for when developmental problems arise. More important, critics suggest that all the traditional models are grounded in European and American worldviews or cultural assumptions.[17] Therefore, few theories have meaningfully incorporated considerations of race in their thinking[18] —a curious fact, since the notion of race came from Europe and the English settlers of the colonies.[19]

Theorists do mention culture and social factors,[20] but few note how historically ingrained beliefs and practices associated with race might affect personality development.[21] Because of the civil rights movement, more attention has been given to the mental health needs of people of color. But what remains constant are the prevailing ideas that undergird how race has been treated and understood by mental health theorists and scholars.[22]

Societal meanings and mechanisms frame the basic assumptions about race in mental health treatment and interventions. And these basic premises permeate mental health services and treatment strategies. In essence, three major paradigms are used to understand mental health where race is concerned (usually, the term *race* meant people of color until the work of racial identity scholars included Whites as a racial group):[23] the belief in inferiority, the notion of cultural and social deprivation, and the idea of cultural difference or the multicultural perspective.[24] The three paradigms overlap and have been employed simultaneously; furthermore, the assumptions derived from each are embedded, to varying degrees, in current social, political, educational, and mental health structures and practices.[25] When a paradigm is ascendant, it takes precedence over other viewpoints, and its adherents seldom seek alternative perspectives.[26] They use the concepts and policies of their point of view to guide problem-solving and to create procedures, programs, and interventions.

The belief in inferiority holds that people of color are limited biologically, that they are genetically inferior to Whites, and that differences in mental health can be attributed to the inherent physical differences.[27] The social activism of the civil rights era saw a shift from inferiority to explanations about cultural deficit or deprivation.[28] This notion combines the social meaning of race with the biological meaning to create a criterion whereby people of color are compared to a White normative standard and are found to be deficient. Proponents of this perspective assert that unevenness or disparities in economic, social, and cultural experiences are responsible for the apparent psychosocial differences among the races.

The cultural difference or cultural diversity idea argues that psychological and behavioral differences between racial groups are best explained in terms of the various racial and cultural influences while at the same time rejecting race as a criterion of difference in favor of the notion of ethnicity or culture.[29] However, the terms *ethnicity* and *culture* seem to be used in ways that refer to racial groups, while *culture* is defined so broadly that any difference creates a cultural group (e.g., age, social class, gender, religion). Social scientists who helped establish the idea of cultural difference, now referred to as *multiculturalism,* focus their efforts on describing the cultures of various groups and studying the psychological and social variables associated with their specific experiences.[30] Scholars argue that consideration of the cultural influences for particular presenting issues or racial groups is warranted and important under the guise of promoting diversity in mental health treatment. Mental health disciplines subsume race within diversity or multicultural perspectives, but race nevertheless retains its status as a central feature of American life even though other ideas such as social class or ethnicity have been introduced and held as more important.

Race continues to be a powerful a force in the minds and hearts of U.S. citizens. Thomas Edsall and Mary Edsall note that when the topic is about our leaders or presidential politics, who should receive government aid, who commits crime, or should have civil rights or the values people should hold or uphold, what is really being discussed is race. They believe that issues of race are deeply entrenched in our politics and society, and in competing ideas about the function and responsibility of government, as well as and in each voter's . . . identity. They observe, "In spite of America's success in eliminating legally protected racial subjugation, race remains a powerful wedge issue." They observe further that

> Racial animosity can be found in community meetings, courtrooms, American legion bars, political rallies, softball clubs, PTA sessions, public parks, and private gatherings across America. . . . On a daily level, a substantial number of whites view blacks [and people of color] as dangerous and as antagonistic to basic American values; these whites do not distinguish between blacks of different . . . classes. . . . A significant number of blacks, in turn, . . . view whites as not only attempting to evade responsibility for the continuing consequences of slavery and discrimination, but as the entrenched wielders of power in a lopsided whites-only system.[31]

Perspective on "race" defines liberal and conservative beliefs. In terms of policy, race still plays a critical role in the creation of a political system that has for years tolerated—if not supported—the growth of the disparity between rich and poor. These issues can be seen in the work of scholars such as Ta-Nehisi Coates,[32] E. J. Dionne and colleagues,[33] and Richard Rothstein.[34]

Although the Edsall's statements were offered over twenty-five years ago, some would argue that their sentiments continue to be relevant, as demonstrated by the most recent presidential election in the United States. The campaign, election, and presidency of Donald Trump have been replete with leanings toward White nationalism and racially tinged language designed to tap into White fear and discontent.[35] Political scientists describe the social dynamics reflected in the 2016 and 2020 presidential elections as being consistent with the enduring legacy of race within American politics,[36] and evidence suggests that racial attitudes are influential in voter patterns, with Whites who perceived a racial threat more likely to vote for Donald Trump and other Republicans.[37] Given that race continues to be such a central aspect of American life, it follows that mental health clinicians are also shaped and influenced by the existing racial landscape within North American life.

MENTAL HEALTH STANDARDS

Mental health professionals learn about race through their socialization process—that is, through their education, families, and communities. As has been outlined previously, much of this learning presumes that people of color are disadvantaged and at worst inferior, and that race does not matter as much as social class, gender, or other social factors. Therefore, it is difficult to help mental health professionals recognize the various forms of race-related stress experienced by people of color.[38] We think that to understand the various forms and effects of avoidant, hostile, and aversive-hostile racism, one should go beyond the strict psychological categories used in mental health practice.[39] Mental health standards are usually applied in a color-blind, universal fashion that does not consider race and that therefore promotes the interest of Whites in sustaining a system of racial stratification without recognizing the mental health effects of racism. Standards applied this way also lessen the ability of therapists to be empathic to concerns associated with race.[40]

Some multicultural guidelines and proposals argue that various forms of cultural diversity should be accounted for in mental health practice.[41] These guidelines are broad and often diffuse and are generally not specific to race or the effects of racism. For example, the 2003 American Psychological Association multicultural guidelines offer this clarification:

> The terms *multiculturalism* and *diversity* have been used interchangeably to include aspects of identity stemming from gender, sexual orientation, disability, socioeconomic status, or age. Multiculturalism, in an absolute sense, recognizes the broad scope of dimensions of race, ethnicity, language, sexual orientation, gender, age, disability, class status, education, religious/spiritual orientation, and other cultural dimensions. All of these are critical aspects of an individual's ethnic/racial and personal identity, and psychologists are encouraged to be cognizant of issues related to all of these dimensions of culture.[42]

Said another way, mental health professionals should consider individual differences; this is essentially a universal standard. What is needed is a race-specific mental health standard.[43] To ignore or subsume race within a large multicultural or diversity effort denies that our society is racially structured and minimizes racial group membership, and it denies the psychological meaning associated with race, which scholars argue is an important aspect of personality development and social participation.[44] To ignore race and racism in therapy and mental health practice means that mental health professionals fail to capture all the complex and dynamic aspects of racism and its effects, so they are unable to provide for the comprehensive needs of a racialized society.[45] Reliance on universal, color-blind, or multicultural principles to account for differences in the experiences, perceptions, behaviors, and attitudes of members of various racial groups will not help mental health professionals understand or assess race-based stress.[46]

RACIAL BIAS: FROM DIFFERING PERSPECTIVES

Racial perspective, or how people view the world based on their racial group membership, defined as their racial identity status, is an important factor in race-related competence in psychotherapy.[47] These perspectives are seen in survey research that shows vast differences in how people from different racial groups perceive their life circumstances. Blacks and Whites have differing views about the life and circumstances of their respective racial groups. Jeffrey Jones reports that 64 percent of White Americans believe that Blacks have the same chances of getting work, housing, and education; by contrast, less than half of Blacks (49 percent) believe they have equal access to education, 67 percent do not think they can afford good housing, and only 32 percent think they have equal job opportunities.[48] A national survey found that 59 percent of Blacks consider racial discrimination the central reason for the lack of progress of Black people in the country, while only 35 percent of White people agreed; Whites (58 percent) are more likely than Blacks (31 percent) to say that Black people are responsible for their own conditions.[49] Whereas these findings highlight different perspectives and opinions about racial discrimination, they also underscore the continuing racial hostility that Blacks and other people of color face in this country.

The ongoing occurrence of racism is well documented in scientific research and the national press as well as in studies posted on the internet and in social media.[50] Many respected social and government organizations identify racism and racially based unfair treatment as sociopolitical issues that contribute to disparities in work, criminal justice, health, mental health, education, and other areas of life.[51] These reports do not question the existence of racism as a feature of everyday life in the United States, particularly for Black Americans.

A survey by the Pew Research Center notes that

black and white adults have widely different perceptions about what life is like for blacks in the U.S. For example, by large margins, blacks are more likely than whites to say black people are treated less fairly in the workplace (a difference of 42 percentage points), when applying for a loan or mortgage

(41 points), in dealing with the police (34 points), in the courts (32 points), in stores or restaurants (28 points), and when voting in elections (23 points). By a margin of at least 20 percentage points, blacks are also more likely than whites to say racial discrimination (70% vs. 36%), lower quality schools (75% vs. 53%) and lack of jobs (66% vs. 45%) are major reasons that blacks may have a harder time getting ahead than whites.[52]

Clearly, if the views of White people dominate the effort to comprehend racism's effects on mental health, the result is that racism would not exist, or, if it did exist, it would not have a strong effect on people of color, since in the minds of Whites race matters less than individual effort or responsibility. Furthermore, it can be argued that differences in perceptions of racism across racial groups are in fact a result of individual and structural racism, which results in individual perceptions being informed by a person's experience of race within a racialized society. Therefore, a new mental health standard is warranted, one that recognizes the ongoing reality of racism, outlines the psychological effects of individual and structural racism, and provides guidelines for clinical management of racism-related stress in psychological practice.[53] However, some would suggest that the real issue is racial bias as reflected in research on implicit bias, the idea that racial bias is subconscious and operates outside of awareness.[54]

MEASURING RACIAL BIAS

Some scholars and researchers argue that racism has become hidden from the awareness of actors and, in some instances, of targets.[55] The shift of racism to subconscious and subtle forms of expression is not currently well understood by mental health professionals. The most common approach to assessing subconscious racial bias is the implicit-association test (IAT), which is presumed to measure subconscious racism and to predict discrimination directed at people of color.[56] The race-focused IAT asks people to respond to stimuli (pictures of faces of Blacks and Whites) and sort them into categories; half the stimuli are of racial groups, and the other half are evaluative words (positive and negative) or attributes. Respondents are given two tasks, one presumed easy and the other hard. The hard task involves associating positive words to Black images. This should take more time to do if the person finds this difficult, and the slower response is taken as evidence of implicit racial bias. In a test of validity of the IAT, Anthony Greenwald and colleagues argue that the IAT is better than self-reported measures in terms of predictive validity.[57] The debate centers on whether the IAT or an explicit measure of discrimination is a better predictor of actual discriminatory bias.

Hart Blanton and James Jaccard reviewed evidence regarding the claim that racist attitudes are prevalent but operate outside of awareness. They observe that "the concept of unconscious racism has taken hold in many psychological circles, and it has even captured the attention of the news media and the popular press."[58] Frederick Oswald and colleagues' meta-analysis of IAT and explicit measures of discrimination and the instruments' ability to predict racial discrimination in a variety of ways found that both IAT and explicit measures are poor predictors, writing that

> explicitly endorsed ethnic and racial biases have become less common, yet societal inequalities persist. In response, psychologists have theorized that implicit biases must be a key sustainer of these inequalities . . . and IAT research has become the primary exhibit in support of this theory. The present results call for a substantial reconsideration of implicit-bias-based theories of discrimination at the level of operationalization and measurement; at least to the extent those theories depend on IAT research for proof of the prevalence of implicit prejudices.[59]

The idea that racism can be explained with theories that contend that one's actions are governed by subconscious motivation is not supported by the meta-analysis of the IAT, the instrument that has been the primary foundation for such contentions.[60] Furthermore, the direct expression and experience of racism is not currently considered in assessment models or diagnostic systems. This reality suggests a disconnection between psychological standards and the experiences of people of color who are subjected to racism. Yet many of the studies cited in our review of racism and racial discrimination in chapter 3 show that such experiences are directly and indirectly associated with negative psychological and emotional effects, primarily but not exclusively borne by people of color.

PSYCHOLOGICAL INJURY

When encountering a new client, most mental health professionals document a history and a description of the presenting problem. As part of the history, demographic information like gender, age, race, relationship status, family composition, and so on are noted.[61] The client is allowed time and attention to describe why she has sought help from a mental health professional. The common practice is to note the client's race/ethnicity as part of demographic information on the intake, but the initial assessment does not usually include consideration of racial factors that may have contributed to her condition.

Mental health professionals do not typically assess clients for exposure to race-related experiences. This is troubling, considering that racism has been demonstrated to be involved in many aspects of daily living and in social and economic opportunity and resources.[62] Yet people who seek help from mental health professionals often do not bring up issues of race and racism.[63] Vetta Sanders Thompson and colleagues report from focus groups that Black people do not discuss "experiences with racism, discrimination, and the stress of . . . life and exposure to community trauma . . . because of fears that the therapist would not understand."[64] It can be argued, given the presence of race and racism in our societal structures, that these factors are likely involved in the development, presenting problems, life adjustments, and transitions for both Whites and people of color.[65] The nature of that involvement is often unstated and for some hidden, but we contend that race is present in the person's overall life situation. As noted by recognized researchers and scholars, "many academics, policy makers, scientists, elected officials, and others responsible for defining and responding to the public discourse remain resistant to identify racism as a root cause of racial health inequities."[66] Evidence for this proposition is both direct and indirect.

Researchers and scholars report that in most studies on stress, PTSD, and discrimination, people experience a range of signs and symptoms, some of which are associated with existing diagnostic criteria for mental disorders like stress-related adjustment reactions, mood and anxiety disorders, and PTSD, they also note that people of color underutilize mental health services.[67] Despite the research results pertaining to the prevalence of racial discrimination and racism, the fifth edition of the *Diagnostic and Statistical Manual of Mental Disorders* (DSM-5)[68] does not include race-based stress or race-based traumatic stress (RBTS) in the etiology of psychological symptoms. Therefore, mental health professionals must instead focus on the client's personal or dispositional characteristics when assessing the cause of the client's problems with respect to race and racism. This strategy prevents the professional from including the situational impact of race-based stress or trauma in the assessment.

We believe it is more accurate and effective to assess the effects of racism (e.g., of racial harassment, racial discrimination, and their combination) as psychological and emotional injuries[69] than as psychiatric disorders since the effects come from the sociopolitical environment and thus are situational rather than dispositional (i.e., intrapsychic).

MEETING THE CHALLENGE: EXPLORING RACIAL INCIDENTS AS A TYPE OF TRAUMA

The conceptual and empirical efforts to measure the effects of racism are guided by the question of whether race-related stress from incidents of racial discrimination and racial harassment qualify as severe stress or traumatic stress. To explore this question, we accessed a large body of literature, including research on stressful life events and PTSD (as presented in part I of this volume). The literature indicates that depression and anxiety are common reactions to stressful life events for all people, irrespective of race,[70] and PTSD is the more typical outcome from uncommon events (natural disasters, combat, community violence). However, racial incidents are common and recurring in the lives of many people of color, and although scholars and researchers acknowledge that racial events are stressful and are related to adverse health and mental health outcomes, few note that the stress could be classified as severe or traumatic.

In a notable exception, Lillian Comas-Diaz and Frederick Jacobsen argue that "ethnic and sociocultural emotional injuries can cause profound changes in the sense of self. . . . Exposure to racism can result in psychological affliction, behavioral exhaustion and physiological distress. . . . [It] wounds healthy narcissism and impairs coping because racism often causes confusion, disillusionment and racial mistrust."[71] Raymond Scurfield and David Mackey propose that "exposure to race-related trauma, in and of itself, may be the primary etiology factor in the development of an adjustment or stress disorder."[72] For these authors, race-related stressors are environmental in nature and include structural circumstances such as poverty and residential segregation, work-related experiences, assault, and life-event stress. According to Scurfield and Mackey, exposure involves discrete (single) or repeated experiences that have a lasting impact (are memorable); exposure may also be covert and subtle or "insidious" (chronic and pervasive). They write, "Over time subjective experience of repetitive and cumulative exposure could be traumatically impactful. Such insidious exposure can reinforce assumptions that the world and life are unfair to people of particular races, that [members of the] dominant White race [are] at best unconcerned and at worst malevolent, and one's life has little positive worth and meaning."[73] More recently, Monnica T. Williams and colleagues and Monnica T. Williams, J. Kanter, and T. H. W. Ching argue for the recognition of race-based PTSD, in which people of color display all the *DSM-5* diagnostic criteria for PTSD due to cumulative and cultural trauma.[74] To support their claim they note that a measure was developed to assess race-based PTSD. However, the fact remains that the onus for proving racism is on the target, and the psychological framework is that of the *DSM*—in which race is not recognized. Nevertheless, these scholars contend that race is responsible for mental distress, and although they present cogent and reasonable arguments, exactly how race and racism's effects could be assessed remains muddled in the descriptions of and references to larger events (e.g., poverty, cultural trauma) that may be difficult to directly link to a person's emotional and psychological reactions.

To grasp the effects of racism more clearly, we consulted the trauma literature. We learned that between 5 percent and 10 percent of individuals exposed to an uncommon stressful life event develop PTSD or PTSD symptoms. However, when considering participants' racial backgrounds, people of color are observed to have higher exposure to stressful life events, and their symptoms are more severe.[75] Regarding natural disasters, Whites have the lowest rate of PTSD, at 15 percent after exposure; Latinos/as have the highest rate (38 percent); and Blacks have a rate of 23 percent. In addition, veterans of color have higher rates of PTSD (21 percent for Blacks, 28 percent for Hispanics, 38–57 percent for Native Americans) compared to Whites (14 percent), statistics that are not explained by the specific exposure to combat for each of these groups.[76]

Trauma researchers speculate that the higher rates of PTSD experienced by people of color might be due to stress associated with racism, as Fran Norris illustrates, stating that "minorities may confront hostility, prejudice, and neglect, which serve to heighten the effects of a crisis."[77] The work of Chalsa Loo and colleagues, however, was the first to demonstrate that the experience of racism could play a direct role in the development of PTSD in people of color.[78] Loo and colleagues measured race-related stress in Asian American veterans as a potential way of accounting for the differential rates of PTSD between veterans of color and White veterans. They found that 37 percent of Asian American veterans they studied met the criteria for PTSD, and that the measure of race-related stress predicts PTSD over and above exposure to combat and other factors. This was the first direct empirical evidence suggesting a link between symptoms of trauma and experiences of racism (i.e., race-related stress). The events that occur in natural disasters and combat involve physical threats to life, so when it is shown that race-related stress particular to Asians adds to the stress from these events, this demonstrates that racism can in fact be considered a potentially severe stressor. We reason that since racism often is not associated with experiences that are direct threats to one's life, then racism-related stress or trauma will not lead to PTSD for people who are not exposed to life threats. We also know that what people exposed to racism feel is different from a threat to their lives; it is emotional pain. We conclude that although some symptoms of RBTS overlap with PTSD, the critical or core criteria for the two differ greatly; therefore, RBTS is not PTSD.[79]

Research shows that racism can damage one's psyche and personality.[80] Nevertheless, we think the mental health impact of racism should be thought of and assessed as psychological and emotional injury, recognizing that it is situational. The *Merriam-Webster* dictionary's definition of *disorder* is "an abnormal physical or mental condition or not functioning in a normal healthy orderly way," or a mental illness that requires psychiatric or psychological treatment. In contrast, the dictionary defines *injury* as an act that damages or hurts and is "a violation of another's rights for which the law allows an action to recover damages." We argue that racism disrupts normal functioning,[81] and we contend that it results in psychological and emotional effects but that these effects do not reflect a pathological disorder. Rather, racism violates a person's rights such that he should be able to seek redress or recover damages.[82] Psychological and emotional pain is the core initial response to racial events, among others, and represents a nonpathological classification of injury that we refer to as race-based stress and RBTS.[83]

Eve Carlson proposes a model of traumatic stress wherein an experience qualifies as a trauma if it is perceived as emotionally painful (highly negative), is sudden or unexpected, and is uncontrollable.[84] In chapter 2 we note that researchers have documented that events that are negative, out of one's control, sudden, ambiguous, and repeated can increase the stress response, deepen emotional pain, and lead to a traumatic response.

The emotional and psychological manifestations of PTSD, acute stress disorder, and race-based stress overlap with the symptoms of reexperiencing, avoidance of stimuli associated with the event, and increased arousal. However, PTSD and acute stress disorder each have specific criteria that must be exhibited in certain ways before an individual qualifies to meet the diagnosis, and these criteria are not the same for RBTS. For RBTS, the symptoms need only cluster, not present in such a way that a checklist could be used to document their presence. More important, the criteria for DSM diagnoses do not account for the person's subjective appraisal of the experience, as is done with RBTS, which research demonstrates has a significant impact on the resulting effects.[85] When a person does meet the DSM criteria, she usually has a mental disorder that is affecting her level of functionality, without emphasis on the fact that the individual feels and believes she has been violated.

As described earlier, RBTS shares some of the symptoms of the DSM trauma and stress disorders (e.g., PTSD, acute stress disorder, adjustment disorders), but the DSM diagnoses do not match the experiences or reactions of persons who encounter race-based stress or severe stress, which is why RBTS is not PTSD. First, an experience of racism involves a sudden, emotionally shocking experience that elicits anxiety, which is often (but not always) related to prior experiences of racial discrimination. Typically, the psychological stress or assault may involve a single encounter but can also involve reoccurring encounters or experiences, with one experience becoming the last straw and triggering a stress response. Second, racial avoidance, aversion, or hostility may be communicated indirectly by symbols or coded language or actions.[86] In a society characterized by racism such as the United States, symbolic language and images can communicate a threat to subordinated racial group members. This sets racial experiences apart from other stressors that can cause trauma, and the fact that racial insult can be delivered through various and multiple mechanisms makes it unique.[87]

Threats communicated and experienced through symbols and coded language do not meet the DSM criteria. Moreover, all people may not understand the subtle and symbolic threats associated with racially coded language since this language changes over time. Whites who typically are not targets of racism may attach different meanings to the subtle language and symbols used to communicate racial messages—for instance, the meaning attached to Confederate statues placed throughout the country. Consequently, actions that may not appear threatening to a dominant group member may appear so to members of the threatened group. For instance, overt, race-specific physical and psychological tortures carried out for centuries have been and continue to be associated with unspoken and accepted racial beliefs and stereotypes. Racial beliefs and attitudes are often embodied in symbols (a noose, the Confederate flag, media portrayals of Blacks and Hispanics as violent and criminal or Asians as devious, etc.) and in coded and demeaning language, such as the use of the N-word or the reference to "boy" and so forth.

Language, symbols, or attitudes and actions toward people of color are based on long-held stereotypes that disregard individual characteristics and are based exclusively on physical markers of racial group membership. This type of thinking has led to policies that are used to justify such actions as racial profiling and police stop-and-frisk activities, often in communities of color. We believe that to be treated based on a stereotype or treated as if you, a unique person, do not exist or are invisible can produce racial stress or RBTS.[88]

THE RBTS MODEL

The RBTS model is a conceptual framework designed to show the emotional effects of various types of racial events and the accompanying psychological impact, most often in the context of stress-and trauma-related symptoms.[89] The ideas behind RBTS emerged from expert witness and consultation for racial discrimination and racial harassment civil legal proceedings in schools, workplaces, and public places,[90] and also from research and scholarship on racial identity status attitudes,[91] racial discrimination, and race-related stress. The work by Carter[92] and by Thompson and Carter[93] on race and racial identity attitudes in psychotherapy serves as the foundation of our thinking about the concepts regarding measuring the effects of racism.[94]

Although details of the legal cases vary according to the nature of the incidents and the ensuing legal proceedings, the cases have one clear and unifying issue: Did the plaintiffs experience psychological and emotional harm from their experiences of racial discrimination or racial harassment? Based on what we understood about racism and race, we thought the answer to the question about possible harm from racism was yes—depending on how the person understood her racial group membership or her racial identity status, and depending on the extent to which her racial identity status attitudes affected her perception of the incident. But the legal context presented other challenges that at the time (in the 1990s) we could not address or answer.

For instance, in the legal context, it was necessary to demonstrate a direct link between the racial event and the possible effect on a person's psychological health. Thus, we needed to learn what happened and how the person felt because of the event. It was also necessary to understand the person's history to assess the event in the context of his or her development and prior experiences, and to isolate the event and its possible effects on emotional functioning to determine whether the event alone was related to his or her emotional and psychological symptoms. But first several problems needed to be addressed. It was clear that clinical interviews and psychological assessments should be conducted to determine the presence of emotional harm, and that the DSM should be consulted; however, as noted, the DSM did not consider race or racial experiences for any mental disorder, nor was race a factor in the development of PTSD or in evaluating the impact of any environmental stressors, of which more than fifty were listed in the DSM.

Given that the DSM was (and still is) the primary standard by which mental health disorders could be legally determined, the assessment of whether the racial event contributed to or was a proximate cause of the person's emotional symptoms was initially approached from the perspective of the DSM. Simply stated, at the time, the DSM offered no guidance. As a noted clinical scholar has observed, the DSM criteria for assessing instances of racial discrimination (with no direct physical violence) did not qualify symptoms as traumatic stressors or as contributing to PTSD because the stressor did not lead to a severe enough reaction and often was not perceived as a threat to life.[95]

The legal cases required that clear and direct links exist between the racial incident and the person's emotional reactions. This condition presented two problems: How racism was defined (see chapter 1) often did not allow for direct links to a person's emotional reactions, and even if it did, how could that reaction be identified? Would the reaction be related to a mental health disorder? Or was it some other kind of reaction?

One realm where racial events were defined was in the law, and here racial harassment was (and is) treated as a component of racial discrimination (considered as disparate treatment or disparate impact), and neither was considered a distinct event. Further complicating the legal definition is the fact that when a complaint is filed, the plaintiff must show that the defendant intended to discriminate specifically based on race and with racial animus.[96] This is a difficult condition to meet, given the history of and varied perceptions about race and racism by members of different racial groups. Furthermore, in most racial discrimination legal proceedings, the issue of emotional distress from racial incidents is often not presented, in part because there is no established way to measure racism's emotional effects or the degree of harm. (Tort claims are injury related and are a different area of the law from civil rights, where most racial discrimination cases are brought.) Moreover, legally the inclusion of emotional distress is considered an injury or tort claim and usually has a physical element; only recently have emotional distress claims alone been included in tort actions.[97] Only a few empirical articles on the impact of racism were published in mental health journals at the time (the mid-1990s to the mid-2000s), and an analysis of forensic psychology journals found that fewer than 10 percent of published articles addressed racial issues.[98]

RBTS IS RACIAL TRAUMA

The idea that racism is associated with traumatic reactions is suggested by several scholars,[99] but their arguments are based on criteria for PTSD as a way to understand racial impacts, a position that we think is not useful or valid. For instance, Scurfield and Mackey suggest that "exposure to race-related trauma, in and of itself, may be the primary etiology factor in the development of an adjustment or stress disorder";[100] thus, race is the basis for these disorders even though the diagnostic criteria lack any reference to race-related experiences. For these authors, race-related stressors are environmental in nature and include structural circumstances such as poverty and residential segregation, work-related experiences, assault, and life-event stress. But these assertions are not supported by the *DSM* since none of the factors they list are acknowledged as environmental stressors in the *DSM*. Although Scurfield and Mackey claim to be capturing psychological processes associated with repeated exposure to racism, they fail to establish a clear link between the racial event and emotional and psychological symptoms.

Bryant-Davis and Ocampo argue that racist incidents are traumatic because the incidents are similar to rape, domestic violence, or physical assaults that produce posttrauma-like symptoms.[101] The various threats to one's emotional and psychological well-being could be sudden or systemic, intentional or not, vague and ambiguous, or direct and specific, and could be perpetrated by a person (individual racism), by an institution (institutional racism), or by cultural oppression and power (cultural racism). Regardless of the form racism takes, Bryant-Davis and Ocampo argue that racist incidents are a form of emotional abuse (even though they compare racism to physical assault, when there is not usually a physical element to racism) and therefore could be traumatic.[102] Moreover, Bryant-Davis and Ocampo highlight the fact that racism, rape, and domestic violence are motivated by power or the need to impose one's will over someone who is less powerful. We agree with the idea that racism is about the use of power by dominant group members, but we do not think the various experiences are equivalent. Again, the reference to the physical nature of racism means that it falls within the purview of PTSD, but emphasizing the physical aspect of racism overlooks other aspects of racialized experiences such as coded language, racial stereotyping, verbal assaults, and invalidations that we think separate RBTS from PTSD.[103]

Using the same medical model that is employed to describe sexual assault and rape to explain the effects of racist assaults presents a cautionary tale. Susan Stefan notes:

> The medicalization of women's reactions to male violence has explicitly supported social assumptions that such violence is aberrational and has served to obscure the fact that violence against women is the norm in this society. Women who report being raped are encouraged to think of the pain they suffer as their own problem rather than to examine the social context, which helps to create the pain and exacerbates it. This pain is then defined by [mental health] "experts" as the problem to be overcome, and the goal is each woman's "readjustment" and "recovery" from the rape.[104]

Here Stefan identifies a significant flaw in using medical criteria (i.e., the rape trauma syndrome) for rape. We think the same fate would befall racism if the *DSM* criteria were used to measure or define its effects.[105] Stefan does an important job by showing how the dispositional attributions associated with a woman's response to sexual violence shift the focus entirely onto the woman who was the target, thus hiding the societal role of violence toward women and the imposition of power by the dominant gender group. We want to avoid this same fate with race and racism, so we reject the reference to PTSD as the only form of trauma and put forward the notion that race-based stress can be traumatic and, as such, is an emotional injury.

The social science scholars and legal experts who advocate for the rape trauma syndrome render rape survivors as passive and disordered victims. Yet much of the behavior that serves as the basis for labels of disorder is the product of strength, struggle, and survival—characteristics of women who still are overlooked and undervalued. The reasons that women behave the way they do has become obscured in the research literature, where "a woman's anger means that her symptoms remain unresolved, or in a courtroom, where only her pathology is admissible."[106]

We do not want the same outcome for RBTS reactions. As Bryant-Davis and Ocampo point out, to sustain power and domination, the oppressors must convince people that victims of acts of oppression are unworthy, lazy, or somehow deserving of different or abusive treatment.[107] People of color have been portrayed in this manner for centuries. Bryant-Davis and Ocampo contend that there are emotional and psychological consequences to how one thinks, feels, and functions when subjugated to racial abuse. People subjected to these oppressive experiences may endure headaches, body pains and aches, have trouble sleeping, and difficulty remembering. They may engage in self-blame or have feelings of confusion, shame, and guilt. These symptom clusters form the basis of RBTS injury, which we further explain in chapter 6.

Bryant-Davis and Ocampo also suggest that perpetrators of acts of racism fail to assume responsibility, and that they avoid social or legal reprisals for their actions; more social and legal focus is placed on the victim's role in the abuse.[108] They state that certain tendencies prevail: to attribute to the person of color behavior that is "arrogant"; to imply that the person does not know his or her place or is attempting to get more than he is entitled to; to suggest that the person is overly sensitive or has a criminal record. These ideas are put forth so the incident will not be viewed as a violation of the person's rights. Perpetrators also use cognitive distortions and project a range of emotions such as fear, anxiety, discomfort, and anger onto their targets as a way to disassociate from their acts. Societal responses are similar in that the victim is usually blamed in some way. In cases of both rape and racism, legal and other types of societal sanctions are most often focused on the character or actions of the victim. Some would argue that the law enforcement shootings of unarmed Black men around the country show the pattern of blaming the person who was shot and killed.[109]

Experimental laboratory research has found that Whites perceive incidents of racial harassment—including blatant racial threats, the use of racially offensive symbols and language, and intimidating acts of vandalism—as less severe or serious than do African Americans and Hispanics.[110] This could be because Whites are not subjected to such behavior and are not targets of racial hostility, so it may be difficult for them to visualize such treatment. Similarly, many men are unable to understand what it is like for women to be sexually harassed on the street, or to carry and give birth to a baby. These experiences are outside their frame of reference.

RBTS INJURY: A NONPATHOLOGICAL FORM
OF EMOTIONAL DISTRESS

Building on the varied conceptualizations of race-related stress and trauma, Carter proposes that RBTS injury be considered a nonpathological response of emotional distress.[111] Racial encounters occur as hostile, avoidant, or aversive-hostile racism. The events that may produce RBTS can occur in many different forms. Racial encounters may be direct and clear or subtle and ambiguous. Racial events can occur on an individual level (a stereotype, verbal abuse, or the use of symbols or coded language) or can be systemic. They may also occur on an institutional level, as reflected in the educational, economic, political, and health disparities that result from application of racial stereotypes, or they may occur in the context of cultural racism. Some examples of cultural racism are when people of color are treated as if they are not American or are assumed to be custodial staff because of their race. People often assume that Asians or Hispanics are foreigners and react with surprise when they speak English. Another manifestation of cultural racism is the failure to recognize and remedy the myriad forms of harm and damage brought to the descendants of those held in bondage, who were denied access and opportunity by slavery and legal segregation from 1619 to 1964 (some 345 years).[112] Derald Wing Sue observes of cultural racism that "it is White folks who dominate and control the institutions and social policies that create and enforce American cultural values and norms. Relative to White people, persons of color are . . . powerless on a societal level."[113]

Race-based events may be severe, moderate, or daily slights that can produce harm or injury through memorable impact (lasting effect) or through cumulative exposure to the various forms of racism. Although the best way to measure cumulative exposure has not yet been established, we think lifelong exposure to racism teaches people of color to cope by adapting to racial events and minimizing the impact. Carter, Johnson, and colleagues, in their meta-analyses of more than 240 studies of racial discrimination and its dimensions, found that events occurring in the past year were more stressful than were cumulative lifetime experiences. Yet the levels of severity of racial events reported by Carter and colleagues are inconsistent with the notions presented by Scurfield and Mackey[114] and Bryant-Davis and Ocampo,[115] and we do not believe that the most severe forms of racism are exclusively physical attacks. Carter, Johnson, and colleagues, in their meta-analyses, which included physical and mental health, as well as substance use and cultural factors, found that direct racial discrimination and being stereotyped had a greater effect on stress levels.[116] Carter notes that stress reactions to acts of blatant racism are unrelated to an increase in blood pressure, an indicator of physical health; rather, more subtle acts are related to negative emotional and physical reactions.[117]

We argue that the severity of racial incidents should be determined by the strength and intensity of the person's subjective reaction or appraisal and the symptom cluster that emerges. Since many aspects of racism can be visited on a person throughout his or her life, severity may be a consequence of the effects of numerous events, or a person may be exposed to several different racial incidents over the course of years with one of them being the "last straw" that leads to overwhelming stress and an inability to cope. But researchers noted that the greater effects were from events that took place in the past year and tended to involve stereotyping or direct racially based events. Although people of color are exposed to racism in various forms over the course of their lives, it is unclear how this contributes to individuals' response to specific events at work, in seeking health care, or while shopping or traveling. In an effort to measure the effects of racism, we propose that the racial event should be specific and contained in terms of time. A seemingly innocuous or minor event could be the one that finally causes a person to feel that he or she can no longer manage the stress and pain of encounters with racism. The number of life events a person endures, the type of social support he or she enjoys both before and after an event, and the person's developmental vulnerability all contribute to whether the stress of an event is severe enough to be traumatic.

ASSESSING RBTS

To assess RBTS, the evaluator must establish that the following conditions are present: (1) the person experienced the racial event (or events) as emotionally painful (highly negative); (2) the event was sudden or unexpected; and (3) the person had no control over what happened. As a consequence of the racial event, the following symptoms may emerge and may still be present: arousal or hypervigilance, intrusion or reexperiencing, and avoidance or numbing. Reactions to RBTS may be expressed as physical symptoms such as bodily pains and aches. For some, somatic symptoms such as headaches may be the primary reaction. The person might also develop physical problems such as high blood pressure, weight gain, or hypersensitivity to reminders of the incident. The symptoms may be exhibited through disrupted cognitions or thoughts, such as insomnia or forgetfulness.

Behavioral expression of RBTS may be shown in aggression, irritability, or withdrawal. Emotional indicators can be seen in symptoms of self-blame or feelings of confusion, shame, and guilt. Such expressions can be signaled by a cluster of symptoms, such as anxiety, anger, depression, and low self-esteem.

Thoughts or images may cause a person to reexperience the event, with flashes of the event returning to consciousness or with thoughts that intrude during the day without warning. There may be manifestations of reexperiencing that take the form of anxiety or anger—a common and acceptable mode of emotional expression for many men—or increased irritability. For example, one may be stressed, but the level of stress may not reach the threshold for being labeled traumatic. The person's interpersonal relationships may become strained, or the person might be more distant than she was prior to the triggering racial event. There may be simply a feeling of discomfort or a knot in the stomach when one returns to the place where the event occurred. Arousal can also be expressed in extremely active or aggressive behavior toward oneself or others.

In reexperiencing, the trigger may be a minor or major event. Many people report that their stress is not due to one event but to a series of emotional blows that are experienced as slights, cuts, and scratches that in time grow into gaping wounds, and these larger wounds might be the basis of racial stress or RBTS injury. And the slights and blows can go on and on. For others the event is sudden and bewildering, thus extremely painful.

One's reactions may be expressed in other ways. They may be subconscious and come to consciousness through flashbacks or nightmares. Or the person may find it hard to focus or concentrate, or may feel restless and become frustrated easily. For example, many men of color must remain perpetually hypervigilant because of anticipated racial incidents. As discussed in this book's review of studies (part I), racism causes people to rehearse reactions, responses, and defensive actions. The review also suggests that anxiety and worry are associated with efforts to cope, and that the mental states associated with being the target of racism can lead to greater physical problems, because living in a highly stressful situation increases heart rate, blood pressure, and blood sugar.[118]

Avoidance can be manifested in several ways. In cognitive avoidance, a person may forget or treat the experience as unreal or as something other than racism (distortion). To live through a lifetime of racism, or even infrequent encounters with racism, requires a certain amount of denial. When the denial turns into a loss of memory of an incident, it could be a sign that the event was severely stressful or traumatic. On an emotional level, a person can become numb to the impact of the constant or sudden assault(s) to his dignity or sense of self, thus compromising his capacity to feel a range of emotions. Or she may split the experience from her emotions, attaching few feelings to it as a way to circumvent emotional pain. If possible, she may select to avoid the circumstances and people that contributed to the incident and its associated stress or trauma, and may retreat physically or psychologically into a safer world where it is harder for the pain of racism to reach her.

These reactions may co-occur with feelings of depression, aggression, shifts in self-esteem, racial identity confusion, complicated interpersonal relationships, and strong feelings of shame and guilt. Targets might feel responsible for the circumstances in which they find themselves, perhaps without being aware that racism plays a major role in those circumstances. Alternately, targets might be aware of racism but might feel helpless to deal with its presence or impact.

At the same time, reactions can be adaptive and positive, as reflected in coping strategies that aid in moderating the effects of the RBTS.[119] The reactions may be unique to the person and may blend and combine in ways that can vary from person to person. Coping and racial identity status attitudes (i.e., a psychological orientation to one's racial group membership) are factors in how one may express signs of RBTS.[120]

The concept of RBTS is grounded in theoretical and empirical literature, but it is the first general framework linking specific types of racial events to specific emotional and psychological responses.[121] The following chapters describe empirical evidence validating the RBTS model and discuss how to measure it using the Race-Based Traumatic Stress Symptom Scale (RBTSSS).[122]

6

MEASURING RACE-BASED TRAUMATIC STRESS

THE MEASUREMENT OF THE MENTAL HEALTH effects of racial discrimination has received some attention in the literature,[1] and research suggests that experiences of racism are indeed associated with psychological distress and dysfunction.[2] The race-based traumatic stress (RBTS) model offers a conceptual framework of propositions about how specific types of incidents of racism are linked to specific emotional reactions that reflect racial-related stress or RBTS. This chapter outlines the development of the Race-Based Traumatic Stress Symptom Scale (RBTSS), the first step toward measuring the traumatic effects of racism.

The empirical research evidence as discussed in previous chapters provides a compelling overview of the psychological impact of racial discrimination; however, we also noted that the information does not offer a way to directly measure race-based traumatic stress as racial trauma. In seeking to develop a direct measure of racism-related trauma, we initially turned to the trauma literature. What did we learn that could guide our process in measuring the effects of racism? We learned that traumatic stress was defined as a reaction to events that were perceived as emotionally painful.[3] We learned that the racial events must be experienced as unexpected or sudden in occurrence, out of the person's control, and based on the individual's racial group markers (e.g., skin color and physical features); after the event there should be signs and symptoms such as intrusion or reexperiencing, arousal or hypervigilance, and avoidance or numbing, as well as associated symptoms like anger, anxiety, and low self-worth. Together the symptoms and the event characteristics could result in a traumatic stress reaction. It is believed that experiences of racism, in the form of racial discrimination or racial harassment, could indeed produce severe stress reactions that were inconsistent with the psychiatric understanding of trauma or with posttraumatic stress disorder

(PTSD) as defined in the DSM. Our thinking about race-based traumatic stress as racial trauma started with the effort to deconstruct how racism is defined such that racism is more specific as to its type of experience, in this way it is possible to connect particular experiences of racism with specific emotional and psychological symptoms.

To begin to construct an instrument to assess race-based stress/trauma we looked at trauma instruments, psychological symptom scales, and stressful life-event inventories. We decided it was important to construct an instrument that would include all the elements of the race-based stress or racial trauma experience, from the event to the symptoms and levels of severity. We initially generated a list of items of racial experiences that in our view included all levels of racism (individual, institutional, cultural) as well as all classes of racial incidents such as hostile and avoidant.[4] This process, however, suggested to us that to learn about lasting effects, perhaps we should not give respondents a list of racial experiences; instead, we should let them report their racial discrimination experiences and then tell us if they endured any lasting effects from their experiences. That way we would be able to learn, by hearing in their own words, what happened and what they considered to be racial discrimination as well as how the event affected them. We proceeded with a descriptive study in which we asked open-ended questions about participants' racial experiences.[5]

We asked the participants to describe three racial discrimination encounters and to select one as the most memorable. We reasoned that the most memorable racial event would be the one that was easily recalled and had the greatest emotional and lasting effects. We also asked participants to identify when and where the racial encounter took place. We wanted to know (through yes-or-no questions) whether the incident was (a) emotionally painful (negative), (b) unexpected, and (c) out of the person's control. A list of emotional symptoms associated with the memorable racial event followed these questions, and participants were asked to indicate for each symptom whether they had the reaction within one month after the event.

The emotional reactions were culled from the collection of trauma instruments, psychological symptom scales, and stressful life-event inventories we reviewed in preparing to create the RBTSSS. We essentially designed an item pool of potential symptoms to capture the reactions that were expected to be associated with a RBTS response. Overall, the process involved trying to describe two aspects of the race-based stress or trauma experience: the types of racism people encountered, and their emotional and psychological reactions to a specific racial encounter or type. To capture (i.e., code) the racism experiences, we used the classes of racism proposed by Robert T. Carter and Janet E. Helms, which we have reviewed in previous chapters.[6] Briefly, Carter and Helms first used the legal referents (i.e., racial discrimination and harassment) that indicated disparate treatment and impact but offered the notion that these could be understood as distinct classes of racial experiences, unlike what was done in the law. In this way they did not refer to generic racial discrimination (i.e., racially based unfair treatment). Carter and Helms made the following distinctions: *racial discrimination* or *avoidant racism* is defined as maintaining distance between racial groups (e.g., being ignored by a salesperson or being denied housing because of your race), and *racial harassment* or *hostile racism* intends to communicate the target's inferior status due to his or her race (e.g., being stopped by the police because of your race; experiencing verbal assaults). (Please note that although we distinguish here between racial discrimination and racial harassment, throughout this book we also use the phrase *racial discrimination* more generally, as a sort of catch-all term to encompass all categories of racial encounters).

Carter and Helms initially thought that a person's psychological or emotional reactions to the various classes of racism should be considered a race-based stress disorder.[7] Their thinking was guided by a definition of PTSD that defines responses to a traumatic event as an intrapsychic process of the individual that is reflective of psychopathology and a mental health disorder. However, as previously described, this idea quickly shifted away from an emphasis on psychopathology to one of emotional injury from environmental events, an idea that is associated with normative responses to stressful life events. What followed next were a series of empirical investigations designed to construct a measure of RBTS consistent with the RBTS model and to provide evidence of acceptable psychometric properties and construct validity as well as measurement equivalence for different groups. Said another way, we sought to subject the ideas of RBTS to empirical verification in several ways so we could measure the effects of racism and do so for all people, not just people of color.

PRELIMINARY EVIDENCE FOR RBTS AND FOR MEASURING THE EFFECTS OF RACISM

STUDY ONE

We have already provided a brief description of the earliest study in which a descriptive approach was used to learn the kinds of racial encounters reported by participants of color and their accompanying emotional responses.[8] That study used an online-based qualitative approach. Researchers solicited participants by sending email announcements to listservs of various organizations throughout the country. They reasoned that to learn what people thought were incidents constituting racial discrimination, they needed to rely on participants' descriptions and on their self-identified emotional effects associated with the incidents. The assumptions were that if the incident was memorable, then it would more than likely be associated with lasting psychological symptoms. To test these ideas, we used open-ended questions: (1) Have you had an experience of racial discrimination? (2) Was it once or more often? (3) When did it happen? (4) Where did it happen? (5) What happened? (6) Did you have any lasting effects?

Of 352 individuals who logged on to the study, 262 completed the study, with 29 (11 percent) saying they did not have an encounter with racial discrimination and 233 (89 percent) saying they did. The participants were 72 percent (n=167) female and 27 percent (n=63) male; some did not report gender. Thirty-nine percent were twenty-one to thirty years old; 24 percent were thirty-one to forty; 15 percent were forty-one to fifty; and 19 percent were older than fifty. Most were Black, Latino/a, or Asian, and some were biracial. Less than half (49 percent) of the participants had a graduate degree; some had a college degree; and the rest had some college or a high school diploma.

Because the participants used their own words to describe what happened, it was necessary to generate categories of racial events and lasting emotional effects. Phenomenological content-based coding procedures were used to group the events and the effects into categories. The primary investigator created the categories for coding from the self-descriptions. The investigator derived ten categories from the participants' responses to the question "What happened?" For the question about whether the participants experienced any lasting effects, nine categories were created to capture the psychological and emotional effects participants reported.

The ten categories of types of racial discrimination were (1) multiple experiences; (2) hostile work environment (e.g., not promoted, lower pay); (3) verbal assault; (4) denied access or service; (5) profiled (e.g., followed in a store, accused or suspected of theft, stopped by police); (6) treated on basis of stereotype; (7) violated racial rules; (8) physical assaults; (9) own-group discrimination; and (10) other.

The nine categories of lasting emotional effects were (1) extreme emotional distress; (2) hypervigilance or arousal; (3) mild emotional distress;

(4) avoidance; (5) intrusion; (6) distrust; (7) lower self-worth; (8) positive outcome; and (9) other.

Two researchers independently used the categories to code participants' responses. Percentage agreement was used to gauge the accuracy of the coding, finding that for the first round there was 68 percent agreement with the racial discrimination categories and 60 percent agreement with the emotional effect categories. After discussion and clarification of the categories, participants' responses were independently recoded and percentage agreement recalculated, finding 83 percent agreement with the racial discrimination categories and 68 percent agreement with the psychological and emotional effect categories. The coders then discussed each of their disagreements over both sets of categories and found their discrepancies to be minor, thereby achieving 100 percent agreement through a process of consensus.

Frequencies of racial events by category were as follows: multiple experiences (18 percent of respondents); hostile work environment (17 percent); verbal assault (14 percent); denied access or service (12 percent); profiled (12 percent); treated as stereotype (9 percent); violated racial rules (8 percent); other (4 percent); physical assault (2 percent); and own-group discrimination (1 percent). The emotional effects were extreme distress (36 percent); hypervigilance (15 percent); mild distress (16 percent); avoidance (8 percent); intrusion (2 percent); distrust (8 percent); lower self-worth (9 percent); positive outcome (3 percent); and other (3 percent).[9]

Overall, the results of this investigation support the contention that people of color are subjected to experiences of racial discrimination, and that the racial discrimination results in lasting emotional reactions. We found that, in general, nearly all the emotional and psychological effects reported by respondents were consistent with Eve Carlson's notion of traumatic stress,[10] and a smaller proportion also fit the narrower criteria for PTSD or acute stress as defined in the *DSM-IV*.[11] Additionally, apparent differences exist between types of racial experiences—that is, racial hostility (i.e., harassment, experienced by 54 percent of the study's respondents) and racial avoidance (i.e., discrimination, experienced by 23 percent of respondents)—and the two result in different emotional effects. This later finding provides support for Carter and Helms's proposal to deconstruct and redefine racism into distinct types or classes, which they designate as racial harassment and racial discrimination, following the legal terms and at the same time showing that racial harassment as hostile racism is different from racial discrimination as avoidant racism, unlike how the terms are used in the law (they are not distinguished from one another).[12]

The study also reveals that racial discrimination is prevalent for all people of color, not just for Black Americans, and that it results in lasting emotional effects similar to what would be expected for traumatic stress, meaning that people report feeling distressed. Some symptoms overlap with PTSD, but not many of the racial events were physical; rather, most seemed to cause emotional distress.

STUDY TWO

To follow the initial investigation, we sought to focus on the issue of whether the classes of racism have different emotional effects.[13] We thought that we could explore this question by classifying the events and emotional effects into four groups. The emotional effects were put into groups that reflected either no injury or injury (stronger, harmful emotional reactions). The racial events were grouped into hostile and avoidant. We used logistic regression (for categorical variables) to see if the classes of racism predicted injury or no injury. The events grouped together as hostile included verbal assault, physical assault, hostile work environment, being profiled, and violating racial rules; the avoidant events included denied access, treated as stereotype, and own-group discrimination. Emotional reactions that reflected injury (severe emotional reactions) included extreme distress, arousal, avoidance, and intrusion (notice the traumatic stress symptoms); in the no-injury group, emotional reactions included no lasting effects, mild distress, distrust, positive outcome, and lower self-worth. We conducted chi-square analysis for demographic differences in racial events and emotional reactions. Results showed that the groupings did not differ by race, gender, or socioeconomic status, and logistic regression found that hostile events (n = 127) predicted psychological injury (n = 108).[14]

The study shows that race-based encounters are related to emotional harm and that the type of racial event might matter in terms of the psychological symptoms that result. The emotional category of psychological injury includes core traumatic stress symptoms (intrusion, arousal, etc.), which offers preliminary evidence for the propositions of the RBTS: that hostile and avoidant racial events could be related to severe stress reactions or race-related traumatic stress. The findings also indicate that types of racism may be associated with emotional symptoms from memorable events, and that racial groups' racial experiences do not seem to differ because of race, gender, or social class. Moreover, more severe emotions seem to be related to the experience of hostile racism.

Additional findings of importance are noted: 11 percent of participants reported not having any experience of racial discrimination, and, of those who did report racial experiences, 24 percent indicated that they did not endure any lasting emotional effects. These findings are contrary to common assumptions that all people of color experience racial discrimination and that experiences of racial discrimination are typically associated with a lasting emotional effect. They highlight individual variations among people of color regarding the perception and impact of racial encounters and illustrate the discussion in chapter 4 of the influence of such factors as racial identity status attitudes, racism-related coping factors, social class, and racial socialization on one's experience of racism and racial discrimination.[15]

It is important to note, however, that the findings of this study are based primarily on the way the investigators coded categories of racial discrimination events and lasting emotional/psychological effects. As such, the findings could have been influenced by potential investigator bias associated with how categories were generated and how emotional reactions were grouped. Therefore, to address potential bias, another study was designed in which participants identified the type of racism experienced and reported emotional reactions using a self-report inventory of emotions.

STUDY THREE

Using a mixed-method approach, Robert T. Carter and Jessica Forsyth's investigation yielded several outcomes, including (1) identifying participants' emotional reactions (self-reported from a checklist) to racial incidents; (2) grouping the self-reported emotions into psychological scales, some of which reflect trauma-related symptoms; (3) having respondents identify the class of racial events by saying whether they thought it was racial discrimination (avoidance) or racial harassment (hostile); and (4) determining how the psychological scales were related to stress responses in reactions to racial events (a series of survey questions about stress were included in the study).[16]

This investigation involved a new online data collection that yielded 260 usable participants of color (Black, Latino/a, Asian, Native, and biracial

Americans). All participants had at least a high school education, 32 percent had a four-year college degree, and 57 percent had completed a graduate degree. Most participants identified as middle to upper-middle class. Participants described in their own words a memorable racial event, when and where it happened, and whether it was racial harassment or racial discrimination. Next, participants identified their emotional reactions and coping strategies, using the Emotions and Coping Checklist (part of the Racism and Life Experiences Scale).[17] This measure allowed participants to select from sixty emotions and thirty-five coping strategies, and they could select as many as they thought applied to their experience. Finally, they also competed questions about the stressfulness of the experience.

Because a specific scoring procedure did not exist for the Emotions and Coping Checklist, we explored whether we could use its list of emotions and coping behaviors to construct psychological symptom scales that would be consistent with the signs and indicators of RBTS proposed by Carter.[18] Four independent raters coded the qualitative descriptions of participants' memorable racial encounters using the racial event categories developed in previous studies.[19] Before we coded their descriptions of events, we used responses from a previous study to establish a baseline agreement for the descriptions of memorable events. We used four coders, and we calculated Cohen's kappa[20] as the measure of interrater reliability among them, yielding a kappa of .94.

To better understand which incidents participants categorized as harassment and which as discrimination, we examined the frequency of incidents. Most participants considered incidents of vicarious racism (100 percent), physical assault (81 percent), verbal assault (67 percent), and profiling (61 percent) to be racial harassment, and incidents of denied access (95 percent), being treated based on a stereotype (77 percent), hostile work environment (73 percent), own-group discrimination (64 percent), and violation of racial rules (56 percent) to be racial discrimination.

Two coders independently assigned the emotion words to psychological scales, doing so with 87–96 percent agreement. Discussions resolved any disagreements, reaching an interrater reliability of .94 using Cohen's kappa. Psychological reaction scales were constructed from the emotion checklist and fourteen coping behavior items. The scales had between six and fifteen items each, and internal consistency ranged from .68 to .78. The scales were identified as intrusion, arousal, avoidance, depression, anxiety, anger, low self-esteem, positive outcome/ vigor, and guilt/shame.[21] That scales could be construed from the emotions list is important because it suggests that symptoms that are proposed to accompany RBTS can be demonstrated to exist independent of the categories used in previous studies.

Participants identified their emotions associated with their racism experience, resulting in a mean number of emotions for each participant at 11.38 (SD = 7.65). Ninety-seven percent of participants reported between one and twenty of the sixty emotions on the checklist, and 2 percent did not report any emotions. Participants described feeling disrespected (75 percent), angry (74 percent), insulted (60 percent), and disappointed (51 percent). Nearly half reported feeling frustrated (45 percent), outraged (44 percent), hurt (43 percent), or shocked (42 percent). Less-frequent reactions seemed to reflect some degree of emotional disturbance such as feeling inferior or being irritated, annoyed, sad, rejected, demoralized, or humiliated. Participants also reported feeling helpless, confused, embarrassed, challenged, isolated, betrayed, and nervous. There were some variations between racial groups in the patterns of emotional responses. For instance, Native Americans and Latino/a respondents tended to react to their experiences with a greater proportion of internalized emotions (e.g., feelings of humiliation, rejection, helplessness, and/or inferiority), and Native Americans were the only group that did not choose anger among the top fifteen emotions.[22]

One objective of the study was to enhance our understanding of the relationship between incidents of racism and emotional stress.[23] The study determined that 78 percent of participants experienced racial incidents as stressful, while 21 percent experienced little or no stress. The duration of stress was also considered, with 51 percent saying they were not stressed for long (from a few days to less than one month) and 44 percent reporting being stressed for two months to one year or longer.

As many as 91 percent of participants had encountered racial discrimination within the past ten years, mostly at work or school, with no racial group or social class variation. The psychological reactions of anxiety, guilt, arousal, positive response, and avoidance were stronger if the incident was hostile or direct rather than vicarious or avoidant. Avoidant experiences were related to anxiety symptoms, while hostile incidents were associated with more hypervigilant reactions. Lastly, participants said they did not seek help from mental health professionals but did talk to friends or family about the event.

The study provided participant-based information about emotions, psychological symptoms, and stress reactions. The psychological scales advanced the understanding of reactions to racial incidents in several ways. First, we learned about people of color's raw emotions. Second, because it was possible to group emotions, we were able to capture psychological symptoms that confirm traumatic stress reactions related to racial incidents. Finally, we learned that stress reactions accompany racial incidents, with 44 percent reporting lasting stress reactions (beyond two months).

These early studies laid the foundation for the development of the Race-Based Traumatic Stress Symptom Scale (RBTSSS). They confirmed that the propositions of the model could be sustained because classes of racism were associated with varied emotional reactions. Additionally, memorable racial incidents were stressful in that emotional and psychological symptoms reflected trauma-related reactions to them. These investigations also provided preliminary support for the notion of RBTS.

DEVELOPMENT OF THE RACE-BASED TRAUMATIC STRESS SYMPTOM SCALE

Following the guidelines for instrument development, we began the work to develop an RBTS assessment tool. In general, scale-development scholars say that several important steps should be followed.[24] First, determine what is to be measured—in other words, what is the conceptual framework for the instrument? In our case, the conceptual framework was the RBTS model. Once the intent of the measure is established, generate an item pool and determine how the scale will be formatted or organized. We knew from the early studies that the format should be open-ended, where participants describe racial incidents and select the one that is the most memorable. We knew that participants needed to indicate what we call the "yes" criteria: whether the event was negative or emotionally painful, unexpected, and out of their control. Next, an appropriate sample is needed with which to evaluate—usually with the statistical procedure of factor analysis—whether the items capture the intended constructs. We knew that an online investigation would not be best, given the instructions and the length of the preliminary measure or data packet. So we arranged to collect data in person in a number of settings and locations.

It was clear from traditional assessment measures of trauma that respondents needed to describe any reactions they may have had at least a month after the memorable event. Analyses of the possible reactions could reflect stress or trauma depending on whether the appropriate clusters of symptoms were found to be present at appropriate cut-off scores.

The focus on developing an instrument to measure emotional reactions to specific encounters with racial discrimination has implications for both practice and research and is useful to mental health professionals in several ways. Such a measure facilitates awareness and recognition on the part of professionals and their clients, and it helps targets of racial discrimination or harassment understand the emotional impact of systematic, covert, subtle, and subconscious forms of such treatment. It also serves as a mental health assessment tool that can be used to determine how a person may have been harmed by an encounter with racial discrimination or harassment. Such a tool would be valuable in forensic cases as well as in research studies focused on psychological outcomes and racism and racial health disparities.[25] Because there is little information about the psychological impact of race-based experiences in the mental health literature, it is imperative to measure the effects of racism in order to determine the type and degree of its emotional impact.

The RBTSSS was constructed from a pool of 147 symptoms drawn from psychological instruments.[26] The stem "As a consequence of the memorable encounter I had with racism" was paired with symptoms like "I experience tiredness and lack of energy," or "I experience mental images of the event," etc., and the response options ranged from 0 (not my reaction) to 4 (would not go away). The response format asked (1) if the person had the reaction thirty days or more *after* the event (2) if they have the reaction *now*, when thinking about the event; and (3) if anyone noticed any changes in their behavior because of the reaction.

The initial scale-development and validation study involved 381 Black, Latino/a, biracial, Asian, and White participants. Because our work in this area is grounded in racial identity status attitudes research and scholarship, we believe that race pertains to all Americans, not just to people of color, so we included Whites in our participant group. Whites have race and can have racial experiences that are stressful.

We tried to capture the symptoms we had found in previous studies, as reported in the literature. We included items that reflected depression, intrusion or reexperiencing, anger, anxiety, avoidance or numbing, loss of self-worth, arousal or hypervigilance, shame, guilt, positive responses, and somatic reactions like headaches, abdominal pain, and discomfort. To be clear, what we had at this point was a set of ideas and a long list of items that we believed reflected race-related psychological symptoms. We were trying to find out whether the list of symptoms could be reduced or reorganized so the items would form smaller groups or clusters (factors) revealing underlying dimensions of the latent (i.e., hidden) constructs we understood to be symptoms of RBTS. The assumption was that if emotional reactions to racial incidents were reported at a level of severity that reflected elevated psychological symptoms, we might be able to show evidence of an RBTS response. To do this, we set out to collect data that would allow us to explore participant responses in a data-reduction procedure (factor analysis) that would identify symptoms and clusters associated with a race-related stress or trauma response or with psychological symptoms that would be components of RBTS. Remember, we did not directly measure each symptom; instead, we assessed the manifestation of a symptom based on an individual's reports of emotional/psychological reactions such as feeling tired, sad, nervous, and so on. We hoped that the collection of reactions or items would reveal common threads associated with a larger psychological experience such as depression or anxiety. Similarly, the emotions checklist identified psychological symptoms in the earlier mixed-methods study. The statistical procedure called *exploratory factor analysis* (EFA) allowed us to assess whether variables or items would group together in smaller clusters with clear underlying dimensions or common themes.

After exposing the items to an EFA with oblique promax rotation given the assumed correlation between the items, the groups of items that loaded on each factor were analyzed to determine the themes. As a result of the EFA, seven distinct factors or groupings seem to reflect seven symptom scales: depression, intrusion, anger, avoidance, low self-esteem, hypervigilance, and physical reactions with internal consistency (Cronbach's alphas) ranging from .67 to .96. Symptom clusters like shame, guilt, and vigor that were found in previous studies did not emerge in the scale-development investigation.

We examined the symptom scale's correlations with one another and found a range of .37 to .58, meaning that the scales were related to one another, not independent. At the same time, with the size of the correlation being small to moderate, we concluded that the scales assessed related but distinct symptoms. Finally, a comparison of symptom scores between participants who reported the racial event as being painful, unexpected, and out of their control and participants who did not experience the racial event in that manner indicated higher total RBTSSS scores among participants who indicated "yes" than those who did not.[27]

The EFA supports the construct validity, and reliability estimates suggest adequate psychometric properties of the RBTSSS. The findings also suggest that the structure of the RBTSSS includes seven scales outlining specific aspects of the RBTS responses, as well as a total scale score that reflects a more general trauma response to memorable racial incidents that have lasting emotional impact. Furthermore, the results of the scale construction illustrate that it is possible to measure the psychological and emotional effects of racism for a multiracial sample. This evidence goes beyond Black Americans as the racial group most impacted by racial encounters and suggests that RBTS symptoms are experienced across gender and racial groups. Is RBTS the same as PTSD? As described in earlier chapters, we argue that it is different, and we present evidence to support our contention. The data we offer come from participants from community-based service agencies in the Northeast region of the country. The reports document the relationships in these individuals between measures of PTSD (the PTSD Checklist Civilian Version, or PCL-C-17, and the Trauma Symptoms Checklist, or TSC-40) and the RBTSSS.

RBTS AND PTSD: ARE THE TWO RELATED?

To explore the question of how or if RBTS is related to or overlaps with PTSD, Robert T. Carter, Veronica Johnson, and Katheryn Roberson report on an inquiry that was conducted with community participants.[28] The participants (n = 92) were forty-nine men (54.3 percent) and forty-two women (45.7 percent) who ranged in age from twenty-six to seventy with an average or mean age of (M = 44.57 years, SD = 10.09). Participants comprised forty-six Whites (50 percent) and forty-eight people of color (48.9 percent), of which thirty were Black (32.6 percent), twelve Hispanic (13 percent), and six biracial (3.3 percent); one identified as other (1.1 percent), and one did not report their racial designation. The group consisted of thirty-seven lower-class participants (40.2 percent), fourteen working-class (15.2 percent), nineteen lower-middle-class (20.7 percent), thirteen middle-class (14.1 percent), three upper-middle-class (3.3 percent), and one upper-class (1.1 percent). With respect to education, the largest group of participants, thirty-eight (41.3 percent), had a high school diploma, thirty-four (37 percent) indicated some high school education or below, and fourteen (15.2 percent) had a college education or higher. (Some demographic data are missing because not all the participants answered all the questions.) The RBTSSS and the PCL-C-17[29] were administered.

The PCL-C-17 is a seventeen-item measure used to assess trauma symptoms experienced over the last month. Participants rated the severity of these symptoms using a five-point Likert scale ranging from 1 (not at all) to 5 (extremely). The total PTSD score is attained by summing all the items. Higher scores indicate the presence of more PTSD symptoms. For this study, the internal consistency score for the total scale was .94.

To examine stress reactions associated with specific experiences of racism, participants' self-reported reactions *after* the event and their *recent* reactions were analyzed. Within the total sample (n = 92), participants' responses to experiences of racism *after* the event were weakly related to the PCL-C-17: RBTSS depression (−.24), intrusion (.36), anger (−.20), hypervigilance (.15), physical symptoms (.27), low self-esteem (.10), and avoidance (−.21). Participants' *recent* responses were generally not related to the PCL-C-17, including depression recently (−.05), intrusion (−.01), anger (−.18), hypervigilance (−.07), physical symptoms (.10), low self-esteem (.12), and avoidance (−.37). The lack of correlation between RBTS reactions experienced both *after* the event and *recently* and the PTSD trauma symptoms supports our hypothesis that RBTS and PTSD are distinctly different reactions.

To detect reactions indicative of a severe stress response, additional analyses were performed to identify elevations in reactions *after* the event and *recently*. To identify elevations, *t*-scores were calculated on each participant for each of the seven symptom scales, for RBTS reactions occurring both *after* the event and *recently*. Respondents with reaction scale scores of 55, one-half a standard deviation above the mean and higher, were considered elevated—that is, their reactions reflect some level of race-based stress. According to Carter's conceptualization of race-based traumatic stress, at least two of the three core reaction scales (intrusion, avoidance, hypervigilance) were needed for a traumatic reaction to be present.[30] The additional reactions, including depression, anger, low self-esteem, and physical symptoms, were considered associated symptoms that occur alongside the two or three core reactions to varying extents.

To obtain a final sample of participants to be used in these additional analyses, the researchers identified the participants with elevations in RBTS (which we labeled the *stress-trauma group*) and who also met three criteria reflective of traumatic reactions—that is, who reported their race-related experience as sudden, negative, and uncontrollable. This process yielded a total of fifty-nine respondents. Of those, thirty had elevated RBTS scores on the *"after"* subscales.

Specific responses to racism in the stress-trauma group were examined in relation to PTSD symptoms as measured by the PCL-C-17. Results revealed a small number of significant negative associations between RBTS symptoms and PTSD symptoms; however, even these associations may have been by chance. A Bonferroni correction was conducted to calculate the significance level appropriate when making multiple comparisons. Based on this correction, our threshold for significance should be $p < .007$. Therefore, many of these associations may have been significant simply by chance. RBTS anger symptoms experienced *recently* inversely correlated with the PCL-C-17 (−.42), and RBTS avoidance symptoms experienced *recently* were also inversely correlated with the PCL-C-17 (−.39), meaning, for instance, if RBTS anger was high, PCL-17 was low. Within the stress-trauma group, no significant relationships were found between RBTS *after* response.

These findings more or less support our contention that RBTS is distinctly different from PTSD. As previously mentioned, the significant associations between some of the RBTS symptoms and the PCL-C-17 might indicate an individual's symptoms following a general experience of stress, and some generalized symptoms may result from any stressful experience (RBTS, PTSD, or otherwise). These relationships seem to be tenuous and weak at best. Finally, results of a multivariate analysis of variance did not reveal any statistically significant group differences between stress/trauma, general stress, and trauma symptoms as measured by the PCL-C-17.

The primary objective of the study was to further establish the psychometric properties and validity of the RBTSSS. We presented some preliminary findings, such as interscale correlations between the RBTSSS reaction scales and symptom scales of the PCL-C-17, which assess DSM diagnostic criteria for a trauma reaction.

With respect to the memorable race-related encounters that participants described, most respondents indicated that the event was unexpected and out of their control and that the effects were emotionally painful. For a large portion of participants, the race-related encounters were not isolated events but rather recurring incidents. It is also important to note that the racial incidents occurred in many aspects of the participants' lives, most frequently in school and neighborhood settings, and at different stages of their lives (e.g., adulthood, childhood, adolescence).

The correlation findings seem to suggest that there are weak positive associations between the various RBTSSS after-reaction scales and the PCL-C-17. Because we hypothesize that PTSD is different from RBTS, the two instruments are dissimilar in that they capture two very different reactions to fundamentally different experiences of trauma. Such findings based on the current sample and study characteristics provide preliminary evidence of discriminant validity for the construct of race-based traumatic stress injury. Although discriminant validity is an important aspect of establishing the psychometric properties of an instrument—or what a scale actually measures—scholars additionally suggest the importance of determining the convergent validity of a measure, which can be evidenced in strong correlations between the scale of interest and scores on theoretically comparable measures.

Robert T. Carter, Sinead Sant-Barket, and Shawna Stotts report that, given the striking prevalence of racism reported and the range of social and environmental stressors that many people of color in the United States encounter, including racial discrimination and segregation, it is critical for researchers to thoroughly explore race-related experiences to gain insight into the specific factors that might increase an individual's risk of developing mental health problems, and in particular traumatic stress reactions.[31]

While it is clear that people are harmed by racism, and findings have shown that people of color experience these events as stressful, less information exists demonstrating how specific experiences of racial discrimination contribute to reactions reflective of trauma. Consequently, an empirically validated approach to measuring individuals' reactions to and psychological symptoms arising from specific encounters with racism is needed.

Studies suggest that examining specific types (rather than broad categories) of race-related encounters can assist researchers in better capturing the nuances of how racial discrimination is experienced,[32] thus providing valuable information regarding the corresponding mental health effects of discrimination and having potential assessment and treatment implications.[33] Additional limitations of existing studies on racism and mental health include a focus on African American populations (i.e., providing only limited evidence on the experiences of stress and racism among other racial-ethnic groups), the indirect approach used to examine the health consequences of racism (i.e., inferred from high rates of PTSD), and the generalized method of obtaining data from surveys that identify and describe race-related experiences rather than capturing the individual's unique description of the event and his or her specific emotional response. Furthermore, researchers who study trauma do not typically consider racial events as sources of traumatic stress reactions. Ultimately, the concept of race-

based traumatic stress contributes to the mental health assessment literature by addressing the aforementioned limitations and offering mental
health professionals a way to recognize and assess the stress that results from
experiences of racism and helping to determine whether that stress has
risen to the level of trauma. To truly understand the emotional impact of
racism, a standardized survey instrument that illustrates the impact of such
experiences by directly relating specific encounters (e.g., verbal assault,
profiling, denial of access or services) to the emotional reactions that follow is
clearly needed. An empirically validated measure of race-based traumatic
stress would enhance our knowledge of the psychological distress associated
with racism.

The study conducted by Robert T. Carter, Sinead Sant-Barket, and Shawna
Stotts mentioned previously was designed to examine RBTS and PTSD reactions using a different measure of PTSD trauma. In the study there were
125 participants and of these, sixty-six were men (53 percent) and fifty-six were
women (45 percent). They ranged in age from nineteen to eighty-six
(M = 42.19 years, SD = 12.62). Fifty-four of the participants (43 percent) were
White, and sixty-eight (54 percent) were people of color, including fifty-nine
who were Black (47 percent), three Hispanic (2 percent), one Asian (1 percent),
one Native American (1 percent), three biracial (2 percent), and one identified as other (1 percent). Forty-four individuals identified themselves as from
the lower socioeconomic class (35 percent), forty as working class (32 percent),
nineteen as lower middle class (15 percent), twelve as middle class (10 percent),
and three as upper middle class (2 percent). With respect to education, the largest group of participants (sixty-one individuals, or 49 percent) had a high school
diploma, the next largest group (thirty-four individuals, or 27 percent) had a
college education or higher, and twenty-seven individuals (22 percent) had
some high school education or below. (Some demographic data are missing
because not all participants answered all the questions.) The RBTSSS was
used to measure the stress associated with specific experiences of racism, and
the Trauma Symptoms Checklist (TSC-40)[34] was used to assess participants'
responses to trauma using the following six scales: dissociation, anxiety, depression, sexual abuse trauma index (SATI), sleep disturbance, and sexual problems. The Cronbach's alpha for each of the six subscales was .82, .86, .86, .83,
.87, and .82, respectively. Study results are presented below. Robert T. Carter,
Katherine Kirkinis, and Veronica Johnson found the same overlap between
RBTSSS and TSC-40 scales in another recent and similar study with a larger
participant group.[35]

In the study, Robert T. Carter, Sant-Barket, and Stotts converted RBTSSS elevations into a group where the group included only those participants who responded "yes" to all three of these questions about their reported memorable racial event. This criterion reduced the sample by forty-four respondents, leaving eighty-one of the 125. The new group had the same demographics as the full sample. A person-specific scoring method was developed to assist researchers and clinicians in determining an RBTS symptom-scale elevation profile for each participant based on their reactions to their memorable encounter with racism.[36]

In order to score the RBTSSS reactions, the summed subscale scores were converted to standardized t-scores. Once t-scores were calculated for each of the seven "*after*" symptom scales for each participant, we identified respondents with reaction scale scores of 55 and higher (one-half a standard deviation above the mean) and treated the scale scores as elevated and reflecting some relative level of stress. Consistent with Carter's conceptualization of race-based traumatic stress,[37] at least two of the three (core) reaction scales (intrusion, avoidance, hypervigilance) were needed for a traumatic reaction to be present; the remaining reactions (depression, anger, physical symptoms, low self-esteem) were considered clustered or associated symptoms that accompany the two or three critical reactions to varying degrees.

Respondents who had an elevation on at least one core scale with no necessary cluster elevations composed the general-stress reaction group. Of the eighty-one participants who reported their memorable race-related event as sudden, negative, and out of their control, forty-five met criteria for the RBTS stress-trauma elevation group, and thirty had no core scale elevations (RBTS no-stress group).

Focusing on the RBTS stress-trauma group (n = 45), interscale correlations were examined to explore the potential relationships or associations between the seven "*after*" RBTSSS reaction scales and the six TSC-40 scales. A total of thirty-five positive, significant correlations were found (twenty-eight at the .01 level and seven at the .05 level), which greatly exceeds the number expected by chance. The largest correlations occurred between the RBTS low self-esteem scale and the TSC dissociation (r = .57, $p < .01$) and SATI (r = .55, $p < .01$) scales, which indicate that these scales were associated with a moderate strength of practical significance ($.30 \leq r^2 \leq .33$). To a lesser degree, the RBTS low self-esteem scale was also positively correlated with the TSC anxiety (r = .48, $p < .01$), depression (r = .48, $p < .01$), and sleep disturbance scales (r = .46, $p < .01$). Additional interscale correlations that approached a medium effect size $(.20 \leq r^2 \leq .25)$ occurred between the TSC dissociation and SATI scales and the RBTSS depression, physical, avoidance, hypervigilance, and intrusion scales, as well as the RBTSS physical and TSC depression scales. While several more positive and significant correlations were found between the seven RBTSS scales and the six TSC scales $(.30 \leq r \leq .40, p < .01 \text{ or } < .05)$, the relatively small effect sizes of these associations suggest that the practical significance of these relationships is relatively weak. Taken together, these significant correlations indicated that, overall, the RBTS low self-esteem reaction scale was the most frequently and moderately correlated RBTS scale to the TSC-40 scales (all except sexual problems), and the TSC dissociation and sexual abuse trauma index were the most frequently and moderately associated TSC-40 scales to the RBTSSSs (low self-esteem, depression, physical, avoidance, hypervigilance, and intrusion); however, the effect sizes of these correlations $(.20 \leq r^2 \leq .33)$ indicated that the strength of these relations was only moderate at best.

The significant and positive associations between the RBTSSSs and the scales of the TSC-40 suggest that although the measures overall are assessing comparable aspects or symptom clusters of a similar construct (i.e., traumatic reactions), the relatively moderate relationships between the scales indicate that the instruments may also measure distinct dimensions of trauma reactions.

PRACTICE AND RESEARCH IMPLICATIONS OF THE RBTSSS

Many mental health studies of racial discrimination and the effects of stress show that people experience psychological distress such as depression and anxiety as a result of racism-related stressors. However, it has not been clear whether specific types of experiences with racial discrimination contribute to the effects of RBTS as racial trauma. Moreover, in the existing literature, trauma has not been considered as a possible reaction to race-related stress.[38] Further, as mentioned, studies and measures of racism-related stress and discrimination have had several limitations. Many of the measures focus on African Americans, and more information is needed about other racial groups and how they are affected by racial encounters.[39] In some cases, evidence of the potential traumatic impact of racism is indirect (e.g., inferred from high rates of PTSD). Few studies[40] have drawn directly from participants' own descriptions of critical encounters with discrimination and their accompanying lasting emotional effects. Some studies use two- or three-item measures of racial discrimination, and overall the instruments used for racial discrimination vary significantly from study to study.[41]

This chapter describes the conceptual and empirical development of a measure specifically designed to capture emotional responses to racial encounters or racism that are sudden, are out of one's control, and result in emotional pain. The structure of the RBTSSS provides support for the concept of RBTS proposed by Carter.[42] He notes that an encounter with racism should be experienced as negative in order to qualify as a traumatizing stressor, which indicates that the experience might have produced emotional pain. More specifically, he suggests that the encounter should be sudden, which contributes to the intensity of the reaction, and experienced as out of one's control. The RBTSSS presented in this chapter can be used to investigate and gain a more accurate understanding of racism-related experiences and their emotional impact.

This information will be helpful to clinicians working with individuals who have experienced incidents that result in RBTS.[43] It could also be useful for professionals dealing with racial harassment or racial discrimination lawsuits, such as attorneys or mental health professionals who might serve as consultants and expert witnesses. The RBTSSS can be used by researchers to shed light on the relationship between the various impacts of classes or types of racial discrimination (e.g., being profiled in a store, being denied access to housing, being assaulted verbally) and the accompanying emotional and psychological responses. The RBTSSS contributes to understanding and measuring the emotional effects of racism and racial discrimination on people of various racial and ethnic groups, and its use should increase knowledge of how particular incidents might produce severe stress reactions and of what types of incidents are most associated with severe symptoms.

7

EMPIRICAL RESEARCH EVIDENCE ASSOCIATED WITH THE RACE-BASED TRAUMATIC STRESS SYMPTOM SCALE

AFTER THE CONSTRUCTION OF THE RBTSSS to measure the effects of racism, several studies were undertaken to address important questions about the scale's validity regarding the constructs that were measured, and how the scale should be used. This chapter presents information about the validity of these investigations.

After publication of the first article about the construction of the RBTSSS, many aspects of the instrument remained unaddressed. First, although there were three questions for every symptom, the only subject of inquiry in the first study involved only the question pertaining to symptoms experienced *after* the event.[1] The thinking was that since a person's reactions following a racial event are more directly related to whether they had a traumatic stress reaction, then that should be the emphasis. It seemed more important to discover any common dimensions in the *after*-the-event items than to address other aspects of the measure.

With the scale-development study, we established the utility of the symptom items, identified common themes, and derived seven scales from the item pool. We were able to show that the scales have internal-consistency reliability and do not overlap (i.e., are not highly correlated). We also were able to show the importance of the "yes" criteria—three questions about the racial event being unexpected, happening out of the person's control, and resulting in emotional pain. Eve Carlson believes that an incident must cause emotional pain,[2] which is a critical or core component of traumatic stress, so it is important that the instrument account for the fact that the racial incident is a source of emotional pain. We think it is meaningful that there is a significant difference between total RBTSSS scores of those who report the "yes" criteria and those who do not. We take this difference to support the notion that the "yes" elements are needed for race-based stress or trauma to be present.

However, other parts of the measure are not explored in the scale-development study. For instance, the questions about having a reaction *"now"* or *"recently"* and whether "anyone noticed a change in your behavior" remain unexamined. These two questions are included in the instrument because they capture important aspects or features of race-based traumatic stress (RBTS) reactions.

With respect to the *"now* "question, when RBTS occurs, it is embedded into one's memory in a way that brings about reexperiencing and flashbacks (intrusion). Reminders of or discussing the event can have a similar effect, bringing back memories of the incident such that the person relives it and the related distress. Race-related stress and trauma also cause symptoms that alters how a person behaves and functions. Many of the related changes are observable by others, hence the "change in behavior" questions for each symptom. The questions help to make the effects of the race-related stress or trauma more objective and verifiable.

Finally, in the scale-development study, we used summed-scale scores for a total score. The total scores were summed across all the scales, a procedure that did not reveal whether any particular scale was higher than the others, nor was there a way to distinguish between race-based stress and RBTS. We decided it would be valuable to have a scoring system that aided in these distinctions. Many of these issues are examined in follow-up investigations to the scale-development study.

"AFTER" AND "NOW" SYMPTOM QUESTIONS ABOUT THE EVENT: ARE THEY RELATED?

The first follow-up study was undertaken by Robert T. Carter and Sinead Sant-Barket, who examined whether participants *"after"* and *"now"* symptom responses were related.[3] (Recall from chapter 6 that we distinguished between symptoms that occurred *after* the event and those that occurred *recently,* or *now.*) For the *"now"* response to be meaningful, we reasoned that it is related to the person's *"after"* response. That is, we expected that if someone reported that a symptom was experienced frequently or would not go away just after the event, they would more than likely give the same or similar responses for the "*now*" option. So if a person frequently felt sad after the event, they would also say, in the present, that they frequently felt sad, "*now.*"

We used canonical-correlation analyses (CCA), a multivariate procedure, to explore whether the "*after*" and "*now*" responses are related. We selected CCA because it allows the researcher to use a set of dependent and independent variables to determine if the combination of variables produces a new "synthetic" variate set. CCA reduces type 1 errors (thinking you have found a significant result when you have not) that might occur if multiple analyses are used (i.e., regression, each with a single dependent variable). Each significant canonical function produces a new variate with variables from both sets in the correlation. Thus, we learn how the variables in question combine and operate together. The CCA generates as many functions as there are independent variables in the analyses. However, since the procedure maximizes the correlations for each function, subsequent functions in the analyses are uncorrelated. Therefore, each function is independent of the others, and each function reveals a distinct set of relationships. It is also the case that each function accounts for a separate amount of variance between the set of variables in the analyses.[4]

Carter and Sant-Barket found that all eight functions generated were statistically significant.[5] The first contained all the scales, combining each "*after*" symptom scales with its "*now*" scale. The following functions combined one "*now*" symptom scale with its "*after*" scale. For instance, "depression after" and "depression now" formed a canonical variate. The pattern of results emerged for all seven scales, meaning each scale has a separate function that only contains the "*after*" and the "*now*" scales. Thus, the analyses suggest that both "*after*" and "*now*" responses can be used to understand the presence of race-based stress or trauma since the study shows that the two responses are related.

This finding points to an important characteristic of race-based stress and race-based trauma-related experiences in which the person relives past events or incidents. When the incident has left a powerful emotional imprint, recalling the symptom can trigger the return of the incident to conscious memory. That said, it remains impossible to know which scales are contributing to the person's race-based stress or possible RBTS without a method to score that is based on a person's responses and where summed scores across scales are not used.

HOW SHOULD THE SYMPTOM SCALES BE SCORED? NEW INDIVIDUAL SCORING METHOD AND INTERPRETATION

Carter and Sant-Barket present a new scoring system and address variation in responses to the "change in behavior" question by comparing people with high RBTS scale scores with those who did not have high RBTS scale scores or elevations.[6] We expect that if people report race-based stress or RBTS, they will also endorse the "change in behavior" items more than those who are not stressed or do not exhibit any race-based stress or trauma.

The scoring for the RBTSSS in the initial development study is group oriented since the focus was to determine if there is evidence to support the construct. Therefore, the scoring that was used totaled the scale scores across individuals or for the sample as a group. But, in this way, the initial evidence for the possible presence of race-based stress was limited to group-based information. If the measure is to be used in clinical or forensic settings to assess the mental health effects of racism, its scoring needs to yield a way to understand the meaning of the scores for an individual—a person-specific score profile.

The person-specific scoring method that Carter and Sant-Barket present involves the conversion of summed scale scores to standardized scores for each person in the participant group.[7] The goal of the person-specific scoring method is for the scale score to be easier to understand and interpret in terms of determining which scores are low and high or elevated on symptom scales, thus giving the scale values clear meaning for clinical, forensic, and research purposes, and making it possible to interpret responses for one person as well as for a larger group of participants.

Using 381 participants from the scale-development study, we converted their raw scores to standard scores. We determined the raw item responses, using one person to illustrate, and summed items for each symptom scale—for example, depression *"after"* (e.g., summed value of ten depression items = 38). Then we did the same for all symptom scales. The resulting summed scores for all seven symptoms could then be used to find the person's mean and standard deviation for both *"after"* and *"now"* reactions. The person's mean (e.g., $M = 26$) and standard deviation (e.g., $SD = 10$) were used to convert the raw summed scores to z-scores for each symptom scale (e.g., Score $(X) - M/SD$; depression $= 38 - 26 / 10 = z$ of 1.20). Then we convert the z-scores to a t-score (where all t-scores have a set mean and standard deviation; $M = 50$, $SD = 10$), multiplying the z-score by 10 and adding 50 to the result (e.g., $1.20 \times 10 = 12 + 50 =$ depression t-score $= 62$). Because t-scores have a mean of 50 and a standard deviation of 10, this score-transformation procedure allows for easy identification of the scale scores' level, that is, when it is either low (below the mean), at mid-range (at the mean), or high or elevated (above the mean by a half or full standard deviation or more). The t-standard score is used to interpret the RBTSSS scores. For example, "high" or "elevated" are scores that are one-half standard deviation above the mean, a t-score of 55, or one standard deviation above the mean, a scale t-score of 60 shows that a symptom is high or elevated. One or more elevations indicates the presence of race-based stress, and three or more elevated scale scores mean RBTS is present.

In addition to the high scale scores, the interpretation of RBTSSS elevations requires that we also consider whether participants report that their most memorable racial event was emotionally painful (negative), sudden, and out of their control. Said another way, RBTS is present if the person endorses the "yes" criteria and had elevated symptom scale scores (one-half or one full standard deviation above the mean). To learn more about the "change in behavior" question, we selected only those participants who endorsed all the "yes" criteria questions about their memorable racial event. This selection reduced the sample size to 253.

To illustrate our score interpretation strategy, we focused solely on participants' reactions "*after*" the event for ease of explanation. Once t-scores were calculated for each of the seven symptom scales for each participant in the sample, we identified respondents with reaction scale scores of 55 or higher (one-half a standard deviation above the mean), which means some level of stress. Consistent with Carter's[8] conceptualization of RTBS, we use participants with at least two of the three reaction scales (intrusion, avoidance, hypervigilance) for a traumatic reaction to be present, and any remaining reactions were thought of as clustered symptoms (depression, anger, physical, low self-esteem).

Therefore for a stress/trauma reaction to be present in this nonclinical participant group, it was determined that a person must have high scores on (1) two or more core reaction scales (e.g., intrusion score of 63, a hypervigilant score of 59) and no other elevated scores; or (2) at least one elevated core scale with at least one elevated cluster scale (e.g., an elevated score of 56 on the avoidance and anger scales). Respondents who did not have any elevated reaction scores were excluded from the stress/trauma group ($n = 76$), which reduced the sample to 177 participants. A total of 74 participants met the stress/trauma reaction criteria, and 103 comprised the no-stress reaction group.

We wanted first to determine whether the change items are a meaningful part of the RBTSSS's three questions after each stem. We compared the no-stress and stress/trauma groups to see if there is a difference in the two groups in terms of whether someone noticed a change in them. We conducted an analysis of variance (ANOVA) in which the total *"change"* reaction scale was the dependent variable and the participants' reaction grouping was the independent variable. Results of the analysis are significant in that participants in the stress/trauma reaction group report that others noticed a change in their behavior to a greater degree than the no-stress group.[9] Thus, it the change question is a valuable way to determine whether the respondent is aware of how his behavior might have been observed by others. At the very least, the change question indicates that the person is aware that his behavior might have resulted in his actions being different.

We conducted further analyses to see if there are any differences based on demographic group (i.e., race, gender, and socioeconomic status). Of the three demographic variables of interest, racial group membership is the only one with significant group differences in the prevalence of reactions. We found that Asian participants are more likely to report significantly higher rates of depression and lower rates of hypervigilance reactions compared to White respondents, and Blacks are more likely to report higher anger reactions than Whites. There are no gender or socioeconomic status group differences. The two investigations we describe establish that the scale should be used with the three responses to each symptom scale, and that the "yes" criterion is of value.

EMPIRICAL VALIDITY EVIDENCE STUDIES

The scale-development studies provide evidence of the merit of the RBTS concept and measure, but further validity evidence is needed (i.e., to establish the extent to which the ideas and measurement are sound, replicable, and capture something stable) from a new sample. More important, since the participants are racially heterogeneous in the scale-development studies, and not exclusively people of color, the validity sample should be similar. Any validity study has to show that the scale's structure is the same and that the structure and scale items are confirmed with new participants from similar and different racial, gender, and social class groups, meaning that people from different groups respond to the items and scales in the same way, and that the scales are measuring the concepts (i.e., symptoms and RBTS) in a similar manner—that is, that there is measurement equivalence across groups (i.e., race, gender, socioeconomic status).

To test the validity of the RBTS theory and instrument, structural equation modeling (SEM) was used, which is a multivariate statistical procedure that allows the investigator to empirically test theoretical propositions and measurements that could confirm the factor structure of a psychological instrument.[10] In addition, SEM permits the investigator to define constructs and to explore how they are associated with a set of variables and other related constructs. A major task of SEM is to determine whether the theoretical ideas are supported by empirical data drawn from study participants, assuming there is some indication that the model or ideas can be supported by the data. SEM makes it possible to test or explore more complex theoretical assumptions if the initial model is valid.[11]

In SEM there are two distinct types of variables, observed or indicators and unobserved or latent (not measured). Latent variables are considered hypothetical factors and are not directly measured (i.e., there are no scores). Instead, we infer from variables that are measured by using scores from physical measures, surveys, self-report instruments, and so on. The observed variables are indicators used to define the hypothetical latent construct.[12]

Variables, either observed or latent, can be independent (i.e., not influenced by any other variable) or dependent (i.e., influenced by other variables). Path and regression analyses use only observed or measured variables. For example, in regression analysis, the number of books at home (independent) could be used to predict school grades (dependent). With SEM, measured or indicator variables are used to show one or more latent variables. For example, "fitness" is a latent variable that is indicated by the measured variables of diet consumed, type and frequency of exercise, and heart rate and blood pressure.

As noted, SEM is a complex statistical procedure that differs from many statistical tests most professionals learn, like ANOVA, bivariate correlation (r), and so forth. SEM has several advantages and challenges. One advantage is that measurement error is accounted for in the models that are tested, and a challenge is that several indices must be evaluated to determine if the model accurately captures the proposed relationships between the latent and observed variables—that is, does the model fit the data? There is no significance level or probability that must be met. Rather, one must consult several fit indices to know if the model matches the data.[13]

Carter and Carrie Muchow examined the construct, predictive validity, and measurement equivalence of the RBTSSS using SEM with eleven hundred racially diverse adults from the community and from colleges and universities.[14] In SEM, confirmatory factor analyses (CFAs) involves testing a theoretical (latent constructs—proposed, not directly measured) and a measurement (variables with scores) model. The measurement model under investigation came from the exploratory factor analysis (EFA) described in chapter 6, the fifty-two after-the-event items and seven scales of the RBTSSS.[15] Carter and Muchow tested the seven-factor structure that made up the measurement model. The theoretical model involves the constructs associated with the seven RBTSSS latent scales and the underlying construct of RBTS.

We should note that, according to William Hoyt and colleagues, there are several types of validity: (a) content related (i.e., a match between the content and the tasks or psychological issues being assessed); (b) criterion related (i.e., the ability of the measure to predict future behavior or related constructs), and (c) construct related (i.e., the elements of a construct that account for variation in scores on the measure). Hoyt and colleagues state that "construct validation then, is an ongoing, theory-guided inquiry into systematic determination of test scores (often called the test's factor structure or internal structure), correlates of test scores (external structure) and the variables (e.g., testing conditions, population under investigation) on which these structures are contingent."[16] Thus, they note that all validity is related to construct validity.

A CFA as part of an SEM is a statistical procedure that is similar to factor analysis. It examines or helps determine whether an instrument captures the intended idea or construct in a manner consistent with what is believed to be the nature of that construct (or factor). For instance, is depression measured by the Beck Depression Inventory? Thus, the goal of a CFA is to test whether the data fit a hypothesized, full structural model. The model is taken from a conceptual framework or theory. In this instance, both the conceptual and measurement aspects of the RBTSSS were investigated. The items composing each *"after"* scale are indicators of the latent symptoms scales. The indicators are presumed to reflect the seven constructs or symptom scales identified in the initial scale-development inquiry. The seven symptom scales are depression, intrusion, anger, hypervigilance, physical reactions, low self-esteem, and avoidance, which meant that the items or indicators that comprised the RBTS depression scale would indicate an unmeasured latent construct as "RBTS depression." These are the unobserved (i.e., not directly measured) latent variables in the CFA. In the validity study, we thought that the same fifty-two after-the-event items and the same seven-scale-factor structure could be confirmed in the analysis of the measurement model. We also believed that the theoretical or second-order model, which included the constructs associated with the seven latent symptom scales and the underlying latent construct of RBTS, could also be confirmed.

In conducting SEM, unlike standard statistical tests in which a level of significance is set and must be met, the researcher must determine whether multiple fit indices reach acceptable levels. In SEM, five indices exist that should meet suitable values for the model to demonstrate a good fit. In evaluating the specified model, the "absolute fit" indices (chi-square [χ^2], root mean square error of approximation [RMSEA], and the standardized root mean square residual [SRMR]) were examined first. A "good-fitting" structural model should yield a nonsignificant χ^2. Given that χ^2 statistics are sensitive to sample size, data from large samples tend to yield significant χ^2 values, and data that violate multivariate normality can lead to model rejection even when the model is specified properly.[17] To account for multivariate nonnormality and the large size of the cross-validation sample in the validity analyses, additional fit indices that are less sensitive to these assumptions were selected and used to evaluate the model fit. The RMSEA tests the extent to which relationships between variables predicted by the model differ from those that emerged in the observed data. In recent years, this estimate has been referred to as the most precise fit index, as confidence intervals are calculated around its value. As noted by Li-tze Hu and Peter Bentler, a good model fit has a RMSEA value of .06 or lower,[18] and the SRMR a value of .08 or lower. Other indices are the comparative fit index (CFI) and the tucker lewis index (TLI), which are incremental indices with values between .90 and .95 to demonstrate acceptable model fit. In assessing model fit, it is important that at least four of the indices meet the criteria described above. Reporting various fit indices is necessary given that different ones reflect varying dimensions of model fit.[19] When testing complex models in SEM, as noted by Rex Kline,[20] reporting multiple fit estimates is necessary given that different statistics reflect different dimensions of model fit.

Examination of the indices yielded by the current CFA reveal that achieved adequate model fit. The fit indices for the RBTSS "*after*" items are as follows: chi-square, $\chi^2 = 3946.172$ ($df = 1253$) $p = .0001$. The χ^2 ratio (the value divided by the degrees of freedom) was 3.14. The ratio is used to determine whether the values fall between 2 and 5, suggesting that χ^2 may provide a good indicator of the overall fit of the model. Additionally, RMSEA = .06 (90 percent CI = .057, .062), CFI = .90 and TLI = .90, and SRMR = .047. The resulting critical values indicate that the model fit the data from the cross-validation sample relatively well.

Evaluation of the fit indices and parameter estimates resulting from the SEM indicate that the second-order model also adequately fit the data. We thus conclude that the latent indicators are associated with the latent construct of RBTS. The indices are as follows: $\chi^2 = 4252.01$, $(df = 1267)$ $p = .0001$, χ^2 ratio = 3.35, RMSA = .06, CFI = .90, TLI = .90, and SRMR = .05. Additionally, all seven latent scale indicators loaded on race-based trauma are at or close to 1.0 or higher, and all are positively associated (depression = 1.0; intrusion = .97; anger = .93; hypervigilance = 1.15; physical symptoms = 1.04; low self-esteem = 1.02; and avoidance = .92). Review of the above fit indices supports the existence of the concept of RBTS. The analysis reveals a good model fit and illustrates that the seven observed variables are associated with the latent construct of RBTS.

It is also important to know whether the RBTSSS measures the same re-actions it is designed to assess in all groups with which it will be used.[21] For this question, tests of measurement equivalence or invariance are calculated for race and gender groups. The results of the invariance tests provide additional evidence supporting the RBTSSS's instrument and what it measures and that its measurement is equivalent with respect to gender but not race. Said another way, racial groups respond differently to the scales and items, but gender groups do not.

FURTHER VALIDITY EVIDENCE

The issue of whether constructs and variables that are similar would be related to the RBTSSS was also examined in a study of concurrent validity with CCA. Each significant canonical function produces a new variate, which is the weighted sum of all the variables in the analysis. Thus, we learn how the variables in question operate together.

Two separate CCAs were conducted to examine the multivariate relationships between two variable sets; independent variables were RBTS symptom scales, and dependent variables were the six subscales (anxiety, depression, loss of control, positive affect, and emotional ties) of the Mental Health Inventory (MHI). One CCA was done with the no-stress group, meaning the group comprised individuals who did not score above the mean for trauma symptoms. The other CCA was done with a stress/trauma group comprising individuals who scored one-half or one standard deviation above the mean on at least one trauma symptom scale.

In the no-stress group ($n = 244$), the analysis yielded only one interpretable function (R^2c) of .178, .098, .042, .012, .003, and .001 for each successive function. The full model was significant (Wilks' $\lambda = .699$ criterion, F [42, 1086.94] = 2.05, $p < .001$), explaining about 30 percent of the variance. The coefficients for the no-stress group were loss of control (−.91), depression (−.65), and anxiety (−.54), which contributed to the variate set. Emotional ties (.37) and positive affect (.31) did not contribute to the variate set. For the predictor set, RBTS avoidance (−.72), low self-esteem (−.66), depression (−.57), hypervigilance (−.56), and anger (−.47) contributed, while physical symptoms (−.38) and intrusion (.02) did not. The structure coefficients for MHI were all in the same direction (negative signs) with the predictive variables, indicating a positive relationship. We labeled the canonical variate for the no-stress group "*emotional distress from racial experiences.*"

In the stress/trauma group ($n = 171$), only the first function was interpreted. The full model was significant, explaining 40 percent of the variance (Wilks' $\lambda = .599$, F [42, 744.54] = 2.05, $p < .001$). The coefficients for the stress/trauma group in order of magnitude were MHI depression (−.99), anxiety (−.81), loss of control (−.80), and positive affect (.42); emotional ties (.38) did not contribute to the variate. All RBTS symptom variables contributed to the predictor set as follows: low self-esteem (−.86), hypervigilance (−.79), anger (−.76), depression (−.75), physical symptoms (−.69), intrusion (−.57), and avoidance (−.55). Finally, RBTS symptom variables were positively related to MHI scales, except for positive affect and emotional ties, which were inversely associated with the RBTS symptom scales. Thus, the canonical variate seems to be best captured as "*race-based trauma.*"

Results of both CCAs were significant with one variate to be interpreted, indicating evidence of convergent and divergent validity, with fewer relationships for the no-stress group and more and stronger relationships between RBTS symptoms and mental health symptoms in the stress/trauma group.

For the no-stress group, the pattern of relationships between the MHI scales and RBTS symptoms shows that, while racial encounters may not be described as "stressful," they are nevertheless experienced as deeply troubling; people felt out of control, accompanied by anxiety, depression, and a lack of well-being. Feelings of needing or wanting to escape, loss of self-worth, depression, anger, and perceiving the need to monitor one's environment merged with the psychological states. This finding is consistent with the results of studies of racial discrimination and racial harassment.[22]

In the case of the participants in the stress/trauma group, the pattern of relationships differs from that of the no-stress group, and more variance is accounted for by the canonical variate. The RBTS symptom scales also have a different order with mental health symptoms, and all scales are part of the canonical variate. The RBTS symptom variables form two sets. For the stress/trauma group, a lower sense of self, a need to survey one's environment, and anger/depression grouped together, while bodily manifestations, intrusive thoughts, and the need to get away from people clustered together more clearly. The findings seem to suggest that participants experienced more than disturbance; rather, they seemed to experience RBTS. Hence, we believe that the patterns that emerged from the CCA indicate evidence of convergent and divergent validity, illustrated by fewer relationships for the no-stress group and more and stronger relationships between RBTS symptoms and mental health symptoms in the stress/trauma group.

RBTSSS VALIDITY FOR BLACK AMERICANS

A study by R.T. Carter, Carrie Muchow, and Alex Pieterse with 527 Black American adults examined whether the RBTSSS would work with a specific racial group.[23] To that end, CFA and a test of measurement invariance across gender and socioeconomic status (SES) as well as a test of predictive validity were conducted. The structure of the RBTSSS was confirmed through tests of the first-order model and measurement invariance using CFA. A second-order SEM supported the RBTS construct. Predictive analyses indicated that the RBTS symptom scales are significantly associated with psychological outcomes including anxiety, depression, and loss of emotional and behavioral control. Overall analyses found support for the construct and predictive validity for the RBTSSS for Blacks.

RBTSSS AND RACIAL IDENTITY STATUS ATTITUDES AMONG PEOPLE OF COLOR

From another perspective, an examination of how RBTSSS is related to racial identity status attitudes and psychological well-being or distress was undertaken. To understand the impact that racial experiences have on people of color, it is important to consider whether there are any RBTS symptoms and within-group differences as reflected in one's racial identity status attitudes. The researchers asked whether the combination of RBTS symptom reactions and racial identity status attitudes related to the psychological functioning for people of color. The study by Carter, Veronica E. Johnson, and colleagues explored the relationships between a person's reactions to memorable racial encounters as assessed by the RBTSSS, their racial identity status attitudes, and psychological functioning (i.e., distress and well-being).[24] Data from 282 adults in the community were used, and cluster analyses were conducted. A two-cluster group solution was found that showed associations between externally defined or less mature racial identity status attitudes and higher RBTS symptoms and psychological distress. Internally defined or more mature racial identity status attitudes are related to decreased psychological distress and lower RBTS symptoms. The findings were unexpected because lower racial identity statuses represent an immature ego status and as such it was thought that there was less vulnerability to RBTS, yet we find in this study that individuals with less mature racial identity status attitudes could be more vulnerable to racism-related stress as represented by higher RBTS symptom levels.

RBTSSS AMONG WHITE AMERICANS

Race is a social construct used to identify, group, categorize, and classify people based on physical features, skin color, or language, and to place them into distinct "racial groups" based on those physical markers.[25] This social tradition of classifying people by race includes everyone, Whites and people of color.[26] Whites comprise a distinct racial group with its own racial identity process and expression.[27] Janet E. Helms and Carter were the first to present a measure of White racial identity development, providing research support for a White racial identity process (i.e., Whites' ability to understand themselves as racial beings).[28] Given that Whites are a racial group, they also experience negative racial incidents and are at risk for experiencing race-based stress. The purpose of this research study was to explore whether the RBTSSS could be used with Whites and whether RBTS is a valid construct for Whites.

Although people of color report higher rates of racial discrimination than do Whites and they hold less power in society, Whites report experiences of racial discrimination and have emotional reactions to these experiences. David Williams and colleagues report that 93 percent of participants in their study attribute unfair treatment to injustice; from Whites' perspective, unfair treatment takes the form of racial minorities getting preference, while Blacks perceive less opportunity.[29] Furthermore, people of lower social status experience greater discrimination than those of higher social status, regardless of their race.

Kelly Bower and colleagues find a positive relationship between racial discrimination and depression and anxiety in a sample of low-income, urban, White adults.[30] Notably, comparison of Whites and people of color on emotional and physical reactions to race-based incidents show that both groups are equally harmed by these experiences and feel anger and frustration.[31] When people undergo experiences of racial discrimination, they are harmed regardless of their race. People have a wide range of interactions with others that could be considered negative racial encounters. Carter and colleagues present a set of categories based on participants' descriptions of racial experiences.[32] This set of categories was used in the current study to accomplish one of the study's aims: to document the various memorable experiences noted by Whites, including verbal assault, denial of access to service, hostile work environment, violation of racial rules, being profiled, treatment on the basis of a stereotype, physical assaults, own-group discrimination, and other experiences.

In addition to the types of racial experiences Whites might report, variation exists in how members of any racial group might assign meaning to their race.[33] Therefore, to understand Whites' racial encounters, it is necessary to know how variation in their psychological orientation to their race or their racial identity status attitudes might influence descriptions of race-based incidents.[34] The White racial identity ego statuses include contact, in which there is a denial of race and its significance (i.e., colorblindness); disintegration, characterized by dissonance and confusion about the meaning of race; reintegration, in which a person reaffirms beliefs of White racial superiority; pseudoindependence, characterized by an idealized and primarily intellectual racial awareness; and autonomy, characterized by the development of a positive White racial identity that is not based on notions of supremacy.[35] Consideration of racial identity is vital in the evaluation of an individual's subjective experience of racial encounters as well as in assessing race-based stress and trauma.[36] Therefore, we explored several questions about Whites' experiences of racial stress, the types of experiences they report, and which of these might be classified as race-related stress. Does the RBTSSS have validity and reliability with a Whites-only participant group, and are there any within-group psychological and demographic differences like racial identity status, socioeconomic status, and gender for Whites (measurement equivalence)? Are Whites' emotional reactions to race incidents similar to or different from those experienced by Blacks?

The study included 284 White adults from several community sites within the northeast United States. About a third were male (31.9 percent, $n = 90$) and two-thirds female (68.1 percent, $n = 192$); two did not report gender. The majority of the participants' SES were working class (13.7 percent), lower class (20.1 percent), and middle class (53.9 percent). Their ages were between seventeen and eighty-six ($M = 32.32$, $SD = 11.69$), and years of education averaged around some college ($M = 13.88$, $SD = 3.38$).

Our first inquiry was whether the RBTSSS was reliable and valid for Whites, and whether the concept of RBTS could be supported. We used SEM and conducted CFA. We hypothesized that the same fifty-two-item, seven-scale structure could be confirmed in the analysis.[37] The theoretical model was the same as for the other validity studies. The specified model was assessed by implementing the robust mean-and variance-adjusted weighted least squares (WLSMV) estimation procedure. As noted in the psychometric literature,[38] the WLSMV approach provides accurate parameter estimates with sample sizes of 200 or greater and non-normal data sets.[39] We found the following fit values: χ^2 (1,253) 1,919.338 ($p < .001$), and the normed χ^2/df ratio was approximately 1.50; the RMSEA was .043 (90 percent CI: .039, .047), the CFI = .98, and the TLI = .97. A model fit was found for both the first- and second-order models (χ^2 [1267] 1930.971 [$p < .001$]). Additionally, RMSEA was .043 (90 percent CI [.039, .047]), CFI .98, and TLI .98 (second order). The latent scale indicators also loaded on race-based trauma at values ranging from 1.0 to 1.1 with significance values of $p \leq .001$. We thus found that the seven latent scales indicated the latent construct of RBTS for Whites.

Regarding measurement equivalence, we found that the configural model demonstrated excellent fit for both first- and second-order models, providing evidence of construct invariance for both gender and SES to the seven-factor first-order model for Whites. These findings suggest that the RBTSSS captures the same basic factor structure across White groups. Similarly, the model fit estimates suggest that the model is an adequate fit to the data for each gender group, and thus, the first- and second-order factor structures hold for both gender and SES groups. Thus, while we found that Whites respond differently than people of color in the previous study, this investigation shows that the RBTSSS does work with Whites separately.

In another study, Carter, Katheryn Roberson, and Veronica E. Johnson examined how White racial identity status attitudes (WRIAS) are related to RBTSSS and psychological well-being and distress.[40] The study involved 145 Whites who had completed the White racial identity scale, the RBTSSS, and the MHI. There were eighty-six females (59.3 percent) and fifty-eight males (40.7 percent), participants' average age was 34.25 years (SD = 12.98), their SES on average was lower-middle class (2.88, SD = 1.43), and average years of education were 14.03.

A hierarchical cluster analysis was conducted to examine how RBTS reactions and WRIAS when grouped together are related to mental health outcomes. The hierarchical cluster analysis grouped participants with similar configurations of RBTS reactions and WRIAS. A multivariate analysis of variance (MANOVA) was used to determine if significant differences between cluster groups exist for psychological distress and well-being. Discriminant analysis was used to determine if the racial events reported by Whites differ based on the cluster grouping. Three cluster groups were generated.

Participants in the first cluster group, called "No RBTS Undifferentiated Racial Identity," consisted of sixty-one White American adults with the same gender makeup as the full sample. Participants in this cluster had higher levels of education (M = 15.51, SD = 2.78) and middle-class SES (M = 3.68, SD = 1.25). The group had RBTS scale scores that were below the mean, with anger the lowest at 41. This group's WRIAS contact scores were at the mean (50), and scores for pseudoindependence (51) and autonomy (51) were about the same, while the scale scores of disintegration and reintegration were both below the mean at 47.

The second cluster, "RBTS Low Stress Disintegration and Reintegration Blend," consisted of sixty-seven participants, thirty-seven females and thirty males, with mean age of thirty-four (M = 34.33, SD = 11.61). Participants in this cluster had lower levels of education (M = 13.22, SD = 3.70) and lower-middle-class SES (M = 2.45, SD = 1.32). The group had RBTS scale scores above 53; the highest was anger, at 54. Their WRIAS scores were at the mean for the scales of disintegration and reintegration, both at 52, and slightly below the mean for contact, pseudoindependence, and autonomy, all with a score of 49.

The third cluster, "RBTS High Reintegration," consisted of seventeen participants, nine females and eight males, with a mean age of thirty-six

(M = 36.24, SD = 9.61); they had the lowest education level (M = 12.12, SD = 1.83) and lower-class SES (M = 1.76, SD = .97). This cluster groups' RBTS scale scores were all above 67, above the mean by more than one and a half standard deviations and, for some scales, almost two full standard deviations; the highest were low self-esteem and intrusion (both 69). Their WRIAS scores were above the mean for disintegration and reintegration (54 and 57, respectively). The group also had scores that were above the mean for contact, autonomy, (54 and 52, respectively) and pseudoindependence (51). We now examine the racial event types for Whites by comparing the three cluster groups for any possible differences in type.

DIFFERENCES BETWEEN CLUSTER GROUPS BASED ON RACIAL DISCRIMINATION EVENT TYPE

The cluster group analyses raise the question of what kind of racial experiences these participants had. To explore this question, participants' racial encounters were categorized based on reported experiences without researcher judgment about accuracy of the participants' perceptions. Eleven participants' events were not used because four participants provided events that we could not code and seven did not report any event. For this analysis we regrouped events with low frequency by putting together hostile work environment (n = 3) and profiling (n = 3) into a new category we called "aversive-hostile," and we excluded own-group discrimination (n = 1) from analysis. The remaining seven racial event categories for Whites were used for analyses: verbal assault (n = 38), vicarious events (n = 25, with no restriction on target's race), violation of racial rules (n = 21), physical assault (n = 20), treatment on the basis of a stereotype (n = 13), denial of access to services (n = 10), and aversive-hostile events (n = 6). A discriminant analysis was conducted to determine which types of racial encounters were more frequently associated with each of the three cluster groups. Discriminant analysis provides information on how strongly and to which cluster each type of racial encounter was related. Discriminant analysis achieves this through creating functions that maximize the difference between the grouping variables. The three clusters were entered as the grouping variables with the racial encounter types as the discriminator variables. Significant functions in this analysis would indicate that the three clusters are different with respect to the types of racial encounters participants described. The function coefficients and structure matrix would then provide further information regarding how specific types of racial encounters relate to the group differences.

The discriminant analysis produced one function that discriminates between the three clusters ($R_c = .29$; $\lambda = .87$; χ^2 [$df = 14, 138$] $= 17.54$, $p = .23$). The analysis indicates that there are no significant differences between the clusters regarding the types of racial encounters. However, the analysis does provide useful descriptive information about how racial events are related to the different cluster groups. Given the exploratory nature of the analysis, we offer details on how the events are associated with the three cluster groups. The sign of the coefficient indicates the direction of the variable; that is, the cluster groups with positive coefficients more frequently report event types with positive coefficients, and the cluster groups with negative coefficients more frequently report event types with negative coefficients. The categories with higher absolute values contribute more strongly to the differentiation between the three clusters.

Examination of the functions shows that vicarious events (.60) and violation of racial rules (.34) have a high positive coefficient, and physical assault (−.68) has a high negative coefficient. The cluster groups with positive relationships to the function are more likely to report events with a positive valence and with high coefficients. Alternatively, the cluster groups that have a negative valence to the function are more likely to report those with negative valence and more strongly report those with low coefficients. The "No RBTS Undifferentiated Racial Identity" cluster (.33) has a positive relationship with the function, indicating that participants in this group report vicarious experiences and violating racial rules more strongly. The cluster groups "RBTS Low Stress Disintegration and Reintegration Blend" (−.19) and "RBTS High Reintegration" both have negative associations with the function (−.49). This indicates that both groups are more likely to report physical assault, yet the "RBTS High Reintegration" cluster reports physical assault with greater strength (see figure 7.1).

To determine if the three clusters are significantly different from one another with respect to mental health variables, a MANOVA was conducted with the three cluster groups as independent variables and MHI scales of psychological well-being and psychological distress as dependent variables. Post hoc tests indicate that psychological distress scores are significantly different between no RBTS and low stress ($p < .001$), no RBTS and RBTS (traumatic stress; $p < .001$), and low stress and RBTS ($p < .001$). Psychological well-being scores are significantly different between no RBTS and low RBTS

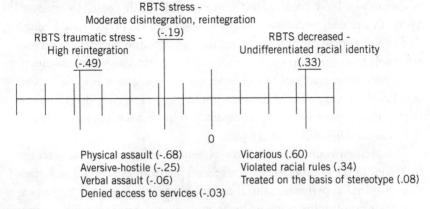

FIGURE 7.1 Cluster group loadings on and composition of the discriminant function

($p < .01$) and no RBTS and RBTS ($p < .001$). However, low RBTS and RBTS do not have significantly different psychological well-being scores ($p > .05$). Cluster group means and standard deviations for RBTS, WRIAS, and psychological well-being and distress are shown in figure 7.1.

Participants in the "No RBTS Undifferentiated Racial Identity" cluster group have significantly less distress ($p < .001$) and higher well-being ($p < .01$) than those in both the "Low Stress Disintegration Reintegration Blend" cluster group and "RBTS High Reintegration" cluster group. Conversely, the participants in the "RBTS High Reintegration" cluster group report significantly more psychological distress ($p < .001$) than participants in the other two cluster groups.

AN EMPIRICAL EXAMINATION OF THE FULL RBTS MODEL

In another investigation, Carter and colleagues examined the full RBTS conceptual model, exploring whether the classes of racism experiences (i.e., hostile, avoidant, and aversive-hostile) would predict RBTS symptoms.[41] Seventy racial experience items were used to explore the notion of classes of racism,[42] and the experiences had two responses for each item: (1) the frequency of exposure to the racial experience (how often the event happened in the past year: 0 = not at all; 1 = on occasion; 2 = several times a year; 3 = several times a month; 4 = several times a week; 5 = several times a day) and (2) the degree of stressfulness (how stressful was the event: 0=not at all; 1=slightly annoyed; 2=mildly irritated; 3=distracted or preoccupied; 4=had trouble functioning).

Scale-development strategies were used to examine the factor structure separately from the classes of racism for both the frequency of racial experiences and stress reactions to the experiences. The goal was to determine whether the items could be grouped into distinct categories (EFA) indicating the classes of racism and, subsequently, if the items could be confirmed (CFA) as valid on a different sample.

The study was divided into three phases. The first phase analyzed the frequency of racial experiences, the second phase analyzed the stress reactions to racial experiences, and the third phase employed two regression analyses using the instruments for frequency and stress reactions to predict RBTS symptoms. Results from the EFAs in phases 1 and 2 show that the racial experience items grouped into three factors for both frequency of racial experience and stress reactions. This provides evidence of the three classes of racism (hostile, avoidant, and aversive-hostile) theorized by Carter.[43] The EFAs were followed by SEM procedures (CFAs) to verify that the items would indicate the latent constructs of the three classes of racism with a new sample of participants.[44] The model fit assessed by the CFAs provides evidence that racism can be measured as comprising three distinct classes of experiences for both frequency (eighteen items) and stress reactions (twenty-three items). The two measures were then used in predictive analyses where the RBTSSSs were dependent variables and the classes of racism measures (hostile, avoidant, and aversive-hostile) for frequency and stress were predictors.

The regression analyses show that for frequency of classes of racism, hostile, aversive-hostile, and avoidant racism are related to RBTS symptoms in that order. Hostile racism is associated with anger and intrusion. Aversive-hostile racism is related to depression, anger, avoidance, and hypervigilance. Avoidant racism is related to depression, anger, physical symptoms, hypervigilance, and low self-esteem. Overall, hostile racism has the strongest effect size but not the greatest number of symptoms. Aversive-hostile and avoidant racism (for frequency of events) are associated with more symptoms.

In the regression analysis of the three classes of racism for stress produced by the experiences, the effect size is larger, suggesting that the relationships are more frequent and robust. The classes of racism for stress have a different order than frequency of experiences. Stress related to hostile racism is associated with three of the seven RBTS symptoms: anger, avoidance, and intrusion. Stress related to avoidant racism is associated with six symptoms: depression, anger, physical symptoms, avoidance, hypervigilance, and low self-esteem. Stress related to aversive-hostile racism is associated with four symptoms: depression, anger, physical symptoms, and low self-esteem.

Stress from racial experiences is connected to thirteen symptoms, while frequency is related to seven symptoms. Additionally, there were more symptoms from avoidant and aversive-hostile racism than from hostile racism. The three RBTS symptoms for stress from hostile racism include two core symptoms and anger. This suggests that although fewer emotional reactions occur, the impact is still quite powerful. The stress reactions to avoidant racism seem to be the most significant, encompassing six of the seven symptoms. Yet regardless of the class of racism one encounters, stress arising from the event and the frequency of events are associated with psychological reactions.

The series of investigations we describe in this chapter provides evidence to support the validity of the RBTSSS. Findings from the investigations indicate that the measure is an accurate representation of the RBTS model, that it is stable across racial groups, and that it demonstrates precision in its measurement of psychological symptoms associated with the experience of racism and racial discrimination. Furthermore, the investigations support the contention that these psychological symptoms should be understood as a type of emotional injury, which is consistent with the description of psychological trauma as outlined by Carlson[45] and conceptualized as race-based trauma by Carter.[46] Thus, the RBTSSS can be used to measure the effects of racism.

8

THE SHORT FORM AND THE INTERVIEW SCHEDULE OF THE RACE-BASED TRAUMATIC STRESS SYMPTOM SCALE

ALTHOUGH THE ADVERSE MENTAL HEALTH effects of racism and racial discrimination have been well documented in psychological literature,[1] there is a noted dearth of assessment tools designed to assess for the presence of race-based traumatic stress (RBTS) symptoms. We have already established that the RBTSSS is the only race-based assessment tool to link a specific experience of racism with accompanying psychological and emotional reactions.[2] Furthermore, standard clinical interviews typically lack a focus on race-based stress or trauma. In this chapter we present two additional tools for the assessment of RBTS: a shortened version of the RBTSSS and an interview schedule. We also illustrate the use of the instruments with a case study.

RACE-BASED TRAUMATIC STRESS SYMPTOM SCALE–SHORT FORM (RBTSSS–SF)

The RBTSSS was developed and validated on a racially heterogeneous sample. Evidence has shows that the RBTSSS has strong validity, as assessed by a range of statistical procedures, including exploratory and confirmatory factor analysis as well as measurement invariance (see the previous chapter). In addition to its use for the clinical assessment of RBTS, the RBTSSS also has utility for forensic application; it has been used in civil suits and in a criminal case dealing with racial discrimination and the emotional effects of work-based racism. A noted drawback to its use is the time required to complete it, which averages around thirty to forty-five minutes, exceeding the recommended fifteen minutes that would maximize participant response rates in legal cases and research studies and would minimize participant fatigue.[3] In general, longer self-report measures tend to have higher rates of missing data and carry the risk of lower levels of participation,[4] thereby introducing the possibly of measurement error.[5] When revising and producing shortened versions of established measures, an important goal is to achieve both economy and accuracy. That is, the advantage of less time should not compromise the accuracy of the measure in relation to both reliability and validity.[6]

Given the concerns with the length of the original RBTSSS we undertook to develop a shorter version (see appendix A) in the hope of increasing its use in both research and clinical domains. We conducted three investigations to accomplish this goal. In the first, we used the original scale-development sample to evaluate whether we could reduce the number of items and maintain the instrument's conceptual and measurement accuracy. Further inquiry involved determining, in a racially heterogeneous community sample, whether the initial structure of the RBTSSS could be replicated by the short form, and we sought to establish reliability and validity evidence for the short form. The third study used the RBTSSS–SF to explore predictive validity through possible relationships to psychological symptoms.

FIRST INVESTIGATION: CAN THE RBTSSS BE SHORTER?

Our first goal was to establish whether it was possible to reduce the number of items for each scale while maintaining internal consistency of items and conceptual clarity. We used the initial scale-development group of 381 adults.[7] Procedures for reducing the number of items while maintaining theoretical consistency of the underlying constructs include selecting RBTSSS items that had the strongest loadings on a scale.[8] We selected items from each RBTS symptom scale with loadings at or above .70 from the original exploratory factor analysis, resulting in twenty-two items (see table 8.1).

We knew from this step that we might be able reduce the RBTSSS by some thirty items. What we did not know was whether the twenty-two items would reflect the same structure that had been previously established using structural equation modeling (SEM) procedures. To test the structure of the RBTSSS–SF, we needed to conduct a confirmatory factor analysis (CFA) with the twenty-two items to see if a model fit could be established. If the model fit the data, it would verify that the twenty-two items captured the structure and the concepts measured by the RBTSSS. In the CFA, the twenty-two items were the indicators of the seven latent symptom-scale variables:

TABLE 8.1 Race-Based Traumatic Stress Symptom Scale—Short Form (RBTSSS—SF): Item Factors and Item Loadings

ITEM NUMBER FROM RBTSSS—LONG FORM	FACTOR						
	DEPRESSION	INTRUSION	ANGER	HYPERVIGILANCE	PHYSICAL REACTIONS	LOW SELF-ESTEEM	AVOIDANCE
1	Nothing to look forward to	0.93					
2	Life was meaningless	0.84					
7	Couldn't experience positive feelings	0.79					
42	Emotionally upset when reminded of event		0.85				
43	Think about what happened		0.80				
44	Experience mental images of event		0.79				
46	Can't get event out of mind		0.77				
9	Getting upset easily			0.89			
11	Getting agitated			0.81			

		F1	F2	F3	F4	F5
12	Easily pissed off	0.76				
35	Easily intimidated		0.94			
38	Worried a lot		0.81			
39	Easily frightened		0.79			
21	Physical reactions			0.87		
22	Trembling			0.76		
25	Aware of heart action			0.70		
48	Sense of responsibility				0.82	
50	Feel useless				0.79	
52	Feel like a failure				0.75	
30	Immune to pain					0.82
31	Feel nothing toward event					0.79
34	Drugs/alcohol usage					0.75

Source: Authors' data.

depression, intrusion, anger, hypervigilance, physical symptoms, low self-esteem, and avoidance. To determine a good model fit, the χ^2 statistic should be nonsignificant, while the root mean square error of approximation (RMSEA) should be .06 or lower, the comparative fit index (CFI) and Tucker-Lewis index (TLI) should be .90 or higher, and the standardized root mean square residual (SRMR) should be .08 or lower.[9] The results showed that all fit indices met criteria ($\chi^2 = 211.95$ [$df = 188$] $p = .111$, RMSEA = .02, CFI = .99, TLI = .99, and SRMR = .04). Moreover, the scales had good internal consistency reliability coefficients: depression (3 items, $\alpha = .76$), intrusion (4 items, $\alpha = .88$), anger (3 items, $\alpha = .79$), hypervigilance (3 items, $\alpha = .86$), physical reactions (3 items, $\alpha = .80$), low self-esteem (3 items, $\alpha = .76$), and avoidance (3 items, $\alpha = .70$).

We followed the CFA with a second-order SEM, in which we examined whether the latent RBTS symptom scales (depression, intrusion, hypervigilance, etc.) would indicate the latent construct of RBTS. The fit indices for this analysis were as follows: $\chi^2 = 250.692$ ($df = 202$) $p = .011$; RMSEA = .03; CFI = .98; TLI = .97, and SRMR = .05. In this analysis, four of the five indices met criteria for the model. The first set of analyses demonstrated that the number of items could be reduced while maintaining the measure's conceptual foundation. Furthermore, its theoretical structure was not compromised in that the symptom scales indicated the latent construct of RBTS.

SECOND INVESTIGATION

A limitation of the item-reduction procedure is that it was conducted with the same sample on which the original scale was developed. It was therefore necessary to establish whether the structure of the RBTSSS–SF could be replicated on a new sample, and whether construct validity could be supported by examining interscale correlations and comparing the means of those who reported their memorable encounter as sudden, negative, and uncontrollable (the "yes" criteria for RBTS reaction) and those who did not. An additional goal of this inquiry was to examine measurement equivalence across gender, race, and social class.

The participants were 736 community residents. Ages ranged from fifteen to eighty-six (M = 38.7, SD = 13.08). There were 351 (47.7 percent) females and 377 (51.2 percent) males; 8 (1.1 percent) did not report their gender. Of the total participants, 194 were White (26.4 percent), 402 were Black (54.6 percent), 74 were Hispanic (10.1 percent), 25 were Asian (3.4 percent), 3 were Native

American (.5 percent), 23 were biracial (3.1 percent), and 10 reported as other (1.4 percent). Five participants omitted this information. The education level of participants was 13.56 years (SD = 3.21). Participants' self-reported socioeconomic status broke down as follows: lower class, 172 (23.4 percent); working class, 195 (26.5 percent); lower-middle class, 130 (17.7 percent); middle class, 148 (20.1 percent); upper-middle class, 53 (7.2 percent); upper class, 6 (.8 percent). Thirty-two (4.3 percent) did not answer this item.

We used the newly constructed RBTSSS–SF (twenty-two items and seven scales), and we transformed scale scores into standardized t-scores (M = 50, SD = 10). For the current participants, Cronbach's alphas for internal-consistency reliability for each of the seven scales were as follows: depression (α = .80), intrusion (α = .85), anger (α = .82), hypervigilance (α = .85), physical reactions (α = .84), low self-esteem (α = .83), and avoidance (α = .77). As with the original RBTSSS measure, we were interested in confirming both the measurement model, which is determined by the relationships between the observed or "measured" variables and the "constructs" or theorized variables, and the structural or theoretical model, which examines the proposed relationships among the latent constructs.

MEASUREMENT MODEL

The same method that was used in the first SEM analysis was used to establish the fit of the data to the model being tested (e.g., χ^2, RMSEA, CFI, TLI, SRMR) for the twenty-two items. We found a model fit based on four of the five indices (e.g., $\chi^2 = 361.95$ [$df = 188$] $p = .01$, RMSEA = .04, CFI = .97, TLI = .97, and SRMR = .03). To test the full structural model, we conducted a second-order SEM with the latent scale constructs as indicators for the latent construct RBTS. The fit indices were $\chi^2 = 505.938$ ($df = 202$) $p = .0001$; χ^2-ratio = 2.50; RMSEA = .05; CFI = .95; TLI = .95; and SRMR = .04. Review of the above fit indices supports the existence of the RBTS construct for the RBTSSS–SF.

INTERSCALE CORRELATIONS

The correlation matrix was also examined to determine the extent to which the factors are correlated, revealing factor correlations ranging from .28 to .53 and confirming that the scales are not independent from one another

TABLE 8.2 Interscale Correlations: RBTSSS-SF

SCALE	1	2	3	4	5	6	7
1. Depression	1	-	-	-	-	-	-
2. Intrusion	0.28	1	-	-	-	-	-
3. Anger	0.39	0.51	1	-	-	-	-
4. Hypervigilance	0.40	0.51	0.38	1	-	-	-
5. Physical Reactions	0.34	0.53	0.49	0.52	1	-	-
6. Low Self-Esteem	0.44	0.44	0.36	0.50	0.40	1	-
7. Avoidance	0.43	0.33	0.37	0.48	0.43	0.42	1

Source: Authors' data.

(see table 8.2). These correlations' effect sizes are within the moderate to small range ($r = .53 - r = .28$), suggesting that the factors could also be viewed as assessing related but distinct symptoms. Therefore, each factor seems to be measuring a distinct type of RBTS symptoms since the shared variance due to the correlations between scales did not exceed 28 percent for the largest correlation.

ONE-WAY ANALYSIS OF VARIANCE

We also wanted to explore whether there are differences between the RBTSSS–SF total score for those who reported their most memorable race-based experience as sudden, outside their control, and emotionally negative ("yes" criteria group; $n = 432$) and those who did not ("no" group; $n = 304$). This analysis is a replication of what was done with the scale-development study. We conducted a one-way analysis of variance (ANOVA) with the two groups ("yes" and "no") serving as independent variables and the RBTSSS–SF composite untransformed total score serving as the dependent variable. We found the groups were significantly different: $F (1, 618) = 7.38$, $p < .01$. The "yes" group's mean was 26.4 (SD = 20.1) while the "no" group's mean was 21.9 (SD = 19.4), indicating a significantly higher scale score for the "yes" group.

We also wanted to learn if the RBTSSS–SF could be used across racial, gender, and socioeconomic status (SES) groups. More important, with the full RBTSSS scale, we found racial group differences but no gender group differences.

MEASUREMENT EQUIVALENCE OR INVARIANCE

Accuracy of psychological measurement requires evidence that the same constructs are being measured in the same manner across different groups or categories of people, otherwise known as measurement equivalence or measurement invariance. For instance, it makes no sense to say that males have higher RBTSSS scores than females if the RBTSSS–SF does not measure the same attribute in both groups. Therefore, it is important to test whether the seven-factor RBTSSS–SF (i.e., the first-order factor model) measures the same latent symptom-scale constructs for men and women, for SES groups, and for racial groups.[10] Additionally, it is important to test whether the hypothesized second-order factor of RBTS is measured similarly for the groups we tested. We employed a latent means procedure in SEM to fit a model to the seven-factor first-order model as this procedure is more sensitive and accurate in detecting between-group differences in latent variables.[11] That is, to evaluate the invariance of the RBTSSS–SF, tests of factorial invariance were employed using multiple group confirmatory factor analysis (MGCFA).[12] Factorial invariance enables one to examine whether a construct of interest, or target construct, has the same meaning across groups. To test for further levels of equivalence, the configural or baseline model must be established for each group separately.

Tests of measurement invariance were carried out at three levels (weak, strong, and strict) in a nested fashion. The establishment of weak invariance provides evidence to argue that the relationships between a latent factor (e.g., depression or RBTS) and its indicators (i.e., items or first-order factors) are the same across groups. The establishment of strong invariance provides evidence to make meaningful comparisons of factor (e.g., depression or RBTS) means across groups.[13] The establishment of strict invariance provides evidence that, within each group, the items were measured with the same reliability or precision.[14]

To test the factorial invariance of the first-order factor model (i.e., seven-factor model), a series of five nested tests that constitute different levels of invariance were carried out through MGCFA. The five tests of invariance were configural, weak, strong, strict, and structural. For each of the MGCFAs, the tests of invariance were nested as follows: configural is nested within weak, strong within weak, strict within strong, and structural within strong.[15] For the second-order factor model, we employed the procedures outlined by Dimiter Dimitrov.[16] Specifically, we employed seven sequentially nested models.

To carry out the invariance tests, all analyses used robust maximum likelihood, which was selected due to the non-normal distribution of the sample data. For SES-based analyses, participants were grouped into the "lower SES" category, which served as the reference group. In the gender group analyses, women were the reference group, and in racial group analyses, Whites served as the reference group. To evaluate the model fit, we examined multiple goodness-of-fit indices as well as comparative fit indices.

When interpreting the invariance test results, the CFI, TLI, RMSEA, and delta CFI were used, as these estimates of fit are less sensitive to sample size than chi-square statistics when conducting invariance tests.[17] In particular, Gordon Cheung and Roger Rensvold found delta CFI (ΔCFI) to be the most powerful test in detecting a lack of invariance in a large sample,[18] so we used it over the chi-square statistic to interpret which nested invariance test was most plausible. Established rules of thumb indicate that fit is considered tenable if the CFI and TLI values are close to .90; however, it is favorable for them to reach or exceed .95.[19] RMSEA is an absolute fit index that evaluates closeness of fit. The cutoff value for RMSEA is .08; however, better fit falls around .05. Delta CFI was computed between two adjacently nested models (e.g., configural versus weak, weak versus strong, and M0 versus M1). The suggested cutoff value of −0.01 is used for interpretation, where delta CFI values of greater than −0.01 indicate poorer fit.[20]

The five models of invariance (i.e., configural, weak, strong, strict, and structural) were tested separately for the seven-factor model for each gender, SES, and racial group. The seven models of invariance (i.e., M0–M6) were also tested separately for each gender, SES, and racial group for the second-order model. Results of the model fits for each group type and model (i.e., seven-factor and second-order fact) are shown in tables 8.3–8.5.

GENDER

For gender (female = 351, male = 377), the practical fit indices in table 8.3 (i.e., RMSEA, CFI, and TLI) suggest that structural invariance was acceptable. Hence, the results provide strong evidence to show that, when using the RBTSSS–SF, gender groups respond to items in a similar manner.

TABLE 8.3 Model Fits for Tests of Invariance Across Gender

	CHI-SQUARE	DF	RMSEA (95% CI)	CFI	TLI	ΔCFI[a]
SEVEN-FACTOR MODEL						
Configural	576.715	376	0.039 (0.032–0.045)	0.969	0.962	—
Weak	595.192	391	0.038 (0.032–0.044)	0.969	0.963	0
Strong	621.181	406	0.038 (0.032–0.044)	0.967	0.962	−0.002
Strict	627.752	428	0.036 (0.030–0.042)	0.969	0.967	0.002
Structural	651.669	434	0.037 (0.031–0.042)	0.966	0.964	−0.001
SECOND-ORDER FACTOR MODEL						
M0	733.092	404	0.048 (0.042–0.053)	0.949	0.942	—
M1	753.812	419	0.047 (0.042–0.053)	0.948	0.943	−0.001
M2	764.621	425	0.047 (0.042–0.053)	0.948	0.943	0.000
M3	807.954	446	0.048 (0.042–0.053)	0.944	0.942	−0.004
M4	813.082	447	0.048 (0.042–0.053)	0.944	0.942	0.000
M5	1289.473	460	0.071 (0.066–0.076)	0.872	0.872	−0.072[a]
M6	1299.971	482	0.069 (0.064–0.073)	0.874	0.879	0.002

Note: [a]ΔCFI < −.01 signals lack of invariance.

Source: Authors' data.

For the gender second-order factor, MGCFA model invariance tests, according to the delta CFI and practical fit indices, indicate that partial factorial invariance was tenable. The first-order factor error covariances (M5–M4) and the item error covariances (M6–M5) were not found to be invariant across gender groups, meaning that this result is not necessarily problematic, as the scholars suggest that testing for the invariance of error covariances can be overly restrictive.

Substantively, the results of the second-order factor MGCFA model invariance tests provide evidence of configural, weak, and strong invariance. The presence of configural invariance suggests the same pattern of free- and fixed-model parameters across gender groups. The presence of weak invari-

TABLE 8.4 Model Fits for Tests of Invariance Across Race

	CHI-SQUARE	DF	RMSEA (95% CI)	CFI	TLI	ΔCFI[a]
SEVEN-FACTOR MODEL						
Configural	836.705	564	0.046 (0.038–0.052)	0.960	0.951	—
Weak	884.597	594	0.046 (0.040–0.052)	0.957	0.950	−0.003
Strong	938.816	624	0.047 (0.041–0.053)	0.954	0.948	−0.003
Strict	983.901	668	0.045 (0.039–0.051)	0.953	0.952	−0.001
Structural	1003.177	680	0.046 (0.039–0.051)	0.952	0.952	−0.002
SECOND-ORDER FACTOR MODEL						
M0	1012.162	606	0.054 (0.048–0.060)	0.94	0.932	—
M1	1060.332	636	0.054 (0.048–0.060)	0.938	0.932	−0.002
M2	1072.261	648	0.053 (0.048–0.059)	0.938	0.933	0.000
M3	1151.437	690	0.054 (0.049–0.059)	0.932	0.932	−0.006
M4	1153.429	692	0.054 (0.048–0.059)	0.932	0.932	0.000
M5	1665.34	712	0.076 (0.072–0.081)	0.86	0.863	−0.072[a]
M6	1696.832	756	0.074 (0.069–0.078)	0.861	0.873	0.001

Note: [a]ΔCFI < −.01 signals lack of invariance.
Source: Authors' data.

ance provides evidence to argue that the relationship between the second-order factor of RBTS and its indicators (i.e., seven first-order factors) is the same across gender groups. Finally, the presence of strong invariance provides evidence to make meaningful comparisons of factor (i.e., RBTS) means across gender groups.

RACE

For the race (White = 194, Black = 402, people of color = 102) seven-factor MGCFA model, the invariance tests, according to the delta CFI in table 8.4

TABLE 8.5 Model Fits for Tests of Invariance Across SES

	CHI-SQUARE	DF	RMSEA (95% CI)	CFI	TLI	ΔCFI[a]
SEVEN-FACTOR MODEL						
Configural	572.604	376	0.039 (0.032–0.045)	0.968	0.960	—
Weak	599.233	391	0.039 (0.033–0.045)	0.966	0.959	−0.002
Scalar	627.547	406	0.040 (0.033–0.043)	0.963	0.958	−0.003
Strict	678.170	428	0.041 (0.035–0.047)	0.959	0.955	−0.004
Structural	671.774	434	0.040 (0.034–0.046)	0.961	0.958	−0.002
SECOND-ORDER FACTOR MODEL						
M0	742.559	404	0.049 (0.044–0.055)	0.944	0.936	—
M1	773.266	419	0.049 (0.044–0.055)	0.942	0.936	−0.002
M2	784.476	425	0.049 (0.044–0.055)	0.941	0.936	−0.001
M3	838.046	446	0.050 (0.045–0.056)	0.935	0.933	−0.006
M4	859.675	447	0.052 (0.046–0.057)	0.932	0.93	−0.003
M5	1317.707	460	0.073 (0.069–0.078)	0.859	0.858	−0.073[a]
M6	1350.957	482	0.072 (0.068–0.077)	0.857	0.863	−0.002

Note: [a]ΔCFI < −.01 signals lack of invariance.
Source: Authors' data.

and the practical fit indices in table 8.4 (i.e., RMSEA, CFI, and TLI), show that structural invariance was tenable, as was factorial invariance (i.e., configural, measurement, and structural invariance). Hence, the results provide strong evidence to suggest that, when using the RBTSSS–SF, members of different racial groups respond to the items in a similar way.

For the race second-order factor MGCFA model, invariance tests indicate that partial factorial invariance was tenable. The partial results mean that the first-order factor error covariances (M5–M4) and the item error covariances (M6–M5) were not invariant across race groups. However, this finding is not considered problematic as researchers point out that testing for the invariance of error covariances is overly restrictive.

Substantively, the results of the second-order factor MGCFA model invariance tests provide evidence of configural, weak, and strong invariance. There is evidence that the same patterns occur across racial groups, and there is evidence to show that the relationships between the second-order factor of RBTS and its indicators (i.e., seven first-order factors) are the same across race groups, and that factor (i.e., RBTS) means across race groups are similar.

SES

For the SES (lower SES = 496, higher SES = 207) seven-factor MGCFA model, invariance tests, according to the delta CFI and the practical fit indices in table 8.5 (i.e., RMSEA, CFI, and TLI), structural invariance was tenable. There is strong evidence to suggest that, when using the RBTSSS–SF, any SES group differences on any item are due only to actual group differences.

For the SES second-order factor MGCFA model invariance tests, according to the delta CFI and practical fit indices, the highest form of invariance tenable was for model 4 (M4). As with the other groups, only the first-order factor error covariances (M5–M4) and the item error covariances (M6–M5) were not invariant; this finding is not necessarily problematic since the invariance test of error covariances can be restrictive.[21]

Overall, the results of the second-order factor MGCFA model invariance tests provide evidence of configural, weak, and strong invariance, and configural invariance means the same patterns of parameters exist across SES groups. Whereas weak invariance indicates evidence to show that the relationships between the factors of RBTS and its indicators (i.e., seven first-order factors) are the same across SES groups, strong invariance provides evidence that it is possible to make meaningful comparisons of factor (i.e., RBTS) means across SES groups.[22]

THE THIRD INVESTIGATION

In the final analysis, we were interested in learning if the RBTSSS–SF would predict psychological distress and psychological well-being. Said another way, would the scale operate in terms of establishing predictive validity in a similar fashion to that of the original RBTSSS? To test this notion, we used the thirty-eight-item Mental Health Inventory (MHI)[23] with internal consistency reliability coefficients of the five subscales as follows: anxiety, $\alpha = .88$; depression, $\alpha = .84$; loss of emotional control, $\alpha = .85$; positive affect, $\alpha = .90$; and emotional ties, $\alpha = .70$.

Only participants who completed the MHI and RBTSSS ($n = 539$) were included in this analysis. Participants' mean age was 38.6 (SD = 13.31). There were 261 females (48.4 percent) and 272 males (50.5 percent); 6 participants (1.1 percent) did not report their gender. There were 143 White participants (26.5 percent), 295 Black (54.7 percent), 49 Hispanic (9.1 percent), 23 Asian (4.3 percent), 3 Native American (.6 percent), 15 biracial (2.8 percent), and 7 who reported as other (1.3 percent). Four participants omitted this information. The education level of participants was 13.85 years (SD = 3.10). Participants' self-reported socioeconomic status broke out as follows: lower class, 128 (23.7 percent); working class, 135 (25.0 percent); lower-middle class, 95 (17.6 percent); middle class, 111 (20.6 percent); upper-middle class, 43 (8.0 percent); upper class, 4 (.7 percent). Twenty-three (4.3 percent) did not answer this item.

The five MHI subscales (depression, anxiety, loss of behavioral/emotional control, positive affect, and emotional ties) and seven RBTSSS–SF scales (depression, anger, avoidance, physical symptoms, hypervigilance, low self-esteem, and intrusion) were entered in canonical-correlation analysis (CCA, see table 8.6). The analysis yielded five functions, but only the first function was used. Collectively, the full model was statistically significant (Wilks' $\lambda = .648$ criterion, $F [35, 2219.32] = 6.90$, $p < .001$) and explained 35 percent of the variance. Examination of the CCA indicated that the MHI scale's loss of control (−.97), anxiety (−.89), and depression (−.88) were positively related to the variate, with positive affect (.56) and emotional ties (.47) making inverse contributions to the variate. Inspection of the predictor variable set showed that RBTS hypervigilance (−.88), avoidance (−.87), low self-esteem (−.86), depression (−.83), anger (−.80), physical symptoms (−.79), and intrusion (−.68) contributed to the variate set. The RBTS predictor variables all were positively related to anxiety, depression, and loss of control in the criterion variable set, and were inversely related to positive affect and emotional ties.

IN SUMMARY

We explored whether a smaller collection of items from the original exploratory factor analysis of the RBTSSS could be used as a short version of the

TABLE 8.6 Canonical Solution for Mental Health Symptoms Predicting Race-Based Traumatic Stress for Function 1 ($N=539$)

VARIABLE	COEF	R_s[a]	R^2_c (%)	H^2 (%)[b]
Hypervigilance	−0.238	−0.876	76.7	76.7
Low Self-Esteem	−0.310	−0.858	73.6	73.6
Avoidance	−0.34	−0.873	76.2	76.2
Physical Symptoms	−0.089	−0.793	62.9	62.9
Depression	−0.044	−0.828	68.6	68.6
Intrusion	0.173	−0.634	40.2	40.2
Anger	−0.302	−0.797	63.5	63.5
Anxiety	−0.396	−0.894	79.9	79.9
Depression	−0.007	−0.878	77.1	77.1
Loss of Control	−0.658	−0.966	93.3	93.3
Positive Affect	−0.026	0.560	31.4	31.4
Emotional Ties	−0.043	0.470	22.1	22.1

Notes: Coef=standardized canonical function coefficient; R_s =structure coefficient; R^2_c =squared structure coefficient; H^2 = communality coefficient.

[a]Structure coefficients (R_s) greater than .45 are in italics.

[b]Communality coefficients (H^2) greater than 45% are in italics.

Source: Authors' data.

RBTSSS. We used SEM and CFA with the smaller set of items to determine if a first- or second-order SEM would fit the data. We tested the model with the original sample, and then we cross-validated on a community sample using SEM procedures. Construct validity was established through confirmatory factor analysis. The results of the CFA support the seven-factor solution consistent with the RBTS model and the RBTSSS measure.[24]

In the second study, we conducted SEM and CFA analyses as well as an ANOVA on a new community sample and performed measurement equivalence (invariance) tests. Construct validity was shown by comparing individuals who reported their memorable racial encounter as sudden, uncontrollable, and emotionally painful with those who did not. Our hypothesis is confirmed, and results show that those who deemed their racial encounters as outside their control, emotionally painful, and sudden have higher scores on RBTS symptoms than individuals who answered "no" to these questions.

Analysis of multiple types of measurement invariance (configural, scalar, metric, etc.) for race, gender, and SES shows that participants respond to the RBTSSS–SF conceptual framework in the same way. This is promising as the measure initially is applicable to individuals across group memberships. The result is inconsistent with findings from the original RBTSSS in which the measure was found to be gender invariant but not race invariant.[25] More broadly, findings about the impact of racial incidents on their targets across gender, race/ethnicity, and SES have been varied. Some studies support the current data suggesting that race, social class, and gender do not influence the impact of racial discrimination, while others suggest that racial group membership and social class standing do influence it.[26] For example, Yin Paradies and colleagues found that although gender and class do not moderate the relationship between racial discrimination and mental health, race does.[27] Elizabeth Pascoe and Laura Smart Richman found no effect for race, gender, or SES on racial discrimination's impact on both mental health, physical health.[28] Further investigation should be conducted into how the RBTSSS–SF and the original RBTSSS are influenced by gender, race, and SES groups.

Study three explores predictive validity through associations between the RBTSSS–SF and the MHI subscales. Overall, mental health symptoms as measured by the MHI are associated with RBTS. The findings support the model and measure, as low mood, negative affect, anxiety, and emotion dysregulation have been associated with trauma in many forms.[29] Further, positive affect is inversely related to RBTSSS–SF symptoms and is consistent with the theory, as we expect that those who experience a traumatic event would not report increased levels of happiness, cheerfulness, and feelings of relaxation. Overall, the analyses show that those who experience racial stress or traumatic events also report mental health symptoms that manifest in hyperarousal, mood dysregulation, and negative affect.

The contribution of low self-esteem to this canonical variate confirms the tendency of some to internalize blame or guilt associated with the race-based experience. To manage the confusion often associated with these events, one may behaviorally avoid or become hypersensitive to stimuli that are similar to or reminiscent of the memorable racial encounter. Further complicating this phenomenon is the fact that the perpetrator is not always easily identified (e.g., cultural or institutional racism). The type of encounter (e.g., aversive-hostile racism) can also impact the constellation of emotional responses that are reported.[30]

Overall, then, the RBTSSS–SF is a valuable addition to the measurement of the effects of racism, and evidence suggests that it can be used with confidence by researchers and clinicians.

THE RACE-BASED TRAUMATIC STRESS INTERVIEW SCHEDULE

As an alternate approach to the assessment of RBTS, Robert T. Carter and T. Vinson constructed the Race-Based Traumatic Stress Interview Schedule (RBTSIS; appendix B). The RBTSIS can be used to capture aspects of people's racial experiences that cannot be explored with the long or short forms of the survey measure. Moreover, the interview also affords the respondent an opportunity to elaborate on his or her reactions to racial experiences. The RBTSIS has a similar format as the survey measure, but the questions are presented verbally and responses are recorded by the interviewer. The RBTSIS protocol contains fifty-seven items and seven symptom scales, and the respondents are asked to reflect on both their reactions *after* the event and their more *recent* reactions. The interview is designed for situations in which it would be better for the person to respond to direct questions than complete a survey on his or her own. The verbal format also provides an opportunity for the interviewee to elaborate on his or her responses. An interview typically takes thirty minutes and is mostly focused on the person's racial experiences and reactions.

To examine the predictive validity of the RBTSIS, individuals were recruited who had experienced upsetting racial experiences. Each respondent met with an interviewer who explained the procedures and purpose of the interview. Participants were sixty-three Black Americans, with eleven (17.5 percent) males and fifty-two (82.5 percent) females ranging in age from eighteen to forty-nine ($M = 26.66$; $SD = 7.73$) and in years of education from twelve to twenty-four years ($M = 16$; $SD = 3$). Given the small sample, analyses were limited to group comparisons and some bivariate correlations. After completing the RBTSIS, participants also completed the following self-report measures: the Trauma Symptom Checklist (TSC), the Symptom

Checklist-90-Revised (SCL-90-R), and the Structured Inventory of Malingered Symptomology (SIMS).

INSTRUMENTS

The scoring for the RBTSIS is similar to that of the RBTSSS in that the scale scores are obtained by summing the items that make up each of the seven symptom scales. Reliability coefficients for the RBTSIS were calculated as follows: depression (nine items; $\alpha = .86$), intrusion (seven items; $\alpha = .82$), anger (five items; $\alpha = .84$), hypervigilance (nine items; $\alpha = .83$), anxiety, (eleven items; $\alpha = .89$), self-esteem (eight items; $\alpha = .81$), and avoidance (eight items; $\alpha = .76$).

In the TSC, forty items are summed to produce a total score and six clinical subscales that evaluate various forms of symptomatology associated with trauma: anxiety, depression, dissociation, sexual abuse, sexual problems, and sleep disturbances.[31] Cronbach's alpha coefficients were as follows: dissociation, $\alpha = .70$; anxiety, $\alpha = .74$; depression, $\alpha = .61$; sexual abuse, $\alpha = .73$; sleep disturbances, $\alpha = .73$; sexual problems, $\alpha = .85$; and the total score, $\alpha = .92$.

The SCL-90-R assesses psychological distress with nine symptoms: somatization, obsessive-compulsive symptoms, interpersonal sensitivity, depression, anxiety, hostility, phobic anxiety, paranoid ideation, and psychoticism.[32] The Global Severity Index indicates the current level or depth of the disorder. Cronbach's alpha coefficients were as follows: somatization, $\alpha = .82$; obsessive-compulsive symptoms, $\alpha = .89$; interpersonal sensitivity, $\alpha = .90$; depression, $\alpha = .92$; anxiety, $\alpha = .88$; hostility, $\alpha = .84$; phobic anxiety, $\alpha = .83$; paranoid ideation, $\alpha = .82$; psychoticism, $\alpha = .76$; and Global Severity Index, $\alpha = .98$.

The SIMS has seventy-five items that yield a total score reflective of a general malingering and a Cronbach's alpha of $\alpha = .86$.[33]

For race-based stress or trauma reaction to be present, in this group it was determined that a participant must have at least one standardized scale score that is one standard deviation above the mean (e.g., an intrusion score of 63). A total of twenty-nine participants had one or more elevated RBTSSS scores. Of this group, nine ($n = 9$) participants had three or more elevated symptom-scale scores; we designated them the "RBTS group." Thirty-four ($n = 34$) had no scale elevations; we designated them the "no-race-based stress group."

We tested whether the RBTSIS scales would be related to the trauma-related symptoms as measured by the instruments described previously. People who undergo racism-related encounters are said by some to exaggerate or misrepresent their experiences. In clinical terms, this type of behavior is considered malingering (i.e., exaggeration). It would be expected that if a person's reactions are exaggerated, they would have high scores on a measure used to assess malingering (e.g., SIMS), and positive relationships would exist between the RBTSIS scales and such a measure.

RACIAL EVENTS

The racism-related incidents described by participants were as follows: verbal assault, (31.3 percent); treatment on the basis of stereotype, (18.8 percent); denial of access or service, (14.1 percent); violation of racial rules, (10.9 percent); being profiled, (9.4 percent); hostile work environment, (6.3 percent); physical assault, (4.7 percent); own-group discrimination, (3.1 percent); and vicarious experiences, (1.6 percent).

Of note is that 91 percent ($n=57$) of participants reported that they did not expect the event to happen; 89 percent ($n=56$) felt that they could not control the incident; and 91 percent ($n=57$) reported that the most memorable racist event was emotionally painful. Participants noted that similar memorable events happened in their lifetime as often as once ($n=12$; 21 percent); two to four times ($n=20$; 32 percent); five to six times ($n=12$; 19 percent); or seven or more times ($n=17$; 27 percent). Given the nature of the study and the small sample size, it was important to present analyses from several perspectives, so we categorized participants into three groups: no elevations ($n=34$), race-based stress group ($n=20$), and the race-based trauma group ($n=9$).

We conducted two MANOVA analyses with the three groups, as well as with gender groups (men, $n=11$; women, $n=52$). The MANOVA with the SIMS total and TSC scales and the three groups was not significant (Wilks' $\lambda=.85$ F $[16,102]=.56$, $p=.91$ $\eta^2=.08$), and there were no gender main effects (Wilks' $\lambda=.78$ F $[8,51]=1.77$, $p=.11$ $\eta^2=.22$) or interactions. Although there were no main effects, post hoc tests were inspected; since the study was exploratory, it also seemed important to look for any possible trends given the small sample size. Bonferroni post hoc tests revealed significant group differences (.10 or lower) on four TSC scales. These were: (1) TSC anxiety (race-based stress and race-based trauma groups were different than the no-elevation group [$p = .08$]); and (2) TSC depression (same pattern [$p = .07$]); (3) sex abuse trauma ($p = .03$); and (4) total TSC ($p = .07$). In all these comparisons, the race-based trauma group had higher mean scores than the other groups.

The MANOVA with the SCL scales and the three groups was also not significant (Wilks' $\lambda = .78$ F [18,100] $= .72$, $p = .78$ $\eta^2 = .12$), and there were no gender main effects (Wilks' $\lambda = .87$ F [9,50] $= .81$, $p = .61$ $\eta^2 = .13$) or interactions. Bonferroni post hoc tests revealed significant group differences on four scales. These were: (1) SCL somatization, race-based stress and race-based trauma groups were different than the no-elevation group [$p = .09$]); (2) SCL depression, which had a similar pattern in that the race-based stress group was different from the no-elevation group ($p = .04$), and the race-based trauma group was different from the race-based stress group ($p = .01$); (3) SCL anxiety ($p = .06$); and (4) SCL Global Severity Index ($p = .08$). In all these comparisons, the race-based trauma group had higher mean scores than the other two groups.

In the correlational analyses, we found no significant relationships between the SIMS total score and RBTSIS *"after"* scales for the group that had no elevations on RBTSIS scales. For the stress-trauma group, two correlations exceed the chance of one possible significant correlation, between total SIMS and RBTSIS scales, which suggests no malingering.

CONCLUSIONS

The objective of the current study was to explore the relationship of RBT-SIS scales to related psychological and trauma measures. The participants reported that they encountered various types of racial discrimination that were unexpected, uncontrollable, and emotionally painful. The incidents occurred in many aspects of the participants' lives, including at school, at work, in their neighborhood, at stores, and in other locations and situations (e.g., at the bank, while driving). Incidents also occurred during different life stages (e.g., childhood, adolescence, adulthood, late adulthood), or across the life span. The stress-trauma group demonstrated more trauma and psychological symptoms than the no-RBTS stress group.

To illustrate an RBTS response and its assessment, we present the case of Z. There are several ways that the RBTSSS (i.e., either the RBTSSS–SF, the interview schedule, or the RBTSSS–Long Form [LF]) can be used: (1) it can be administered to a group of people and used like a survey measure, in which sample scores are used to predict or relate to other variables; (2) it can be given to an individual to complete, following the occurrence of a possible racial situation, which may have resulted in emotional distress; or (3) a small group of people can complete it and have it scored for discussion purposes to aid in healing or to impart information. Sample administration of the scale to a larger group of clients can be used to provide feedback about the incidence of RBTS in the agency's client population as well as whether the RBTSSS is related to other psychological instruments given at the same time.

CASE EXAMPLE: CLIENT DESCRIPTION AND BACKGROUND

Z is a forty-year-old middle-class Black woman who claims she was harmed by a racially hostile work environment. She was born and raised in the Northeast region of the country and is the eldest sister to three brothers. After graduating from high school, she worked as a clerk for several organizations and started a family. Although she was aware of race relations, she did not think of herself in racial terms until she reached adolescence, when a man called her brother the N-word. She recalled feeling hurt by the comment and noted that her family members did not speak up or act when her brother was verbally assaulted. Her awareness of her Blackness grew more acute when she had children, and while working as a dispatcher she noticed the different treatment received by Black and White coworkers. Because she was unclear about the basis for the different treatment, she resolved to always initially consider her contribution to any situation. She had no history of behavioral or medical issues as a child or adult.[34]

One year, Z's work evaluations suddenly changed. After years of outstanding appraisals, she started to receive average evaluations. Around the same time, her employer had appointed a new leader, and she learned that other dispatchers were being paid more. The only difference she could determine for the unequal pay was that her coworkers were White and she was not. According to her immediate supervisor, the new leader seemed to want to control everything, unlike prior leaders, which resulted in a change in the evaluation process. Z's immediate supervisor was no longer asked about employee performance; rather, the new leader, who did not observe the day-to-day work, completed the evaluations without consulting Z's immediate supervisor. Z was also asked to work longer hours than usual and take on more mandatory overtime, despite having informed her superiors that in order to care for her children she could not work longer shifts and could not work unannounced overtime. Z's spouse worked an opposite shift (nights for him; days for her), which meant she needed to get home after her regular work hours so her young children would not be alone.

Z described how the leader would visit her work area and speak to her co-workers but not to her. This occurred on several occasions, which led Z to conclude that the leader simply "did not like her." Z was initially okay with not being liked as long as she was paid on time, but she later realized the racial basis of the treatment. She also learned that her shift schedule, pay, and how she was supervised were all influenced by her race.

Z filed a racial discrimination complaint with the human resources (HR) department about the shift, pay, and performance evaluation issues and was told that there was insufficient cause to find discrimination. After her complaint, she was subjected to increased supervision, which she believed was intended as punishment for her complaint. She filed another complaint about how she was being supervised, and this time Z was threatened with being fired. The close supervision of her work continued, and she was later suspended for alleged absenteeism. Z challenged the cause of the suspension, and it was discovered that the HR office had double-counted her authorized sick leave. Following this event, Z was so upset that she became ill and needed to be rushed to the emergency room. She believed it was due to the stress caused by her work environment. The pattern of the racially hostile work environment continued for several years before she took her concerns outside the organization for some relief.

USING THE RBTSSS

Here, we present an example of scale administration to an individual. In this instance, the RBTSSS is not simply administered by itself, as might be the case with other psychological instruments that are given and scored and used to generate information about the person's mental state and psychological functioning. Instead, we use it as part of a clinical interview to aid the person in describing how she or he may have been affected by the racial incident. The interview is usually conducted over the course of days. At the end of the first day or session, we give the participant the RBTSSS- LF and ask her to complete it and bring it to the next session. Once the full interview is completed and the person has talked about her experiences and background and about how the racial incident affected her emotionally, we review the RBTSSS with the participant, discussing only the items that she indicates produce reactions that are frequent or do not go away. The evaluator asks about the reactions and why they were selected, and asks the participant to elaborate further. Because the person has discussed her emotional reactions earlier in the interview, sometimes she has already explained the reaction and how it operates. In our experience, when it comes to racial incidents, people are at a loss for words to describe how they feel, and the list of reactions from the RBTSSS helps them provide detail to their story or helps them elaborate on the nature of the harm they have experienced.

The RBTSSS–SF and the RBTSIS are important new tools for the assessment of race-based traumatic stress as racial trauma, for both clinical intervention and forensic evaluation. Both provide evidence of construct and predictive validity. The following case illustrates how they can be used in the clinical setting.

RBTS CLINICAL INTERVIEW AND ASSESSMENT

Z stated during the clinical assessment interview that one day at home, around the time that she filed her complaints of racial discrimination, she experienced chest pains, numbing in her arm, and pain in her hand. Because of these symptoms, she was taken to the emergency room and was kept in the hospital to determine the cause of her ailments. The doctors ordered her not to return to work, which led Z to take a disability leave for several months. Once she returned to her job, the same type of distressing incidents continued.

The physical episode turned out to be a panic attack. She also reported high levels of anxiety, headaches, and episodes of trembling before she would go to work. After the second racial discrimination complaint and after returning to work, she started to experience memory loss that seemed to get worse over time. She found she was unable to fully attend to her duties, to calm her thoughts, or to concentrate at work, and these symptoms lingered during days when she was off work. The situation affected many aspects of her relationship with her husband and family. She says she would become angry with him even when she knew he was not at fault. She also was agitated and irritable with family members. She became distant, and she and her relatives were not as close as they had been before the situation started at work. She was often depressed and withdrawn.

A key aspect of the RBTSSS clinical interview is documentation of the person's racial history and background. When did he become aware of race and racial issues? How did these issues get discussed, if at all, in the family and community? How did the person come to think of himself as a racial being? Did he encounter racial incidents, and, if so, how were they handled? Were race and racial issues discussed in school? If so, how; if not, how was that understood? Racial history is explored from early recollections to the present without discussing the current situation (i.e., the memorable event), which is done later in the interview. Then the memorable incident is discussed, and how the person was affected is detailed as much as possible. The interviewee should be asked to explain his responses to these reactions. By reviewing these responses, the evaluator can ensure that the interviewee understands the questions, and also that the reactions are related to the person's memorable racial event and not some other experience. Assuming the interviewee understands the questions, and his reactions are relevant to the event in question, the RBTSSS can be scored and integrated into the interview findings as a means to assess whether and to what extent the person has been affected by the racial encounter. Lastly, if possible, as part of the interview, it can help to talk to someone close to the interviewee who can corroborate and also describe the interviewee's history, behavior, and emotional reactions before and since the racial encounter in question.

RBTSSS–LF ASSESSMENT CONCLUSIONS

Z had enough general and personal knowledge and self-awareness regarding race to be able to recognize her situation as a racially hostile work environment. She indicated that the racial experiences at work were beyond her control, unexpected, and emotionally painful or negative. She also tried to cope with the stress of the situation by filing complaints with HR and by taking a leave from work. She exhibited signs and symptoms of RBTS injury, confirmed by her clinical interview, the corroborative interview, the RBTSSS t-score results, and the medical and psychiatric evidence showing panic attacks attributed to work-related stress.

As part of the scoring method, the evaluator should record each item's answer (0–4). The scores should be recorded on a key that organizes the items by reaction type or symptom (e.g., intrusion, depression, avoidance). Each set of reaction items should be summed for a total raw score (x). As noted previously, the summed scores should be used to derive a person-specific mean or average (M) score and standard deviation (SD) for both the *"after"* and the *"now"* or *"more recent"* reaction values for the seven scales. The scores should be totaled and converted to z- and t-scores. With the information and the RBTSSS scale scores, the evaluator can assess whether and to what extent the client was affected by the events associated with the racial encounter.

Based on Z's interview responses and her RBTSSS–LF scores, she was depressed (RBTSSS t-score 62), angry (RBTSSS t-score 54), had intrusive thoughts (RBTSSS t-score 53), and showed signs of arousal (hypervigilance) and exhibited compromised functioning (RBTSSS t-score, physical reactions, 54). Her close relationships were significantly altered and became difficult to manage. She reported experiencing significant anxiety while working and was in a constant state of tension, to the point where she was unable to perform tasks essential to her job. She noted that her reactions were observed by others, which was confirmed by the corroborative interview. She was visibly distraught during our interview and in considerable emotional pain as she recalled the events. She still had significant impairment from the racially hostile work environment, and her experiences at work were the cause of the psychological and emotional harm she endured.

DISCUSSION OF CASE ILLUSTRATION AND CLINICAL APPLICATION

In their guide to the forensic assessment of RBTS injury, Carter and Jessica Forsyth discuss considerations and provide recommendations for the clinical evaluation of an individual who has had an encounter with racism that may be the proximate cause of psychological harm or impairment.[35] They suggest that the evaluator document the situation and the emotional and psychological elements that may be associated with damages to the client. The evaluator should also try to determine the extent and degree of the client's possible impairment, both previously and at the time of the evaluation.

The assessment should be conducted as part of a clinical interview that also collects information about the person's personal, educational, employment, medical, and racial history. Since the scope of information is broad and collecting it can be time consuming, the interview should ideally take place over more than one day (to give the person an opportunity to reflect on the interview process and content). The RBTSSS should be given to the person to complete between interview meetings. Preexisting conditions should be explored, and, when possible, the evaluator should obtain records that confirm and document the reported history. In addition to the interview with the client, the evaluator should aim to interview someone who can corroborate the information or offer an external perspective on the person's mental health status, social history, and racial background.

Given the racial content of the individual's encounter, it is essential to learn about the person's racial background, including what they were taught about race, what their racial environment was during their upbringing, and how they understood their racial experiences—essentially, what was and is the person's racial identity status and functioning. Keep in mind that these thoughts and experiences may not be readily available to one's recall and may require probing and patience.

It is important to learn about the person's racial experience(s) without attribution or embellishment. What about the incident caused the person harm or emotional pain? What were her feelings about what happened? Irrespective of whether the events could be confirmed, how the person felt and feels should be accepted as valid. As we pointed out in previous chapters, stress levels are related to one's appraisal of the situation. The interviewee should explain how the event is racial, and she should explain the basis for her emotional pain. Did the harm manifest in ways that produced emotional and psychological impairment? What did the person do to cope with and address the situation, and what were the results of her coping efforts? What was the racial environment of the situation? Did others (e.g., employer, coworkers, other parties) think of the event in racial terms? How do they characterize what happened? For Z, the evaluator concluded that harm and impairment were evident and that the racially hostile environment at her workplace was the direct basis for her emotional and psychological harm. Thus, it was determined that Z had exhibited RBTS injury.

A SITUATIONAL FRAMEWORK ANALYSIS

If the report is for forensic purposes, it is important to include a situational framework that places the issues into a research and social context. What evidence in the research literature shows that people are harmed by racial discrimination? Does scholarly evidence exist about the situation (e.g., workplace racial harassment) and its outcomes?

SUMMARY

In part II of this volume, we have focused on the conceptual development of the RBTS model and have outlined the construction and validation of three instruments designed to assess the presence of RBTS: the RBTSSS (or RBTSSS-LF), the RBTSSS–SF, and the RBTSIS. In part III we turn to the application of the RBTS model and other measures in the clinical, forensic, and scholarly domains, and we conclude the book by focusing on future directions for the model in terms of clinical and forensic applications, training of mental health clinicians in the area of racial trauma, and using the model in prevention and social policy.

PART THREE

WHAT TO DO WITH WHAT WE KNOW:
PRACTICE APPLICATIONS

9

CLINICAL APPLICATIONS OF THE RACE-BASED TRAUMATIC STRESS MODEL

WE HAVE EXAMINED THE MENTAL HEALTH consequences of racial discrimination for various racial groups. We have looked at the RBTSSS and related measures and their supporting empirical evidence. We now turn to the issues of application. In general, the literature we have reviewed thus far indicates that racial discrimination or racial harassment at all levels involves experiences characterized by hostility (e.g., verbal assault/rejection, disrespect), avoidance (denial of service or access), or aversive-hostility (e.g., people acting as if they are intimidated).

The various types of interpersonal and institutional racial discrimination are associated with higher levels of negative mental health outcomes for many racial-ethnic group members. These effects are related to lower general well-being, higher psychological distress, lower life satisfaction, anger, sadness, depression, anxiety, intrusive thoughts, hyperarousal, emotional numbing, and guilt. People encounter racism and racial discrimination at home, in the workplace, at school, in public places, while driving, and while shopping, and they are exposed to racism through television, movies, videos, newspapers, social media, and magazines. With the exposure to racism and racial discrimination so prevalent and the impact so adverse, it is important to consider how best to use interventions and treatment approaches.

We reviewed the literature on treatment interventions for experiences with racism and racial discrimination and found a limited number of articles.[1] More important are the numerous policy statements and guidelines in the mental health literature aimed at addressing the needs of people of color or underserved populations.

Since the 1980s, mental health professionals from various disciplines have issued numerous policy statements aimed at enhancing practices to ensure competent, effective, and ethical delivery of services to people of color, who are typically underserved. These include the American Psychological Association's (APA's) "Guidelines for Providers of Psychological Services to Ethnic, Linguistic, and Culturally Diverse Populations";[2] the "Guidelines on Multicultural Education, Training, Research, Practice, and Organizational Change for Psychologists";[3] and the newer "Multicultural Guidelines: An Ecological Approach to Context, Identity and Intersectionality."[4] The updated "Ethical Principles of Psychologists and Code of Conduct"[5] now calls for psychologists to be "aware of and respect cultural, individual, and role differences, including those based on age, gender, gender identity, race, ethnicity, culture, national origin, religion, sexual orientation, disability, language, and socioeconomic status, and [to] consider these factors when working with members of such groups."[6] As of 2019, there are updated guidelines for attending to race and ethnicity published by the American Psychological Association.[7]

However, critical commentary can be found addressing how these ethical principles or codes should apply to people of color.[8] These critics illustrate the gaps within American psychology and the pain that ethical principles have caused to indigenous people and people of color. The most recent version of the "Multicultural Guidelines" presents a biosociocultural approach to cultural context and identity.[9] Context in relation to environment, history, and contemporary experiences is noted, as is the need to address social justice, human rights, and access to resources to combat institutional barriers and disparities. The ethical principles/codes and the multicultural guidelines emphasize that psychologists must address the unique experiences of the various populations they serve. However, little specific focus has been directed to the harm caused by experiences of racism and racial discrimination, and the policies have failed to change how mental health services are provided or how mental health professionals are trained.

In 1992, professional psychology and the mental health arena in general were part of a changing health care system.[10] The managed-care movement had taken hold, traditional practices were being challenged to contain costs, and professional judgment was overtaken by the application of business principles. Decisions about treatment were no longer at the sole discretion of the care provider. During this era most psychologists were in private practice; psychiatry had become more focused on medication and hospital stays, and psychologists delivered psychotherapy and psychological testing. Today new challenges confront the field of mental health. One is the growing number of nondoctoral mental health care providers offering therapy services, thus increasing competition and lowering the cost of psychotherapy. The private-practice model has been replaced with institutional service-delivery systems, in part due to changes in health laws.[11] In addition, the profession is beginning to alter its identity from that of a mental health–oriented discipline to that of a health care profession, with a larger role in the health care system. People have begun to recognize that mental health plays a role in overall health by virtue of stress management, wellness, and disease prevention. The new ways of providing mental health care have brought demands for treatment guidelines, evidence-based therapies, and better services for culturally diverse groups or people of color.[12]

Since evidence-based practice is now a "federal standard" as specified in the ACA,[13] providers need to show that their treatments are effective, yet few specific treatment guidelines have been issued, and only recently have treatment guidelines been issued for posttraumatic stress disorder (PTSD) and depression. The shift in focus to overall health means that the medical model has become more dominant in mental health practice, resulting in greater reliance on randomized clinical trials to demonstrate a treatment approach's effectiveness. Yet the medical profession and the applied social sciences (i.e., the mental health disciplines) have troubled histories regarding people of color.

Both the medical profession and psychiatry have well-documented histories of racism and racial oppression.[14] Still, there is little hope even today that treatment guidelines will include much about racial issues or race-related stress/trauma. We take this view because racial-cultural considerations, despite the policy statements and despite having received considerable rhetoric, remain unimportant in the mental health professions. A recent paper on treating depression gives little mention of race or culture,[15] and the APA's latest clinical practice guidelines for the treatment of PTSD includes statements about cultural competence but nothing specific to race:

> Competence regarding culture and diversity involves the recognition that all humans have multiple and intersecting social identities based on . . . gender identity and gender expression, race, ethnicity, sexual orientation, socioeconomic class and socio-demographic characteristics, spiritual and religious identification, and linguistic status. . . . Many other issues . . . involved in addressing issues of culture and diversity . . . should be recognized and addressed.[16]

In essence, this quote from the PTSD guidelines reflects the view that in-dividual differences should be recognized, and thus there is no reference to race or racism. We point to this guidance, or lack thereof, regarding race because most scholars who have written about treating race-related stress and trauma have used the framework for treating PTSD to do so,[17] and although we agree with some of the points these scholars make about the symptoms, we disagree that the PTSD approach should guide treatment for RBTS. We recognize that, to be reimbursed for services, it is necessary to use the codes from the *DSM*. And we acknowledge that there is some overlap in how we conceptualize RBTS injury and PTSD symptoms, but we argue that the over-lap does not make them the same. The key and essential difference is that, with RBTS injury, the core criterion is emotional pain, not a physical threat to life, as is the case with the current Criterion A for PTSD.[18] In fact, Sa-mantha Holmes and colleagues point out that Criterion A ignores experi-ences of oppression.

OBSTACLES TO TREATMENT

Evidence suggests that mental health professionals might have difficulty with matters pertaining to race. They seem unprepared to address such issues, so clients avoid directly discussing their experiences with racism,[19] and clini-cians often lack the training—nor do they seek it—to grasp the significance of racial-cultural issues or experiences.[20] Vetta Thompson and colleagues conducted some twenty-four focus groups with about two hundred Black Americans to explore their attitudes toward therapists and psychotherapy.[21] The participants were two-thirds women and were on average around thirty-five years old. In general, they were reluctant to seek help from mental health professionals due to their cultural traditions of being strong in the face of rac-ism and oppression, of keeping issues within the family, and of believing that seeking therapy was a sign of weakness. This view is supported in a study of perceived need for mental health care that included people from all ra-cial groups and that used clinical and nonclinical samples, finding that people of color are less likely to see the need for mental health care.[22] Regarding psychologists and therapy, Thompson and colleagues observe that

> variations in views were encountered as discussions of psychology and psy-chologists ensued. Psychologists were described as older White males, who

were unsympathetic, uncaring, and unavailable. A common characterization was that psychologists were "impersonal." Psychologists were described as elitist and too far removed from the community to be of assistance to most African Americans. Those participants with prior therapy experience gave the most realistic descriptions of psychologists; however, this did not always result in a positive image.[23]

In terms of trust, focus group members believed that although

psychotherapy might be beneficial, most therapists lacked an adequate knowledge of African American life and struggles to accept or understand them. Participants discussed the stereotypes of African Americans in the larger society and challenged the ability of psychologists to remain unbiased. Also of interest were participants' fears, which included misdiagnosis, labeling, and brainwashing. Psychologists were perceived as predisposed to viewing African Americans as "crazy" and prone to labeling strong expressions of emotion as illness.[24]

However, when therapists show real concern and connect with their clients, the issue of trust can be overcome. Thompson and colleagues note that over half their participants preferred mental health services and believed that race did not matter and at the same time feared that it did matter. Focus group members believed that therapists should know about American history and how Black people were treated because they also believed that therapists would be influenced by the common and negative stereotypes of them. They also thought that a Black therapist would be too removed from their racial-cultural background to understand them and their experiences and issues, saying that "experiences with racism, discrimination, the stress of 'paying bills,' balancing work and family life, and exposure to community trauma, were avoided because of fears that the therapist would not understand. . . . This fear led to a tendency to edit or limit what was discussed."[25] Blacks in this study thought that therapists were out of touch with them and their needs, a perspective that other people of color might share.

What about from the perspective of therapists? How might they be prepared to treat Blacks and other people of color? Nancy Downing Hansen and colleagues conducted a survey of doctoral-level psychologists (44 percent men and 56 percent women, most upper-middle class and White, and with an average of twenty years of experience).[26] The authors note that over their careers, participants reported that they saw predominantly European American clients (64% of career caseload), with 14% of their clients being African American, 10% Hispanic, 5% multiracial/multiethnic, 4% Native American, and 3% Asian American. Taking into account the various clinicians' racial/ethnic identifications, over their careers, on average, 36% of participants' caseloads ($SD = 22.8$) were racially/ethnically different from themselves.[27]

The survey included several questionnaires focusing on multicultural practice and psychotherapy-related multicultural competencies drawn from the APA's Multicultural Guidelines and therapy behaviors. Several behaviors were reported to be used rarely, including utilizing the *DSM-IV* cultural formulations and engaging in actions to improve one's multicultural competence. Other such actions might include

> using various resources to augment treatment (the literature, translators, an indigenous healer), referring a client to a more qualified provider, and using racially/ethnically sensitive data-gathering techniques. Most troubling are the findings that 42% of the sample rarely or never implemented a professional development plan to improve their multicultural competence, 39% rarely or never sought culture-specific case consultation, and 27% rarely or never referred a client to a more culturally qualified provider. Clearly, these respondents are not consistently implementing a number of the multicultural recommendations found in the literature.[28]

We have speculated about how racial issues might be handled by mental health professionals. A recent study provides more information on this issue. Carrie Hemmings and Amanda Evans created a twenty-item survey to examine counselors' experiences when dealing with race-based stress and trauma in their work with clients.[29] Survey respondents were 106 mostly White, middle-aged, licensed professional counselors, more than 70 percent of whom reported that they had worked with clients who presented with race-based trauma; 29 percent had not. They were asked what factors (from among nine choices) had contributed to their clients' racial trauma. The list and the reported frequencies were as follows: covert acts of racism (88.7 percent), hate crimes (84 percent), institutional racism (84 percent), microaggressions (80 percent), out-group comments (76 percent), overt racism acts (86.5 percent), racial discrimination (86 percent), racial profiling (83 percent), own-group racial comments (71 percent). Participants were asked whether they were trained to deal with race-related stress and trauma issues that clients might present. Nineteen percent said they had received such training and 81 percent had not. For those who were trained, their training took place during continuing education activities or after their formal education and training.

Counselors reported working with clients who had undergone distressing racial experiences, but these counselors had received no training to assess or treat the resulting symptoms, nor did they report knowing of any professional policies on race-related stress/trauma with treatment recommendations. More important, the policy, training, and treatment associated with race-related stress/trauma were found to be inversely related to competencies, perhaps indicating that the counselors knew they were ill equipped to deal with racism-related issues in clients.[30] Even with the existence of policy statements about attending to racial-cultural differences, little has been done, as these researchers document, to include consideration of the effects of racism.

Although the idea that mental health professionals are ill-prepared to deal with racial issues has been cited for years, the fact that practice remains unaffected by the guidelines and codes is disturbing. It suggests that because race is merely one criterion in a long list of group memberships, racial learning gets short shrift in both graduate and postgraduate training. However, Benuto and colleagues examined in a mixed-methods study the cultural competency–training experiences of psychologists.[31] The investigation involved two steps: interviews with nine psychologists followed by a survey of 143 psychologists that was based on the interview responses. Most reported that their training had included a class in diversity (85 percent), that they had undergone supervised clinical experience with diverse populations (83 percent), and that they had received training about cultural competency (82 percent). More important, most also reported that exploring personal biases was a part of their training (76 percent). However, fewer had participated in experiential activities (67 percent) and cultural immersion (38 percent).

As we have pointed out, it is hard to know what the concept of diversity means. Still, we will highlight that much of what was reported was intellectual and cognitive learning rather than direct practice. We argue that it is impossible to address an issue in treatment in the absence of assessment or identification. Mental health professionals are typically taught how to discern life experiences and behaviors that are considered abnormal or outside expected social norms. So assessment must precede any effort to intervene.

ASSESSMENT OF RACE-RELATED EXPERIENCES

Traditional assessment practices are insufficient to document the effects of race-related experiences.[32] To assess and treat the impact of racial discrimination, the practitioner must understand how race might influence both the client and the therapist's own perceptions and behavior.[33] For some, the underlying issue is patient engagement. Johanne Eliacin and colleagues note that client engagement is crucial to health care, and the actions taken in health care delivery are influenced by the characteristics of the respective actors.[34] They find that communication and mental health treatment decisions for people of color are less collaborative, and that people of color are more likely to terminate early.[35] Contributing factors to the low level of client engagement are "distrustful interactions, and weak working alliances between minority patients and their providers."[36] A positive working alliance is associated with positive therapy outcomes and symptom relief.[37]

Sandra Matter, writing about the state of racial-cultural considerations in trauma psychology, observes, "Training models in the United States emphasize traditional clinical approaches and the objective stance of the therapist and researcher. . . . There are very few [psychology or mental health training] programs . . . that teach . . . cultural self-awareness and self-examination as a training tool."[38] Moreover, she states that scholars focus on demographics rather than on "explorations of power dynamics, immigration, historical legacies of slavery, societal violence, systemized discrimination against nondominant groups." So the clinician is often unprepared for clients who present with race-related stress or trauma.

Matter believes that training should go beyond the "us versus them" approaches used by many multicultural educators "to increase clinical trainees' effectiveness with different . . . populations, [and] training should also incorporate the trainees' understanding of their own cultural backgrounds."[39]

Krista Malott and Scott Schaefle write that there is "no single and comprehensive guide for practice in supporting clients who experience racism."[40] They offer a four-stage model that includes addressing the therapist's racial-cultural competence. They suggest beginning the conversation with clients with what they call "counseling frameworks" that recognize racism's role in the etiology of the clients' concerns, and they suggest interventions. Enrique Neblett also calls for a broader approach to addressing the effects of racism on mental health.[41]

Malott and Schaefle note that the mental health professional must have acquired racial-cultural competence, particularly the awareness, knowledge, and skills to engage in racism-focused therapy.[42] Awareness means that the professional knows about her own biases and knows something about the worldview or cultural practices of her clients. Specific to race, the therapist must know historical and current racial dynamics and social practices directed at members of different racial groups in the United States. Additional competencies include skills in cross-racial case conceptualizations and knowledge and awareness of White norms and of personal and systemic racism. The racial identity statuses of both parties will influence the process and outcome of the interaction.[43]

Assessing the role and impact of race and the client's experiences of racism must be done throughout the therapeutic encounter. This phase of the interaction is affected by what Malott and Schaefle call the counseling framework or theoretical orientation,[44] or what Matter calls traditional approaches or "westernized, intrapsychic perspectives [that] may inadvertently view a clients' behavior as pathological rather than a rational coping response to racism. Such counseling approaches may over emphasize the client's role in developing and maintaining symptoms rather than [recognizing] the need for a wider, contextual lens that considers the role of environmental stressors in the client's presenting concerns."[45] Alternative theoretical models exist and can be used, such as the biopsychosocial model, which considers the interplay between one's emotions and the environment; multimodal therapy, which uses biopsychosocial perspectives; and a trauma-focused approach,[46] which "allows counselors to recognize historical and ongoing experiences of racism as trauma-inducing for persons of Color."[47] Which model is used may be less important than the therapist's ability to grasp the racial issues.

Although addressing RBTS requires the same fundamental therapy skills common to all types of psychotherapy, clinicians' effectiveness in applying these skills when dealing with racial stress or racial trauma hinges on their ability to understand their own personal experiences and their identity as racial beings within a racialized society.[48] Researchers have shown that, for clinicians, raising awareness of one's personal experience of race has been associated with a range of strong emotional reactions—including guilt, shame, confusion, and anger—that may hamper growth in this area.[49] Still, the clinician must learn to be open and nondefensive when confronting these feelings within both themselves and the client, and they must bring this level of racial awareness and self-understanding to their role in the therapeutic encounter.

Clinical interviews may include a focus on traumatic events but typically have not included consideration of RBTS.[50] The RBTS model and accompanying instruments—the RBTSSS,[51] the RBTS Interview Schedule, the classes-of-racism measures for frequency and stress,[52] the racism-related coping scale,[53] the appropriated oppression (internalized racism) scale,[54] and racial identity status attitudes measures[55]—can fill a void in the clinical assessment of race-related experiences. They can allow a client to elaborate on his experiences, his emotional responses, his coping methods, his racial identity status attitudes, and the impacts on his current life.

RACIAL IDENTITY STATUS ATTITUDES

To date, racial identity status attitude development models and measures have been used in empirical research for all racial groups, as discussed in chapter 4. Racial identity ego statuses range from less mature (i.e., identification with the external, dominant racial-cultural group) to more mature (i.e., identification that is internal and associated with one's own racial-cultural group). Models of racial identity exist for Whites, Blacks, and other people of color. What follows is a discussion of the statuses and the interaction models that inform practice.[56]

Racial identity for Whites is characterized by abandonment of racism and the development of a nonracist identity. For people of color it is characterized by the abandonment of reliance on White culture for self-definition and an acceptance of a positive racial-cultural identity.[57] Patterns of resolution, however, are similar across racial groups. The least mature and more external racial identity status attitudes are contact (Whites), conformity (Native Americans, Asians, and Hispanics), and pre-encounter (Blacks), which are associated with the denial of racism or endorsement of a color-blind worldview. Disintegration (Whites), dissonance (Native Americans, Asians, and Hispanics), and encounter (Blacks) statuses are also externally defined, characterized by conflict or confusion about the meaning of one's race. Reintegration, resistance, immersion/emersion (Blacks) and pseudo-independence (Whites, intellectual only) are characterized by in-racial-group idealization and active out-racial-group rejection, while immersion/emersion attitudes (Native Americans, Asians, Hispanics, and Whites) reflect recognition of one's race and group membership and the accompanying emotions. Emotional awareness makes it possible to integrate race into one's personal identity structure, leading to the more mature and internally derived racial identity status attitudes of internalization (also referred to as integrative awareness for Native Americans, Asians and, Hispanics), and autonomy (Whites), which is generally associated with resolution of conflicts regarding the meaning of race for self and others, acceptance of self as a racial being, and the development of a racial identity that is free from notions of inferiority or supremacy.

Janet E. Helms's interaction model for therapy process and outcome[58] and Carter's racially inclusive model of therapy[59] describe four types of interactions in the therapist-client dyad that are determined by the pairing of patient-therapist racial identity status attitudes. Regardless of their respective racial groups, the pairings (e.g., parallel and crossed, progressive and regressive) set the context for a racism-related stress/trauma environment.[60] The models focus on how racial identity status attitudes interact in therapy relationships and how the interaction affects the process and outcome of clinical encounters. Each pair is described as a relationship type. Thus, in Helms's model, it is not the participants' races as such that characterize relationship types but how their racial identity status attitudes combine.[61] Moreover, Carter presents evidence to show that varied cognitive processes, affective states, actions, and reactions to the therapy relationship characterize the different types of relationships.[62]

A parallel relationship is one in which the counselor and client are at similar levels of racial identity development. Thus, both may hold level-one attitudes, or both may be confused or immersed in their respective racial groups. A crossed relationship occurs when the therapist and patient hold basically opposite attitudes about racial groups. For instance, a therapy dyad consisting of a Black client and a Black therapist would be crossed if the therapist held anti-Black/pro-White attitudes and the patient held pro-Black/anti-White attitudes. A progressive relationship involves a therapist whose racial identity status attitudes are at least one status more advanced than the patient's—for instance, an Asian therapist who has developed more mature status attitudes (e.g., resistance) working with a Native American patient who expresses a lower status (dissonance) and is thus confused about her racial identity. A progressive relationship may be associated with the therapist's ability to recognize various referents to race and racial issues, to express genuine race-based empathy and acceptance, and thus to guide the client in self-exploration. In a progressive relationship, one would expect the session to be perceived as positive and perhaps beneficial by both parties, and one might also find moderate levels of anger and anxiety.[63] In a regressive relationship the patient has a more mature racial identity status development than the therapist, so the relationship is conflictual; the parties have more negative perceptions about the sessions and higher levels of anxiety and hostility due to both of them struggling for control of the session when racial issues are the topic.[64]

Treatment of race-related issues in therapy must be understood in the context of racial identity status relationship types. The most effective relationship type is progressive, but even with this perspective, the medical model and the traditional view of treatment that we presented in this chapter would suggest that the person's race-based stress and RBTS should be treated from the perspective of people in power and not from the perspective of the person who experienced the racial stress or trauma.

TREATMENT OF RBTS INJURY AS RACIAL TRAUMA

Two primary perspectives prevail regarding treatment of race-based stress and RBTS. One is the view that racial trauma should be defined and treated as a type of PTSD, and the other is that RBTS injury should be treated as an emotional harm that results from racism.

In treating RBTS injury, a comprehensive appraisal of the racial encounter should be conducted, including assessing the client's symptomatology and identifying the client's psychological resources.[65] Bryant-Davis and Ocampo also recommend that a thorough trauma history be taken.[66] We worry about resistance, on the part of clients to reveal the pain of their trauma or emotional injury, and thus she may be reluctant to share her experiences and history, a point we have discussed previously; it seems to us that history should be collected during the course of the interaction, depending on the dyad's relationship type. Bryant-Davis and Ocampo suggest that the trauma-based multimodal assessment be used, which involves consulting collateral informants, checking records, and administering psychological and other tests (race-based instruments should be included),[67] but these methods must account for the influence of racial discrimination in the assessment process, given that most psychological tests are developed without regard to race or racial differences.

Bryant-Davis and Ocampo[68] and other scholars[69] argue that treatments for general trauma—such as cognitive-behavioral therapy, eye movement desensitization and reprocessing, exposure therapy, and feminist psychodynamic therapy—could be applied to RBTS. At the same time, these same authors note that no evidence supports their claim that racial incidents or race-related stress/trauma can be treated effectively with these methods. They call for the methods to be modified for race-related issues, including the therapist taking an antiracist perspective. Given the history and current state of knowledge about race and racism, it seems unlikely that therapists would adopt such a perspective. Instead we advance the notion that mental health professionals should learn about themselves as racial-cultural beings so they are able—regardless of race and culture—to grasp the presence of racism and its effects. Through developing a positive, nonracist identity, they could see themselves and others through the lens of race. The assessment should be geared to the specific racial incident, not simply to racism generally, such as when a professional conducts an RBTS injury assessment as part of a clinical interview.

Generally, people who experience race-related stress/trauma also endure physiological strain, which in turn exacerbates mental health reactions such as anxiety, depression, psychological distress, and cultural mistrust. Therefore, an assessment of both physiological and psychological symptoms is necessary to inform the course of treatment. To contextualize our discussion, we present a case description drawn from a legal proceeding in which the plaintiff sued for damages associated with charges of racial harassment and racial discrimination.

CASE HISTORY

H.K. was a thirty-six-year-old, college-educated, middle-class Black male working in law enforcement. He was mentally and physically healthy and had an unblemished educational and employment history. He was passed over for promotion and was subjected to various acts of racial hostility in his workplace over a period of years. He described being accused of faking a work injury, having his integrity questioned, and being treated in a demeaning manner. He was investigated by internal affairs in a manner that was inconsistent with policy. After filing a lawsuit, H.K. was promoted to detective, but he was the only detective who had to work nights and weekends, while others rotated those shifts.

H.K.'s case highlights a central aspect of RBTS: the inexplicable nature of the event. In harmful racial encounters, reasonable explanations for the incident are notably missing.[70] The case shows how the actions directed at H.K. were about his race. This type of personal assault is distinct from a natural disaster or combat; racism, as Holmes and colleagues note, has an "insidious nature . . . , which is often covert and implicit rather than overt or intentionally obtrusive. . . . [It involves] exchanges that send denigrating messages or convey messages . . . about . . . intelligence, morality, value, or culture simply based on [a person's] belonging to a racial group."[71]

H.K. stated that he was demeaned, and he felt helpless and disrespected by the leaders's degrading treatment. He was unable to advance. He felt depressed, withdrawn, and agitated. He had trouble sleeping, and his eating habits changed. He was afraid that he would lose his job. He said the worry and fear caused him to tremble and to be terrified for his well-being. He held in his feelings and fear, and he says he worked hard to suppress his emotions. After his promotion, he felt mostly bad because he believed that the change in his schedule and status was due to retaliation.

EVALUATION OF THE CASE USING THE RBTS MODEL

H.K. exhibited signs and symptoms of race-based traumatic stress. He demonstrated *depression and anger,* had *intrusive thoughts,* showed signs of *arousal or hypervigilance* and of *compromised self-esteem.* His *close relationships were significantly altered.* He was *anxious* and felt in a *constant state of tension.* A family member, who was interviewed, noted significant changes in him that were attributed to his work situation. The family member said he was originally happy and highly engaged in his job. He laughed, joked, and was a lot of fun to be around. But after he applied for detective, he stopped talking about his job. When asked about it, he was evasive. He would typically talk about topics in depth, so the change in his behavior was odd and troubling. On one occasion, when family members were talking about racial issues at their jobs, he suddenly broke down crying. He withdrew from friends and family and for the most part stayed at home alone. He was particularly upset about how the promotion made it impossible for him to spend time with his family. H.K.'s symptoms caused clinically significant impairment.

Most who have undergone distressing racial encounters do not seek help from mental health professionals. There are no specific interventions or techniques to teach your client to help them avoid or end their exposure to racism. There is a "both/and" quality to racial encounters that makes the client's emotional experience complex. The client can feel good about herself (self-esteem) while simultaneously feeling ashamed. Moreover, the client can intellectually know that the aggressor was wrong but still be hurt, bewildered, and emotionally injured by the experience. The client's emotions become merged and fused with her thoughts and behaviors. In other words, emotions, cognitions, and behaviors are interconnected and difficult to tease apart.

Another quality of the client's reaction may be intense emotions. There seems to be an increased depth of feeling in the client who has experienced a racial encounter that is different from everyday events. Many times these intense feelings are overwhelming and promote the secondary reactions of anger, confusion, and resentment. The therapist may observe a nonpathological focus on the details of the racial encounter. Or a client may focus on her anger in a subconscious attempt (defense) to avoid the extreme hurt and pain she is suffering. Sometimes a client displays a nonclinical paranoia. Most often clients are left feeling helpless at lacking any control over what happened to them.

A client may be reluctant to discuss the racial encounter due to shame or guilt, internalized racism, or avoidant or denial coping strategies. The clinician should assess whether the client is ready to talk about the incident or requires more time or exploration into what makes it difficult for her to discuss. Recall that avoidance, denial, and minimizing are common defenses after exposure to a traumatic event.

Consistent with racial identity status theory,[72] if the client does not hold race as a salient part of her identity or does not believe that it bears an impact on her life, she may well be unaware of the effect of racial encounters yet also note that there still maybe a considerable effect based on our research findings presented in chapter 7. This type of client has a dominant preencounter or conformity status; she may rationalize the aggressor's actions and may not identify race as the basis of an encounter or even consider it discriminatory. Personality and other individual factors (e.g., past experiences) may also contribute to her reluctance.

Although addressing RBTS requires the same skills used in all aspects of psychotherapy, clinicians' effectiveness in applying these skills hinges in part on their ability to understand their own personal experiences and identity as racial beings within a racialized society. As stated above, clinicians must learn to be open and nondefensive regarding these emotional processes within both themselves and their clients, and they must bring a higher level of racial awareness and self-understanding to their role. This is a process that can only be undertaken with proper supervision.

Clients may assume that the professional lacks the knowledge and experience to comprehend their race-based history, even if the professional is a person of color or shares their demographic racial group. Patients and therapists often avoid the topic of race for the same reason our society avoids it: the subject is difficult to discuss or understand and often evokes strong emotions. The tendency for clinicians, given their traditional training, is often to make the client feel better by teaching them coping skills or ways to more effectively negotiate racism. Given the nature of racism and the resulting RBTS associated with an experience that is sudden, unexpected, irrational, inexplicable, and out of the client's control, an attempt to console the client could be experienced as an indirect form of invalidation. Carter has shown how discussions of race in therapy have been used against clients,[73] and it is unclear if this practice has changed over time.[74] Efforts to console or help the client cope could be misplaced and often fail to facilitate healing. Such an approach may even convey the message that the client is deficient in his ability to deal with race-related stressors.

Conducting an assessment of the racial trauma can facilitate a healing process, especially if the approach is based on collaboration, respect, compassion, personal racial awareness (i.e., a mature racial identity status attitude), and openness.[75] The core of the work in the case of RBTS treatment lies with the mental health professional, who must seek training and supervision from someone who is qualified to guide him on the journey of racial self-discovery. We think it inadvisable that therapists adopt traditional or accepted treatments and apply them to RBTS, mostly because the critical element of the therapist's readiness goes unaddressed in such situations.

To effectively treat RBTS, the practitioner must be able to see and understand how race might influence her own development and behavior as a therapist and also those of the client.[76] Without this important capacity, we fear that the practitioner will be unable to understand the client's experience or to provide validation.[77]

VALIDATION OF RACE-BASED TRAUMATIC STRESS

In the case study presented above, in addition to responding to the concerns associated with depression and family conflict, the therapist also needed to address H.K.'s racial encounter and the ensuing RBTS as a bona fide area of clinical focus and intervention. Therapists who change the subject or trivialize a client's experience of racism may enact a type of retraumatization by exacerbating the feelings of confusion and anxiety that tend to accompany a racial event. Clients' emotional responses to a race-based incident should always be accepted as valid, irrespective of whether the event is objectively confirmed or not.

Given the hesitancy for people of color to identify racial concerns as the reason for seeking treatment, the client may present with feelings of depression and strained family relationships, as was the case with H.K., rather than highlighting the racial situation. Typically, clinicians might focus on the depression and family conflict and view the racial experience as possibly contributing to the depression. Yet if a working alliance is formed, the RBTS might be revealed. If a client has been involved in a legal case that is now resolved, and the work situation has improved, but the effects of the ordeal linger, an assessment of the RBTS is essential. Not only does attending to the RBTS contribute to a strong working alliance, it also communicates to the client that the inexplicable event is viewed as a legitimate source of distress, thereby validating the client's experience.

As mentioned, standard clinical interviews may include a focus on traumatic events but typically do not include consideration of RBTS.[78] The RBTSSS can be used as part of the clinical interview to help fill that void.

THE CLINICIAN'S ROLE IN TREATING RACE-BASED TRAUMATIC STRESS

RBTS involves events that present a direct threat to an individual's sense of self. After absorbing the shock and reality of what has happened to them, the person realizes it could not have happened to "anyone," as is the case with other kinds of assaults such as sexual assault or robbery; rather, they were targeted specifically because of the visible and identifiable nature of their race. The clinician can focus on the client's reactions to the event and work toward decreasing the intensity of his symptoms.

The course of treatment for RBTS should be divided into three parts: (1) containment, (2) symptom reduction, and (3) recovery and reformation of the wounded self.[79] Recovery means that the mental health professional gives attention to coping behaviors and considers moving beyond the limited role of therapist to engage in advocacy or to help the client access resources that can aid with the healing process (e.g., social support, legal advice, referral to an advocacy agency).[80]

The therapist must also take into consideration the client's symptoms following the racial encounter. Depression, anxiety, and psychological distress specific to the event may require particular treatment interventions. Although the symptoms associated with race-related stress and trauma share some characteristics, expression of the symptoms may vary from person to person. Therefore, a particular client's symptoms should be noted and assumed to be a consequence of the racial encounter. Primary goals of treatment are to reduce the acute symptoms, to reframe aversive out-group attitudes (i.e., a negative view of Whites or other people of color), to alleviate any disturbance of in-group identity (i.e., feeling that the unfair treatment was deserved), and to eradicate avoidant intergroup behaviors.[81] Below we take a closer look at each of these.

The clinician should focus on decreasing the intensity of postevent symptoms because they can cause the person to withdraw from friends and family, creating disruptions in primary relationships. If the event has generated strong negative feelings toward members of the out-group or toward other racial groups, the client would be helped by finding a balance in such attitudes and by learning to avoid using broad strokes in her views of those groups. Treatment efforts should also focus on helping the client have positive interactions across racial lines or at least be able to trust some people from the racial group in question. Although it may be hard for the client to admit, the encounter may have diminished her racial group identity; treatment could restore or heal this type of wound. Paying attention to coping and the moderating effects of other variables (e.g., church and family support) may enhance treatment by alleviating the effects of racial discrimination and racism.

An additional treatment issue involves healing the harm to the person's sense of self. Kellina Craig-Henderson and L. Ren Sloan note that a racial encounter is an assault on the core of self, on "a central part of their identity."[82] Among other actions, the therapist can provide education about the incidence of racial encounters, review the legal implications and options,[83] and allow the client to revisit the incident (retelling and reenacting, etc.).[84] These strategies aim to help the person restore their sense of dignity and self-worth.

GROUP INTERVENTIONS FOR RACIAL TRAUMA

Group therapy as an intervention for individuals experiencing racism has been viewed as an important strategy in the counseling and psychotherapy literature.[85] For these authors, the value of group approaches (which have been referred to as *therapeutic support groups*) lies primarily in the area of support and validation. Positive results include a decrease in anger and frustration, a sense of camaraderie with other group members, insight into the experience of interpersonal conflict, self-empowerment and resilience, and testing one's experience against that of others (referred to by Franklin and Boyd-Franklin as a "sanity check").[86]

The multicultural counseling movement has highlighted the role of group interventions in the context of psychological distress associated with experiences of discrimination and oppression.[87] Kira, Ahmed, Wasim, Mahmoud, and colleagues illustrate how groups can be instrumental in facilitating recovery after experiences of torture. Although racial trauma is not considered a type of torture, aspects of the group process described by Kira and colleagues have particular relevance for addressing experiences of racial trauma. They write, "Community healing—working with the traumatized collective identities and damaged collective self-esteem of the individuals—is an essential task in these groups. . . . Addressing discrimination and oppression is also important work in these groups, given that they are central to our clients' worries and feelings of insecurity, helplessness, loss of control, and loss of personal and collective identity."[88] Note that the dynamics of insecurity, helplessness, loss of control, and loss of identity are core aspects of the race-based traumatic stress model.[89]

Group processes that are germane to the experience of racial trauma include the establishment of safety and trust, psychoeducation on stress and trauma, normalization of racial trauma symptoms as natural responses to the experience of being injured, restoring a sense of personal control though such activities as the collective establishment of group rules, and learning behavioral strategies of stress reduction and relief from intrusive thoughts such as relaxation techniques and mindfulness practices. Given that in an incident of racial trauma one is the recipient of hostility because of one's racial group membership, the collective identity that develops in a group process can be a powerful healing experience.

An additional benefit of group intervention is the cohesion and sense of solidarity that can arise through the establishment of a racially homogenous group.[90] Individuals from the same racial group are engaged in a structured dialogue in which they explore their experience of racist events, their emotional and psychological reactions to the events, and actions they have taken in response. As participants listen and reflect on each other's experiences, the group facilitator focuses on each individual's story, identifies similarities across the stories, and explores members' "in the moment" emotional reactions. The power of a racially homogenous groups lies in the sense of safety that is gained through similarity of experience, which allows for deeper exploration and greater authenticity. Racial incidents have been noted to lead to a "breach of trust and a lack of safety";[91] group processes might provide a corrective emotional experience.

Carlson and colleagues have described a group intervention designed to address the experience of racial trauma among veterans of color.[92] The Race-Based Stress and Trauma (RBST) group is a structured approach that includes many of the elements of group interventions described above. The following themes are addressed in a structured manner, accompanied by relevant content and counseling interventions drawn from cognitive behavioral therapy (CBT), dialectical behavior therapy (DBT), and acceptance and commitment therapy (ACT): (1) introductions and establishing a safe place; (2) interpersonal, intrapersonal, and systemic racism; (3) the physical and psychological toll of chronic exposure to race-based stressors; (4) race-based stressors and mental health; (5) race-based stressors and physical health; (6) race-based stressors and military experiences; (7) challenges to addressing the emotional impact of racism with health care providers; (8) resilience and empowerment. Although this intervention includes content that is unique to the experiences of military veterans, it could be easily adapted to other populations. Additionally, the structure of the RBTS group lends itself to empirical investigations of therapeutic efficacy, thereby providing a platform for evidenced-based practice that is consistent with the requirements of the Affordable Care Act and the RBTS model.[93]

10

A GUIDE TO FORENSIC ASSESSMENT: CLINICAL APPLICATIONS

IN RECENT DECADES, empirical evidence has demonstrated the mental health impact of racial discrimination and racial harassment on people of color. Researchers have found that exposure to racial discrimination is frequent, and they have uncovered significant relationships between racism and the negative emotional reactions of its targets.[1] Much of this work has implications for the forensic assessment and evaluation of civil racial discrimination and racial harassment cases.[2] In this chapter we discuss legal issues of racial discrimination as well as the forensic applications of the Race-Based Traumatic Stress Symptom Scale (RBTSSS), and the RBTS model.[3]

Despite evidence that people of color who are exposed to racial discrimination report psychological and emotional consequences, little has been written in the psychiatric and forensic literature describing or examining the effects of racism.[4] Robert T. Carter and Jessica Forsyth[5] and James Hicks[6] argue that forensic mental health professionals fail to adequately incorporate considerations of race and culture into forensic evaluations, citing, for instance, empirical evidence of misdiagnoses and higher rates of involuntary commitment for people of color, suggesting that people of color are maladjusted rather than targets of racism and racial discrimination.[7] Forensic mental health professionals have limited guidance in understanding and addressing issues germane to race and racism.[8]

Nevertheless, mental health professionals are increasingly called on to provide assessments and to testify about the psychological damages associated with a variety of legal claims, including for civil and criminal cases involving race and racism. Some scholars[9] note that psychological reactions to racial discrimination and other forms of oppression[10] do not fit criteria for disorders as outlined in the *DSM*,[11] especially Criterion A. And the *DSM* still does not include consideration of the racial-cultural context of diagnoses. Samantha Holmes and colleagues observe that in the face of

> overwhelming evidence for the deleterious effects of oppression on the mental health of members of subjugated groups . . . very few forms of oppression have the potential of meeting Criterion A as it is currently written. The wording of Criterion A arguably best lends itself to interpersonal forms of oppression and, even so, has the potential of capturing only a narrow subset of interpersonal oppression (e.g., physically violent hate crimes) while neglecting other frequent iterations.[12]

Traditional assessment tools fail to capture people's emotional and psychological reactions to racism and racial oppression. A person may experience emotional pain because of objectively verifiable or subjective acts of racism.

Our guide to the forensic assessment of the emotional impact of race-based encounters can be used in preparing expert reports. We begin with a discussion of legal options and limitations specific to racial discrimination, racial harassment, and racially hostile work environments, and we provide an analysis of some of the considerations specific to the forensic evaluation of psychological damages in claims of such race-related incidents.

REMEDIES FOR LEGALLY PROHIBITED RACIAL DISCRIMINATION

Some civil rights laws offer three avenues through which targets of racism can seek legal remedy or redress: the Civil Rights Act of 1866, section 1891; the Civil Rights Act of 1964; and the Civil Rights Act of 1991, Title VII, which prohibits discrimination in the workplace. They can also seek recovery of compensatory damages for infliction of emotional distress under civil tort law. Each of these avenues allows for the testimony of forensic expert witnesses to substantiate claims of emotional distress and other forms of psychiatric and psychological impairment, although such testimony is not required. Yet limits to legal redress exist, and the law itself may act as a barrier in several ways to the pursuit of remedy for race-related encounters. Thus, despite the availability of legal remedies, challenges must be overcome when filing claims for racism-related encounters.[13]

First, work or school claims must follow an organization's grievance procedures prior to a complaint being filed with the Equal Employment Opportunity Commission (EEOC), the federal agency tasked with reviewing claims of discrimination and determining whether there is enough evidence for the person to file a lawsuit. But many organizations lack procedures for filing complaints specifically about racial matters. Instead, most discrimination complaints for all protected groups are typically addressed within the general procedures for discrimination, except in the instance of sexual harassment or sexual assault. Given the lack of specific guidelines for racial issues, targets may struggle to determine if they have been subject to treatment for which legal protection is provided. The first step in filing a complaint can be ambiguous, complicated, and compromised. If the issue is not resolved within the organization, the target must follow the procedures established by the EEOC to file a complaint but must do so within strict time limits. The complaint is followed by an EEOC investigation, which preferably leads to a settlement. When a settlement cannot be reached, the EEOC can authorize further legal steps such as a civil suit. It is possible to pursue legal action without going through this process, perhaps by seeking legal assistance from organizations like the National Association for the Advancement of Colored People (which maintains a legal defense fund), the American Civil Liberties Union, or the Legal Aid Society.

Second, the standards for substantiating in a court of law one's claim of legally prohibited racial discrimination or harassment or of hostile work environment (i.e., disparate treatment or impact) present challenges. The burden rests on the plaintiffs to prove that (1) the act was severe and pervasive; (2) it was because of race; (3) it was intentional with racial animus; and (4) it caused extreme emotional distress or some type of psychological or functional impairment.

FORENSIC ASSESSMENT OF MENTAL HEALTH

A forensic mental health assessment assists legal decision makers by providing evidence about a person's mental health. The forensic professional is guided by the legal question being considered. In situations involving race and racism, the evaluator should depart from traditional psychological assessments or tests and include a research-based analysis of the situation in addition to the race-based traumatic stress (RBTS) clinical interview or psychological evaluation.

The questions confronting the mental health forensic evaluator differ from those dealt with in clinical practice in that they must inform decisions related to a body of law. Usually clinical assessments focus on the person's clinical needs and on how best to intervene and assist the course of treatment. Forensic assessment focuses on determining the "capabilities, abilities, or behavioral tendencies that must be understood in order to decide how to resolve the legal questions."[14] Thus, the evaluator should know how the law applies to the situation, even though a mental health professional's training differs from a lawyer's. The audience for the forensic assessment is not other mental health professionals but usually legal professionals or citizens (jury members).

Much of the forensic mental health assessment literature focuses on one's mental state and on legal questions in criminal matters like competence to stand trial, to plead, or to be sentenced. In civil law, the legal issues might include addressing mental injury in a worker's compensation claim, or torts for emotional distress. Administrative matters, antidiscrimination laws, family and child issues (custody), and abuse and neglect disputes might also require expert testimony.

Mental health care and the law hold different assumptions about human behavior. The law assumes that a person acts on free will, whereas in the mental health field people assume that behavior is influenced by various intrapsychic and external forces of which the person may or may not be aware. Gary Melton and colleagues write that "the paradigm in which mental health professions work would appear to be in inherent conflict with legal worldviews."[15] The resolution to this conflict is that mental health professionals should not give opinions on the "ultimate legal issue."[16] Rather, she or he should assist in fact finding.

Yet the disciplines also differ in the process of fact finding. The law emphasizes certainty, whereas mental health professionals can offer only probabilistic statements. Related to this issue is that much of the knowledge in the behavioral sciences is built on normative or group evidence based on samples from which inferences are drawn about populations, while legal issues are usually person-specific.

Cases involving racial discrimination are most often civil, rather than criminal, matters (although racial issues can and should be considered in criminal cases). Civil courts handle disputes between private parties, rather than between a person and the city, state, or federal government, as in criminal matters. Court procedures for civil matters differ from those for criminal matters, as do the standards for legal decisions. In a criminal case, the standard is usually proving beyond a reasonable doubt that a crime was committed. In a civil dispute, the plaintiff must show through a "preponderance of the evidence" that the facts contained in the "complaint" are accurate. Upon receiving a complaint, the defendant responds with answers to the various elements of the complaint, and a trial is held later. Prior to the trial, the two sides request information to "discover" relevant details through documents or other evidence, which may include a mental health examination conducted by an expert mental health professional. In a civil case, the claim may be that the party was harmed or suffered emotional pain due to the actions of the defendant. The evaluation may be intended to gauge the extent of the pain and suffering. The expert typically submits a report containing her opinions, and she may be deposed at any time. A deposition "involves questioning of the witness by the deposing party's attorney with the witness's attorney present."[17]

We argue that RBTS should be considered an instance of intentional infliction of emotional distress (IIED) or negligent infliction of emotional distress (NIED).[18] As noted in previous chapters, racial experiences are stressful, and that stress is associated with a range of emotional reactions that can result in psychological impairment.[19]

Contemporary acts of racism tend to be subtle, ambiguous, and complex. Sometimes they are embedded into organizational policies and procedures. Research indicates that subtle acts of racism can and often do have a strong psychological impact on targets. One study found that subtle or ambiguous racial discrimination is more strongly associated with negative affect than overt discrimination.[20] Another study found that subtle discrimination predicts distress, arguing that because it often occurs within the target's close social network (e.g., among coworkers and supervisors), its psychological impact may be greater.[21] Although adhering to the facts of a legal claim is important, so is assessing and treating the impact of the alleged events to understand the target's subjective perception.

Advances have been made in establishing legal definitions of subtle acts of sexual harassment, making it less important to prove intent, but the same is not true of racial discrimination.[22] Proving intent and showing that the racially discriminatory conduct was sufficiently severe and pervasive can be extremely challenging, especially when the encounter is the proximate cause of the emotional distress or functional impairment.[23] Two separate analyses of racial harassment cases found that 80 percent did not prevail.[24] Furthermore, in the 20 percent of claims that were successful, the plaintiff was subjected to blatant forms of racism in which explicit racial animus was found, the plaintiff endured hostile treatment over long periods of time, or both,[25] which suggests that the courts only find in favor of plaintiffs who have been exposed to particularly severe and overt racial discrimination or harassment. These statistics underscore the importance of the role of mental health forensic experts in assessing claims of emotional distress that arise from racial discrimination, especially those that are ambiguous.

Although forensic evaluations of racial discrimination share similarities with evaluations of other types of psychological damage, a number of unique factors should be considered. As noted above, forensic evaluation in race-related cases has two objectives. The first is to determine whether the incident in question is the proximate cause of the plaintiff's psychological damage or emotional injury and to assess the extent of functional impairment; this is the RBTS assessment.[26] To document functional impairment, if it exists, the evaluator must assess the event's current and long-term effects on the claimant's functioning. First, the evaluator must determine causation through the collection of a thorough history of all aspects of the claimant's life prior to the event, including family background and personality, and developmental, psychological, medical, educational, and occupational history. The evaluator should, where possible, seek corroborating information about the alleged incident and its possible impact on the plaintiff from family members, friends, colleagues, and witnesses, as well as from medical, psychiatric, and employment records. This is particularly important in cases where there may be a history of psychological issues, which would need to be addressed in the evaluation process.

A second objective of the forensic evaluation is establishing the social environment surrounding the racial incident, which includes documenting information on the forms that racism takes in society and its prevalence in the setting in question. The evaluator must present information from the research and other sources describing reported incidents and targets' reactions to them. This research-based analysis helps the court and jury place the events in a proper social-cultural context.

THE CLINICAL INTERVIEW ABOUT THE RACIAL INCIDENT

It is important to discover during the clinical interview how the person recognized racial discrimination and, if they did, how they were harmed by the
encounter. Although some ambiguous racial incidents fail to meet the requirements for legal remedy, they may nonetheless seriously affect a person.
Research on general stress provides support for the impact of ambiguous
events. Studies have found that stress increases if an event is negative, unpredictable, and uncontrollable. Negative events in personal relationships
(e.g., work and family) tend to be stronger predictors of depression. Stress reactions occur whether the stressor is objective or subjective, and both types
independently predict psychological and health effects.[27]

Some people who are exposed to stressful situations can adapt and cope
effectively, while others may not. Thus, in ascertaining the impact of even a
subtle racist event, the evaluating mental health professional should assist the
claimant in exploring the meaning the event held for her—both the event as
a whole and specific aspects of it. The clinical interview should address the
following: (1) the characteristics of the actors involved (race/ethnicity, extent
of power, and influence over the claimant); (2) the number, nature, and duration of the events; (3) the claimant's perception of the negativity, control-
lability, and suddenness of the event; (4) the extent to which the event
constituted a threat or caused feelings of fear and helplessness; and (5) how
the claimant tried to adapt or respond to the incident.[28] Other instruments
besides the Race-Based Traumatic Stress Symptom Scale assess the stress of
racism.[29] However, they do not connect a specific event to specific reactions
or symptoms the way the RBTSSS does.

It is also important to consider the influence of previous or concurrent
stressors on the claimant's emotional reactions.[30] Although widespread, racism continues to be a taboo topic. It is common for a person who has made
a claim of racism to be ridiculed and accused of being overly sensitive, which
can isolate him from social support, thereby intensifying his reactions to the
incident.[31] The perception of hypersensitivity is often reinforced when courts
regularly dismiss all but the most blatant and severe acts of racial discrimination or harassment as insignificant or unworthy of legal remedy.[32] The clinician may find it useful to use the classes-of-racism categories (see part II of
this book) to capture critical characteristics of the person's experiences and
to uncover which elements of the incident contribute to affective, cognitive,
and behavioral responses. Some research indicates that exposure to hostility

(i.e., harassment) or avoidant racism is associated with more extreme emotional and psychological reactions than exposure to other forms of racism.[33]

Research indicates that a person's appraisal of an event is more predictive of the intensity of the stress response than is the nature of the event itself,[34] and that the appraisal is influenced by individual differences. How one appraises an event (e.g., as positive or negative, or as a threat) influences how one copes with it and the psychological responses it elicits. Further, research has found that when different individuals are exposed to the same event, the incidence of traumatic stress varies; certain dispositional characteristics could make some people more vulnerable to traumatic stress than others. Eve Carlson identifies five factors that may influence reactions to traumatic stressors: (1) a person's biological predispositions to stress; (2) a person's developmental level at the time of the event; (3) the severity of the traumatic event; (4) a person's social resources (e.g., socioeconomic status); and (5) a person's prior life events.[35]

For these reasons, reliance on a specific diagnosis may be inappropriate and even misleading in forensic mental health assessment. Stuart Greenberg and colleagues recommend a focus on impairment rather that on *DSM* diagnoses.[36] One consideration is the variety of ways that people process racial information.

THE ROLE OF RACIAL IDENTITY STATUS ATTITUDES

One factor that influences how a person process racial information is his or her racial identity ego status. According to Carter, Johnson, and colleagues, racial identity refers to one's psychological orientation to their demographic racial group.[37] Research into racial identity has shown that people have distinct psychological resolutions regarding their racial group membership.[38] Each racial identity status is associated with a constellation of distinct thoughts, behaviors, attitudes, values, and emotions related both to one's racial group and to the dominant racial group. Racial identity ego statuses differ from what is typically referred to as "race identity," or one's membership in a sociodemographic group based on skin color. Racial identity ego status models exist for Blacks, other people of color, and Whites. The process of maturing as it relates to one's racial identity ego status attitudes differs for each racial group because of varied social, political, and historical experiences. Some examples of racial identity ego status across racial groups include: (1) being color-blind and thinking that race is not salient for self or for others and adopting the cultural values of the dominant group; (2) feeling confused about race and culture; and (3) realizing the meaning of one's race while working to internalize the culture of one's racial group. Ultimately, whether you are White or a person of color, you can evolve a racial identity ego status in which your race and culture are positive and valued aspects of your personality. A White person can be nonracist, feel positive about their Whiteness, and work against oppression, as can people of color (although people of color would be free of prejudice since it is not possible for them to be racist since they do not have sociopolitical power).

An RBTS injury assessment should include an examination of the racial composition and climate of the claimant's family, neighborhood, schools, and other organizations, and how they may have influenced his experiences. It is important to explore memorable racial events that occurred during the claimant's formative years, and the frequency of exposure to both minor and major discrimination across his life span. A history of race-related encounters could predispose him to more acute reactions to racial discrimination. The evaluator should be attentive to experiences that may have borne racial undertones, such as being assigned to special education, conflict with teachers, or involvement in the criminal justice system, and should carefully consider how the person understands that race may have contributed to those events.

In addition to assessing the claimant's racial identity ego status, the collection of a racial-cultural history allows the forensic evaluator to determine whether the claimant may have developed vulnerabilities from past exposure to racial events that may influence her reaction to the present encounter. For some claimants, a seemingly minor racial event following a lifetime of stressful or traumatic racial encounters could be the one that finally erodes her capacity to cope. A thorough racial-cultural assessment can provide a context for reactions that may appear extreme, given a relatively subtle incident. The "thin-skull" doctrine may come into play here. In tort law, the defendant is liable for harm even if the person harmed had existing vulnerabilities. In the case of racism, one scholar observes that "underlying vulnerability does not conceptually preclude recovery."[39]

ASSESSMENT OF RBTS INJURY OR IMPAIRMENT

No accepted legal definition of psychological injury currently exists.[40] William Koch and colleagues define psychological injuries as "stress-related emotional conditions resulting from real or imagined threats or injuries" that must include "causation by a third party."[41] Although a variety of emotional and psychological reactions have been used in support of legal claims of psychological damages,[42] traumatic stress is perhaps the most common diagnosis because, unlike most *DSM* diagnoses, causation is an element of the diagnosis and is also implicit in its criteria. Although not all incidents of racial harassment and discrimination will result in a traumatic reaction, several scholars have posited that the stress associated with racial events may produce emotional reactions that rise to the level of trauma.[43] Consistent with other scholars, Carter and Forsyth argue that the reliance on diagnosable disorders as evidence of emotional distress could cause clinicians to underestimate the true emotional impact of racist experiences.[44] The lack of racial events recognized as stressors in the diagnostic criteria makes it difficult to link the mental health effects of racism to specific types of experiences. Since the law does not require a *DSM* diagnosis to show evidence of injury, and because the *DSM* does not currently consider the racial or social context of the stressors that cause psychological injury, we recommend that mental health professionals expand their perspectives beyond the *DSM*.[45]

Some scholars note that, due to a history of being unfairly pathologized by the mental health disciplines, many people of color resist being misdiagnosed and may be reluctant to accept being labeled as "disordered" even under normal conditions.[46] Other scholars argue that behaviors that might be considered adaptive responses to racism or other forms of oppression are often misinterpreted as evidence of pathology.[47] Exposure to racial discrimination or harassment is likely to heighten these sensitivities and could potentially hamper willing participation in the assessment interview.

We argue that it is more effective clinically to consider the effects of racism as psychological injury rather than as a mental disorder since those effects arise from environmental stressors rather than from the target's abnormality. Holmes and colleagues argue that for individuals who suffer trauma from oppression, the distinction between being labeled "sick" or disordered, rather than being recognized as normal people who were exposed to unjust mistreatment, is clinically significant.[48] From this perspective, general mental health diagnoses have limited utility in capturing the full scope of a race-related incident.

Using the concept of injury, in contrast, means that the person was exposed to an unjust race-based experience that has produced a cluster of symptoms leading to emotional and psychological impairment or injury. In contrast to the notion of disorder, focusing on injury indicates that the rights of the person were unfairly violated and seeking redress is an option. The concept of injury can be conveyed in the expert report by illustrating the manifestation of damage through indexes of psychological functioning and by describing how symptoms operate as a cluster, indicating the presence of an RBTS injury. The designation of RBTS injury (rather than a diagnosis of disorder) could make it easier for some people to accept the impairment and to work toward healing, and it could facilitate establishing a claim for legal or administrative redress.

In summary, we note that it is beyond the evaluator's purview to determine the veracity of a plaintiff's claims. The evaluator can only use valid resources (e.g., medical and employment records; interviews with family members, coworkers, and treating psychologists or psychiatrists) to determine whether a claimant's reactions arose from or were made worse by the racial incident in question. Family members' or coworkers' perceptions of the claimant's psychological or emotional functioning before and after the incident, as well as witnesses' accounts of the event, may serve to corroborate or conflict with the target's claims. Nonetheless, some scholars caution against interviewing defense witnesses (whether employees or employers) in workplace cases because they may have personal agendas or may be afraid of retaliation by their employer.

CASE ILLUSTRATION

Ms. R is a forty-eight-year-old, married, lower-middle-class African American woman. She was employed in a dental office for twenty years. The purpose of this assessment was to determine whether Ms. R was injured emotionally and psychologically by an alleged racially hostile work environment and by acts of racial harassment at the office.

The incidents began when a hygienist was hired. The new person reported that she hated where she had last lived because "too many 'niggers' lived there." The hygienist told Ms. R that she stank, and that she was ugly, fat, dirty, lazy, and worthless; the office manager observed these interactions without saying a word. Ms. R was especially scared because the hygienist had served in the Navy and said she owned a gun. The next month the hygienist shifted from verbal to physical acts, when she pushed Ms. R out of her way. Ms. R had difficulty falling asleep and wondered if she would be safe at the office.

RELEVANT BACKGROUND AND SOCIAL HISTORY

Ms. R was raised in the Northeast. Her father worked as a bus driver, and her mother did factory work. She completed high school when she was eighteen years old. She was an average student, and she attended predominately Black schools. She worked summers during high school. She reported being in good health and had no behavioral or health issues while growing up or during adulthood. She has held several jobs over the years, with breaks for having and caring for her children. She studied to be a dental assistant and has worked as one ever since.

RACIAL EXPERIENCES AND MEDICAL HISTORY

Ms. R grew up in a city that was not racially segregated, and she encountered few racial incidents while growing up. She described harsh treatment by White teachers while she was in elementary school but did not experience the events as racial in nature at the time. Only later did she come to understand that they might have been racially motivated. She was taught in school about race and race relations. She was exposed to the teachings of Martin Luther King Jr. and Malcolm X. When she was in middle school, a friend's mother called her the N-word. She was proud to be a woman and Black. But it was important to her to be a good person above all else. After the experiences at her office, she saw a psychiatrist for about five sessions to help her cope with the incidents.

ASSESSMENT FINDINGS: EMOTIONAL AND PSYCHOLOGICAL IMPACT OF THE EVENTS

Ms. R states that she was demeaned, humiliated, and made to feel helpless. She indicates that she felt like a fool who was betrayed and treated in a way that she did not deserve.

COLLABORATIVE INTERVIEW: FAMILY MEMBER

J, Ms. R's daughter, relayed some of Ms. R's history, including where she went to school and work positions she held. J reported being close to her mother, and she described her as having been a happy-go-lucky person who exhibited a lot of energy and was very active at home and work.

During and after the events at the office, Ms. R became sad and withdrawn. J stated that Ms. R would come home from work crying and upset about what she called racial harassment. Ms. R was shocked that racism existed and that she was the target. J said that her mother knew about racism but did not expect to experience it directly.

J reported that all her mother could do was tell her boss, Dr. B, about what was occurring, and she did so repeatedly. Yet her boss did nothing. This fact made the experience more difficult for her mother. She was let go and was given poor references, and she had difficulty finding a new job because other positions required skills she did not have (e.g., speaking Spanish). These facts compounded the psychological, emotional, and economic effects on her mother. J said that her mother was not the same; she was mostly sad and weepy and seemed lost, and she was often paranoid and worried about what people might say to her. Her mother did not want to go out or be around people. J thought that her mother was depressed and noted that her mother was sleeping less than she used to. Ms. R had changed so much that it was affecting the family, who depend on her for many things.

Ms. R had enough general and personal knowledge of race to be able to recognize her encounter as constituting racial discrimination and her workplace as a racially hostile work environment. She indicated that the racial experiences at the office were beyond her control, unexpected, and emotionally painful. She tried to cope with the stress of the situation. Her options for help within the office were limited to her immediate supervisors (the office manager and Dr. B). None of her efforts to adapt and cope with the racial harassment were successful. Two witnesses, Ms. C and M, submitted statements in which they attested to observing the alleged harassment. In addition, the collaborative interviewee, her daughter, confirmed that Ms. R had changed emotionally and psychologically since her experiences at the office.

Ms. R exhibited signs and symptoms of race-based traumatic stress injury; she is and has been depressed and angry, has intrusive thoughts, engages in avoidance behavior, and shows signs of physical reactions and shame. She reports experiencing significant anxiety while and after working at the office. She has problems sleeping and reports decreased intimacy in her marriage and avoidance of family and friends. She notes that she has flashbacks and nightmares from the harassment. In her interview, she noted that her reactions were observed and experienced by others, which was reflected in the collaborative interview with her daughter. She was visibly upset and in emotional pain during the interview when she recalled the events. She talked about feelings of humiliation arising from actions taken and not taken by Dr. B and the office manager. Her racial experiences at work were and are the proximate cause of her psychological and emotional injury or the IIED. She continues to suffer. To a reasonable degree of professional certainty, the RBTS injury and associated symptoms have caused Ms. R clinically significant psychological distress and emotional impairment.

CONCLUSION

The existing body of research, as well as clinical experience, tends to support the notion that exposure to racism in various forms causes psychological and emotional reactions that may rise to the level of traumatic stress. Experiences of RBTS from racial discrimination or racial harassment of various types (e.g., discrimination in housing, employment, and service provision; interpersonal assaults; racial profiling) are likely involved in the development of presenting problems and may contribute to poor health. Nevertheless, most, although perhaps not all, clinicians still rarely assess patients for exposure to race-related experiences. This chapter provides forensic mental health professionals with guidance in using the appropriate empirical and clinical resources, and in providing effective assessment and support to targets of racial harassment and discrimination.

11

TRAINING MENTAL HEALTH PROFESSIONALS
TO TREAT RACIAL TRAUMA

OVER THE PAST FEW DECADES, the diversity or multicultural counseling movement has assumed great importance in the field of mental health, at times being referred to as the "fourth force" in psychology.[1] Some, however, believe that the focus on multiculturalism has perhaps unintentionally obscured the ongoing need to attend to race and racism in counseling and psychotherapy.[2] This chapter examines current training approaches for mental health professionals to be competent with racial issues and/or racial stress/trauma, with a focus on pedagogical strategies in the counseling and psychotherapy context. Our discussion is critical for the training of mental health professionals, including social workers; health care providers; guidance counselors; nurses; psychiatrists; clinical, counseling, and school psychologists; and teachers. We emphasize strategies for teaching students and professionals in these fields to negotiate and cope with issues of race, racism, and racial identity with the goal of including race as a core consideration in the mental health services they provide.

CURRENT APPROACHES TO TRAINING
FOR RACIAL AWARENESS

Training for professional psychology or mental health practice typically includes an undergraduate education in psychology or a related discipline, graduate education (a master's or doctoral program), doctoral internship training for one year, and postgraduate training and supervision, leading to licensure as a mental health professional.[3]

Although variation occurs across training programs with regard to points of emphasis, diversity or multicultural issues is one of the areas of learning required for some mental health professionals (usually didactic in nature), whether master's or doctoral.[4] Typically, a single course or workshop focused on cultural diversity or multiculturalism provides the typical training for students and professionals, but many programs do not require such a course.[5] In doctoral training the maximum number of classes might involve forty didactic and practice experiences. Racial- or cultural-oriented training usually might be one or two courses, at best. So for graduate training, typically one class out of twenty to forty classes and in some programs no multicultural courses are offered. One study found that some 89 percent of counseling-psychology programs offered at least one course with a cultural focus,[6] although the cultural focus may or may not include race.[7]

It is important to put the training in perspective. The minimum training period for a person to become a mental health professional is two years for social workers and mental health counselors, and the maximum is four to six years for psychologists or counselor educators. A two-year program includes about twenty classes that represent a mix of experientially based helping skill-development courses, theoretical and professional content is usually delivered via didactic instruction, and practicums (e.g., field placements, externships at service provider agencies, supervised practicums at clinics). The lone class in diversity or multiculturalism is generic, and for the most part, the overall training in helping skills and techniques assumes that the therapy principles taught are universal.

To have racial awareness requires racial-cultural competence which is often not offered when diversity or multicultural issues are the focus. Racial-cultural competence is defined by Teceta Thomas Tormala and colleagues as follows: "Cultural competence reflects cultural awareness of self and others that facilitates effective treatment of clients from differing [racial-]cultural groups and interpersonal or intergroup problem-solving skills that shift with the [racial-]cultural dynamics within a therapeutic setting."[8] Jose Abreu and colleagues define multicultural counseling, which assumes cultural competence, as involving therapeutic relationships that cross race and ethnicity and therefore require the development of knowledge, awareness, and skills so the mental health professional can work in a racially and ethnically diverse society.[9]

Alex Pieterse and colleagues point out that even though scholars emphasize the need to infuse multiculturalism into all aspects of counseling training, the single-course approach is still the tool most frequently used.[10] Moreover, little agreement exists regarding what and how to teach about race and culture; in experiential and didactic training, especially regarding race and culture, these classes elicit various forms of resistance among students and faculty,[11] a dynamic that might also shape the type of material emphasized by instructors in multicultural counseling courses.

Traditional theories of personality and human development continue to dominate mental health training programs. Trainees, regardless of race, usually are taught to apply established theory, techniques, and methods of treatment and human development to matters of race and culture.[12] These universal ideas are used in treatment to understand and explain race. We would argue that these theories and approaches are limited and are victim-focused when the topic is race or racial differences.[13] A training approach that integrates race and its role in human development is preferable. Yet obstacles work against the inclusion of race in mental health training. The faculty would have to see a focus on race as important and needed, but the extent to which faculty members are invested in training around these topics varies considerably.[14] The worldviews of the dominant racial-cultural group seem to dictate the content of most training programs.

THE AMERICAN WORLDVIEW AND CULTURAL LEARNING

One would expect that how mental health professionals are trained and the ideas they bring to and learn in their training and practice are central to the health and well-being of the people they seek to serve. To the extent that the values, attitudes, and beliefs of these professionals are congruent with those of the people they help, their effectiveness is greatly enhanced. Likewise, if incongruities exist between the professional's values and attitudes and those of the client, the care will likely be ineffective.[15]

Mental health training and practice are shaped by several interrelated factors. A significant factor is the worldview or the cultural patterns and beliefs of the dominant racial-cultural group. Psychology and psychotherapy began in Europe and the Unites States in the nineteenth century, and at that time the perspectives and life experiences of people of color and women were not heard or considered important.[16] The beliefs of the dominant group—white men—shaped the norms and structure of institutions in the United States, including those involved in mental health services and training.[17]

All institutions are linked in that they exist to serve the goals and pass on the teachings and values of society as reflected in the worldview of the dominant racial-cultural group.[18] Even measures of cultural competence are infused with a dominant-culture perspective. Zofia Kumas-Tan and colleagues write, "Many of the measures we examined either assume that both dominant and marginalized groups have the same experiences of multiculturalism, or they take the dominant group's experience as the norm."[19] Outlooks that place European and American perspectives at the center dominate personality theories and practice in mental health professions and in society in general, which has resulted in the marginalization of other cultural worldviews. The prevailing understanding is that mental health professionals assume that the dominant racial-cultural worldview is universal.[20] Differing worldviews that would allow mental health professionals to be racially and culturally competent and effective are not taught.[21]

FOUNDATIONS OF RACIAL-CULTURAL COMPETENCE

Although the need for racial and cultural competence within psychology and the mental health professions has long been recognized,[22] the emphasis has tended to be on the ability of the practitioner to work with people of color. Don Davis and colleagues observe that the multicultural competencies (MCC) movement has been around for decades, growing out of mental health disparities among people of color. They note that these competencies "are now included in accreditation requirements and guidelines for all areas of psychological science. . . . Similar emphasis on MCCs has occurred across several disciplines, including education, social work, counseling, law, and medicine."[23] At the same time, they point out that the clinical efficacy of MCCs has received little attention, and little evidence indicates that they are effective in mental health practice.

Given that all individuals are racial beings, we disavow the emphasis on multicultural counseling competence for people of color. Instead, we argue that racial-cultural competence should fundamentally encompass conscious knowledge of one's own racial-cultural group (e.g., race, gender, ethnicity, social class, religion). This means recognizing the versatility of knowing, feeling, and behaving that might occur because of one's racial-cultural worldview. Racial-cultural competence also means recognizing and knowing about people who belong to groups other than one's own. Such knowledge includes information about each group's (including one's own) social-political history and an understanding of how that history influences each person's status and participation in society.[24] One's self-knowledge, coupled with an understanding of one's racial-cultural group, must be enhanced by individual racial-cultural self-exploration and development.[25] One must evolve a personal identity that is free of bias or in which the existence of bias is recognized and monitored.[26] Said another way, effective and competent mental health professionals should evolve advanced racial and ethnic group identities so they are able to facilitate growth and exploration in others as educators, advocates, policy makers, or practitioners.[27]

The approach we advocate treats all racial-cultural groups as important to understand. We should avoid the practice of describing the ills of our social system and the outcomes of exploitation and oppression by focusing on the victims of oppression. Emphasis on the victims of oppression, regardless of the group of interest, is a limited view that blocks a grasp of sociocultural norms and institutional policies that would aid our understanding of the development of illness, abnormality, or health, all of which are culture bound and influenced by sociopolitical trends and currents. Recent evidence suggests

> a cultural (mis)attribution bias in American psychology: the tendency to see racial/ethnic minorities as members of a group whose traits, beliefs, and behaviors are shaped primarily by culture, and to perceive the White racial/ethnic majority as autonomous and independent actors who are instead largely influenced by psychological processes. Because this bias rests on assumptions about human behavior that are not supported by evidence and may lead to differential treatment of members of specific social groups, it constrains psychologists' explanations of behavior and cognition.[28]

José Causadias and colleagues found that studies in psychology that focus on "culture" tend to have large proportions of people of color, thus supporting the notion that culture or race "still occupies a secondary place in mainstream psychology, as it is often associated with marginal or exotic groups and thought to contribute little to understanding basic psychological processes."[29] They also report on a survey of psychologists showing that psychologists, irrespective of race, rated as "favorable" studies of culture with people of color in the samples, and as "less favorable" noncultural studies with people of color:

The cultural (mis)attribution bias has negative consequences for the psychological sciences. It compromises the external validity of noncultural psychology because what we know about minorities remains restricted or distorted. . . . It negates that Whites are also cultural beings and that cultural processes—including cultural values, ideologies, and religious beliefs—also shape their perceptions and behavior in meaningful ways. . . . The cultural (mis)attribution bias situates White behavior as the gold standard of human experience against which all other groups should be compared. When minorities depart from this norm, they are considered deviant and deficient.[30]

The findings of this research support our contention that we are all racial-cultural beings and that the dominant cultural worldview is used in racial oppression.

American culture has evolved from White ethnic upper- and middle-class values and beliefs. American cultural systems are superordinate to ethnic group values. Some of the dimensions of White American cultural patterns, according to Edward Stewart and Milton Bennet[31] and Martin Marger,[32] are individualism expressed through personal preferences; self-expression reflected in a social conformity and achievement of goals based on external criteria (e.g., school grades, good job); authority and power that is hierarchical; communication patterns that are verbal and use standard English; a future-time orientation; a Judeo-Christian religious system; a belief that the nuclear family structure is ideal; and standards of music, beauty, and social traditions (holidays, monuments, etc.) that are grounded in European-American history and culture.

Members of racial-cultural groups vary in how much they identify with and are invested in their own group and how acculturated they are to the dominant culture. These variations influence the meaning and significance of one's group and its culture (i.e., one's racial identity status). Social and economic resources also influence one's vulnerability to stressors from life events.[33] Fewer resources and lower social status are associated with greater vulnerability to such stressors.[34] One's community and its organizations can have both positive and negative effects on mental health. Support systems that address and seek to reduce the effects of social, personal, and economic resources can protect individuals from the harm of stressors, reducing the incidence of negative mental and physical outcomes. These contextual factors should be included in the training of mental health professionals. However, as can be seen from our discussion, trainees are often not taught that race or culture pertain to all members of society.

TYPOLOGIES OF DIFFERENCE

It is easy to see differences when people are visibly dissimilar, speak another language, or wear distinctive clothes. It is harder to see and understand racial-cultural differences in views of the world, in thinking, and in interpersonal relationships when there is more perceived similarity. It is even more difficult in the United States, where many groups of Americans have been in the society for hundreds of years and are acculturated but not integrated into mainstream social, economic, and political institutions. Under these circumstances, discerning less obvious racial-cultural variation can be challenging. Moreover, the process of learning about and understanding racial-cultural differences conflicts with dominant American cultural patterns.[35] One way to learn about racial-cultural variation is by using what is called the typologies of difference model.[36]

The history of race in psychology and the social sciences reveals various approaches for understanding variation between and among people and groups. Effective practice for addressing RBTS must incorporate a historical understanding of the treatment of race within the social sciences, psychology, and the helping professions.

Carter and Pieterse describe the historical development of race and discuss how it is distinct from ethnicity and culture.[37] One way that most people distinguish race from culture and ethnicity is through a perception that culture and ethnicity are fluid and flexible; they can change over time, usually within a few generations. Race and the characteristics associated with it are thought to be permanent. Carter and Pieterse show how race has come to be the context for culture in the United States.[38] It is also important to understand the historical legacy of how race and culture have been conceptualized and taught in the social sciences, psychology, and related disciplines.

Said another way, a considerable history regarding race and culture must be overcome, including some beliefs that remain prominent in mental health training and practice. People are socialized with ideas about race, and they bring these assumptions into their learning. For training to be effective, these unstated ideas need to be confronted and examined. For instance, researchers have shown how people learn about race through the developmental and socialization processes. As we noted previously, people think that race is about genetics and biology rather than a social construction. Tara Mandalaywala and colleagues write:

> Evidence from multiple scientific disciplines, including genetics . . . , evolutionary biology . . . and anthropology . . . confirms that race is a socially constructed category. Nevertheless, people often think about race as if it is deterministically rooted in biology. . . . The beliefs that racial categories reflect real distinctions found in nature, and that race is an inherently meaningful part of identity, are widespread. . . . These beliefs reflect psychological *essentialism*—a set of cognitive biases that lead people to view members of a category as sharing a deep, underlying essence that causes them to be fundamentally similar to one another in both obvious and non-obvious ways.[39]

In a study of Black and White children between five and six years old and their parents, Mandalaywala and colleagues found that the children did think that skin color was inherited but did not hold essentialist views. The researchers conclude that when an essentialist view does emerge, it is because of "protracted developmental processes and require[s] ample cultural input."[40]

Many ideas about race come from what is communicated in other disciplines, such as anthropology and cultural psychology. Paul Pedersen and Juris Draguns separately describe the relationship between anthropology (the first discipline to study culture) and cultural psychology.[41] Much of the science of anthropology during the late nineteenth and early twentieth centuries was comparative. Western culture was held out as the standard for what was considered civilized and moral. Other races and worldviews were described in many instances as underdeveloped and uncivilized. Racial classifications were the primary mechanism used to make distinctions about a mature society.[42]

Carter and Robert Guthrie each note that nineteenth-century anthropologists developed racial classification systems by measuring skin color, hair texture, and lip thickness.[43] Psychology during that era was a science that studied the mind by building on biology and physics. Yet psychology as a discipline adopted the racial systems used by anthropology to explain and justify differences among human groups. Thus, early anthropological research associated with race and culture was devoted to psychological investigations that affirmed the prevalent paradigm of the times, which held that Whites were psychologically and genetically superior. The belief in White superiority and non-White inferiority by American and European scientists is well documented and was held by leading health professionals, including G. Stanley Hall, the first president of the American Psychological Association, and Louis Terman, another influential psychologist who adapted intelligence tests in the United States. Both Hall and Terman claimed that Americans who were not White were unable to benefit from education and could not be productive citizens because they lacked intelligence. Similar views were restated in the mid-1960s by Arthur Jensen, and in the 1990s by Charles Murray and Richard J. Herrnstein.[44]

Beliefs in racial group inferiority are challenged and rejected by many researchers and scholars.[45] Yet ideas based on the notion of racial-cultural differences remain influential in many spheres of American life. In the mental health professions, certain practices that produce disparities in access and treatment reflect to some degree the established belief that poor people, working-class people, and people of color cannot benefit from education, training, or treatment. Irrespective of the scientific fact that race as a biological construct is nonexistent, Marger captures the ongoing tension by stating that people continue to treat race as a biological reality and therefore attach meaning and significance to racial differences.[46] Health and mental health disparities are understood to reflect deficiencies in people of color (based on the notion of cultural deprivation and/or inferiority) rather than being attributed to the systems of racial oppression.

In describing racial inequalities in health, Margaret Hicken and colleagues state that "cultural racism . . . at once dynamically maintains structural racism over time and serves as a 'cloak of invisibility' that renders racialized and racially-hierarchical structures as racially-neutral and rational."[47] The systems of racial oppression operate in a way that masks themselves and delegitimizes those who seek to challenge them. Thus, efforts to train people to recognize these aspects of racism require considerable effort and resolve.

When language is used to refer to people of color as "disadvantaged" and to Whites as "privileged," it disregards the many factors that contribute to a person being disadvantaged, such as poverty, discrimination, and imposed social and family disorganization—factors that are presumed to determine the mental functioning of people of color rather than to be effects of external stressors. Mental health scholars propose interventions for people of color that are designed to address psychological and behavioral dysfunction. Yet such patterns of behavior are emblematic of low self-esteem, psychological distress, poor impulse control, and unhealthy expressions of anger, and the systemic structures that create these adaptive states are seldom acknowledged.

Researchers and scholars observe that the norm used to assess "cultural deprivation" was White, middle-class society, and they argue that people of color (Blacks, Asians, Native Americans, and Hispanics/Latinos) were not deprived of culture; rather, they were culturally different. The focus on racial difference was foundational to what is now called the multicultural movement or cultural competence.[48] The perspective at the beginning of the MC movement essentially held that Americans from historically disenfranchised groups who identified based on racial characteristics (i.e., skin color) had retained distinct aspects of their cultures of origin because they were segregated from mainstream American society. As immigrants of color came to the country, they, too, were often segregated, whereas White immigrants eventually were able to overcome the initial resistance to their assimilation into mainstream society.[49]

Although the notion of racial-cultural difference has replaced or is used as an alternative to the paradigms of inferiority and cultural deprivation, it is unfortunate that any of these constructs still exist in the twenty-first century—perhaps in slightly different forms but with the same messages and assumptions. The emphasis on difference continues for people of color, in the absence of an examination of White cultural patterns associated with the construction of what is considered normal and the imposition of those standards on everyone.[50]

Carter and Pieterse[51] and Carter[52] point out that race and identity, both personal and social, are intertwined. As such, race and racial identity (one's psychological orientation to race) are central aspects of human development and mental health practice and training. Carter states that "to understand racial influences in psychotherapy, one must first understand how race is integrated into personality."[53] The importance of understanding race as an aspect of personality lies in the reality of our present-day society and is shaped by our past, and each person who trains to be a mental health professional or educator has been socialized in a society where race remains an integral part of daily life.[54]

PEDAGOGICAL STRATEGIES FOR EFFECTIVE PRACTICE WITH RBTS

Various approaches are suitable for incorporating training to address RBTS as racial trauma in the core clinical competencies required of, psychologists, counselors, social workers, and other mental health and health professionals. The following discussion is guided by the content areas identified by Shelley Harrell[55] as essential for working with the effects of racism, including racial identity theory;[56] racial socialization;[57] White privilege or White-conferred dominance;[58] the history of race within psychology;[59] racism-related stress;[60] contemporary racism;[61] and prejudice reduction and antiracism strategies.[62]

DEVELOPMENT OF RACE-BASED CRITICAL CONSCIOUSNESS

Critical race theory (CRT) focuses on the oppressive aspects of society to generate societal and individual change.[63] The goal of CRT is the "transformation of social relationships through dialogues and social relations."[64] CRT provides an important vehicle by which to increase racial awareness, which is particularly important for mental health clinicians who prize the therapy relationship as the mechanism of change.[65]

In addition, scholars outline some other methods that could be used to promote racial awareness, including experiential approaches such as the Racial-Cultural Counseling Lab (a course taught to graduate students that employs didactic, experiential, and therapy simulations with a focus on race, ethnicity, social class, and religion);[66] racial engagement through intergroup dialogues;[67] active racial awareness through examining the process of socialization;[68] and racial immersion experiences to facilitate a greater understanding of individuals who are from a different racial background.[69] All these approaches aim to generate interpersonal interactions between individuals who are racially similar and those who are dissimilar for the express purpose of talking about one's understanding of their own racialized experience, both as an individual and as part of a racial group. The goal of facilitating racial awareness is to ensure greater appreciation of the way race-related interactions inform social relationships, and to raise students' understanding of how racial incidents can evoke powerful emotions, even when harm is not intended. Chalmer Thompson and Helen Neville note that to "resolve the problems that arise from racial socialization in the United States, scholars have asserted that people need to work through rather than suppress race as an integral aspect of their identities."[70] Opportunities that involve dialogue about, exploration of, and confrontation of one's experience and socialization as a racial being are critical to one's ability to appreciate the importance of race and culture in the experience of one's clients or patients.[71]

KNOWLEDGE OF RACISM AND PSYCHOLOGICAL OUTCOMES

We have underscored the need for mental health clinicians to understand and appreciate both historical and contemporary realities of racism within American society.[72] In addition to understanding how race and culture informs one's worldview, a clinician needs to understand the impact of racial oppression on the day-to-day life experiences of clients of color.[73] Effective instruction in this area includes a focus on racism-related stress and reactions such as racism-related fatigue, confusion, and frustration.[74] An understanding of the role that intergenerational trauma plays in RBTS is also essential.[75] The question is where and how to provide this type of instruction. Standalone courses are available.[76] In addition, instruction can be infused throughout training programs, including in courses on life-span development, personality, assessment and measurement, prevention and consultation, and counseling theory and practice. We think infusion works best.

KNOWLEDGE OF RACIAL IDENTITY AND RACIAL SOCIALIZATION

Josh Miller and Ann Marie Garran[77] emphasize the need for mental health professionals to understand the central role of racism in the history and development of the United States by drawing on ethical guidelines of various professional bodies that highlight extending justice, affirming the dignity of all individuals,[78] being aware of cultural values and biases,[79] and meeting the needs of and empowering those who are vulnerable and oppressed.[80]

We have addressed many of these topics in this volume; the following discussion focuses on how to include these content areas in the training of mental health professionals. As noted, content on racism and antiracism training tends to be lacking from multicultural course syllabi or from the training curriculum in general.[81] There are, however, other vehicles through which racism-related content and a focus on interventions for RBTS can be infused across a program's curricula. The social work training program at Smith College presents a comprehensive approach to dealing with racism. It offers a program-level commitment to addressing racism through pedagogy, experiential learning, and practicum placements. Indeed, the program intentionally invites applicants to engage in a struggle against the insidious effects of racism within our society.[82] Given that most training programs in the mental health professions lack this explicit commitment, we focus on how core content associated with understanding and treating RBTS as racial trauma can be infused throughout a program.

Racial socialization and racial identity theory are noted aspects of personality development.[83] As described earlier in this book, racial identity and racial socialization account for variability in perceptions of racism and the manner in which individuals are affected by racist incidents. Adding content on racial socialization and racial identity to human-development courses and teaching these constructs to clinicians as part of how to assess of a client's psychological profile are important tools for teaching about RBTS. Shawn Utsey and colleagues outline a semester-long course titled Race and Racial Identity.[84] The first class includes an assessment of the students' racial identity statuses,[85] providing a lens through which students are exposed to a range of content, including the historical aspects of racism within American society, the role of culture and worldview, the construct of White privilege, the emotional aspects of racial identity development, and awareness of racism. The racial identity frame is thought to decrease defensiveness and allow the student to understand the material on race and racism from the perspective of identity and racial identity development.

FACILITATING AWARENESS OF AVERSIVE RACISM AND BIAS

We have noted that racial aggressions are linked to symptoms of RBTS,[86] and that racial bias (i.e., prejudicial attitudes) is understood to be directly associated with racial micro- and macroaggression.[87] Furthermore, racial bias is thought to influence a mental health clinician's decision-making process and their attributions of a client's behavior.[88] Strategies to reduce racial bias are viewed as central to a clinician's development of racial and cultural competence.[89]

Structured dialogue among individuals who belong to different racial groups is offered as an important approach to reducing prejudice and increasing racial awareness.[90] Intergroup dialogue is defined as a "facilitated group experience that may occur once or may be sustained over time and is designed to give individuals and groups a safe and structured opportunity to explore attitudes about polarizing societal issues."[91] Some scholars identify various approaches to implementing intergroup dialogue within the training of mental health professionals. Brent Mallinckrodt and colleagues describe the use of intergroup dialogue within a counseling-psychology doctoral program as an approach to facilitating attitudes and action toward social justice advocacy.[92] The authors view intergroup dialogue as central to the consciousness-raising aspects of the curriculum. In a review of educational strategies to improve race relations in the areas of negative affective reactions, discrimination, stereotypes, and prejudice, Mark Engberg identifies intergroup dialogue as one strategy that shows promise based on current empirical findings.[93] Rebecca Willow, in a study of adults from various racial groups participating in a structured interracial dialogue, identifies themes of empathy, moral consciousness, and the benefits of interracial contact as emerging from the discussion.[94] Although the focus on racial bias and raising consciousness about race and racism does not directly relate to interventions for RBTS as racial trauma, it does allow practitioners to develop an understanding and appreciation of the potential role of race and racism in the lives of their clients, thereby making direct interventions potentially more effective.[95]

TEACHING ASSESSMENT OF RBTS

One of the most fundamental tasks of mental health clinicians is conducting assessments, including mental health status, evidence of psychopathology, understanding of developmental history, and identification of psychological strengths.[96] Although scholars suggest that an assessment for RBTS be included as part of the standard intake assessment,[97] typical templates for conducting assessment/intake interviews continue to omit a specific focus on trauma, whether race-based or not. In a taxonomy of trauma assessment, Ibrahim Aref Kira presents a comprehensive approach to understanding both personal and collective trauma but does not specifically identify race-based trauma as an area of inquiry.[98]

We have outlined the utility of the RBTSSS and the accompanying RBTS clinical interview in the assessment of RBTS as racial trauma. One approach to centralizing training in racial-trauma assessment is to provide trainees exposure to these instruments as part of the standard curriculum for psychological assessment. The goal here is to enhance awareness of the need to consider RBTS as racial trauma, especially when working with individuals of color. Given racial dynamics that often occur in same or cross-racial therapy dyads,[99] clients of color are likely to be less forthcoming about their experiences with race and racism, even if such experiences are their primary concern.[100] By including a focus on RBTS as a routine practice, the mental health clinician conveys to the client that issues of race and racism are legitimate topics of attention. Whether one employs an information-gathering approach or a therapeutic approach to assessment, both models allow for the insertion of race and racism. We believe that the reluctance toward doing so is primarily associated with a lack of training and a fear of discomfort.

TEACHING THERAPY SKILLS FOR RBTS AS RACIAL TRAUMA

Many opportunities within the current skills-training curricula of mental health professionals allow for a focus on race-based stress and RBTS as racial trauma. Clara Hill and colleagues describe training procedures for the facilitation of basic counseling skills.[101] Employing the helping-skills model, these authors encourage a step-by-step approach to training that teaches one skill at a time. They emphasize the need to focus first on exploration skills, which are critical to building and facilitating the counseling relationship through conveying understanding and empathy. Relational skills are identified as part of the foundational competency for mental health clinicians in the area of intervention.[102]

Given that the development of basic counseling skills is fundamental to effective practice, we believe that these foundational courses are an important place in which to develop racial competence. A focus on race and racism in counselor training elicits strong emotions.[103] Two fundamental aspects of training for novice therapists are learning to manage emotions and becoming self-aware. We argue that the training of clinicians already includes a vehicle through which therapy skills for treating RBTS as racial trauma could be developed, although these skills are not often presented within the context of race, racism, and race-related stress or trauma. Mental health trainees are taught to ask the most invasive and intrusive questions associated with very sensitive information, such as histories of general trauma, loss, and abuse. In our teaching experiences, trainees often feel more authorized asking these questions and less authorized—and indeed more uncomfortable with—asking about their clients' racial background or race-related experiences. The introductory helping-skills course allows for the normalization of racial content in the therapy process and provides a way for trainees to attend to areas of discomfort associated with discussing racial content with their clients.

THE ROLE OF CLINICAL SUPERVISION

Supervision is an important area of skill development for attending to racial trauma.[104] Effective supervision, however, requires racial self-awareness and a specific knowledge of racial trauma, including the role of intergenerational trauma, on the part of the supervisor. In addition, a willingness to talk about racial dynamics within the supervisory process is an important aspect of maintaining a strong working alliance.[105] Supervision provides an opportunity for a trainee to examine potential conflicts between their own racial-cultural worldview and that of the clients they work with as well as to confront possible biases associated with their worldview. Effective supervision can help the trainee work through the discomfort and fear associated with initiating race-related dialogues and probing a client's experience of racial trauma. Finally, in supervision, a trainee can gain familiarity with more specific interventions, such as using the RBTS clinical interview; facilitating strategies for coping with and resisting acts of racial discrimination; processing strong emotions elicited by the experience of RBTS, including anger, guilt, and shame; working with cognitive distortions to shift the focus from self-blame to a realistic understanding of the racial-based trauma as reflective of an external source of distress (i.e., "something happened to me" instead of " I did something wrong"); and employing strategies to help the client reduce intrusive thoughts, prolonged rumination, and hypervigilance, such as nonjudgmental acceptance, mindfulness practice, skills training for increasing distress tolerance, and acting opposite one's emotions.[106]

SKILLS TRAINING AND GATEKEEPING

Skills training (through both simulated and live counseling sessions) and skills assessment are perhaps the most critical aspects of development for mental health professionals.[107] In addition, several personal attributes are identified for success in the practice of psychotherapy and counseling, including cognitive flexibility and tolerance of ambiguity, emotional receptivity and well-being, and strong relational skills.[108] Both skills training and the development of these attributes have direct application to training for racial competence and effective intervention in racial trauma. Education and training of mental health professionals should therefore prioritize elements viewed as essential for overall efficacy and should also integrate the specific requirements of knowledge and awareness of RBTS. Furthermore, the gate-keeping role of educators in mental health training should be clearly outlined. If mental health trainees do not demonstrate foundational competency in skills, awareness, and knowledge when dealing with race, they should not be allowed to move forward for advanced training opportunities. Candice Presseau and colleagues demonstrate the value of such training and how it helps to promote social justice activities.[109] Finally, advanced training for intervention in racial-based trauma should include specific practicum sites where students are more likely to encounter individuals experiencing or exposed to RBTS as racial trauma.

In this chapter we have outlined the influence of worldview in the training of helping, health and mental health professionals and have called for an emphasis that prioritizes race and culture as central to the lives of all individuals. We have outlined the way that the dominant, Eurocentric approach in psychology has limited the discipline's ability to attend to systemic factors that affect the well-being of people of color. Finally, we have outlined several pedagogical strategies that could be used to more effectively respond to the stress associated with racial group membership. In our final chapter we turn to emerging areas of inquiry and areas of needed focus in the assessment and treatment of RBTS as racial trauma.

12

EMERGING ISSUES IN PRACTICE AND RESEARCH

AS WE HAVE SEEN, the literature consistently supports the finding of an adverse relationship between experiences of racism and psychological distress.[1] The focus of this volume is a specific type of stress, which we identify as race-based traumatic stress (RBTS). We have shown that the RBTS model and accompanying assessment tools (the Race-Based Traumatic Stress Symptom Scale [RBTSSS], long and short forms, and the RBTS Interview Schedule) are critical additions to mental health practice and represent important developments in the assessment and treatment of race-related stress and RBTS.[2] Given the ongoing and ubiquitous nature of racism within American society, this final chapter focuses on emerging issues in research and practice for the understanding of RBTS as racial trauma, including assessing the developmental impact of RBTS as racial trauma on children and adolescents; further differentiating race-based trauma from posttraumatic stress disorder (PTSD); incorporating the phenomenon of intergenerational transmission of trauma within our understanding of race-related stress and RBTS as racial trauma; incorporating prevention more explicitly within mental health practice; and employing novel research approaches to enhance our understanding of RBTS. We also discuss the role and place of liberation psychology, racial socialization, limitations associated with the RBTS model, and complex trauma.

DEVELOPMENTAL IMPACT OF RBTS ON CHILDREN AND ADOLESCENTS

Much has been written on the developmental impacts of childhood trauma. Scholars conceive of childhood trauma in the context of how it shapes mental representations of the physical and social worlds (e.g., instilling an idea that the world is an unsafe place),[3] and report neurobiological correlates of trauma that include structural changes in brain anatomy associated with the later development of disorders such as anxiety and depression.[4] Additionally, researchers identify the impact of trauma and adverse childhood experiences on patterns of attachment later in life, with findings suggesting that traumatic experiences may influence the quality of relationships in adulthood, including the child-parent bond.[5] Finally, exposure to childhood maltreatment and abuse is associated with a wide range of psychopathology later in life, including PTSD, substance abuse, anxiety, personality disorders, and suicidal ideation.[6]

What is conspicuously absent from the research, however, is a focus on race-related stress and RBTS and how it impacts childhood well-being and development. The Core Curriculum on Childhood Trauma (CCCT) provides a good example of this absence. The CCCT was developed as a tool for training graduate students (and practicing professionals) in foundational concepts of trauma-informed care in preparation for advanced training in specific trauma-focused, evidence-based treatments.[7] Yet, irrespective of the fact that ample evidence suggests that experiences of racial discrimination and racism influence mental health outcomes for children and adolescents,[8] the CCCT fails to mention racism, race-related-stress, or RBTS. Evidence of racism's impact on children's health include a review by Lee Pachter and Cynthia Coll of forty articles outlining positive associations in children and adolescents between racism and symptoms that include depression, anxiety, lowered self-esteem, externalizing behaviors such as conduct disorders and school delinquency, substance use, and low birth weight.[9] Pachter and Coll report that 70 percent of the articles focus on African Americans, and most of the associations are in the areas of externalizing behaviors, health symptoms, or psychological outcomes. Naomi Priest and colleagues reviewed the literature on racism and health, focusing on children and adolescents ages twelve to eighteen.[10] Seventy-six percent of studies indicate an inverse association between racism and psychological health, highlighting symptoms like depression, anxiety, and lowered self-esteem. Although these findings are consistent with the literature that focuses on the adult experience of racism and racial discrimination, it is important to note that Priest and colleagues do not review evidence of trauma or trauma-related symptoms as an outcome of racism. They identify the lack of psychometrically sound measures designed to assess the frequency and intensity of stress responses to racism among children and adolescents.

The experience of race-related stress and RBTS among children and adolescents is an emerging and needed area of inquiry. Maryam Jernigan and Jessica Henderson Daniel write, "Black children and adolescents are particularly vulnerable to race-based traumatic stress because they may not have yet developed a sophisticated cognitive understanding or the affective language with which to process the ongoing effects of racism."[11] They suggest that important areas for ongoing examination include attention to RBTS within the school environment and research examining the role of racial identity and racial socialization in providing psychological protection from the traumatic effects of racism. Given children's limited range of coping skills, the likelihood of a negative outcome associated with a traumatic event is significantly increased.[12] Furthermore, evidence suggests that childhood trauma predisposes individuals to mood- and anxiety-related disorders and personality disorders later in life. Yet race-related stress and RBTS has not been included in this body of research. In fact, the well-known Adverse Childhood Experiences (ACEs) study, which outlines adult effects of adverse childhood experiences, does not provide one reference to racial events or the experience of racism as a type of adverse childhood experience.[13]

Scholars including Andres Pumariega have encouraged the examination of historical trauma on the current life experiences of children and adolescents of color.[14] One important area of future inquiry is the application of race-based traumatic symptoms to the types of racial events experienced by children and adolescents. Understanding the mechanism through which childhood and adolescent RBTS affects neurobiological, psychosocial, and psychological outcomes is another one. Treatment recommendations that emerge from these areas of inquiry might have implications for reducing or ameliorating the adult effects of childhood trauma.

FURTHER DELINEATING RACE-BASED TRAUMA FROM PTSD

Given the criteria for PTSD and the ongoing lack of attention to race-related trauma within those criteria, a need exists to more clearly outline how RBTS both overlaps with and is distinct from PTSD. Scholars including Lillian Comas-Díaz,[15] Comas-Díaz and colleagues,[16] and Monnica Williams and colleagues[17] suggest that evidenced-based treatment approaches for PTSD, such as prolonged exposure to trauma stimuli, might have efficacy for racism-induced PTSD. Although some types of racial incidents, such as physical assault, might meet the criteria for PTSD, we argue in this volume that race-based traumatic stress is a broader construct than PTSD; therefore, applying concepts and treatments associated with PTSD to RBTS might result in both an inaccurate understanding of the RBTS and ineffective treatments.

Throughout this volume we point out that the current conceptualization of trauma (i.e., trauma as a neurobiological disorder) fails to capture the role of race-based stress in terms of both the exposure event(s) and the psychological and behavioral responses to the exposure. Even though changes in the *DSM-5* Criterion A, now include exposure to non-life-threatening traumatic events, research shows that *DSM*-informed criteria for PTSD do not include experiences of race-related stress or RBTS.[18] Drawing on a cross-sectional sample of 2,853 American adults, Dean Kilpatrick and colleagues identify the most frequent trauma exposure events as disaster (50 percent), physical or sexual assault (53 percent), and death of a close family member or friend due to violence, accident, or disaster (52 percent); most individuals report more than one category.[19] Although the sample included 689 individuals who self-identified as either Black, Native American, Asian, or multiracial, no attention was given to the extent to which any of the exposure events were race related. Additionally, when looking at responses to racial events as measured by the RBTSSS, we note that avoidance, hypervigilance, intrusion, and physical or somatic responses are consistent with the *DSM-5* criteria for PTSD; however, depression, anger, and lowered self-esteem are not. We have consistently stated that RBTS does not fit the *DSM* criteria for PTSD. We believe that the medically oriented approach to PTSD is not the best conceptualization for the effects of racism, which have been identified as an emotional injury. It is important, however, to continue to examine the extent to which the emotional injury of RBTS is associated with other life experiences such as career trajectory and work productivity, quality of interpersonal and romantic relationships, general subjective well-being and quality of life, and ongoing sense of self and self-efficacy. In this context, work by scholars focusing on posttraumatic growth[20] might also have implications for an expanded understanding of the psychological effects of RBTS by providing insights into adaptation, coping, and psychological flexibility in response to racial discrimination and racism.

HISTORICAL LOSS AND INTERGENERATIONAL TRAUMA

Another emerging area of focus that could lead to a more complete understanding of RBTS is that of historical loss and intergenerational transmission of trauma as it applies to the experience of people of color living within the United States. Michelle Sotero conceptualizes historical or intergenerational trauma as having four elements: (1) mass trauma deliberately and systematically inflicted on a target population by a subjugating, dominant population; (2) trauma not limited to a single catastrophic event but continuing over an extended period; (3) traumatic events that reverberate throughout the population, creating a universal experience of trauma; and (4) a traumatic experience of such magnitude that it derails the population from its natural, projected historical course and results in a legacy of physical, psychological, social, and economic disparities that persists across generations.[21] The genocide of Native Americans and the World War II Holocaust, which primarily affected individuals of Jewish descent, are the two historical events that have received the most attention in the empirical and conceptual literature.[22] Although the notion of intergenerational trauma has also been applied to African Americans[23] and Japanese Americans,[24] given the distinctive nature of the racially oppressive experiences each group endured, it is challenging to provide a comprehensive model of intergenerational trauma that applies to both. To illustrate, the Native American experience is defined by conquest, relocation, loss of language and culturally informed rituals, and forced assimilation.[25] The African American experience is characterized by enslavement, legal segregation, restriction of human rights, and hyperincarceration.[26] Furthermore, given the ongoing nature of structural (individual, institutional, and systemic) racism within the United States, the notion of intergenerational trauma for people of color encompasses both historical and continuing effects.[27] Laurence Kirmayer and colleagues provide a model for understanding the transmission of trauma across generations for various racial groups affected by mass trauma events.[28] It includes consideration of effects at the level of community, family, and individual.[29]

Historical loss and intergenerational trauma are illustrated by the work of Les Whitbeck and colleagues through the construction of the Historical Loss Associated Symptoms Scale.[30] The measure provides some evidence for trauma-related symptoms associated with historical loss as noted by the anger/avoidance and depression/anxiety subscales.[31] The application and adaptation of models of intergenerational trauma and historical loss to the experience of Black Americans and Japanese Americans present an important area of future research for scholars interested in RBTS.[32]

THE APPLICATION OF MODELS OF PREVENTION TO RBTS

Although scholars identify the impact of societal oppression as an important factor when calling for mental health disciplines to adopt a greater focus on prevention,[33] only within the last few decades has prevention assumed a more prominent place within psychological research and practice.[34] Partly driven by the growing appreciation of the psychological impact of life stressors and oppressive societal conditions, prevention scholars challenge the field to move beyond focusing on the individual. Sally Hage and colleagues state, "A focus on individual change, while disregarding the need for social change, minimizes the important role of the community in personal development; ignoring social structures can serve to sustain existing inequities."[35]

In this volume we represent racism as a social structure associated with inequitable experiences and outcomes across racial groups. We document how racism at all levels—individual, cultural, and institutional—is associated with adverse health-related outcomes and health disparities.[36] We also note that trauma-related disorders are influenced by race, given the higher rates of PTSD among people of color following a traumatic event.[37] For these reasons, a focus on the prevention of racism seems to be a logical area of emphasis.[38] Furthermore, because health outcomes are associated with such social phenomena as segregation and discrimination, some scholars call for racism to be conceptualized as a public health concern[39] and for public health scholars and educators to employ a greater focus on structural racism as an important determinant of health.[40] It is important to note, however, that the elimination of racism and racial discrimination has never been a focus of the public health initiatives promoted by the Centers for Disease Control and Prevention or the Department of Health and Human Services, which include vaccinations, tobacco cessation, containment of infectious diseases, nutrition, motor vehicle safety, and fluoridation of water.[41] Still, public health scholars view eliminating racism as central to the goal of achieving health equity,[42] urging federal support for policy initiatives designed to outline the effects of racism and explicate ways in which the prevalence of racism at all levels can be decreased. The prevention of racism is an emerging issue that deserves greater attention.[43]

PREVENTION OF RBTS AS RACIAL TRAUMA

The prevention of racism should be considered a primary level of activity.[44] Within psychology, the goal of primary prevention is defined as forestalling "dysfunction by reducing the occurrence of disorder, and . . . promot[ing] psychological health and well-being."[45] Research indicates that even the anticipation of discriminatory or prejudicial behavior associated with one's racial group triggers a greater cardiovascular stress response than anticipating a nonprejudicial interaction.[46] The role of prevention should be viewed as a public health necessity and should focus on a reduction in the frequency of racial events and other forms of social injustice that affect health.[47]

Larisa Buhin and Elizabeth Vera argue that the most critical area of prevention in racism is shifting attitudes and beliefs.[48] They advocate person-centered interventions whereby individuals can learn about systems of racial oppression and societal racism through interpersonal interactions in the contexts of teaching, counseling, and higher education. They believe that to target racial systems, one must shift racial beliefs that inform decisions made by policymakers as well as prejudicial and racial attitudes that shape interpersonal interactions and relationships.

Even though the mental health literature over the past few decades has focused on diversity or multicultural competence and has paid less attention to racial-cultural competence,[49] specific competence with RBTS appears to be lacking.[50] Also missing is a focus on antiracism and on interventions and policies designed to prevent RBTS and mitigate the psychological impact of consistent exposure to racism.[51] A major critique of the multicultural and diversity agenda[52] is seen in the following statement by George Dei: "The pleasant poetry of 'diversity' and 'multiculturalism' would suggest that when we learn about each other's differences, we will learn to appreciate and celebrate what might otherwise be perceived as threatening and unknowable. But these naïve interpretations of difference do not implicate power relations or internalized oppression in the equation."[53]

Reducing RBTS through intervention and prevention would incorporate the following areas of focus, as described by Simon Corneau and Vicky Stergiopoulos:[54]

- Education: Educating mental health practitioners and society at large about the ongoing presence of racism, the ways White racism continues to be supported and maintained, and the impact of racism on health and social well-being

- Empowerment: Assisting individuals who have been affected by RBTS to regain control of their lives through developing a strong racial identity and engaging in activities to challenge oppressive structures that shape their lives
- Building alliances: Facilitating partnerships across health care providers, service delivery organizations, and groups affected by racism in order both to challenge racial attitudes and structures and to provide competent interventions to individuals experiencing psychological injury as a result of racial encounters
- Language: Using language that challenges, does not stigmatize, and fosters egalitarian relationships between clients and providers. Particularly important here are the accurate application of assessment and the use of language that describes psychological distress and dysfunction in the larger social context.
- Alternative health strategies: Using healing strategies that move beyond the medical model of locating disorder within the individual and adopt a psychosocial model of mental distress. This approach allows for the incorporation of a wider range of racially-culturally informed interventions that focus more closely on mind-body interactions, spirituality, and cultural narratives of distress and healing.[55]
- Advocacy, social justice, activism: Promoting strategies that advocate for social change through the elimination of discrimination, greater inclusion of people of color as service providers and policy makers, and direct advocacy to support those in society who are "disenfranchised, marginalized, and oppressed."[56]
- Fostering reflexivity: Continually examining personal values, biases, and attitudes. For White individuals, this includes the acceptance of responsibility for racism and awareness and rejection of negative racial attitudes and behaviors; for people of color, it includes an understanding of their worldview and personal belief system and examining internalized racism or appropriated oppression.[57]

PREVENTION AND REDUCTION OF RACISM AS PUBLIC POLICY

Earlier we drew attention to scholars who view the health effects of racism as a matter of public health policy.[58] A massive volume of literature outlines the harmful effects of racism; in fact, the effect sizes associated with the relationship between racism and health[59] are similar to those associated with other well-known risk factors, such as increased soft drink consumption and obesity.[60] Obesity has been given considerable attention as a public health concern, with recommendations focused on school-based and workplace interventions.[61] Given the emphasis on collaboration for health improvement at both the national and global levels,[62] what appears to be lacking in the area of racism as a public health concern is commitment, prioritization, and urgency. For the health-related outcomes associated with racism and RBTS, we imagine an initiative that defines racism; articulates ways in which racism operates at all levels (individual, institutional, and cultural); operationalizes racism, not race, in health-related research; recognizes the disease burden and the accompanying economic toll associated with racism; and includes specific racism-related initiatives in considering funding and resource allocation. Clearly, this approach requires a significant shift in the way we conceptualize public health to center the life and experiences of people of color.[63] We agree with Rachel Hardeman and colleagues, who state that if we more consistently "acknowledge and name racism in our work, writing, research, and interactions with patients and colleagues, we can advance understanding of the distinction between racial categorization and racism and clear the way for efforts to combat the latter."[64] Although our vision for a public health initiative associated with the reduction of racism and RBTS might be viewed as naïve and idealistic, we agree with Martin Luther King Jr.'s 1968 description of injustice in health as the most shocking and inhumane of all forms of inequality. If health professionals are going to be true to their ethical mandates of beneficence, fidelity, and justice,[65] a focus on racism is a moral and ethical imperative.[66]

RESEARCH AS A TOOL FOR THE REDUCTION OF RBTS

An important tool for reduction of race-related stress and RBTS is theoretically driven and informed research.[67] The areas of focus outlined in 2012 by Corneau and Stergiopoulos[68] typically fall outside traditional approaches to empirical inquiry and therefore might suffer from a less robust evidence base. Future directions for the reduction of RBTS therefore need to focus on building a body of empirical evidence regarding racial awareness, social justice activism as a means of preventing RBTS, and empowerment-based strategies in which the targets of racism engage in acts of resistance at both individual and institutional levels. Resisting racism is an important aspect of coping with racism-related stress.[69]

Western approaches to the construction of knowledge are critiqued for employing research participants as passive observers. Research that challenges entrenched systems of domination and oppression is framed as "participatory, action-oriented, and emancipatory."[70] Action research prioritizes the voices of its participants and, in the context of oppression, allows voices and experiences of marginalized groups to be heard and seen. Brett Stoudt and colleagues write, "With roots in critical and liberation psychology, PAR [participatory action research] actively challenges traditional conceptions of objectivity by democratizing the 'right to research.' Participatory research collectives of varied expertise upend the belief that only university-based or trained researchers have the right to research and possess the tools of theoretically informed inquiry."[71] Engaging individuals and groups that endure racial oppression in the act of constructing knowledge by using their subjective experience as a central aspect of the research process is an important approach to the recognition of RBTS and is a prerequisite for racially competent care.[72] An additional approach to understanding the psychological impact of RBTS is regarding it through the eyes of practitioners who have worked with individuals reporting race-related stress or RBTS.[73] Systematically investigating racism-related phenomenon as witnessed by therapists and counselors provides a perspective of RBTS that does not rely only on self-reporting. Observational studies have been a hallmark of psychological science,[74] and this approach could afford a deeper understanding of the effects of RBTS, of coping strategies, and of acts of resistance. Interview and survey studies are also needed.

THE APPLICATION OF LIBERATION PSYCHOLOGY TO RBTS

Psychology has been critiqued for having a narrow focus on the individual and overlooking larger sociopolitical constructs that bear directly on the psychological health of individuals and groups.[75] Liberation psychology, which was developed as a model for working with oppressed communities living under the politically repressive regimes of Latin America, offers an approach to understanding and intervening in systems of oppression.[76] Geraldine Moane describes it as "an analysis of the social conditions in which people live their lives, an understanding of internalized oppression, and a set of practices or interventions that will transform psychological and social patterns associated with oppression."[77]

Liberation psychology most clearly applies to RBTS in its focus on challenging internalized representations of oppression among people of color.[78] A critical element of historical trauma is the collective loss of identity. A psychology of liberation allows collective identity to be reclaimed through recognizing oppressive practices and structures that have supported negative and harmful stereotypes of marginalized groups. Roderick Watts and colleagues apply the principles of liberation psychology to the development of critical consciousness, the process through which "oppressed or marginalized people learn to critically analyze their social conditions and act to change them."[79]

Liberation psychology promotes taking action to raise awareness of one's oppression, challenge stereotypical notions of self based on oppressive histories, engage in activism to challenge oppressive structures, and redefine one's identity from an empowerment-based perspective rather than a victim- or survivor-based perspective.[80] This shift in perspective can offer an important antidote to the symptoms of race-related stress and RBTS; it builds self-esteem that is typically diminished by RBTS and challenges the limited sense of agency associated with depressed affect.

THE APPLICATION OF RACIAL SOCIALIZATION TO RBTS

In earlier parts of this book, we address individual variation associated with the psychological impact of racism. We identify ways in which racial socialization affords a protective effect for individuals exposed to racial incidents, and we identify racial socialization as a moderating (i.e., restraining) variable in the relationship between racism and psychological distress.[81] One of the mechanisms through which racial socialization works is that of educating and preparing an individual for the likelihood of encountering racism during their lifespan.[82] In our definition of RBTS, we highlight the unexpected and sudden nature of an event as a criterion for exposure. Racial socialization may play an important role in decreasing the extent to which a racial incident is experienced as "unexpected." Think of the following situation. A siege mentality—a belief that the rest of the world has negative intentions toward you—is a type of paranoia that is inconsistent with well-being. Yet if your experience is truly that your well-being is threatened by social forces and societal structures, then your stance of viewing yourself as under siege could in fact be protective and helpful in maintaining your safety and well-being. Although this example does not perfectly capture the experience of living in a racialized society, it serves to highlight the potential role of racial socialization in providing a protective barrier against the traumatic effects of racial incidents. The concept of racial socialization has typically been applied to the Black American experience, but more recently it has been extended to other racial and ethnic groups.[83] Understanding the precise mechanism in which racial socialization counters the traumatic effects of racism is therefore viewed as an important and emerging area in the understanding of RBTS and factors that reduce or ameliorate its symptoms across racial and ethnic groups.

TOWARD A MORE COMPLETE UNDERSTANDING OF RBTS

The RBTS model is the first and only model that addresses the experience of racism from the perspective of traumatic stress. Although researchers increasingly acknowledge both the limits of PTSD in defining traumatic stress and the wide range of psychological and emotional responses associated with traumatic stress, racism-related experiences are still viewed as outside the accepted definition.[84] With an eye toward remedying this deficiency, we have described RBTS and how to measure it, and we have presented empirical evidence to support these concepts. We believe that scholars and clinicians can feel confident in using the model to further the understanding of RBTS and to inform clinical interventions and treatment approaches. Yet there may be aspects of RBTS that the model does not yet fully capture. Shawn Utsey and colleagues outline a set of what they define as acute reactions to the experience of racism.[85] The following are particularly relevant to RBTS:

- Racism-related fatigue: A type of psychological exhaustion associated with consistent exposure to racism
- Anticipatory racism reactions: A group of defense mechanisms associated with fear and threat
- Racism-related frustration: A sense of powerlessness in the face of chronic exposure to racism that results in anger, aggravation, disappointment, and lowered life satisfaction
- Racism-related confusion: A questioning of identity and meaning associated with racial events, which leads to uncertainty and lowered self-confidence

Although elements of these reactions are captured in the RBTS model, the notions of confusion and fatigue are not. Furthermore, the conceptualization of these reactions is largely built on the experiences of African Americans, and while they might be useful in understanding the experiences of other groups of color, no evidence exists to support such a conclusion. Because trauma can cast a lifelong influence on an individual's well-being, the development of a more complete picture of the way RBTS affects people remains important and urgent.

COMPLEX TRAUMA

Finally, the notion of complex trauma has been applied to traumatic experiences that are reoccurring and sustained over long periods.[86] For people of color, membership in a racial group that has endured either historical trauma or cultural dislocation influences how they respond to current and reoccurring racial events.[87] Scholars refer to this dynamic as *cumulative trauma*.[88] It is important to further develop the RBTS model to incorporate cumulative experiences of racism within the frame of complex trauma. Additional examination of factors such as adaptation, personality style, spirituality, social support, and political activism can also provide insight into circumstances that might offer psychological protection from racism-related incidents.

Those in the mental health professions have a responsibility for the health and well-being of individuals and society at large. The ongoing and persistent nature of racism within American society underscores the need to more fully understand the nature of racial trauma and to respond to it more effectively. This book represents an important step in that direction.

Appendix A

RBTSSS SHORT FORM (RBTSSS-SF)

Robert T. Carter, Alex L. Pieterse,
Carrie Muchow, Veronica E. Johnson, Corrine E. Galgay,
and Dakota Clintron

REACTION SURVEY

In the lines below, please list and briefly describe up to three of the most memorable events of racism you have experienced in your life, the setting where the event(s) occurred (e.g., school, work, store), the location where the event(s) occurred (e.g., city, state, or country), and when in your life the event took place (e.g., childhood, adolescence, adulthood, later adulthood).

Event #1: _____

_____

Setting: _____
Location (city/state): _____
Period of Life: _____

Event #2: _____

_____

Setting: _____
Location (city/state): _____
Period of Life: _____

Event #3: _____

_____

Setting: _____
Location (city/state): _____
Period of Life: _____

OF THE EVENTS DESCRIBED ABOVE, PLEASE
CIRCLE THE <u>ONE</u>
MOST MEMORABLE EXPERIENCE
AND USE IT TO ANSWER THE REMAINING QUESTIONS.

How often has this type of event occurred? (Circle one.)

Please check the box next to each period in your life when you experienced the event.

	(3–12 yrs)	(13–18 yrs)	(19–60 yrs)	(61+ yrs)
a. Only ONE time:	in ☐ childhood,	☐ adolescence,	☐ adulthood,	☐ later adulthood.
b. A FEW (3–4) times:	in ☐ childhood,	☐ adolescence,	☐ adulthood,	☐ later adulthood.
c. SEVERAL (5–6) times:	in ☐ childhood,	☐ adolescence,	☐ adulthood,	☐ later adulthood.
d. ALL the time:	in ☐ childhood,	☐ adolescence,	☐ adulthood,	☐ later adulthood.

Did you find that this event was out of your control?   ☐ Yes   ☐ No
Did you find that this event was unexpected?   ☐ Yes   ☐ No
Did you find that this event was a negative experience?   ☐ Yes   ☐ No

Using the ONE experience you described and circled above, respond to the following reactions. Read each reaction carefully and circle the number that best describes your reactions or feeling *right after the event (within one month)* and then, the best description of your reactions or feelings *more recently* when you think about, speak about, or are reminded of the event. In the third column, please circle whether or not (Y/N) *others (i.e., friends, family, or co-workers) noticed a change* in your behavior or personality following the event.

1. As a consequence of the memorable encounter I had with racism, I felt that I had nothing to look forward to.

RIGHT AFTER EVENT (CIRCLE ONE)

Does not describe my reactions	Had this reaction infrequently	Had this reaction sometimes	Had this reaction frequently	This reaction would not go away
0	1	2	3	4

MORE RECENTLY (CIRCLE ONE)

Does not describe my reactions	Had this reaction infrequently	Had this reaction sometimes	Had this reaction frequently	This reaction would not go away
0	1	2	3	4

Did others notice a change in you? (Circle one.)   Yes   No

2. As a consequence of the memorable encounter I had with racism, I feel emotionally upset when I am reminded of the event.

RIGHT AFTER EVENT (CIRCLE ONE)

Does not describe my reactions	Had this reaction infrequently	Had this reaction sometimes	Had this reaction frequently	This reaction would not go away
0	1	2	3	4

MORE RECENTLY (CIRCLE ONE)

Does not describe my reactions	Had this reaction infrequently	Had this reaction sometimes	Had this reaction frequently	This reaction would not go away
0	1	2	3	4

Did others notice a change in you? (Circle one.)   Yes   No

3. As a consequence of the memorable encounter I had with racism, I found myself getting upset rather easily.

RIGHT AFTER EVENT (CIRCLE ONE)

Does not describe my reactions	Had this reaction infrequently	Had this reaction sometimes	Had this reaction frequently	This reaction would not go away
0	1	2	3	4

MORE RECENTLY (CIRCLE ONE)

Does not describe my reactions	Had this reaction infrequently	Had this reaction sometimes	Had this reaction frequently	This reaction would not go away
0	1	2	3	4

Did others notice a change in you? (Circle one.)　　　　Yes　　　　No

4. As a consequence of the memorable encounter I had with racism, I feel easily intimidated (as if someone is going to hurt you as they walk past you in the street).

RIGHT AFTER EVENT (CIRCLE ONE)

Does not describe my reactions	Had this reaction infrequently	Had this reaction sometimes	Had this reaction frequently	This reaction would not go away
0	1	2	3	4

MORE RECENTLY (CIRCLE ONE)

Does not describe my reactions	Had this reaction infrequently	Had this reaction sometimes	Had this reaction frequently	This reaction would not go away
0	1	2	3	4

Did others notice a change in you? (Circle one.)　　　　Yes　　　　No

5. As a consequence of the memorable encounter I had with racism, I experience physical reactions (e.g., heart pounding, trouble breathing, sweating) when something reminds me of the event.

RIGHT AFTER EVENT (CIRCLE ONE)

Does not describe my reactions	Had this reaction infrequently	Had this reaction sometimes	Had this reaction frequently	This reaction would not go away
0	1	2	3	4

MORE RECENTLY (CIRCLE ONE)

Does not describe my reactions	Had this reaction infrequently	Had this reaction sometimes	Had this reaction frequently	This reaction would not go away
0	1	2	3	4

Did others notice a change in you? (Circle one.)		Yes		No

6. As a consequence of my most memorable encounter with racism, I feel a sense of responsibility for the event.

RIGHT AFTER EVENT (CIRCLE ONE)

Does not describe my reactions	Had this reaction infrequently	Had this reaction sometimes	Had this reaction frequently	This reaction would not go away
0	1	2	3	4

MORE RECENTLY (CIRCLE ONE)

Does not describe my reactions	Had this reaction infrequently	Had this reaction sometimes	Had this reaction frequently	This reaction would not go away
0	1	2	3	4

Did others notice a change in you? (Circle one.)		Yes		No

7. As a consequence of the memorable encounter I had with racism, I feel like I am immune to pain.

RIGHT AFTER EVENT (CIRCLE ONE)

Does not describe my reactions	Had this reaction infrequently	Had this reaction sometimes	Had this reaction frequently	This reaction would not go away
0	1	2	3	4

MORE RECENTLY (CIRCLE ONE)

Does not describe my reactions	Had this reaction infrequently	Had this reaction sometimes	Had this reaction frequently	This reaction would not go away
0	1	2	3	4

Did others notice a change in you? (Circle one.)   Yes   No

8. As a consequence of the memorable encounter I had with racism, I felt that life was meaningless.

RIGHT AFTER EVENT (CIRCLE ONE)

Does not describe my reactions	Had this reaction infrequently	Had this reaction sometimes	Had this reaction frequently	This reaction would not go away
0	1	2	3	4

MORE RECENTLY (CIRCLE ONE)

Does not describe my reactions	Had this reaction infrequently	Had this reaction sometimes	Had this reaction frequently	This reaction would not go away
0	1	2	3	4

Did others notice a change in you? (Circle one.)   Yes   No

9. As a consequence of the memorable encounter I had with racism, I find myself thinking about what happened even when I don't want to.

RIGHT AFTER EVENT (CIRCLE ONE)

Does not describe my reactions	Had this reaction infrequently	Had this reaction sometimes	Had this reaction frequently	This reaction would not go away
0	1	2	3	4

MORE RECENTLY (CIRCLE ONE)

Does not describe my reactions	Had this reaction infrequently	Had this reaction sometimes	Had this reaction frequently	This reaction would not go away
0	1	2	3	4

Did others notice a change in you? (Circle one.)　　　　Yes　　　　No

10. As a consequence of the memorable encounter I had with racism, I found myself getting agitated.

RIGHT AFTER EVENT (CIRCLE ONE)

Does not describe my reactions	Had this reaction infrequently	Had this reaction sometimes	Had this reaction frequently	This reaction would not go away
0	1	2	3	4

MORE RECENTLY (CIRCLE ONE)

Does not describe my reactions	Had this reaction infrequently	Had this reaction sometimes	Had this reaction frequently	This reaction would not go away
0	1	2	3	4

Did others notice a change in you? (Circle one.)　　　　Yes　　　　No

11. As a consequence of the memorable encounter I had with racism, I feel worried a lot (for example, walking down the street).

RIGHT AFTER EVENT (CIRCLE ONE)

Does not describe my reactions	Had this reaction infrequently	Had this reaction sometimes	Had this reaction frequently	This reaction would not go away
0	1	2	3	4

MORE RECENTLY (CIRCLE ONE)

Does not describe my reactions	Had this reaction infrequently	Had this reaction sometimes	Had this reaction frequently	This reaction would not go away
0	1	2	3	4

Did others notice a change in you? (Circle one.)   Yes   No

12. As a consequence of the memorable encounter I had with racism, I experienced trembling (e.g., in the hands).

RIGHT AFTER EVENT (CIRCLE ONE)

Does not describe my reactions	Had this reaction infrequently	Had this reaction sometimes	Had this reaction frequently	This reaction would not go away
0	1	2	3	4

MORE RECENTLY (CIRCLE ONE)

Does not describe my reactions	Had this reaction infrequently	Had this reaction sometimes	Had this reaction frequently	This reaction would not go away
0	1	2	3	4

Did others notice a change in you? (Circle one.)   Yes   No

13. As a consequence of my most memorable encounter with racism, I certainly feel useless at times.

RIGHT AFTER EVENT (CIRCLE ONE)

Does not describe my reactions	Had this reaction infrequently	Had this reaction sometimes	Had this reaction frequently	This reaction would not go away
0	1	2	3	4

MORE RECENTLY (CIRCLE ONE)

Does not describe my reactions	Had this reaction infrequently	Had this reaction sometimes	Had this reaction frequently	This reaction would not go away
0	1	2	3	4

Did others notice a change in you? (Circle one.)   Yes   No

14. As a consequence of the memorable encounter I had with racism, when I describe the event, I feel nothing, as if I'm not "really there."

RIGHT AFTER EVENT (CIRCLE ONE)

Does not describe my reactions	Had this reaction infrequently	Had this reaction sometimes	Had this reaction frequently	This reaction would not go away
0	1	2	3	4

MORE RECENTLY (CIRCLE ONE)

Does not describe my reactions	Had this reaction infrequently	Had this reaction sometimes	Had this reaction frequently	This reaction would not go away
0	1	2	3	4

Did others notice a change in you? (Circle one.)   Yes   No

15. As a consequence of the memorable encounter I had with racism, I couldn't seem to experience any positive feelings at all.

RIGHT AFTER EVENT (CIRCLE ONE)

Does not describe my reactions	Had this reaction infrequently	Had this reaction sometimes	Had this reaction frequently	This reaction would not go away
0	1	2	3	4

MORE RECENTLY (CIRCLE ONE)

Does not describe my reactions	Had this reaction infrequently	Had this reaction sometimes	Had this reaction frequently	This reaction would not go away
0	1	2	3	4

Did others notice a change in you? (Circle one.)		Yes		No

16. As a consequence of the memorable encounter I had with racism, I experience mental images of the event.

RIGHT AFTER EVENT (CIRCLE ONE)

Does not describe my reactions	Had this reaction infrequently	Had this reaction sometimes	Had this reaction frequently	This reaction would not go away
0	1	2	3	4

MORE RECENTLY (CIRCLE ONE)

Does not describe my reactions	Had this reaction infrequently	Had this reaction sometimes	Had this reaction frequently	This reaction would not go away
0	1	2	3	4

Did others notice a change in you? (Circle one.)		Yes		No

17. As a consequence of the memorable encounter I had with racism, I become easily pissed off (as if you can't control your temper during an otherwise normal conversation).

RIGHT AFTER EVENT (CIRCLE ONE)

Does not describe my reactions	Had this reaction infrequently	Had this reaction sometimes	Had this reaction frequently	This reaction would not go away
0	1	2	3	4

MORE RECENTLY (CIRCLE ONE)

Does not describe my reactions	Had this reaction infrequently	Had this reaction sometimes	Had this reaction frequently	This reaction would not go away
0	1	2	3	4

Did others notice a change in you? (Circle one.)　　　　Yes　　　　No

18. As a consequence of the memorable encounter I had with racism, I become easily frightened (e.g., when you hear subtle noises).

RIGHT AFTER EVENT (CIRCLE ONE)

Does not describe my reactions	Had this reaction infrequently	Had this reaction sometimes	Had this reaction frequently	This reaction would not go away
0	1	2	3	4

MORE RECENTLY (CIRCLE ONE)

Does not describe my reactions	Had this reaction infrequently	Had this reaction sometimes	Had this reaction frequently	This reaction would not go away
0	1	2	3	4

Did others notice a change in you? (Circle one.)　　　　Yes　　　　No

19. As a consequence of the memorable encounter I had with racism, I was ware of the action of my heart in the absence of physical exertion (e.g., racing heart).

RIGHT AFTER EVENT (CIRCLE ONE)

Does not describe my reactions	Had this reaction infrequently	Had this reaction sometimes	Had this reaction frequently	This reaction would not go away
0	1	2	3	4

MORE RECENTLY (CIRCLE ONE)

Does not describe my reactions	Had this reaction infrequently	Had this reaction sometimes	Had this reaction frequently	This reaction would not go away
0	1	2	3	4

Did others notice a change in you? (Circle one.)　　　Yes　　　No

20. As a consequence of my most memorable encounter with racism, I am inclined to feel that I am a failure.

RIGHT AFTER EVENT (CIRCLE ONE)

Does not describe my reactions	Had this reaction infrequently	Had this reaction sometimes	Had this reaction frequently	This reaction would not go away
0	1	2	3	4

MORE RECENTLY (CIRCLE ONE)

Does not describe my reactions	Had this reaction infrequently	Had this reaction sometimes	Had this reaction frequently	This reaction would not go away
0	1	2	3	4

Did others notice a change in you? (Circle one.)　　　Yes　　　No

21. As a consequence of the memorable encounter I had with racism, I have used alcohol or other drugs to help me sleep or to make me forget the event.

RIGHT AFTER EVENT (CIRCLE ONE)

Does not describe my reactions	Had this reaction infrequently	Had this reaction sometimes	Had this reaction frequently	This reaction would not go away
0	1	2	3	4

MORE RECENTLY (CIRCLE ONE)

Does not describe my reactions	Had this reaction infrequently	Had this reaction sometimes	Had this reaction frequently	This reaction would not go away
0	1	2	3	4

Did others notice a change in you? (Circle one.)   Yes   No

22. As a consequence of the memorable encounter I had with racism, I can't seem to get the event out of my mind even when I try.

RIGHT AFTER EVENT (CIRCLE ONE)

Does not describe my reactions	Had this reaction infrequently	Had this reaction sometimes	Had this reaction frequently	This reaction would not go away
0	1	2	3	4

MORE RECENTLY (CIRCLE ONE)

Does not describe my reactions	Had this reaction infrequently	Had this reaction sometimes	Had this reaction frequently	This reaction would not go away
0	1	2	3	4

Did others notice a change in you? (Circle one.)   Yes   No

RBTSSS–SHORT FORM: SCORING KEY

The numbers in parentheses indicate the number of items for the scale.

Depression (3) = 1, 8, 15
Intrusion (4) = 2, 9, 16, 22
Anger (3) = 3, 10, 17
Hypervigilance (3) = 4, 11, 18
Physical symptoms (3) = 5, 12, 19
Self-esteem (3) = 6, 13, 20
Avoidance (3) = 7, 14, 21

Appendix B

CARTER-VINSON RACE-BASED TRAUMATIC STRESS INTERVIEW SCHEDULE

BACKGROUND INFORMATION

1. What is your age?
2. What is your gender?
3. What is your religious affiliation?
4. What is your highest level of education, in years? *(Translate to years.)*
5. What is your annual income? You may provide me a range. (E.g., $0–$5,000; $5,001–$10,000)
6. How many people live in your household, including yourself?
7. What is your country of origin?
   If you were born outside of the U.S., how many years have you lived in the U.S.?
8. What is your ethnicity? *(E.g., American, Japanese)*
9. How would you describe your race? *(E.g., Black, White, Asian, Native American, biracial, other)*
10. How has your race affected you? For example, ... *(E.g., positively, negatively)*
11. Have you ever been treated in a way that was upsetting because of your race?

(If participant responds NO to question 11, skip interview.)

MEMORABLE EVENT INFORMATION

I'd like you to take a moment to think about three of the most memorable encounters with racism you have experienced. Think of where each of the events occurred, the geographic location, and when the events took place.

12. Event #1:
    Please tell me a little about the first event. *(Write full description.)*
    What happened?
    What was the setting of the event *(e.g., school, work, a store)*?
    What was the location of the event *(e.g., city, state, country)*?
    When did this event occur *(e.g., childhood, adolescence, adulthood, later adulthood)*?

13. Event #2:
    Please tell me a little about the second event. *(Write full description.)*
    What happened?
    What was the setting of the event *(e.g., school, work, a store)*?
    What was the location of the event *(e.g., city, state, country)*?
    When did this event occur *(e.g., childhood, adolescence, adulthood, later adulthood)*?

14. Event #3:
    Please tell me a little about the third event. *(Write full description.)*
    What happened?
    What was the setting of the event *(e.g., school, work, a store)*?
    What was the location of the event *(e.g., city, state, country)*?
    When did this event occur *(e.g., childhood, adolescence, adulthood, later adulthood)*?

Now, out of those three events, which was the ONE most memorable experience?

MEMORABLE EVENT REACTIONS

I'm going to ask you several questions about the event you chose as your most memorable.

Could you tell me more about this? Give me a little more detail? How was this event sudden? How was it out of your control? Could you describe how you felt about the incident? Was it emotionally painful or negative?

15. For the following questions, I want you to respond either "yes" or "no." Did you feel that this event was . . . (Circle yes or no.)
    . . . something you did not expect?   Yes   No
    . . . something you could not stop?   Yes   No
    . . . emotionally painful or a negative experience? Yes   No

16. How often has this type of event occurred in your life? For example, one time, a couple of times, several times, many times. (Circle one.)
    1 time   2–4 times   5–6 times   ?+ times

17. During what period of your life would you say these events occurred? For example, during childhood, adolescence, adulthood, later adulthood, or more than one period. (Circle all that apply?)
    Childhood   Adolescence   Adulthood   Later Adulthood

I would like to ask you several questions about your reactions to the memorable event you described. Think about both your reactions *immediately following* the event and your reactions *more recently when you think about the event*, and I'll ask you about your reactions in more detail.

(To interviewer: Using the following scale, try to discern frequency of reactions occurring both after the event and more recently when the interviewee is reminded of the event.)

Provide participant with the next page, which lists the response options.

As a consequence of the racial event you recalled, did you have these reactions immediately following the event, did you . . . [reaction]?

0 = No, I *did not* have this reaction
1 = Yes, but I *did not* have this reaction often
2 = Yes, I *sometimes* had this reaction
3 = Yes, I *often* had this reaction
4 = Yes, I *always* had/have this reaction

When you think about the event more recently, do you . . . [reaction]?

o= No, I *do not* have this reaction
1= Yes, but I *do not* have this reaction often
2= Yes, I *sometimes* have this reaction
3= Yes, I *often* have this reaction
4= Yes, I *always* have this reaction

DEPRESSION

First I would like to ask you questions about how this event may have affected your mood. As a consequence of the racist event you recalled, did you have these reactions?

o *No, I did/do not have this reaction*
1 *Yes, but I did/do not have this reaction often*
2 *Yes, I sometimes had/have this reaction*
3 *Yes, I often had/have this reaction*
4 *Yes, I always had/have this reaction*

18. As a reaction immediately following the event, did you feel sad? o 1 2 3 4
When you think about the event more recently or today, do you feel sad?
o 1 2 3 4

19. As a consequence of the racist event you recalled, did you have these reactions?
. . . did you feel you had nothing to look forward to? o 1 2 3 4
. . . do you feel you have nothing to look forward to? o 1 2 3 4

20. . . . did you lose interest in things you used to enjoy? o 1 2 3 4
. . . do you feel you lose interest in things you used to enjoy? o 1 2 3 4

21. . . . did you find yourself feeling tired and with less energy? o 1 2 3 4
. . . do you find yourself feeling tired and with less energy? o 1 2 3 4

22. . . . did you feel hopeless? o 1 2 3 4
. . . do you feel hopeless? o 1 2 3 4

23. . . . did you have trouble experiencing any positive feelings at all? 0 1 2 3 4
    . . . do you have trouble experiencing any positive feelings at all? 0 1 2 3 4

24. . . . did you feel you could do few things right? 0 1 2 3 4
    . . . do you feel you could do few things right? 0 1 2 3 4

25. . . . did you experience poor appetite? 0 1 2 3 4
    . . . do you experience poor appetite? 0 1 2 3 4

26. . . . did you experience difficulty in getting to sleep at night? 0 1 2 3 4
    . . . do you experience difficulty in getting to sleep at night? 0 1 2 3 4

DEPRESSION (AFTER) TOTAL   _____

DEPRESSION (RECENT) TOTAL   _____

ANGER

Now I would like to ask about how this event affected your anger.

0 *No, I did/do not have this reaction*
1 *Yes, but I did/do not have this reaction often*
2 *Yes, I sometimes had/have this reaction*
3 *Yes, I often had/have this reaction*
4 *Yes, I always had/have this reaction*

27. As a consequence of the racial event you recalled, did you have these
    this reaction immediately following the event, did you find yourself get-
    ting upset very easily? 0 1 2 3 4
    When you think about the event more recently or today, do you find
    yourself getting upset very easily? 0 1 2 3 4

28. . . . did you find that you were very irritable? 0 1 2 3 4
    . . . do you find that you are very irritable? 0 1 2 3 4

29. . . . did you find it hard to calm down after something upset you? 0 1 2 3 4
    . . . do you find it hard to calm down after something upsets you? 0 1 2 3 4

30. . . . did you find it difficult to tolerate interruptions to what you were doing? 0 1 2 3 4
. . . do you find it difficult to tolerate interruptions to what you are doing? 0 1 2 3 4

31. . . . did you become defensive when receiving feedback about something? 0 1 2 3 4
. . . do you become defensive when receiving feedback about something? 0 1 2 3 4

ANGER (AFTER) TOTAL   _____

ANGER (RECENT) TOTAL   _____

ANXIETY

Now I would like to ask you about whether as a consequence of the racial event you recalled, did the event make you anxious?

0 *No, I did/do not have this reaction*
1 *Yes, but I did/do not have this reaction often*
2 *Yes, I sometimes had/have this reaction*
3 *Yes, I often had/have this reaction*
4 *Yes, I always had/have this reaction*

32. As a consequence of the racial event you recalled, did you have this reaction immediately following the event, did you feel scared without good reason? 0 1 2 3 4
When you think about the event more recently or today, do you feel scared without good reason? 0 1 2 3 4

33. . . . did you feel terrified? 0 1 2 3 4
. . . do you feel terrified? 0 1 2 3 4

34. . . . did you find it difficult to relax? 0 1 2 3 4
. . . do you find it difficult to relax? 0 1 2 3 4

35. . . . did you find yourself in situations that made you so anxious you were relieved when they ended? 0 1 2 3 4
. . . do you find yourself in situations that make you so anxious you are relieved when they end? 0 1 2 3 4

36. . . . did you worry about situations in which you might embarrass yourself? 0 1 2 3 4
. . . do you worry about situations in which you might embarrass yourself? 0 1 2 3 4

37. . . . did you feel on edge (unable to settle down)? 0 1 2 3 4
. . . do you feel on edge (unable to settle down)? 0 1 2 3 4

38. . . . did you feel worried a lot? 0 1 2 3 4
. . . do you feel worried a lot? 0 1 2 3 4

39. . . . did you experience heart pounding, trouble breathing, or sweating when something reminded you of the event? 0 1 2 3 4
. . . do you experience heart pounding, trouble breathing, or sweating when something reminds you of the event? 0 1 2 3 4

40. . . . did you feel as though your heart was beating hard and fast, as if it might pop out of your chest? 0 1 2 3 4
. . . do you feel as though your heart is beating hard and fast, as if it might pop out of your chest? 0 1 2 3 4

41. . . . did you feel shaky? 0 1 2 3 4
. . . do you feel shaky? 0 1 2 3 4

42. . . . did you experience trembling (e.g., hands)? 0 1 2 3 4
. . . do you experience trembling (e.g., hands)? 0 1 2 3 4

ANXIETY (AFTER) TOTAL　　　　_____

ANXIETY (RECENT) TOTAL　　　　_____

AVOIDANCE

Now I would like to ask you as a consequence of the racial event you recalled, did the event affect your behaviors?

 o No, I did/do not have this reaction
 1 Yes, but I did/do not have this reaction often
 2 Yes, I sometimes had/have this reaction
 3 Yes, I often had/have this reaction
 4 Yes, I always had/have this reaction

43. As a consequence of the racial event you recalled did you have this re-action immediately following the event, did you experience reluctance to meet new people or attempt new experiences? o 1 2 3 4
 When you think about the event more recently or today, do you experi-ence reluctance to meet new people or attempt new experiences? o 1 2 3 4

44. . . . did you try not to think about, talk about, or have feelings about the event? o 1 2 3 4
 . . . do you try not to think about, talk about, or have feelings about the event? o 1 2 3 4

45. . . . did you seem to not remember some details of the event? o 1 2 3 4
 . . . do you seem to not remember some details of the event? o 1 2 3 4

46. . . . did you seem to not recall the order of the event? o 1 2 3 4
 . . . do you seem to not recall the order of the event? o 1 2 3 4

47. . . . did you find it hard to believe the event really happened to you? o 1 2 3 4
 . . . do you find it hard to believe the event really happened to you? o 1 2 3 4

48. . . . did you feel you could not talk about the event? o 1 2 3 4
 . . . do you feel you cannot talk about the event? o 1 2 3 4

49. . . . did you tend to stay away from people or places that reminded you of the event? o 1 2 3 4

. . . do you tend to stay away from people or places that remind you of the event? 0 1 2 3 4

50.   . . . did you feel cut off or distant from others? 0 1 2 3 4
. . . do you feel cut off or distant from others? 0 1 2 3 4

AVOIDANCE (AFTER) TOTAL   _____

AVOIDANCE (RECENT) TOTAL   _____

HYPERVIGILANCE/AROUSAL

Now I would like to ask you as a consequence of the racial event you recalled, did the event affect your level of apprehension?

0 *No, I did/do not have this reaction*
1 *Yes, but I did/do not have this reaction often*
2 *Yes, I sometimes had/have this reaction*
3 *Yes, I often had/have this reaction*
4 *Yes, I always had/have this reaction*

51. As a consequence of the racial event you recalled, did you have this re-action immediately following the event, did you experience trouble stay-ing asleep? 0 1 2 3 4
When you think about the event more recently or today, do you experi-ence trouble staying asleep? 0 1 2 3 4

52. . . . did you find yourself getting impatient when delayed in any way (e.g., traffic lights)? 0 1 2 3 4
. . . do you find yourself getting impatient when delayed in any way (e.g., traffic lights)? 0 1 2 3 4

53. . . . did you feel as if you were trapped or cornered? 0 1 2 3 4
. . . do you feel as if you are trapped or cornered? 0 1 2 3 4

54. . . . did you become more alert (for example, checking to see who is around you, being uncomfortable with your back to a door, etc.)? 0 1 2 3 4

. . . do you become more alert (for example, checking to see who is around you, being uncomfortable with your back to a door, etc.)? 0 1 2 3 4

55. . . . did you become jumpy or easily startled? 0 1 2 3 4
. . . do you become jumpy or easily startled? 0 1 2 3 4

56. . . . did you feel easily embarrassed (as if others knew something about you that you wished they did not)? 0 1 2 3 4
. . . do you feel easily embarrassed (as if others know something about you that you wished they did not)? 0 1 2 3 4

57. . . . did you feel paranoid (for example, when people looked at you when you walked into a room)? 0 1 2 3 4
. . . do you feel paranoid (for example, when people look at you when you walk into a room)? 0 1 2 3 4

58. . . . did you feel generally uneasy? 0 1 2 3 4
. . . do you feel generally uneasy? 0 1 2 3 4

59. . . . did you feel a need to have more control over your environment?
0 1 2 3 4
. . . do you feel a need to have more control over your environment?
0 1 2 3 4

HYPERVIGILANCE (AFTER) TOTAL _____

HYPERVIGILANCE (RECENT) TOTAL _____

INTRUSION

Now I would like to ask as a consequence of the racial event you recalled, did the event affect your thinking.

0 *No, I did/do not have this reaction*
1 *Yes, but I did/do not have this reaction often*
2 *Yes, I sometimes had/have this reaction*
3 *Yes, I often had/have this reaction*
4 *Yes, I always had/have this reaction*

60. As a consequence of the racial event you recalled, did you have this re-action immediately following the event, did you become emotional when you were reminded of it? 0 1 2 3 4
When you think about the event more recently or today, do you become emotional when you are reminded of it? 0 1 2 3 4

61. . . . did you find yourself thinking about what happened even when you didn't want to think about it? 0 1 2 3 4
. . . do you find yourself thinking about what happened even when you don't want to think about it? 0 1 2 3 4

62. . . . did you experience mental images of the event? 0 1 2 3 4
. . . do you experience mental images of the event? 0 1 2 3 4

63. . . . did you have times when you felt and thought that the event was happening again? 0 1 2 3 4
. . . do you have times when you feel and think that the event is happening again? 0 1 2 3 4

64. . . . did you find it hard to get the event out of your mind even when you tried? 0 1 2 3 4
. . . do you find it hard to get the event out of your mind even when you try? 0 1 2 3 4

65. . . . did you find that unrelated people, places, or occurrences reminded you of the event? 0 1 2 3 4
. . . do you find that unrelated people, places, or occurrences remind you of the event? 0 1 2 3 4

66. . . . did you find yourself reacting physically when you thought about, talked about, or were reminded of the event? 0 1 2 3 4
. . . do you find yourself reacting physically when you think about, talk about, or are reminded of the event? 0 1 2 3 4

INTRUSION (AFTER) TOTAL _____

INTRUSION (RECENT) TOTAL _____

COMPROMISED SELF-ESTEEM

Now I'd like to ask you some if as a consequence of the racial event you recalled, did the event affect your self-esteem?

0 *No, I did/do not have this reaction*
1 *Yes, but I did/do not have this reaction often*
2 *Yes, I sometimes had/have this reaction*
3 *Yes, I often had/have this reaction*
4 *Yes, I always had/have this reaction*

67. As a reaction immediately following the event, did you feel inferior to those around you? 0 1 2 3 4
When you think about the event more recently or today, do you feel inferior to those around you? 0 1 2 3 4

68. . . . did you feel a sense of responsibility for the event? 0 1 2 3 4
. . . do you feel a sense of responsibility for the event? 0 1 2 3 4

69. . . . did you blame yourself for not responding differently to the event?
0 1 2 3 4
. . . do you blame yourself for not responding differently to the event?
0 1 2 3 4

70. . . . did you feel less satisfied with your life? 0 1 2 3 4
. . . do you feel less satisfied with your life? 0 1 2 3 4

71. . . . did you feel you were unable to do things as well as most other people? 0 1 2 3 4
. . . do you feel you are unable to do things as well as most other people?
0 1 2 3 4

72. . . . did you feel useless at times? 0 1 2 3 4
. . . do you feel useless at times? 0 1 2 3 4

73. . . . did you feel that you were not a person of worth, at least on an equal plane with others? 0 1 2 3 4

... do you feel that you are not a person of worth, at least on an equal plane with others? 0 1 2 3 4

74. ... did you wish you could have more respect for yourself? 0 1 2 3 4
... do you wish you could have more respect for yourself? 0 1 2 3 4

COMPROMISED SELF-ESTEEM (AFTER) TOTAL   _____

COMPROMISED SELF-ESTEEM (RECENT) TOTAL   _____

INTERVIEW SCORE SHEET

SUBSCALE	AFTER TOTAL	RECENT TOTAL
Depression (9)		
Anger (5)		
Anxiety (11)		
Avoidance (8)		
Hypervigilance/Arousal (9)		
Intrusion (7)		
Compromised Self-Esteem (8)		

Notes: Raw scores need to be converted to *z*-scores—with the mean and standard deviation for the person or sample—and then to *t*-scores (*z*-scores × 10 + 50 = *t*-score).

NOTES

Introduction

1. Michelle Alexander, *The New Jim Crow: Mass Incarceration in the Age of Colorblindness* (New York: New Press, 2012); Paul Finkelman, *Supreme Injustice: Slavery in the Nation's Highest Court* (Cambridge, MA: Harvard University Press, 2018); Ibram X. Kendi, *Stamped from the Beginning: The Definitive History of Racist Ideas in America* (New York: Nation Press, 2016); Martin Marger, *Race and Ethnic Relations: American and Global Perspectives*, 10th ed. (Stamford, CT: Cengage Learning, 2015); Audrey Smedley and Brian D. Smedley, "Race as Biology Is Fiction, Racism as a Social Problem Is Real: Anthropological and Historical Perspectives on the Social Construction of Race," *American Psychologist* 60 (January 2005), https://doi.org/10.1037/0003-066X.60.1.16; Jake Silverstein, "1619 Editor's Note," *New York Times Magazine*, August 20, 2019, 4–5.

2. George Marsh Fredrickson, *The Arrogance of Race: Historical Perspectives on Slavery, Racism and Social Inequity* (Middleton, CT: Wesleyan University Press, 1988); Kendi, *Stamped from the Beginning*; Nikole Hannah-Jones, "The Idea of America: 1619 Project," *New York Times Magazine*, August 20, 2019, 14–26.

3. Lerone Bennett Jr., *Before the Mayflower: A History of Black America* (Chicago: Johnson, 1988), 86.

4. Fredrickson, *The Arrogance of Race.* 189.

5. Ibram X. Kendi, *Stamped from the Beginning: The Definitive History of Racist Ideas in America* (New York: The Nation Press), 11.

6. Bennett, *Before the Mayflower*; James Oliver Horton and Lois E. Horton, *Slavery and the Making of America* (New York: Oxford University Press, 2005).

7. Horton and Horton, *Slavery and the Making of America*; Kendi, *Stamped from the Beginning.*

8. Howard Dodson, *Jubilee: The Emergence of African American Culture* (Washington, DC: National Geographic Books, 2002); John K. Thornton, *A Cultural History of the Atlantic World, 1250–1820* (New York: Cambridge University Press, 2012).

9. Fredrickson, *The Arrogance of Race*, 193.

10. Horton and Horton, *Slavery and the Making of America*, 29.

11. Dodson, *Jubilee*; Kendi, *Stamped from the Beginning*; Thornton, *A Cultural History of the Atlantic World*.

12. Horton and Horton, *Slavery and the Making of America*.

13. Fredrickson, *The Arrogance of Race*, 204.

14. Bennett, *Before the Mayflower*.

15. Stephen Jay Gould, *The Mismeasure of Man* (Harmondsworth: Penguin, 1984).

16. Fredrickson, *The Arrogance of Race*, 205.

17. Horton and Horton, *Slavery and the Making of America*; David R. Williams and Selina A. Mohammed, "Racism and Health I: Pathways and Scientific Evidence," *American Behavioral Scientist* 57 (August 2013): 1152–73, doi:10.1177/0002764213487340.

18. Eduardo Bonilla-Silva, *Racism Without Racists: Color-Blind Racism and the Persistence of Racial Inequality in America*, 5th ed. (Lanham, MD: Rowman and Littlefield, 2017); Kendi, *Stamped from the Beginning*.

19. Fredrickson, *The Arrogance of Race*, 205.

20. Sari Horwitz and Emma Brown, "Justice Department Plans a New Project to Sue Universities Over Affirmative Action Policies," *Washington Post*, August 1, 2017.

21. E. J. Dionne Jr., Norman J. Ornstein, and Thomas E. Mann, *One Nation After Trump: A Guide for the Perplexed, the Disillusioned, the Desperate, and the Not-Yet Desperate* (New York: St. Martin's, 2017), 159.

22. Dionne, Ornstein, and Mann, *One Nation After Trump*, 160.

23. Ta-Nehisi Coates, *We Were Eight Years in Power: An American Tragedy* (New York: One World, 2017), xvi.

24. Brian F. Schaffner, Matthew Macwilliams, and Tatishe Nteta, "Understanding White Polarization in the 2016 Vote for President: The Sobering Role of Racism and Sexism." *Political Science Quarterly* 133 (Spring 2018): 9–34, https://doi.org/10.1002/polq.12737.

25. German Lopez, "The Past Year of Research Has Made It Clear: Trump Won Because of Racial Resentment," *Vox*, December 15, 2017, https://www.vox.com/identities/2017/12/15/16781222/trump-racism-economic-anxiety-study.

26. Ian Austen, "Canada to Pay Millions in Indigenous Lawsuit over Forced Adoptions," *New York Times*, October 6, 2017, https://www.nytimes.com/2017/10/06/world/canada/indigenous-forced-adoption-sixties-scoop.html.

27. BBC, "Why the Fuss Over Confederate Statues?" August 17, 2017, https://www.bbc.com/news/world-us-canada-40966800.

28. Joe R. Feagin, *Racist America: Roots, Current Realities, and Future Reparations*, 3rd ed. (New York: Routledge, 2014).

29. Michelle Alexander, *The New Jim Crow: Mass Incarceration in the Age of Colorblindness* (New York: New Press, 2012); Vanessa Williamson and Isabella Gelfand, "Trump and Racism: What Do the Data Say?" Brookings Institution, August 14, 2019, brookings.edu/blog/fixgov/2019/08/14/trump-and-racism-what -do-the-data-say/.

30. David A. Graham, Adrienne Green, Cullen Murphy, and Parker Richards, "An Oral History of Trump's Bigotry," *The Atlantic*, June 2019, 1–24.

31. Daniel Patrick Moynihan, "Employment, Income, and the Ordeal of the Negro Family," in *The Negro American*, ed. Talcott Parsons and Kenneth Bancroft Clark (Boston: Houghton-Mifflin, 1966), 134–59.

32. Isabel Wilkerson, "Our Racial Moment of Truth," *New York Times*, July 19, 2015, https://www.nytimes.com/2015/07/19/opinion/sunday/our-racial-moment-of -truth.html.

33. Jim Rutenberg, "A Dream Undone: Inside the 50-Year Campaign to Roll Back the Voting Rights Act," *New York Times*, July 29, 2015, https://www.nytimes.com /2015/07/29/magazine/voting-rights-act-dream-undone.html.

34. New York Times Editorial Board, "Ending the Cycle of Racial Isolation," *New York Times*, October 17, 2015, https://www.nytimes.com/2015/10/18/opinion /sunday/ending-the-cycle-of-racial-isolation.html.

35. Daniel Funke and Tina Susman, "From Ferguson to Baton Rouge: Deaths of Black Men and Women at the Hands of Police," *LA Times*, July 12, 2016, http:// www.latimes.com/nation/la-na-police-deaths-20160707-snap-htmlstory.html.

36. Robert Pearl, "Why Health Care Is Different If You're Black, Latino. or Poor," *Forbes*, March 5, 2015, https://www.forbes.com/sites/robertpearl/2015/03/05 /healthcare-black-latino-poor/#152a3ffa7869; Samuel Walker, Cassia Spohn, and Miriam DeLone, *The Color of Justice: Race, Ethnicity, and Crime in America* (Boston: Cengage Learning, 2012).

37. Alex L. Pieterse and Robert T. Carter, "An Examination of the Relationship Between General Life Stress, Racism-Related Stress, and Psychological Health Among Black Men," *Journal of Counseling Psychology* 54, no. 1 (2007): 102–9, doi:10.1037/0022-0167.54.1.101; Alex L. Pieterse, Robert T. Carter, and Kilynda A. Ray, "The Relationship Between Perceived Racism, Stress, and Psychological Functioning Among Black Women," *Journal of Multicultural Counseling and Development* 41 (January 2013): 36–46, doi:10.1002/j.2161-1912.2013.00025.x.

38. Elizabeth A. Pascoe and Laura Smart Richman, "Perceived Discrimination and Health: A Meta-Analytic Review," *Psychological Bulletin* 135 (July 2009): 531–54, doi:10.1037%2Fa0016059; Yin Paradies et al., "Racism as a Determinant of Health: A Systematic Review and Meta-Analysis," *PloS one* 10 (September 2015): 1–48, doi:10.137/journal.pone.0138511; Alex L. Pieterse et al., "Perceived Racism

and Mental Health Among Black American Adults: A Meta-Analytic Review," *Journal of Counseling Psychology* 59 (January 2012): 1–9, https://doi.org/10.1037/a0026208.

39. Marger, *Race and Ethnic Relations*, 19.

40. Feagin, *Racist America* 220.

41. Williams and Mohammed, "Racism and Health I." 23.

42. Robert T. Carter et al., "Racial Discrimination and Health Outcomes Among Racial/Ethnic Minorities: A Meta-Analytic Review," *Journal of Multicultural Counseling and Development* 45, no. 4 (2017): 232–59, doi:10.1002/jmcd.12076; Robert T. Carter et al., "A Meta-Analytic Review of Racial Discrimination: Relationships to Health and Culture," *Race and Social Problems* 11, no. 1 (March 2019): 15–32, doi:10.1007/s12552-018-9256-y; Nikole Hannah-Jones. The Idea of American: 1619 Project. August 20 (2019). The New York Times Magazine. Alex L. Pieterse and Shantel Powell, "A Theoretical Overview of the Impact of Racism on People of Color," in *The Cost of Racism for People of Color: Contextualizing Experiences of Discrimination*, ed. Alvin N. Alvarez, Christopher T. H. Liang, and Helen A. Neville (Washington, DC: American Psychological Association, 2016), 11–30; Pieterse et al., "Perceived Racism and Mental Health Among Black American Adults"; Paradies et al., "Racism as a Determinant of Health"; Williams and Mohammed, "Racism and Health I."

43. Robert T. Carter et al., "Initial Development of the Race-Based Traumatic Stress Symptom Scale: Assessing the Emotional Impact of Racism," *Psychological Trauma: Theory, Research, Practice, and Policy* 5 (January 2013): 1–9, doi:10.1037/a0025911.

44. Robert T. Carter, "Racism and Psychological and Emotional Injury: Recognizing and Assessing Race-Based Traumatic Stress," *Counseling Psychologist* 35 (January 2007): 13–105, doi:10.1177/0011000006292033.

1. Terms and Concepts Defined

1. Elena Schatell, "Challenging Multicultural Disparities in Mental Health," National Alliance on Mental Illness, July 10, 2017, https://www.nami.org/Blogs/NAMI-Blog/July-2017/Challenging-Multicultural-Disparities-in-Mental-He.

2. U.S. Department of Health and Human Services (USDHHS), *Mental Health: Culture, Race and Ethnicity: A Supplement to Mental Health: A Report of the Surgeon General* (Washington, D.C.: USDHHS, 2001).

3. J. Landrum-Brown, "Black Mental Health and Racial Oppression," in *Handbook of Mental Health and Mental Disorder Among Black Americans*, ed. Dorothy Smith-Ruiz (New York: Greenwood, 1990), 113.

4. Derald Wing Sue et al., *Counseling the Culturally Diverse: Theory and Practice*, 8th ed. (Hoboken, NJ: Wiley, 2019); Suman Fernando, *Mental Health, Race and Culture* (New York: Palgrave Macmillan, 2010); Paul Finkelman, *Supreme*

Injustice: Slavery in the Nation's Highest Court (Cambridge, MA: Harvard University Press, 2018).

5. Lerone Bennett Jr., *Before the Mayflower: A History of Black America* (Chicago: Johnson, 1988); James Oliver Horton and Lois E. Horton, *Slavery and the Making of America* (New York: Oxford University Press, 2005); John K. Thornton, *A Cultural History of the Atlantic World 1250–1820* (New York: Cambridge University Press, 2012); Veronica E. Johnson and Robert T. Carter, "Black Cultural Strengths and Psychosocial Well-Being: An Empirical Analysis with Black Adults," *Journal of Black Psychology* (2019): 1–35.

6. World Health Organization (WHO), "Mental Health: A State of Well-Being," 2014, http://www.who.int/features/factfiles/mental_health/en/.

7. Martin Marger, *Race and Ethnic Relations: American and Global Perspectives*, 10th ed. (Stamford, CT: Cengage Learning, 2015).

8. Chalmer E. Thompson and Helen A. Neville, "Racism, Mental Health, and Mental Health Practice," *Counseling Psychologist* 27 (March 1999): 162.

9. Robert T. Carter and Alex L. Pieterse, "Race: A Social and Psychological Analysis of the Term and Its Meaning," in *Handbook of Racial-Cultural Psychology and Counseling*, ed. Robert T. Carter, vol. 1, *Theory and Research* (Hoboken, NJ: Wiley, 2005a), 41–63; Linda Faye Williams, *Constraint of Race: Legacies of White Skin Privilege in America* (University Park: Pennsylvania State University Press, 2004).

10. Marger, *Race and Ethnic Relations*; Edward C. Stewart and Milton J. Bennett, *American Cultural Patterns: A Cross-Cultural Perspective*, 2nd ed. (London: Nicholas Brealey, 2005).

11. Hector Betancourt and Steven Regeser López, "The Study of Culture, Ethnicity, and Race in American Psychology," *American Psychologist* 48 (June 1993): 629–37, doi.org/10.1037/0003-066X.48.6.629.

12. Robert T. Carter, "Cultural Values: A Review of Empirical Research and Implications for Counseling," *Journal of Counseling and Development* 70 (September–October 1991): 164–73; Carter, ed., *Handbook of Racial-Cultural Psychology and Counseling*, vol. 1; Florence Rockwood Kluckhohn and Fred L. Strodtbeck, *Variations in Value Orientations* (Evanston, IL: Row, Peterson, 1961).

13. Marger, *Race and Ethnic Relations*.

14. Robert T. Carter, *Race and Racial Identity in Psychotherapy: Toward a Racially Inclusive Model* (New York: Wiley, 1995b); Carter, ed., *Handbook of Racial-Cultural Psychology and Counseling*, vol. 1.

15. Stewart and Bennett, *American Cultural Patterns*.

16. Schatell, "Challenging Multicultural Disparities in Mental Health."

17. Richard J. Castillo, *Culture and Mental Illness: A Client-Centered Approach* (Pacific Grove, CA: Brooks/Cole, 1997); Ethan Watters, *Crazy Like Us: The Globalization of the American Psyche* (New York: Free Press, 2010).

18. Schatell, "Challenging Multicultural Disparities in Mental Health."
19. Schatell, "Challenging Multicultural Disparities in Mental Health."
20. Arthur L. Whaley, "Cultural Mistrust: An Important Psychological Construct for Diagnosis and Treatment of African Americans," *Professional Psychology, Research, and Practice* 32 (December 2001): 555–62.
21. Lisa Dixon et al., "Variables Associated with Disparities in Treatment of Patients with Schizophrenia and Co-Morbid Mood and Anxiety Disorders," *Psychiatric Services* 52 (September 2001): 1216–22, doi:10.1176/appi.ps.52.9.1216.; Shula Minsky et al., "Diagnostic Patterns in Latino, African American, and European American Psychiatric Patients," *Archive of General Psychiatry* 60 (June 2003): 637–44, doi:10.1001/archpsyc.60.6.637.; Whaley, "Cultural Mistrust."
22. Schatell, "Challenging Multicultural Disparities in Mental Health."
23. Joshua Breslau et al., "Lifetime Risk and Persistence of Psychiatric Disorders Across Ethnic Groups in the United States," *Psychological Medicine* 35 (March 2005): 317–27; J. S. Jackson et al., "The National Survey of American Life: A Study of Racial, Ethnic and Cultural Influences on Mental Disorders and Mental Health," *International Journal of Methods in Psychiatric Research* 13, no. 4 (2004): 196–207, doi.org/10.1002/mpr.177; Schatell, "Challenging Multicultural Disparities in Mental Health."
24. Schatell, "Challenging Multicultural Disparities in Mental Health."
25. Christine J. Yeh and Carla D. Hunter, "The Socialization of Self: Understanding Shifting and Multiple Selves Across Cultures," in *Handbook of Racial-Cultural Psychology and Counseling*, ed. Carter, 1: 78–93.
26. Hazel Rose Markus and Shinobu Kitayama, "Cultures and Selves: A Cycle of Mutual Constitution," *Perspectives on Psychological Science* 5 (August 2010): 420–30.
27. Derald Wing Sue and David Sue, *Counseling the Culturally Diverse: Theory and Practice* (Hoboken, NJ: Wiley and Sons, 2016).
28. Harry C. Triandis, *Individualism and Collectivism* (Boulder, CO: Routledge, 2018).
29. Audrey Smedley and Brian D. Smedley, *Race in North America: Origin and Evolution of a Worldview*, 4th ed. (Boulder, CO: Westview, 2012).
30. Carter and Pieterse, "Race: A Social and Psychological Analysis of the Term and Its Meaning"; Robert Carter and Veronica Johnson, "Racial Identity Statuses: Applications to Practice," *Practice Innovations* 4, no. 1 (2019): 42–58, dx.doi.org/10.1037/pri0000082; Janet E. Helms and Donelda A. Cook, *Using Race and Culture in Counseling and Psychotherapy: Theory and Process* (Boston: Allyn and Bacon, 1999); Chalmer E. Thompson and Robert T. Carter, ed., *Racial Identity Theory: Applications to Individual, Group, and Organizational Interventions* (New York: Routledge, 2012 [1997]).
31. See Carter, ed., *Handbook of Racial-Cultural Psychology and Counseling*, vol. 1.

32. Helms and Cook, *Using Race and Culture in Counseling and Psychotherapy*; Janet E. Helms, "A Review of White Racial Identity Theory: The Sociopolitical Implications of Studying White Racial Identity in Psychology," in *Psychology Serving Humanity: Proceedings of the 30th International Congress of Psychology*, ed. Saths Cooper and Kapano Ratele, vol. 2, *Western Psychology* (New York: Psychology Press), 12–27.

33. Carter and Johnson "Racial Identity Statuses: Applications to Practice"; Janet E. Helms, "An Update of Helms's White and People of Color Racial Identity Models," in *Handbook of Multicultural Counseling*, ed. Joseph G. Ponterotto et al. (Thousand Oaks, CA: Sage, 1995), 181–98.

34. Eduardo Bonilla-Silva, "Rethinking Racism: Toward a Structural Interpretation," *American Sociological Review* 62 (July 1997): 465–80; Eduardo Bonilla-Silva, *Racism Without Racists: Color-Blind Racism and the Persistence of Racial Inequality in America*, 5th ed. (Lanham, MD: Rowman and Littlefield, 2017); John F. Dovidio and Samuel L. Gaertner, *Prejudice, Discrimination, and Racism* (San Diego, CA: Academic Press, 1986); John F. Dovidio et al., "Reducing Intergroup Bias Through Intergroup Contact: Twenty Years of Progress and Future Directions," *Group Processes and Intergroup Relations* 20 (June 2017): 606–20; James M. Jones, *Prejudice and Racism*, 2nd ed. (New York: McGraw-Hill, 1997).

35. Jones, *Prejudice and Racism*, 372.

36. Joe Feagin, *Systemic Racism: A Theory of Oppression* (New York: Routledge, 2006), xii.

37. Fred R. Harris and T. Wicker, *The Kerner Report: The 1968 Report of the National Advisory Commission on Civil Disorders* (New York: Pantheon, 1988); Otto Kerner Jr., *Kerner Report: The 1968 Report of the National Advisory Commission on Civil Disorders* (Washington, DC: Knopf, 1968).

38. Kerner Jr., *Kerner Report*, 10.

39. David Williams and Ruth Williams-Morris, "Racism and Mental Health: The African-American Experience," *Ethnicity and Health* 5, nos. 3–4 (2000): 243–68.

40. Rodney Clark et al., "Racism as a Stressor for African Americans: A Biopsychosocial Model," *American Psychologist* 54 (October 1999): 805, doi:10.1037/0003-066X.54.10.805.

41. Hussein Abdilahi Bulhan, *Frantz Fanon and the Psychology of Oppression* (New York: Plenum, 1985).

42. Michael Omi and Howard Winant, *Racial Formation in the United States: From the 1960s to the 1990s*, 2nd ed. (New York: Routledge, 1994).

43. Thompson and Neville, "Racism, Mental Health, and Mental Health Practice."

44. Williams and Williams-Morris, "Racism and Mental Health: The African-American Experience."

45. Marger, *Race and Ethnic Relations.*

46. Thompson and Neville, "Racism, Mental Health, and Mental Health Practice."

47. Bonilla-Silva, *Racism Without Racists*, 5th ed.

48. Helen A. Neville et al., "Color-Blind Racial Ideology: Theory, Training and Measurement Implications in Psychology," *American Psychologist* 68 (September 2013): 455–66, doi.org/10.1037%2Fa0033282; Alvin N. Alvarez, Christopher T. H. Liang, and Helen Neville, ed., *The Cost of Racism for People of Color: Contextualizing Experiences of Discrimination* (Washington, DC: American Psychological Association, 2016).

49. For example, Bonilla-Silva, *Racism Without Racists*, 5th ed.; Jones, *Prejudice and Racism*; Marger, *Race and Ethnic Relations.*

50. Joe R. Feagin, *Systemic Racism*; Joe R. Feagin, *How Blacks Built America* (New York: Routledge, 2016).

51. Feagin, *Systemic Racism*; xiii.

52. Colleen Flaherty, "More Faculty Diversity, Not on Tenure Track," Inside Higher Education, August 22, 2016, https://www.insidehighered.com/news/2016/08/22/study-finds-gains-faculty-diversity-not-tenure-track.

53. Paula Denise McClain and Jessica D. Johnson Carew, *"Can We All Get Along": Racial and Ethnic Minorities in American Politics*, 7th ed. (New York: Westview, 2018); Derald Wing Sue, *Overcoming Our Racism: The Journey to Liberation* (San Francisco: Jossey-Bass, 2003); Richard L. Zweigenhaft, "Diversity Among CEOs and Corporate Directors: Has the Heyday Come and Gone?" Who Rules America? website, August 21, 2013, https://whorulesamerica.ucsc.edu/power/diversity_among_ceos.html.

54. James M. Jones and Robert T. Carter, "Racism and White Racial Identity: Merging Realities," in *Impacts of Racism on White America*, 2nd ed., ed. Raymond G. Hunt and Benjamin P. Bowser (Thousand Oaks, CA: Sage, 1996), 1–23.

55. Sue, *Overcoming Our Racism*, 34.

56. McClain and Carew, *"Can We All Get Along*," 291.

57. Elizabeth Brondolo et al., "Racism and Mental Health: Examining the Link Between Racism and Depression from a Social Cognitive Perspective," in *The Cost of Racism for People of Color: Contextualizing Experiences of Discrimination*, ed. Alvin N. Alvarez, Christopher T. H. Liang, and Helen A. Neville (Washington, DC: American Psychological Association, 2016), 109.

58. Jones and Carter, "Racism and White Racial Identity," 3.

59. David Williams and Selina Mohammed, "Racism and Health I: Pathways and Scientific Evidence," *American Behavioral Scientist* 57 (August 2013): 1153, doi:10.1177/0002764213487340.

60. Robert T. Carter, "Racism and Psychological and Emotional Injury: Recognizing and Assessing Race-Based Traumatic Stress," *Counseling Psychologist* 35 (January 2007): 13–105, doi:10.1177/0011000006292033.
61. Shelley Taylor, *Health Psychology*, 9th ed. (Boston: McGraw-Hill, 2015).
62. Bruce P. Dohrenwend, "Toward a Typology of High-Risk Major Stressful Events and Situations in Posttraumatic Stress Disorder and Related Psychopathology," *Psychological Injury and Law* 3 (June 2010): 89–99; Ronald C. Kessler, "The Effects of Stressful Life Events on Depression," *Annual Review of Psychology* 48 (February 1997): 191–214; Peggy A. Thoits, "Stress and Health: Major Findings and Policy Implications," *Journal of Health and Social Behavior* 51 (October 2010): S41–S53.

2. Understanding Reactions to Stress

1. Peggy A. Thoits, "Stress and Health: Major Findings and Policy Implications," *Journal of Health and Social Behavior* 51, no. 1 (2010): S41–S53.
2. Yin Paradies, "A Systematic Review of Empirical Research on Self-Reported Racism and Health," *International Journal of Epidemiology* 35, no. 4 (2006): 888–901; Tanja C. Link and Carrie B. Oser, "The Role of Stressful Life Events and Cultural Factors on Criminal Thinking Among African American Women Involved in the Criminal Justice System," *Criminal Justice and Behavior* 45 (January 2018): 8–30.
3. Shelley Taylor, *Health Psychology*, 9th ed. (Boston: McGraw-Hill, 2015).
4. Edward Sarafino and Timothy Smith, *Health Psychology: Biopsychosocial Interactions*, 8th ed. (Hoboken, NJ: Wiley, 2014).
5. Taylor, *Health Psychology*, 113.
6. Sarafino and Smith, *Health Psychology*.
7. Richard S. Lazarus and Susan Folkman, *Stress, Appraisal, and Coping* (New York: Springer, 1984), 22–24.
8. Susan Folkman, "Stress: Appraisal and Coping," in *Encyclopedia of Behavioral Medicine*, ed. Marc D. Gellman and J. Rick Turner (New York: Springer, 2013), 1913–15.
9. Sarafino and Smith, *Health Psychology*, 60.
10. Shelley E. Taylor, "Mechanisms Linking Early Life Stress to Adult Health Outcomes," *Proceedings of the National Academy of Sciences* 107, no. 19 (2010): 8507–12.
11. Taylor, *Health Psychology*.
12. Taylor, *Health Psychology*, 117.
13. Suzanne Pieper et al., "Prolonged Cardiac Effects of Momentary Assessed Stressful Events and Worry Episodes," *Psychosomatic Medicine* 72 (2010): 570–707.

14. Paolo Palatini and Stevo Julius, "Heart Rate and the Cardiovascular Risk," *Journal of Hypertension* 15, no. 1 (1997): 3–17.

15. Marianne Frankenhaeuser, "A Psychobiological Framework for Research on Human Stress and Coping," in *Dynamics of Stress*, ed. Mortimer H. Appley and Richard A. Trumbull (Boston: Springer, 1986), 101–16.

16. Suzanne C. Segerstrom et al., "Pause and Plan: Self-Regulation and the Heart," in *How Motivation Affects Cardiovascular Response: Mechanism and Applications*, ed. Rex A. Wright and Guido H. E. Gendolla (New York: American Psychological Association, 2012), 181–98.

17. Julian Thayer et al., "Heart Rate Variability, Prefrontal Neural Function, and Cognitive Performance: The Neurovisceral Integration Perspective on Self-Regulation, Adaptation, and Health," *Annals of Behavioral Medicine* 37 (April 2009): 141–53, doi:10.1007/s12160-009-9101-z.

18. Susan Folkman and Richard S. Lazarus, "The Relationship Between Coping and Emotion: Implications for Theory and Research," *Social Science and Medicine* 26, no. 3 (1988): 309–17; Richard S. Lazarus, *Stress and Emotion: A New Synthesis* (New York: Springer, 2006), 86–90.

19. Ilan H. Meyer, Sharon Schwartz, and David M. Frost, "Social Patterning of Stress and Coping: Does Disadvantaged Social Statuses Confer More Stress and Fewer Coping Resources?" *Social Science and Medicine* 67 (August 2008): 368–79; R. Jay Turner and William R. Avison, "Status Variations in Stress Exposure: Implications for the Interpretation of Research on Race, Socioeconomic Status, and Gender," *Journal of Health and Social Behavior* 44 (December 2003): 488–505, http://www.jstor.org/stable/1519795.

20. Elizabeth Brondolo et al., "Racism as a Psychosocial Stressor," in *Handbook of Stress Science: Biology, Psychology, and Health*, ed. Richard J. Contrada and Andrew Baum (New York: Springer, 2011), 167–84; Tarani Chandola and Michael G. Marmot, "Socioeconomic Status and Stress," in *Handbook of Stress Science: Biology, Psychology and Health*, ed. Richard J. Contrada and Andrew Baum (New York: Springer, 2011), 185–95.

21. Brondolo et al., "Racism as a Psychosocial Stressor."

22. Gregory E. Miller et al., "Low Early-Life Social Class Leaves a Biological Residue Manifested by Decreased Glucocorticoid and Increased Proinflammatory Signaling," *PNAS Proceedings of the National Academy of Sciences of the United States of America* 106, no. 34 (2009): 14716–721, doi:10.1073/pnas.0902971106.

23. Sarafino and Smith, *Health Psychology*, 68; see also Naomi I. Eisenberger, "The Neural Bases of Social Pain: Evidence for Shared Representations with Physical Pain," *Psychosomatic Medicine* 74, no. 2 (February–March 2012): 126–35, doi.org/10.1097/PSY.0b013e3182464dd1.

24. Nayeli Y. Chavez-Dueñas et al., "Healing Ethno-Racial Trauma in Latinx Immigrant Communities: Cultivating Hope, Resistance, and Action," *American*

Psychologist 74, no. 1 (2019): 49–62; Shelley P. Harrell, "A Multidimensional Conceptualization of Racism-Related Stress: Implications for the Well-Being of People of Color," *American Journal of Orthopsychiatry* 70, no. 1 (2000): 42–57, doi.org/10.1037/h0087722; Donna K. Nagata, Jacqueline H. J. Kim, and Kaidi Wu, "The Japanese American Wartime Incarceration: Examining the Scope of Racial Trauma," *American Psychologist* 74, no. 1 (2019): 36–48.

25. Monica C. Skewes and Arthur W. Blume, "Understanding the Link Between Racial Trauma and Substance Use Among American Indians," *American Psychologist* 74, no. 1 (2019): 88–100; Taylor, *Health Psychology*.

26. Ronald C. Kessler, "The Effects of Stressful Life Events on Depression," *Annual Review of Psychology* 48, no. 1 (1997): 191–214; Kimberly A. Bell et al., "Emotional Response to Perceived Racism and Nocturnal Heart Rate Variability in Young Adult African Americans," *Journal of Psychosomatic Research* 121 (2019): 88–92; Tse-Chuan Yang and Danhong Chen, "A Multi-Group Path Analysis of the Relationship Between Perceived Racial Discrimination and Self-Rated Stress: How Does It Vary Across Racial/Ethnic Groups?" *Ethnicity and Health* 23, no. 3 (2018): 249–75.

27. Tyan Parker Dominguez et al., "Racial Difference in Birth Outcomes: The Role of General, Pregnancy, and Racism Stress," *Health Psychology* 27 (2008): 194–203, doi.org/10.1037/0278-6133.27.2.194.; Sierra E. Carter et al., "The Effect of Early Discrimination on Accelerated Aging Among African Americans," *Health Psychology* (advance online publication, 2019),http://dx.doi.org.tc.idm.oclc.org/10.1037/hea0000788; Bridget Goosby, Jacob Cheadle, and Mitchell Colter, "Stress-Related Biosocial Mechanisms of Discrimination and African American Health Inequities," *Annual Review of Sociology* 44, no. 1 (2018): 319–40.

28. Shawn O. Utsey et al., "Cultural, Sociofamilial, and Psychological Resources that Inhibit Psychological Distress in African Americans Exposed to Stressful Life Events and Race-Related Stress," *Journal of Counseling Psychology* 13 (January 2008): 49–62, doi:10.1037/0022-0167.55.1.49.

29. David Williams, "Stress and the Mental Health of Populations of Color: Advancing Our Understanding of Race-Related Stressors," *Journal of Health and Social Behavior* 59, no. 4 (2018): 466–85.

30. Michelle J. Sternthal, Natalie Slopen, and David R. Williams, "Racial Disparities in Health: How Much Does Stress Really Matter?" *Du Bois Review* 8, no. 1 (2011): 95–113.

31. Robert T. Carter, Veronica E. Johnson, Katherine Kirkinis, Katheryn Roberson, Carrie Muchow, and Corinne Galgay, "A Meta-Analytic Review of Racial Discrimination: Relationships to Health and Culture." *Race and Social Problems* 11, no. 1 (March 2019): 15–32. doi.org/10.1007/s12552-018-9256-y; Darlene Lu, Julie R. Palmer, Lynn Rosenberg, Alexandra E. Shields, Esther H. Orr, Immaculata Devivo, and Yvette C Cozier, "Perceived Racism in Relation to Telomere

Length Among African American Women in the Black Women's Health Study," *Annals of Epidemiology* (2019), doi.org/10.1016/j.annepidem.2019.06.003.

32. Thoits, "Stress and Health," S49.

33. Fran H. Norris et al., "60,000 Disaster Victims Speak: Part I. an Empirical Review of the Empirical Literature, 1981–2001," *Psychiatry* 65, no. 3 (2002): 207–39; Nicholas J. Sibrava et al., "Posttraumatic Stress Disorder in African American and Latinx Adults: Clinical Course and the Role of Racial and Ethnic Discrimination," *American Psychologist* 74, no. 1 (2019): 101–16; Monnica T. Williams et al., "Assessing Racial Trauma Within a DSM-5 Framework: The UConn Racial/Ethnic Stress and Trauma Survey," *Practice Innovations* 3, no. 4 (2018): 242–60, doi.org/10.1037/pri0000076.

34. Thema Bryant-Davis, "The Cultural Context of Trauma Recovery: Considering the Posttraumatic Stress Disorder Practice Guideline and Intersectionality," *Psychotherapy* 56, no. 3 (2019): 400–408.

35. See Bruce P. Dohrenwend, "Inventorying Stressful Life Events as Risk Factors for Psychopathology: Toward Resolution of the Problem of Intra-Category Variability," *Psychological Bulletin* 132, no. 3 (May 2006): 477–95.

36. Taylor, *Health Psychology*.

37. Brian D. Smedley, Adrienne Y. Stith, and Alan R. Nelson, ed., *Unequal Treatment: Confronting Racial and Ethnic Disparities in Health Care* (Washington, DC: National Academies Press, 2003).

38. Substance Abuse and Mental Health Services Administration (SAMHSA), *Racial/Ethnic Differences in Mental Health Service Use Among Adults* (Washington, DC: SAMHSA, 2015).

39. U.S. Department of Health and Human Services (USDHHS), *Mental Health: Culture, Race and Ethnicity: A Supplement to Mental Health: A Report of the Surgeon General* (Washington, DC: USDHHS, 2001).

40. For example, Aisha N. Griffith, Noelle M. Hurd, and Saida B. Hussain. "'I Didn't Come to School for This': A Qualitative Examination of Experiences with Race-Related Stressors and Coping Responses Among Black Students Attending a Predominantly White Institution," *Journal of Adolescent Research* 34, no. 2 (2019): 115–139; Ronald L. Simons, Man-Kit Lei, Steven R. H. Beach, Ashley B. Barr, Leslie G. Simons, Frederick X. Gibbons, and Robert A. Philibert, "Discrimination, Segregation, and Chronic Inflammation: Testing the Weathering Explanation for the Poor Health of Black Americans," *Developmental Psychology* 54, no. 10 (2018): 1993–2006, search.proquest.com/docview/2155147166/; David R. Williams and Selina A. Mohammed, "Racism and Health I: Pathways and Scientific Evidence," *American Behavioral Scientist* 57, no. 8 (2013): 1152–73, doi:10.1177/0002764213487340.

41. Lazarus and Folkman, *Stress, Appraisal, and Coping*, 21.

42. American Psychiatric Association, *Diagnostic and Statistical Manual of Mental Disorders*, 5th ed. (Washington, DC: American Psychiatric Association, 2013), 271.

43. Eve B. Carlson, *Trauma Assessments: A Clinician's Guide* (New York: Guilford Press, 1997).

44. Eve B. Carlson and Constance J. Dalenberg, "A Conceptual Framework for the Impact of Traumatic Experiences," *Trauma, Violence, and Abuse* 1, no. 1 (2000): 4–28.

45. For example, Thema Bryant-Davis and Carlota Ocampo, "Racist-Incident-Based Trauma," *Counseling Psychologist* 33, no. 4 (2005a): 479–500; Robert T. Carter et al., "Racial Discrimination and Race-Based Traumatic Stress: An Exploratory Investigation," in *Handbook of Racial-Cultural Psychology and Counseling*, vol. 2, *Training and Practice*, ed. Robert T. Carter (Hoboken, NJ: Wiley, 2005), 447–76; Robert T. Carter, "Racism and Psychological and Emotional Injury: Recognizing and Assessing Race-Based Traumatic Stress," *Counseling Psychologist* 35, no. 1 (2007): 13–105, doi:10.1177/0011000006292033; Raymond Monsour Scurfield and David W. Mackey, "Racism, Trauma and Positive Aspects of Exposure to Race-Related Experiences: Assessment and Treatment Implications," *Journal of Ethnic and Cultural Diversity in Social Work* 10, no. 1 (2001): 23–47.

46. J. Gayle Beck and Denise M. Sloan, *The Oxford Handbook of Traumatic Stress Disorders* (New York: Oxford University Press, 2012); H. Rutherford Turnbull III and Ann P. Turnbull, *Free Appropriate Public Education: The Law and Children with Disabilities*, 5th ed. (Denver, CO: Love, 1998).

47. Judith Lewis Herman, *Trauma and Recovery: The Aftermath of Violence from Domestic Abuse to Political Terror* (New York: Basic Books, 1992).

48. Turnbull and Turnbull, *Free Appropriate Public Education: The Law and Children with Disabilities* (Denver: Love Publishing, 1998).

49. M. L. Boone, D. W. Neumeister, and C. L. Charney, "Trauma," *Trauma and Disaster Responses and Management*, ed. Robert J. Ursano and Ann E. Norwood, 1–30, *Review of Psychiatry Series* 22, no. 1 (Washington, DC: American Psychiatric Publishing, 2003), 7.

50. Beck and Sloan, *The Oxford Handbook of Traumatic Stress Disorders*.

51. John P. Wilson and Terence Martin Keane, *Assessing Psychological Trauma and PTSD*, 2nd ed. (New York: Guilford, 2004).

52. See American Psychiatric Association, *Diagnostic and Statistical Manual of Mental Disorders* (1987, 1994, 2000, 2013).

53. American Psychiatric Association, *Diagnostic and Statistical Manual of Mental Disorders*, 5th ed., 271.

54. American Psychiatric Association, *Diagnostic and Statistical Manual of Mental Disorders*, 5th ed.

55. Nnamdi Pole, Laurie Fields, and Wendy D'Andrea, "Stress and Trauma Disorders," in APA *Handbook of Clinical Psychology*, vol. 4, *Psychopathology and Health*, ed. John C. Norcross, Gary R. VandenBos, and Donald K. Freedheim (Washington, DC: American Psychological Association, 2016), 99.

56. Robert T. Carter, "Racism and Psychological and Emotional Injury: Recognizing and Assessing Race-Based Traumatic Stress," *Counseling Psychologist* 35, no. 1 (2007): 13–105, doi:10.1177/0011000006292033.

57. Herman, *Trauma and Recovery*.

58. Thema Bryant-Davis and Carlota Ocampo, "Racist-Incident-Based Trauma," *Counseling Psychologist* 33, no. 4 (2005): 479–500; Bryant-Davis, "The Cultural Context of Trauma Recovery," 400–408.

59. M. Williams et al., "Assessing Racial Trauma Within a DSM-5 Framework."

60. Andrea L. Roberts et al., "The Stressor Criterion for Posttraumatic Stress Disorder: Does It Matter?" *Journal of Clinical Psychiatry* 73 (2012): 269, doi:10.4088/JCP.11m07054.

61. Pole, Fields, and D'Andrea, "Stress and Trauma Disorders," 98–99.

62. Gilbert Singletary, "Beyond PTSD: Black Male Fragility in the Context of Trauma," *Journal of Aggression, Maltreatment, and Trauma* (2019), doi.org/10.1080/10926771.2019.1600091.

63. Samantha C. Holmes, Vanessa C. Facemire, and Alexis M. DaFonseca, "Expanding Criterion A for Posttraumatic Stress Disorder: Considering the Deleterious Impact of Oppression," *Traumatology* 22, no. 4 (2016): 315–16.

64. John. C. Norcross and Bruce E. Wampold, "Relationships and Rresponsiveness in the Psychological Treatment of Trauma: The Tragedy of the APA Clinical Practice Guideline," *Psychotherapy* (advance online publication 2019), http://dx.doi.org/10.1037/pst0000228.

65. Fran H. Norris, "Epidemiology of Trauma Frequency and Impact of Different Potentially Traumatic Events on Different Demographic Groups," *Journal of Consulting and Clinical Psychology* 60, no. 3 (1992): 409–18.

66. Norris, "Epidemiology of Trauma Frequency," 409.

67. Carlson, *Trauma Assessments*, 28

68. Herman, *Trauma and Recovery*; Pole, Fields, and D'Andrea, "Stress and Trauma Disorders."

69. Beck and Sloan, *The Oxford Handbook of Traumatic Stress Disorders*; Zuleka Henderson, "In Their Own Words: How Black Teens Define Trauma," *Journal of Child and Adolescent Trauma* 12 (2019): 141–51, doi.org/10.1007/s40653-017-0168-6.

70. Carlson, *Trauma Assessments*, 5-6

71. Carlson, *Trauma Assessments*, 29.

72. Lazarus and Folkman, *Stress, Appraisal, and Coping*.

73. Carlson, *Trauma Assessments*, 32.

74. See Carlson, *Trauma Assessments*, 36

75. David R. Williams and Harold Neighbors, "Racism, Discrimination and Hypertension: Evidence and Needed Research," *Ethnicity and Disease* 11 (2001): 800–16; Rebecca Rangel Campón and Robert T. Carter, "The Appropriated Racial Oppression Scale: Development and Preliminary Validation," *Cultural Diversity and Ethnic Minority Psychology* 21, no. 4 (2015): 497–506, http://dx.doi.org/10.1037/cdp0000037; Suzette L. Speight, "Internalized Racism: One More Piece of the Puzzle," *Counseling Psychologist* 35, no. 1 (2007): 126–34.

76. Williams and Neighbors, "Racism, Discrimination and Hypertension," 112.

77. Carlson, *Trauma Assessments*, 37.

78. Williams and Mohammed, "Racism and Health I."

79. Herman, *Trauma and Recovery*, 121

80. Robert T. Carter et al., "A Meta-Analytic Review of Racial Discrimination: Relationships to Health and Culture," *Race and Social Problems* 11, no. 1 (March 2019): 15–32, doi.org/10.1007/s12552-018-9256-y; Robert T. Carter and Veronica E. Johnson, "Racial Identity Statuses: Applications to Practice," *Practice Innovations* 4, no. 1 (2019): 42–58, dx.doi.org/10.1037/pri0000082; Jessica Forsyth and Robert T. Carter, "The Development and Preliminary Validation of the Racism-Related Coping Scale," *Psychological Trauma: Theory, Policy, Research, and Practice* 6, no. 6 (2014): 632–43, doi.org/10.1037/a0036702.2014; Veronica Elaine Johnson, "Testing a Model of Black Cultural Strength Using Structural Equation Modeling" (PhD diss., Teachers College, Columbia University, 2017).

81. Henderson, "In Their Own Words"; Julia L. Perilla, Fran H. Norris, and Evelyn A. Lavizzo, "Ethnicity, Culture, and Disaster Response: Identifying and Explaining Ethnic Differences in PTSD Six Months After Hurricane Andrew," *Journal of Social and Clinical Psychology* 21, no. 1 (2002): 20–45; Andrea L. Roberts et al., "Race/Ethnic Differences in Exposure to Traumatic Events, Development of Post-Traumatic Stress Disorder, and Treatment-Seeking for Post-Traumatic Stress Disorder in the United States," *Psychological Medicine* 41, no. 1 (2011): 71–83; Williams et al., "Assessing Racial Trauma Within a DSM-5 Framework."

82. Hugh F. Butts, "The Black Mask of Humanity: Racial/Ethnic Discrimination and Post-Traumatic Stress Disorder," *Journal of the American Academy of Psychiatry and the Law* 30, no. 3 (2002): 336–39.

3. Redefining Racism

1. Nancy Krieger, "Discrimination and Health Inequities," *International Journal of Health Services* 44 (2014): 643–710, doi.org/10.2190/HS.44.4.b.

2. Rodney Clark et al., "Racism as a Stressor for African Americans: A Biopsychosocial Model," *American Psychologist* 54, no. 10 (1999): 805–16, doi:10.1037/0003-066X.54.10.805.

3. Nnamdi Pole, Laurie Fields, and Wendy D'Andrea, "Stress and Trauma Disorders," in APA *Handbook of Clinical Psychology*, vol. 4, *Psychopathology and Health*, ed. John C. Norcross, Gary R. VandenBos, and Donald K. Freedheim (Washington, DC: American Psychological Association, 2016), 97–133.

4. David R. Williams et al., "Research on Discrimination and Health: An Exploratory Study of Unresolved Conceptual and Measurement Issues," *American Journal of Public Health* 102 (2012): 975–78, doi.org/10.2105/AJPH.2012.300702.

5. David R. Williams, "Stress and the Mental Health of Populations of Color: Advancing Our Understanding of Race-Related Stressors," *Journal of Health and Social Behavior* 59, no. 4 (2018): 1153.

6. American Psychological Association, *Stress in America: The Impact of Discrimination: Stress in America Survey* (Washington, DC: American Psychological Association, 2016).

7. Shervin Assari, Frederick X. Gibbons, and Ronald L. Simons, "Perceived Discrimination Among Black Youth: An 18-Year Longitudinal Study," *Behavioral Sciences* 8, no. 5 (April 2018): 44.

8. See Rahshida Atkins, "Instruments Measuring Perceived Racism/Racial Discrimination: Review and Critique of Factor Analytic Techniques," *International Journal of Health Services* 44, no. 4 (2014): 711–34; Nancy R. Kressin, Kristal L. Raymond, and Meredith Manze, "Perceptions of Race/Ethnicity–Based Discrimination: A Review of Measures and Evaluation of Their Usefulness for the Health Care Setting," *Journal of Health Care for the Poor and Underserved* 19 (2008): 697–730, doi.org/10.1353/hpu.0.0041; Joao Luiz Bastos et al., "Racial Discrimination and Health: A Systematic Review of Scales with a Focus on Their Psychometric Properties," *Social Science and Medicine* 70, no. 7 (2010): 1091–99.

9. Robert T. Carter, "Racism and Psychological and Emotional Injury: Recognizing and Assessing Race-Based Traumatic Stress," *Counseling Psychologist* 35, no. 1 (2007): 13–105, doi:10.1177/0011000006292033; Robert T. Carter et al., "Race-Based Traumatic Stress Symptom Scale and White Americans: Construct Validity," unpublished manuscript, 2018; Robert T. Carter and Veronica E. Johnson, "Racial Identity Statuses: Applications to Practice," *Practice Innovations* 4, no. 1 (2019): 42–58, dx.doi.org/10.1037/pri0000082; Sumie Okazaki, "Impact of Racism on Ethnic Minority Mental Health," *Perspectives on Psychological Science* 4, no. 1 (2009): 103–7, doi.org/10.1111/j.1745-6924.2009.01099.x; Yin Paradies et al., "Racism as a Determinant of Health: A Systematic Review and Meta-Analysis," *PloS one* 10, no. 9 (2015): 1–48, doi:10.137/journal.

pone.0138511; Nicholas J. Sibrava et al., "Posttraumatic Stress Disorder in African American and Latinx Adults: Clinical Course and the Role of Racial and Ethnic Discrimination," *American Psychologist* 74, no. 1 (2019): 101–16; Gilbert Singletary, "Beyond PTSD: Black Male Fragility in the Context of Trauma," *Journal of Aggression, Maltreatment, and Trauma* (2019), https://doi.org/10.1080 /10926771.2019.1600091; David R. Williams, Harold W. Neighbors, and James S. Jackson, "Racial/Ethnic Discrimination and Health: Findings from Community Studies," *American Journal of Public Health* 93, no. 2 (2003): 200–8, doi.org/10.2105/AJPH.93.2.200.

10. Yvette C. Cozier et al., "Perceived Racism in Relation to Weight Change in the Black Women's Health Study," *Annals of Epidemiology* 19, no. 6 (2009): 379, doi.org/10.1016/j.annepidem.2009.01.008.

11. Stephen L. Buka, "Disparities in Health Status and Substance Use: Ethnicity and Socioeconomic Factors," *Public Health Reports* 117 (2002): 118–25; Frederick X. Gibbons et al., "Exploring the Link Between Racial Discrimination and Substance Use: What Mediates? What Buffers?" *Journal of Personality and Social Psychology* 99 (2010): 785–801, doi.org/10.1037%2Fa0019880.

12. Luisa N. Borrell et al., "Self-Reported Racial Discrimination and Substance Use in the Coronary Artery Risk Development in Adults Study," *American Journal of Epidemiology* 166, no. 9 (2007): 1069, doi.org/10.1093/aje/kwm180; Carter et al., "Race-Based Traumatic Stress Symptom Scale and White Americans: Construct Validity"; Hannah L. F. Cooper et al., "Residential Segregation and Injection Drug Use Prevalence Among Black Adults in US Metropolitan Areas," *American Journal of Public Health* 97, no. 2 (2007): 344–52, doi.org/10.2105 /AJPH.2005.074542; Frederick X. Gibbons et al., "Perceived Discrimination and Substance Use in African American Parents and Their Children: A Panel Study," *Journal of Personality and Social Psychology* 86, no. 4 (2004): 517–29, doi.org/10.1037/0022-3514.86.4.517.

13. A. B. de Castro, Gilbert C. Gee, and David T. Takeuchi, "Job-Related Stress and Chronic Health Conditions Among Filipino Immigrants," *Journal of Immigrant and Minority Health* 10 (2008): 551–58, doi.org/10.1007/s10903-008-9138-2.

14. Rebecca Din-Dzietham et al., "Perceived Stress Following Race-Based Discrimination at Work Is Associated with Hypertension in African Americans: The Metro Atlanta Heart Disease Study," *Social Science and Medicine* 58 (2004): 449–61, doi.org/10.1016/S0277-9536(03)00211-9.

15. Rosalind M. Peters, "Racism and Hypertension Among African Americans," *Western Journal of Nursing Research* 26 (2004): 612–31, doi.org/10.1177/0193945 904265816.

16. Carter, "Racism and Psychological and Emotional Injury: Recognizing and Assessing Race-Based Traumatic Stress"; Carter et al., "Race-Based Traumatic

Stress Symptom Scale and White Americans: Construct Validity"; Robert T. Carter et al., "Racial Discrimination and Health Outcomes Among Racial/ Ethnic Minorities: A Meta-Analytic Review," *Journal of Multicultural Counseling and Development* 45, no. 4 (2017): 232–59, doi.org/10.1002/jmcd.12076; Robert T. Carter et al., "A Meta-Analytic Review of Racial Discrimination: Relationships to Health and Culture," *Race and Social Problems* 11, no. 1 (March 2019): 15–32; Pascoe and Richman, "Perceived Discrimination and Health: A Meta-Analytic Review"; Williams and Mohammed, "Discrimination and Racial Disparities in Health: Evidence and Needed Research"; Paradies et al., "Racism as a Determinant of Health: A Systematic Review and Meta-Analysis."

17. Brenda Major et al., "Perceived Discrimination as Worldview Threat or Worldview Confirmation: Implications for Self-Esteem," *Journal of Personality and Social Psychology* 92, no. 6 (2007): 1068–86, doi.org/10.1037/0022-3514.92.6.1068.

18. Sherrill L. Sellers et al., "Effects and Health Behaviors on Mental and Physical Health of Middle-Class African American Men," *Health Education and Behavior* 36, no. 1 (2009): 31–44, doi.org/10.1177/1090198106293526.

19. Carol D. Ryff, Corey L. M. Keyes, and Diane L. Hughes, "Status Inequalities, Perceived Discrimination, and Eudaimonic Well-Being: Do the Challenges of Minority Life Hone Purpose and Growth?" *Journal of Health and Social Behavior* 44, no. 3 (2003): 275–91. http://www.jstor.org/stable/1519779.

20. Gilbert C. Gee et al., "Self-Reported Discrimination and Mental Health Status Among African Descendants, Mexican Americans, and Other Latinos in the New Hampshire REACH 2010 Initiative: The Added Dimension of Immigration," *American Journal of Public Health* 96, no. 10 (2006): 1821–28.

21. Christopher T. H. Liang and Carin M. Molenaar, "Beliefs in an Unjust World: Mediating Ethnicity-Related Stressors and Psychological Functioning," *Journal of Clinical Psychology* 72, no. 6 (2016): 552–62, doi.org/10.1002/jclp.22271.

22. Delida Sanchez et al., "Exploring Divergent Patterns in Racial Identity Profiles Between Caribbean Black American and African American Adolescents: The Links to Perceived Discrimination and Psychological Concerns," *Journal of Multicultural Counseling and Development* 44, no. 4 (2016): 285–304, doi.org /10.1002/jmcd.12054.

23. Asani H. Seawell, Carolyn E. Cutrona, and Daniel W. Russell, "The Effects of General Social Support and Social Support for Racial Discrimination on African American Women's Well-Being," *Journal of Black Psychology* 40, no. 1 (2014): 3–26, doi.org/10.1177/0095798412469227.

24. Dawnsha R. Mushonga and Angela K. Henneberger, "Protective Factors Associated with Positive Mental Health in Traditional and Nontraditional Black Students," *American Journal of Orthopsychiatry* (March 28, 2019), dx.doi.org. /10/1037/ort0000409.

25. Aprile D. Benner et al., "Racial/Ethnic Discrimination and Well-Being During Adolescence: A Meta-Analytic Review," *American Psychologist* 73, no. 7 (2018): 855–83.

26. Ada Robinson-Perez, Miesha Marzell, and Woojae Han, "Racial Microaggressions and Psychological Distress Among Undergraduate College Students of Color: Implications for Social Work Practice," *Clinical Social Work Journal* (June 1, 2019): 1–8.

27. Naa Oyo A. Kwate and Melody S. Goodman, "Cross-Sectional and Longitudinal Effects of Racism on Mental Health Among Residents of Black Neighborhoods in New York City," *American Journal of Public Health* 105, no. 4 (2015): 711–18.

28. Ann W. Nguyen et al., "Discrimination, Serious Psychological Distress, and Church-Based Emotional Support Among African American Men Across the Life Span," *Journals of Gerontology*, Series B 73, no. 2 (2018): 198–207.

29. Naa Oyo A. Kwate et al., "Experiences of Racist Events Are Associated with Negative Health Consequences for African American Women," *Journal of the National Medical Association* 95, no. 6 (2003): 450–60.

30. Bonnie Moradi and Cristina Risco, "Perceived Discrimination Experiences and Mental Health of Latina/O American Persons," *Journal of Counseling Psychology* 53, no. 4 (2006): 411–21.

31. Emma Wadsworth et al., "Racial Discrimination, Ethnicity, and Work Stress," *Occupational Medicine* 57, no. 1 (2007): 18–24, doi.org/10.1093/occmed/kq1088.

32. Alex L. Pieterse and Robert T. Carter, "The Role of Racial Identity in Perceived Racism and Psychological Stress Among Black American Adults: Exploring Traditional and Alternative Approaches," *Journal of Applied Social Psychology* (2010), https://doi.org/10.1111/j.1559-1816.2010.00609.x.

33. Robert M. Sellers and J. Nicole Shelton, "The Role of Racial Identity in Perceived Racial Discrimination," *Journal of Personality and Social Psychology* 84, no. 5 (2003): 1079–92, doi.org/10.1037/0022-3514.84.5.1079.

34. Sellers and Shelton, "The Role of Racial Identity in Perceived Racial Discrimination," 1087.

35. Laura Castro-Schilo et al., "When Discrimination Hurts: The Longitudinal Impact of Increases in Peer Discrimination on Anxiety and Depressive Symptoms in Mexican-Origin Youth," *Journal of Youth and Adolescence* 48, no. 5 (2019): 864–75, http://search.proquest.com/docview/2191942447/.

36. Hans Oh et al., "Discrimination and Suicidality Among Racial and Ethnic Minorities in the United States," *Journal of Affective Disorders* 245 (2019): 517–23.

37. Monnica T. Williams et al., "Discrimination and Symptoms of Obsessive–Compulsive Disorder Among African Americans," *American Journal of Orthopsychiatry* 87, no. 6 (2017): 636–45, doi.org/10.1037/ort0000285.

38. Donte Bernard et al., "Imposter Phenomenon and Mental Health: The Influence of Racial Discrimination and Gender," *Journal of Counseling Psychology* 64, no. 2 (2017): 155–66, https://doi.org/10.1037/cou0000197.

39. Shervin Assari, "Educational Attainment Better Protects African American Women than African American Men Against Depressive Symptoms and Psychological Distress," *Brain Sciences* 8, no. 10 (2018): 182, doi.org/10.3390/brainsci8100182.

40. Kathy Sanders-Phillips et al., "Perceived Racial Discriminations, Drug Use, and Psychological Distress in African American Youth: A Pathway to Child Health Disparities," *Journal of Social Issues* 70, no. 2 (2014): 279–97.

41. Rheeda Walker et al., "A Longitudinal Study of Racial Discrimination and Risk for Death Ideation in African American Youth," *Suicide and Life-Threatening Behavior* 47, no. 1 (2017): 86–102, doi.org/10.1111/sltb.12251.

42. Irene J. K. Park et al., "Does Anger Regulation Mediate the Discrimination-Mental Health Link Among Mexican-Origin Adolescents? A Longitudinal Mediation Analysis Using Multilevel Modeling," *Developmental Psychology* 53, no. 2 (2017): 340–52, doi.org/10.1037/dev0000235.

43. Robert T. Carter et al., "Racial Discrimination and Race-Based Traumatic Stress: An Exploratory Investigation," in *Handbook of Racial-Cultural Psychology and Counseling*, vol. 2, *Training and Practice*, ed. Robert T. Carter (Hoboken, NJ: Wiley, 2005), 447–76.

44. Eve B. Carlson, *Trauma Assessments: A Clinician's Guide* (New York: Guildford Press, 1997): 43–60.

45. Carter et al., "Racial Discrimination and Race-Based Traumatic Stress: An Exploratory Investigation."

46. Carlson, *Trauma Assessments*, 43–60.

47. Anna Khaylis, Lynn Waelde, and Elizabeth Bruce, "The Role of Ethnic Identity in the Relationship of Race-Related Stress to PTSD Symptoms Among Young Adults," *Journal of Trauma and Dissociation* 8, no. 4 (2007): 91–105, doi.org/10.1300/J229v08n04_06.

48. Elena Flores et al., "Perceived Racial/Ethnic Discrimination, Posttraumatic Stress Symptoms, and Health Risk Behaviors Among Mexican American Adolescents," *Journal of Counseling Psychology* 57, no. 3 (2010): 264–73, doi.org/10.1037/a0020026.

49. Alex L. Pieterse, Robert T. Carter, Sarah A. Evans, and Rebecca A. Walter, "An Exploratory Examination of the Associations Among Racial and Ethnic Discrimination, Racial Climate, and Trauma-Related Symptoms in a College Student Population," *Journal of Counseling Psychology* 57, no. 3 (2010): 255–63.

50. T. B. Loeb et al., "Predictors of Somatic Symptom Severity: The Role of Cumulative History of Trauma and Adversity in a Diverse Community Sample," *Psychological Trauma-Theory Research Practice and Policy* 10, no. 5 (2018): 491–98.

51. Katherine Kirkinis et al., "Racism, Racial Discrimination, and Trauma: A Systematic Review of the Social Science Literature," *Ethnicity and Health* (August 2018): 1–21, doi.org/10.1080/13557858.2018.1514453.

52. Carter, "Racism and Psychological and Emotional Injury: Recognizing and Assessing Race-Based Traumatic Stress."

53. Sibrava et al., "Posttraumatic Stress Disorder in African American and Latinx Adults: Clinical Course and the Role of Racial and Ethnic Discrimination."

54. Robert T. Carter, Katherine Kirkinis, and Veronica Johnson, "Race-Based Traumatic Stress and General Trauma Symptoms," *Traumatology* 26, no. 1 (2020): 11–18.

55. Alex L. Pieterse and Robert T. Carter, "An Examination of the Relationship Between General Life Stress, Racism-Related Stress and Psychological Health Among Black Men," *Journal of Counseling Psychology* 54, no. 1 (2007): 102–9, doi:10.1037/0022-0167.54.1.101.

56. Alex L. Pieterse, Robert T. Carter, and Kilynda A. Ray, "The Relationship Between Perceived Racism, Stress, and Psychological Functioning Among Black Women," *Journal of Multicultural Counseling and Development* 41 (2013): 36–46, doi.org/10.1002/j.2161-1912.2013.00025.x.

57. American Psychiatric Association, *Diagnostic and Statistical Manual of Mental Disorders*, 4th ed., text revision (Washington, DC: American Psychiatric Association, 2000).

58. Deidre M. Anglin et al., "Racial Discrimination Is Associated with Distressing Subthreshold Positive Psychotic Symptoms Among US Urban Ethnic Minority Young Adults," *Social Psychiatry and Psychiatric Epidemiology* 49, no. 10 (2014): 1545–55, doi.org/10.1007/s00127-014-0870-8.

59. Deidre M. Anglin et al., "Race-Based Rejection Sensitivity Partially Accounts for the Relationship Between Racial Discrimination and Distressing Attenuated Positive Psychotic Symptoms," *Early Intervention in Psychiatry* 10, no. 5 (2016): 411–18, doi.org/10.1111/eip.12184.

60. Henry A. Willis and Enrique W. Neblett, "OC Symptoms in African American Young Adults: The Associations Between Racial Discrimination, Racial Identity, and Obsessive-Compulsive Symptoms," *Journal of Obsessive-Compulsive and Related Disorders* 19 (2018): 105–15.

61. Deidre M. Anglin et al., "Ethnic Identity, Racial Discrimination and Attenuated Psychotic Symptoms in an Urban Population of Emerging Adults," *Early Intervention in Psychiatry* 12, no. 3 (2018): 380–90.

62. Li Maio, "Discrimination and Psychiatric Disorder Among Asian American Immigrants: A National Analysis by Subgroups," *Journal of Immigrant and Minority Health* 16, no. 6 (2014): 1157–66, doi.org/10.1007/s10903-013-9920-7.

63. Gilbert C. Gee et al., "The Association Between Self-Reported Racial Discrimination and 12-Month DSM-IV Mental Disorders Among Asian Americans,"

Social Science and Medicine 64, no. 10 (2007): 1984–96, doi.org/10.1016/j .socscimed.2007.02.013.

64. Nnamdi Pole et al., "Why Are Hispanics at Greater Risk for PTSD?" *Cultural Diversity and Ethnic Minority Psychology* 11, no. 2 (2005): 144–61, doi.org/10.1037 /1099-9809.11.2.144.

65. Dennis R. Combs et al., "Perceived Racism as a Predictor of Paranoia Among African Americans," *Journal of Black Psychology* 32, no. 1 (February 2006): 87–104, doi.org/10.1177/0095798405283175.

66. Sirry M. Alang, "Mental Health Care Among Blacks in America: Confronting Racism and Constructing Solutions," *Health Services Research* 54, no. 2 (2019): 346–55.

67. See, for example, Carter, "Racism and Psychological and Emotional Injury: Recognizing and Assessing Race-Based Traumatic Stress"; Alex L. Pieterse, Nathan R. Todd, Helen A. Neville, and Robert T. Carter, "Perceived Racism and Mental Health Among Black American Adults: A Meta-Analytic Review," *Journal of Counseling Psychology* 59, no. 1 (January 2012): 1–9, doi.org/10.1037 /a0026208; Williams and Mohammed, "Discrimination and Racial Disparities in Health: Evidence and Needed Research."

68. Borrell et al., "Self- Reported Racial Discrimination and Substance Use in the Coronary Artery Risk Development in Adults Study"; Haslyn E. Hunte and Adam E. Barry, "Perceived Discrimination and DSM-IV–Based Alcohol and Illicit Drug Use Disorders," *American Journal of Public Health* 102, no. 12 (2012): e111–e117, doi.org/10.2105/AJPH.2012.300780.

69. Carter et al., "A Meta-Analytic Review of Racial Discrimination: Relationships to Health and Culture."

70. Pascoe and Richman, "Perceived Discrimination and Health: A Meta-Analytic Review."

71. Schmitt et al., "The Consequences of Perceived Discrimination for Psychological Well-Being: A Meta-Analytic Review."

72. "Race-Based Traumatic Stress Symptom Scale and White Americans: Construct Validity"; Pieterse et al., "Perceived Racism and Mental Health Among Black American Adults: A Meta-Analytic Review"; María del Carmen Triana, Mevan Jayasinghe, and Jenna R. Pieper, "Perceived Racial Discrimination and Its Correlates: A Meta-Analysis," *Journal of Organizational Behavior* 36 (2015): 491–513, doi.org/10.1002/job.198.

73. Angelitta M. Britt-Spells et al., "Effects of Perceived Discrimination on Depressive Symptoms Among Black Men Residing in the United States: A Meta-Analysis," *American Journal of Men's Health* 12, no. 1 (2016): 52–63, doi.org/10 .1177/1557988315624509.

74. Debbiesiu L. Lee and Soyeon Ahn, "Discrimination Against Latina/os: A Meta-Analysis of Individual-Level Resources and Outcomes," *Counseling Psychologist* 40, no. 1 (2012): 28–65, doi.org/10.1177/0011000011403326.

75. Debbiesiu L. Lee and Soyeon Ahn, "The Relation of Racial Identity, Ethnic Identity, and Racial Socialization to Discrimination-Distress: A Meta-Analysis of Black Americans," *Journal of Counseling Psychology* 60, no. 1 (2013): 1–14, doi.org/10.1037/a0031275.

76. Paradies et al., "Racism as a Determinant of Health: A Systematic Review and Meta-Analysis."

77. Carter et al., "Racial Discrimination and Health Outcomes Among Racial/Ethnic Minorities: A Meta-Analytic Review."

78. Carter et al., "A Meta-Analytic Review of Racial Discrimination: Relationships to Health and Culture."

79. Priscilla Lui and Lucia Quezada, "Associations Between Microaggression and Adjustment Outcomes: A Meta-Analytic and Narrative Review," *Psychological Bulletin* 145, no. 1 (2019): 45–78.

80. Kwame Mackenzie and Kamaldeep Buhi, "Institutional Racism in Mental Health Care," *British Medical Journal* 334 (2007): 649, doi.org/10.1136/bmj.39163 .395972.80.

81. Karyn D. McKinney, *Being White: Stories of Race and Racism* (London: Taylor and Francis, 2013).

82. Robert T. Carter et al., "Racial Discrimination and Race-Based Traumatic Stress: An Exploratory Investigation"; Robert T. Carter et al., "Does Racism Predict Psychological Harm or Injury: Mental Health and Legal Implications," *Law Enforcement Executive Forum* 7, no. 5 (2007): 129–54.

83. Robert T. Carter et al., "The Development of Classes of Racism Measures for Frequency and Stress Reactions: Relationships to Race-Based Traumatic Symptoms," *Traumatology* 22, no. 1 (2016): 63–74.

84. Robert T. Carter and Janet Helms, "Racial Discrimination and Harassment: A Racially Based Trauma" (paper presented at the American College of Forensic Examiners Conference, Orlando, FL, September 2002).

85. Carter, "Racism and Psychological and Emotional Injury: Recognizing and Assessing Race-Based Traumatic Stress."

86. Carter, "Racism and Psychological and Emotional Injury: Recognizing and Assessing Race-Based Traumatic Stress"; Carter and Helms, "Racial Discrimination and Harassment: A Racially Based Trauma."

87. Carter, "Racism and Psychological and Emotional Injury: Recognizing and Assessing Race-Based Traumatic Stress."

88. John F. Dovidio and Samuel L. Gaertner, "On the Nature of Contemporary Prejudice: The Causes, Consequences and Challenges of Aversive Racism," in *Racism: The Problem and the Response*, ed. Jennifer L. Eberhardt and Susan T. Fiske (Thousand Oaks, CA: Sage, 1998), 3–32.

89. For example, J. B. McConahay, "Modern Racism, Ambivalence, and the Modern Racism Scale," in *Prejudice, Discrimination and Racism*, ed. John F. Dovidio and Samuel L. Gaertner (New York: Academic, 1986), 91–126.

90. John F. Dovidio et al., "Reducing Intergroup Bias Through Intergroup Contact: Twenty Years of Progress and Future Directions," *Group Processes and Intergroup Relations* 20, no. 5 (2017): 606–20.

91. Carter et al., "The Development of Classes of Racism Measures for Frequency and Stress Reactions: Relationships to Race-Based Traumatic Symptoms."

4. Variations in Responses to Racial Discrimination

1. Robert T. Carter et al., "Racial Discrimination and Race-Based Traumatic Stress: An Exploratory Investigation," in *Handbook of Racial-Cultural Psychology and Counseling*, vol. 2, *Training and Practice*, ed. Robert T. Carter (Hoboken, NJ: Wiley, 2005), 447–76; Alex L. Pieterse and Robert T. Carter, "The Role of Racial Identity in Perceived Racism and Psychological Stress Among Black American Adults: Exploring Traditional and Alternative Approaches," *Journal of Applied Social Psychology* (2010), https://doi.org/10.1111/j.1559-1816.2010.00609.x.

2. Robert T. Carter et al., "Race-Based Traumatic Stress, Racial Identity Status, and Psychological Functioning: An Exploratory Investigation," *Professional Psychology: Research and Practice* 48, no. 1 (2017): 20–37, doi.org/10.1037/pro0000116; Robert T. Carter and Veronica E. Johnson, "Racial Identity Statuses: Applications to Practice," *Practice Innovations* 4, no. 1 (2019): 42–58, dx.doi.org/10.1037/pri0000082.

3. Hector Betancourt and Steven Regeser López, "The Study of Culture, Ethnicity, and Race in American Psychology," *American Psychologist* 48, no. 6 (1993): 629–37, doi.org/10.1037/0003-066X.48.6.629; Robert T. Carter and Amy L. Reynolds, "Race-Related Stress, Racial Identity Statuses and Emotional Reactions of Black Americans," *Cultural Diversity and Ethnic Minority Psychology* 17, no. 2 (2011): 156–62, doi.org/10.1037/a0023358; Jean S. Phinney, "When We Talk About American Ethnic Groups, What Do We Mean?" *American Psychologist* 51, no. 9 (1996): 918, doi.org/10.1037/0003-066X.51.9.918.

4. Robert T. Carter et al., "Race-Based Traumatic Stress, Racial Identity Status, and Psychological Functioning"; Janet E. Helms, Maryam Jernigan, and Jackquelyn Mascher, "The Meaning of Race in Psychology and How to Change It: A Methodological Perspective," *American Psychologist* 60, no. 1 (2005): 27–36, doi.org/10.1037/0003-066X.60.1.27; Chalmer E. Thompson and Robert T. Carter, eds., *Racial Identity Theory: Applications to Individual, Group, and Organizational Interventions* (Mahwah, NJ: Lawrence Erlbaum, 2012 [1997]).

5. Martin Marger, *Race and Ethnic Relations: American and Global Perspectives*, 10th ed. (Stamford, CT: Cengage/ Learning, 2015),18; Audrey Smedley and Brian D. Smedley, "Race as Biology Is Fiction, Racism as a Social Problem Is Real: Anthropological and Historical Perspectives on the Social Construction of Race," *American Psychologist* 60, no. 1 (2005): 16, doi.org/10.1037/0003-066X .60.1.16.

6. Robert T. Carter and Jessica M. Forsyth, "Reactions to Racial Discrimination: Emotional Stress and Help-Seeking Behaviors," *Psychological Trauma: Theory, Research, Practice, and Policy* 2, no. 3 (2010): 183–91, doi.org/10.1037/a0020102; Edward A. Delgado-Romero, Nallely Galván, Peggy Maschino, and Marcy Rowland, "Race and Ethnicity in Empirical Counseling and Counseling Psychology Research: A 10-Year Review," *Counseling Psychologist* 33, no. 4 (2005): 419–48, doi.org/10.1177/0011000004268637.

7. Marger, *Race and Ethnic Relations.*

8. Sirry M. Alang, "Mental Health Care Among Blacks in America: Confronting Racism and Constructing Solutions," *Health Services Research* 54, no. 2 (2019): 346–55; Lora L. Black, Rhonda Johnson, and Lisa VanHoose, "The Relationship Between Perceived Racism/Discrimination and Health Among Black American Women: A Review of the Literature from 2003–2013," *Journal of Racial and Ethnic Health Disparities* 2 (2015): 11–20, doi.org/10.1007/s40615-014-0043-1; Aprile D. Benner et al., "Racial/Ethnic Discrimination and Well-Being During Adolescence: A Meta-Analytic Review," *American Psychologist* 73, no. 7 (2018): 855–83; Schekeva P. Hall and Robert T. Carter, "The Relationship Between Racial Identity, Ethnic Identity, and Perceptions of Racial Discrimination in an Afro-Caribbean Descent Sample," *Journal of Black Psychology* 32, no. 2 (2006): 155–75, doi.org/10.1177/0095798406287071.; Robert M. Sellers and J. Nicole Shelton, "The Role of Racial Identity in Perceived Racial Discrimination," *Journal of Personality and Social Psychology* 84, no. 5 (2003): 1079–92, doi.org/10.1037/0022-3514.84.5.1079.

9. Deidre M. Anglin et al., "Ethnic Identity, Racial Discrimination and Attenuated Psychotic Symptoms in an Urban Population of Emerging Adults," *Early Intervention in Psychiatry* 12, no. 3 (2018): 380–90; Alvin N. Alvarez, Christopher T. H. Liang, and Helen Neville, ed., *The Cost of Racism for People of Color: Contextualizing Experiences of Discrimination* (Washington, DC: American Psychological Association, 2016); Tiffany Yip, Gilbert C. Gee, and David T. Takeuchi, "Racial Discrimination and Psychological Distress: The Impact of Ethnic Identity and Age Among Immigrant and United States–Born Asian Adults," *Developmental Psychology* 44, no. 3 (2008): 787–800, doi.org/10.1037/0012-1649.44.3.787.

10. Sha'Kema Blackmon et al., "Linking Racial-Ethnic Socialization to Culture and Race-Specific Coping Among African American College Students," *Journal of Black Psychology* 42, no. 6 (2016): 549–76, doi.org/10.1177/0095798415617865; Elizabeth Brondolo et al., "Coping with Racism: A Selective Review of the Literature and a Theoretical and Methodological Critique," *Journal of Behavioral Medicine* 32, no. 1 (2009): 64–88, https://link.springer.com/article/10.1007%2Fs10865-008-9193-0.

11. Tawanda M. Greer, "Measuring Coping Strategies Among African American Women: An Exploration of the Latent Structure of the COPE Inventory,"

Journal of Black Psychology 33, no. 3 (2007): 260–77, doi.org/10.1177/009579 8407302539; Anita Jones Thompson, Karen McCurtis Witherspoon, and Suzette L. Speight, "Gendered Racism, Psychological Distress, and Coping Styles of African American Women," *Cultural Diversity and Ethnic Minority Psychology* 14, no. 4 (2008): 307–14, doi.org/10.1037/1099-9809.14.4.307.

12. Shawn O. Utsey et al., "Racial Discrimination, Coping, Life Satisfaction, and Self-Esteem Among African Americans," *Journal of Counseling and Development* 78, no. 1 (2000): 72–80, doi.org/10.1002/j.1556-6676.2000.tb02562.x.

13. Lauri L. Hyers, "Resisting Prejudice Every Day: Exploring Women's Assertive Responses to Anti-Black Racism, Anti-Semitism, Heterosexism, and Sexism," *Sex Roles* 56, nos. 1–2 (2007): 1–12, doi.org/10.1007/s11199-006-9142-8.

14. Veronica J. Smith et al., "Implicit Coping Responses to Racism Predict African Americans' Level of Psychological Distress," *Basic and Applied Social Psychology* 30 (2008): 246–77, doi.org/10.1080/01973530802375110.

15. Janelle R. Goodwill et al., "An Exploratory Study of Stress and Coping Among Black College Men," *American Journal of Orthopsychiatry* (January 2018), advance online publication, https://doi.org/10.1037/ort0000313.

16. Vetta L. Sanders Thompson, "Coping Responses and the Experience of Discrimination," *Journal of Applied Social Psychology* 36, no. 5 (2006): 1198–214, doi.org/10.1111/j.0021-9029.2006.00038.x.

17. Delida Sanchez et al., "Racial-Ethnic Microaggressions, Coping Strategies, and Mental Health in Asian American and Latinx American College Students: A Mediation Model," *Journal of Counseling Psychology* 65, no. 2 (2018): 214–25, doi.org/10.1037/cou0000249.

18. Sha'Kema Blackmon et al., "Linking Racial-Ethnic Socialization to Culture and Race-Specific Coping among African American College Students"; Jessica Forsyth and Robert T. Carter, "The Influence of Racial Identity Status Attitudes and Racism-Related Coping on Mental Health Among Black Americans," *Cultural Diversity and Ethnic Minority Psychology* 18, no. 2 (2012): 128–40, doi .org/10.1037/a0027660; Jessica Forsyth and Robert T. Carter, "The Development and Preliminary Validation of the Racism-Related Coping Scale," *Psychological Trauma: Theory, Policy, Research, and Practice* 6, no. 6 (2014): 632–43, doi .org/10.1037/a0036702.

19. Elizabeth Brondolo, Linda C. Gallo, and Hector F. Myers, "Race, Racism and Health: Disparities, Mechanisms, and Interventions," *Journal of Behavioral Medicine* 32, no. 1 (2009): 1–8, doi.org/10.1007/s10865-008-9190-3.

20. Forsyth and Carter, "The Development and Preliminary Validation of the Racism-Related Coping Scale"; Meifen Wei et al., "Development and Validation of a Coping with Discrimination Scale: Factor Structure, Reliability, and Validity," *Journal of Counseling Psychology* 57, no. 3 (2010): 328, doi.org/10.1037 /a0019969.

21. David Mellor, "Responses to Racism: A Taxonomy of Coping Styles Used by Aboriginal Australians," *American Journal of Orthopsychiatry* 74, no. 1 (2004): 56–71, doi.org/10.1037/0002-9432.74.1.56.

22. For example, Brondolo et al., "Coping with Racism: A Selective Review of the Literature and a Theoretical and Methodological Critique"; Forsyth and Carter, "The Development and Preliminary Validation of the Racism-Related Coping Scale"; Aisha N. Griffith, Noelle M. Hurd, and Saida B Hussain, "'I Didn't Come to School for This': A Qualitative Examination of Experiences with Race-Related Stressors and Coping Responses Among Black Students Attending a Predominantly White Institution," *Journal of Adolescent Research* 34, no. 2 (2019): 115–39; Shelly P. Harrell, "A Multidimensional Conceptualization of Racism-Related Stress: Implications for the Well-Being of People of Color," *American Journal of Orthopsychiatry* 70, no. 1 (2000): 42–57, doi.org/10.1037/h0087722; Rafael J. Hernández and Miguel Villodas, "Collectivistic Coping Responses to Racial Microaggressions Associated with Latina/o College Persistence Attitudes," *Journal of Latinx Psychology* 7, no. 1 (2019): 76–90; Darrell L. Hudson et al., "Racial Discriminations, John Henryism, and Depression Among African Americans," *Journal of Black Psychology* 42, no. 3 (2016): 221–43, doi.org/10.1177/0095798414567757; Lionel D. Scott, Jr., "The Relation of Racial Identity and Racial Socialization to Coping with Discrimination Among African American Adolescents," *Journal of Black Studies* 33, no. 4 (2003b): 520–38, doi.org/10.1177/0021934702250035; Smith et al., "Implicit Coping Responses to Racism Predict African Americans' Level of Psychological Distress," *Basic and Applied Social Psychology* 30 (2008): 246–77, doi.org/10.1080/01973530802375110.

23. Deborah L. Plummer and Steve Slane, "Patterns of Coping in Racially Stressful Situations," *Journal of Black Psychology* 22, no. 3 (1996): 302–15, doi.org/10.1177/00957984960223002.

24. For example, Sharon Danoff-Burg, Hazel M. Prelow, and Rebecca R. Swenson, "Hope and Life Satisfaction in Black College Students Coping with Race-Related Stress," *Journal of Black Psychology* 30 (2004): 208–28, doi.org/10.1177/0095798403260725; Utsey et al., "Racial Discrimination, Coping, Life Satisfaction, and Self-Esteem Among African Americans"; Shawn O. Utsey et al., "Examining the Role of Culture-Specific Coping as a Predictor of Resilient Outcomes in African Americans from High Risk Urban Communities," *Journal of Black Psychology* 33, no. 1 (2007): 75–93, doi.org/10.1177/0095798406295094.

25. Danoff-Burg et al., "Hope and Life Satisfaction in Black College Students Coping with Race-Related Stress."

26. Forsyth and Carter, "The Influence of Racial Identity Status Attitudes and Racism-Related Coping on Mental Health Among Black Americans."

27. Ma'at E. Lyris Lewis-Coles and Madonna G. Constantine, "Racism-Related Stress, Africultural Coping, and Religious Problem-Solving Among African

Americans," *Cultural Diversity and Ethnic Minority Psychology* 12, no. 3 (2006): 433, doi.org/10.1037/1099-9809.12.3.433; Utsey et al., "Examining the Role of Culture-Specific Coping as a Predictor of Resilient Outcomes in African Americans from High Risk Urban Communities."

28. Karina L. Walters and Jane M. Simoni, "Reconceptualizing Native Women's Health: An 'Indigenist' Stress-Coping Model," *American Journal of Public Health* 92, no. 4 (2002): 520–24, doi.org/10.2105/AJPH.92.4.520.

29. For example, Ramona Benkert and Rosalind M. Peters, "African American Women's Coping with Health Care Prejudice," *Western Journal of Nursing Research* 27, no. 7 (2005): 863–89, doi.org/10.1177/0193945905278588; Alfrieda Daly et al., "Effective Coping Strategies of African Americans," *Social Work* 40, no. 2 (1995): 240–48; Hudson et al., "Racial Discriminations, John Henryism, and Depression Among African Americans"; Kumea Shorter-Gooden, "Multiple Resistance Strategies: How African American Women Cope with Racism and Sexism," *Journal of Black Psychology* 30, no. 3 (2004): 406–25, doi .org/10.1177/0095798404266050.

30. Griffith, Hurd, and Hussain, "'I Didn't Come to School for This'"; Hernández and Villodas, "Collectivistic Coping Responses to Racial Microaggressions Associated with Latina/o College Persistence Attitudes"; Sanchez et al., "Racial-Ethnic Microaggressions, Coping Strategies, and Mental Health in Asian American and Latinx American College Students: A Mediation Model."

31. Tawanda M. Greer, "Coping Strategies as Moderators of the Relationship Between Race and Gender-Based Discrimination and Psychological Symptoms for African American Women," *Journal of Black Psychology* 37, no. 1 (2011): 42–54, doi.org/10.1177/0095798410380202; Helen A. Neville, Puncky Paul Heppner, and Li-fei Wang, "Relations Among Racial Identity Attitudes, Perceived Stressors, and Coping Styles in African American College Students," *Journal of Counseling and Development* 75 (1997): 303–11, doi.org/10.1002/j.1556-6676.1997 .tb02345.x; Utsey et al., "Examining the Role of Culture-Specific Coping as a Predictor of Resilient Outcomes in African Americans from High Risk Urban Communities"; Lindsey M. West, Roxanne A. Donovan, and Lizbeth Roemer, "Coping with Racism: What Works and Doesn't Work for Black Women?" *Journal of Black Psychology* 36, no. 3 (2010): 331–49, doi.org/10.1177/0095798409353755.

32. Lionel D. Scott Jr., "The Relation of Racial Identity and Racial Socialization to Coping with Discrimination Among African American Adolescents"; Lionel D. Scott Jr., "Cultural Orientation and Coping with Perceived Discrimination Among African American Youth," *Journal of Black Psychology* 29, no. 3 (2003a): 235–56, doi.org/10.1177/0095798403254213.

33. Robert T. Carter and Alex L. Pieterse, "Race: A Social and Psychological Analysis of the Term and Its Meaning," in *Handbook of Racial-Cultural Psychology*

and Counseling, vol. 1, *Theory and Research*, ed. Robert T. Carter (Hoboken, NJ: Wiley, 2005), 41–63; Thompson and Carter, *Racial Identity Theory*.

34. Carter et al., "Race-Based Traumatic Stress, Racial Identity Status, and Psychological Functioning: An Exploratory Investigation"; Carter et al., "A Meta-Analytic Review of Racial Discrimination: Relationships to Health and Culture," *Race and Social Problems* 11, no. 1 (March 2019): 15–32, https://doi.org/10.1007/s12552-018-9256-y; Lori S. Hoggard, Shawn C. T. Jones, and Robert M. Sellers, "Racial Cues and Racial Identity: Implications for How African Americans Experience and Respond to Racial Discrimination," *Journal of Black Psychology* 43, no. 4 (2017): 409–32, doi.org/10.1177/0095798416651033; Robert M. Sellers et al., "Racial Identity, Racial Discrimination, Perceived Stress, and Psychological Distress Among African American Young Adults," *Journal of Health and Social Behavior* 44, no. 3 (2003): 302–17, doi.org/10.2307/1519781.

35. Carter et al., "Race-Based Traumatic Stress, Racial Identity Status, and Psychological Functioning: An Exploratory Investigation"; Carter and Johnson, "Racial Identity Statuses: Applications to Practice"; Thompson and Carter, *Racial Identity Theory*; William E. Cross Jr. et al., "Identity Work: Enactment of Racial-Ethnic Identity in Everyday Life," *Identity* 17, no. 1 (2017): 1–12, doi.org/10.1080/15283488.2016.1268535; Tiffany Yip, "Ethnic/Racial Identity—A Double-Edged Sword? Associations with Discrimination and Psychological Outcomes," *Current Directions in Psychological Science* (May 2018), https://doi.org/10.1177/0963721417739348.

36. For example, Janet E. Helms, "An Update of Helms's White and People of Color Racial Identity Models," in *Handbook of Multicultural Counseling*, ed. Joseph G. Ponterotto et al., (Thousand Oaks, CA: Sage, 1995), 181–98; Thompson and Carter, *Racial Identity Theory*.

37. Robert T. Carter, *The Influence of Race and Racial Identity in Psychotherapy: Toward a Racially Inclusive Model* (New York: Wiley, 1995a).

38. Helms, "An Update of Helms's White and People of Color Racial Identity Models."

39. For example, Carter et al., "Race-Based Traumatic Stress, Racial Identity Status, and Psychological Functioning: An Exploratory Investigation"; Carter and Johnson, "Racial Identity Statuses: Applications to Practice"; Pei-Han Cheng, Robert T. Carter, and Donald Y. Lee, "Racial Identity Status Attitudes and Acculturation of Korean and Chinese Americans: Criterion-Related Profile Analyses," *Journal of Multicultural Counseling and Development* 43, no. 2 (2015): 97–108, doi.org/10.1002/j.2161-1912.2015.00067.x.

40. Robert M. Sellers and Mia A. Smith, J. Nicole Shelton, Stephanie, A. J. Rowley, and Tabbye M. Chavous, "Multidimensional Model of Racial Identity: A Reconceptualization of African American Racial Identity," *Personality and*

Social Psychology Review, 2 no. 1 (1998): 18–39; Robert M. Sellers, Cleopatra Howard Caldwell, Karen H. Schmeelk-Cone, and Marc Zimmerman, "Racial Identity, Racial Discrimination, Perceived Stress, and Psychological Distress Among African American Young Adults," *Journal of Health and Social Behavior* 44, no. 3 (2003): 302–17, doi.org/10.2307/1519781; Robert M. Sellers and J. Nicole Shelton, "The Role of Racial Identity in Perceived Racial Discrimination," *Journal of Personality and Social Psychology* 84, no. 5 (2003): 1079–92, doi.org /10.1037/0022-3514.84.5.1079; Sherrill L. Sellers, Vence Bonham, Harold W. Neighbors, and James W. Amell, "Effects and Health Behaviors on Mental and Physical Health of Middle-Class African American Men," *Health Education and Behavior* 36, no. 1 (2009): 31–44, doi.org/10.1177/1090198106293526; Frank C. Worrell, William E. Cross Jr., and Beverly J. Vandiver, "Nigrescence Theory: Current Status and Challenges for the Future," *Journal of Multicultural Counseling and Development* 29 (2001): 201–13.

41. Helms, "An Update of Helms's White and People of Color Racial Identity Models."

42. For example, Robert T. Carter, Janet E. Helms, and Heather L. Juby, "The Relationship Between Racism and Racial Identity for White Americans: A Profile Analysis," *Journal of Multicultural Counseling and Development* 32, no. 1 (January 2004): 2–17, doi.org/10.1002/j.2161-1912.2004.tb00357.x; Jessica Forsyth, Schekeva Hall, and Robert T. Carter, "Racial Identity Among African Americans and Black West Indian Americans," *Professional Psychology: Research and Practice* 46, no. 2 (2015): 124–31, psycnet.apa.org/doi/10.1037/a0038076; Carter and Johnson, "Racial Identity Statuses: Applications to Practice"; Deidre Franklin-Jackson and Robert T. Carter, "The Relationships Between Race-Related Stress, Racial Identity, and Mental Health for Black Americans," *Journal of Black Psychology* 33, no. 1 (2007): 5–26, doi.org/10.1177/0095798406295092; Sellers and Shelton, "The Role of Racial Identity in Perceived Racial Discrimination"; Matthew P. Siegel and Robert T. Carter, "Emotions and White Racial Identity Status Attitudes," *Journal of Multicultural Counseling and Development* 42, no. 3 (2014): 218–31, doi.org/10.1002/j.2161-1912.2014.00056.x; Roderick J. Watts, "Racial Identity and Preferences for Social Change Strategies Among African Americans," *Journal of Black Psychology* 18, no. 2 (1992): 1–18, doi.org/10.1177/00957984920182002; Roderick J. Watts and Robert T. Carter, "Psychological Aspects of Racism in Organizations," *Group and Organization Studies* 16 (1991): 328–44, doi.org/10.1177/105960119101600307.

43. David H. Chae et al., "The Role of Racial Identity and Implicit Racial Bias in Self-Reported Racial Discrimination: Implications for Depression Among African American Men," *Journal of Black Psychology* 43, no. 8 (2017): 789–812, doi.org/10.1177/0095798417690055.

44. Shawn C. T. Jones et al., "Emotional Response Profiles to Racial Discrimination: Does Racial Identity Predict Affective Patterns?" *Journal of Black Psychology* 40, no. 4 (2014): 334–58, doi.org/10.1177/0095798413488628.

45. Franklin-Jackson and Carter, "The Relationships Between Race-Related Stress, Racial Identity, and Mental Health for Black Americans."

46. Sellers and Shelton, "The Role of Racial Identity in Perceived Racial Discrimination."

47. Anna Khaylis, Lynn Waelde, and Elizabeth Bruce, "The Role of Ethnic Identity in the Relationship of Race-Related Stress to PTSD Symptoms Among Young Adults," *Journal of Trauma and Dissociation* 8, no. 4 (2007): 91–105, doi.org/10.1300/J229v08n04_06.

48. Neville, Heppner, and Wang, "Relations Among Racial Identity Attitudes, Perceived Stressors, and Coping Styles in African American College Students."

49. Sellers, and Shelton, "The Role of Racial Identity in Perceived Racial Discrimination."

50. Hoggard, Jones, and Sellers, "Racial Cues and Racial Identity."

51. Melissa L. Greene, Niobe Way, and Kerstin Pahl, "Trajectories of Perceived Adult and Peer Discrimination among Black, Latino, and Asian American Adolescents: Patterns and Psychological Correlates," *Developmental Psychology* 42, no. 2 (2006): 223, doi.org/10.1037/0012-1649.42.2.218.

52. Tamika C. B. Zapolski et al., "Collective Ethnic–Racial Identity and Health Outcomes Among African American Youth: Examination of Promotive and Protective Effects," *Cultural Diversity and Ethnic Minority Psychology* 25, no. 3 (2019): 388–96.

53. For example, Forsyth and Carter, "The Influence of Racial Identity Status Attitudes and Racism-Related Coping on Mental Health Among Black Americans"; Neville, Heppner, and Wang, "Relations Among Racial Identity Attitudes, Perceived Stressors, and Coping Styles in African American College Students."

54. Watts, "Racial Identity and Preferences for Social Change Strategies Among African Americans."

55. Robert T. Carter, "Racism and Psychological and Emotional Injury: Recognizing and Assessing Race-Based Traumatic Stress," *Counseling Psychologist* 35, no. 1 (2007): 13–105, doi:10.1177/0011000006292033; David H. Chae et al., "The Role of Racial Identity and Implicit Racial Bias in Self-Reported Racial Discrimination"; Delida Sanchez et al., "Exploring Divergent Patterns in Racial Identity Profiles Between Caribbean Black American and African American Adolescents: The Links to Perceived Discrimination and Psychological Concerns," *Journal of Multicultural Counseling and Development* 44, no. 4 (2016): 285–304, doi.org/10.1002/jmcd.12054; Dawn M. Szymanski and Jioni A. Lewis, "Race-Related Stress and Racial Identity as Predictors of African American

Activism," *Journal of Black Psychology* 41, no. 1 (2015): 170–91, doi.org/10.1177 /0095798414520707; David R. Williams and Selina A. Mohammed, "Discrimination and Racial Disparities in Health: Evidence and Needed Research," *Journal of Behavioral Medicine* 32 (2009): 20–47, doi:10.1007/s10865-008-9185-0.

56. For example, Forsyth and Carter, "The Influence of Racial Identity Status Attitudes and Racism-Related Coping on Mental Health Among Black Americans"; Diana T. Sanchez et al., "Confronting as Autonomy Promotion: Speaking Up Against Discrimination and Psychological Well-Being in Racial Minorities," *Journal of Health Psychology* 21, no. 9 (2016): 1999–2007, doi.org/10.1177 /1359105315569619.

57. See also Tabbye Chavous et al., "Shifting Contexts and Shifting Identities: Campus Race-Related Experiences, Racial Identity, and Academic Motivation Among Black Students During the Transition to College," *Race and Social Problems* 10, no. 1 (2018): 1–18, http://search.proquest.com/docview/1993643837/.

58. Forsyth and Carter, "The Influence of Racial Identity Status Attitudes and Racism-Related Coping on Mental Health Among Black Americans."

59. Smith et al., "Implicit Coping Responses to Racism Predict African Americans' Level of Psychological Distress."

60. Forsyth and Carter, "The Influence of Racial Identity Status Attitudes and Racism-Related Coping on Mental Health Among Black Americans."

61. Robert T. Carter and Sinead Sant-Barket, "Assessment of the Impact of Racial Discrimination and Racism: How to Use the Race-Based Traumatic Stress Symptom Scale in Practice," *Traumatology* 21, no. 1 (2015): 32–39.

62. Delida Sanchez, Leann Smith, and Whitney Adams, "The Relationships Among Perceived Discrimination, Marianismo Gender Role Attitudes, Racial-Ethnic Socialization, Coping Styles, and Mental Health Outcomes in Latina College Students," *Journal of Latina/o Psychology* 6, no. 1 (2018): 1–15, doi.org /10.1037/lat0000077.

63. Gilbert C. Gee et al., "Racial Discrimination and Health Among Asian Americans: Evidence, Assessment, and Directions for Future Research," *Epidemiologic Reviews* 31 (2009): 130–51, doi.org/10.1093%2Fepirev%2Fmxp009; Enrique W. Neblett Jr., Donte L. Bernard, and Kira Hudson Banks, "The Moderating Roles of Gender and Socioeconomic Status in the Association Between Racial Discrimination and Psychological Adjustment," *Cognitive Behavioral Practice* 23, no. 3 (2016): 385–97, doi.org/10.1016/j.cbpra.2016.05.002.

64. Lucas Torres, Mark W. Driscoll, and Maria Voell, "Discrimination, Acculturation, Acculturative Stress, and Latino Psychological Distress: A Moderated Mediational Model," *Cultural Diversity and Ethnic Minority Psychology* 18 (2012): 17–25, doi.org/10.1037/a0026710.

65. Enrique W. Neblett Jr. et al., "Patterns of Racial Socialization and Psychological Adjustment: Can Parental Communications About Race Reduce the Im-

pact of Racial Discrimination?" *Journal of Research on Adolescence* 18, no. 3 (2008): 477–515, doi.org/10.1111/j.1532-7795.2008.00568.x.

66. Michael W. Kraus, Jun Won Park, and Jacinth J. X. Tan, "Signs of Social Class: The Experience of Economic Inequality in Everyday Life," *Perspectives on Psychological Science* 12, no. 3 (2017): 422, doi.org/10.1177/1745691616673192.

67. Matthew A. Diemer et al., "Best Practices in Conceptualizing and Measuring Social Class in Psychological Research," *Analyses of Social Issues and Public Policy* 13, no. 1 (2013): 77–113, doi.org/10.1111/asap.12001; Nancy Krieger et al., "Racism, Sexism, and Social Class: Implications for Studies of Health, Disease, and Well-Being," *American Journal of Preventive Medicine* 9, no. 6 (Suppl., 1993): 82–122, doi.org/10.1016/S0749-3797(18)30666-4.

68. Alex L. Pieterse and Robert T. Carter, "An Examination of the Relationship Between General Life Stress, Racism-Related Stress and Psychological Health Among Black Men," *Journal of Counseling Psychology* 54, no. 1 (2007): 102–9, doi:10.1037/0022-0167.54.1.101.

69. Robert T. Carter and Janet E. Helms, "The Relationship Between Racial Identity Attitudes and Social Class," *Journal of Negro Education* 37, no. 1 (1988): 22–30.

70. Sarah S. Townsend et al., "Influencing the World Versus Adjusting to Constraints: Social Class Moderates Responses to Discrimination," *Social Psychological and Personality Science* 5, no. 2 (2014): 226–34, doi.org/10.1177 /1948550613490968.

71. Naa Oyo A. Kwate and Melody S. Goodman, "Racism at the Intersections: Gender and Socioeconomic Differences in the Experience of Racism Among African Americans," *American Journal of Orthopsychiatry* 85, no. 5 (2015): 397–408, doi.org/10.1037/ort0000086.

72. Samantha L. Moore-Berg and Andrew Karpinski, "An Intersectional Approach to Understanding How Race and Social Class Affect Intergroup Processes," *Social and Personality Psychology Compass* 13, no. 1 (2019): 1–14, doi.org.10.1111 /spc3.12426.

73. John W. Berry, "Acculturation: Living Successfully in Two Cultures," *International Journal of Intercultural Relations* 29, no. 6 (2005): 697–712, doi.org/10.1016 /j.ijintrel.2005.07.013.

74. Saul G. Alamilla et al., "Acculturation, Enculturation, Perceived Racism and Psychological Symptoms Among Asian American College Students," *Journal of Multicultural Counseling and Development* 45, no. 1 (2017): 37–65, doi.org/10 .1002/jmcd.12062.

75. Saul G. Alamilla, Bryan S. K. Kim, and Alexandra Lam, "Acculturation, Enculturation, Perceived Racism, Minority Status Stressors, and Psychological Symptomatology Among Latino/as," *Hispanic Journal of Behavioral Sciences* 32, no. 1 (2010): 55–76, doi.org/10.1177/0739986309352770.

76. Torres, Driscoll, and Voell, "Discrimination, Acculturation, Acculturative Stress, and Latino Psychological Distress: A Moderated Mediational Model."

77. Beverly Araújo Dawson, "Discrimination, Stress, and Acculturation Among Dominican Immigrant Women," *Hispanic Journal of Behavioral Sciences* 31, no. 1 (2009): 96–111, doi.org/10.1177/0739986308327502.

78. John W. Berry and Feng Hou, "Acculturation, Discrimination and Wellbeing Among Second Generation of Immigrants in Canada," *International Journal of Intercultural Relations* 61 (2017): 29–39, doi.org/10.1016/j.ijintrel.2017.08.003.

79. B. Heidi Ellis et al., "Discrimination and Mental Health Among Somali Refugee Adolescents: The Role of Acculturation and Gender," *American Journal of Orthopsychiatry* 80, no. 4 (2010): 564–75, doi.org/10.1111/j.1939-0025.2010.01061.x.

80. William Liu et al., "Racial Trauma, Microaggressions, and Becoming Racially Innocuous: The Role of Acculturation and White Supremacist Ideology," *American Psychologist* 74, no. 1 (2019): 143–155, dx.doi.org/10.1037/amp0000036.

81. See Beverly Y. Araújo and Luisa N. Borrell, "Understanding the Link Between Discrimination, Mental Health Outcomes, and Life Chances Among Latinos," *Hispanic Journal of Behavioral Sciences* 28, no. 2 (May 2006): 245–66, doi.org/10.1177%2F0739986305285825.

82. Diane Hughes et al., "Parents' Ethnic-Racial Socialization Practices: A Review of Research and Directions for Future Study," *Developmental Psychology* 42 (2006): 747–70, doi.org/10.1037/0012-1649.42.5.747.

83. Howard Carlton Stevenson and Edith G. Arrington, "Racial/Ethnic Socialization Mediates Perceived Racism and the Racial Identity of African American Adolescents," *Cultural Diversity and Ethnic Minority Psychology* 15 (2009): 125–36, doi.org/10.1037/a0015500.

84. Neblett et al., "Patterns of Racial Socialization and Psychological Adjustment: Can Parental Communications About Race Reduce the Impact of Racial Discrimination?"

85. Mia A. Smith Bynum, E. Thomaseo Burton, and Candace Best, "Racism Experiences and Psychological Functioning in African American College Freshmen: Is Racial Socialization a Buffer?" *Cultural Diversity and Ethnic Minority Psychology* 13, no. 1 (2007): 64–73, doi.org/10.1037/1099-9809.13.1.64.

86. April Harris-Britt et al., "Perceived Racial Discrimination and Self-Esteem in African American Youth: Racial Socialization as a Protective Factor," *Journal of Research on Adolescence* 17 (2007): 669–82, doi.org/10.1111/j.1532-7795.2007.00540.x.

87. Riana E. Anderson et al., "EMBRacing Racial Stress and Trauma: Preliminary Feasibility and Coping Responses of a Racial Socialization Intervention," *Journal of Black Psychology* 44, no. 1 (2017): 25–46, doi.org/10.1177/0095798417732930.

88. Riana Elyse Anderson and Howard C. Stevenson "RECASTing Racial Stress and Trauma: Theorizing the Healing Potential of Racial Socialization in Families," *American Psychologist* 74, no. 1 (2019): 63–75.

89. See Christina J. Thai et al., "Microaggressions and Self-Esteem in Emerging Asian American Adults: The Moderating Role of Racial Socialization," *Asian American Journal of Psychology* 8, no. 2 (2017): 83, doi.org/10.1037/aap0000079.

90. Linda P. Juang, Hyung Chol Yoo, and Annabelle Atkin, "A Critical Race Perspective on an Empirical Review of Asian American Parental Racial-Ethnic Socialization," in *Asian American Parenting: Family Process and Intervention*, ed. Yoonsun Choi and Hyeouk Hahm (Cham, Switz.: Springer, 2017), 11–35, https://doi.org/10.1007/978-3-319-63136-3_2.

91. Juang et al., "A Critical Race Perspective on an Empirical Review of Asian American Parental Racial-Ethnic Socialization," 25.

92. Sanchez, Smith, and Adams, "The Relationships Among Perceived Discrimination, Marianismo Gender Role Attitudes, Racial-Ethnic Socialization, Coping Styles, and Mental Health Outcomes in Latina College Students."

93. Noé Rubén Chávez and Sabine Elizabeth French, "Ethnicity-Related Stressors and Mental Health in Latino Americans: The Moderating Role of Parental Racial Socialization," *Journal of Applied Social Psychology* 37, no. 9 (2007): 1974–98, doi.org/10.1111/j.1559-1816.2007.00246.x.

94. Christopher T. H. Liang, Alvin N. Alvarez, Linda Juang, and Mandy Liang, "The Role of Coping in the Relationship Between Perceived Racism and Racism-Related Stress for Asian Americans: Gender Differences," *Journal of Counseling Psychology* 54 (2007): 132–41, doi.org/10.1037/0022-0167.54.2.132.

95. Yin Paradies et al., "Racism as a Determinant of Health: A Systematic Review and Meta-Analysis," *PloS One* 10, no. 9 (2015): 1–48, doi:10.137/journal.pone.0138511; Elizabeth A. Pascoe and Laura Smart Richman, "Perceived Discrimination and Health: A Meta-Analytic Review," *Psychological Bulletin* 135, no. 4 (2009): 531–54, doi.org/10.1037%2Fa0016059.

96. Anderson and Stevenson, "RECASTing Racial Stress and Trauma"; Carter et al., "Race-Based Traumatic Stress, Racial Identity Status, and Psychological Functioning: An Exploratory Investigation"; Carter and Johnson, "Racial Identity Statuses: Applications to Practice"; William R. Concepcion, Eric L. Kohatsu, and Christian J. Yeh, "Using Racial Identity and Acculturation to Analyze Experiences of Racism Among Asian Americans," *Asian American Journal of Psychology* 4, no. 2 (2013): 136–42, doi.org/10.1037/a0027985; Liu et al., "Racial Trauma, Microaggressions, and Becoming Racially Innocuous"; Hyung Chol Yoo and Richard M. Lee, "Does Ethnic Identity Buffer or Exacerbate the Effects of Frequent Racial Discrimination on Situational Well-Being of Asian Americans?" *Journal of Counseling Psychology* 55, no. 1 (2008): 63–75, doi.org/10.1037/1948-1985.S.1.70.

97. David R. Williams et al., "Racial Differences in Physical and Mental Health: Socioeconomic Status, Stress and Discrimination," *Journal of Health Psychology* 2, no. 3 (1997): 335–51, doi.org/10.1177/135910539700200305; David R. Williams, "Stress and the Mental Health of Populations of Color: Advancing Our Understanding of Race-Related Stressors," *Journal of Health and Social Behavior* 59, no. 4 (2018): 466–85.

5. Race-Based Traumatic Stress as Racial Trauma

1. Nadine J. Kaslow et al., "Facilitating the Pipeline Progress from Doctoral Degree to First Job," *American Psychologist* 73, no. 1 (2018): 47–62, dx.doi.org /10.1037/amp0000120; Teceta Thomas Tormala et al., "Developing Measurable Cultural Competence and Cultural Humility: An Application of the Cultural Formulation," *Training and Education in Professional Psychology* 12, no. 1 (2018): 54–61, dx.doi.org/10.1037/tep0000183.

2. Robert T. Carter, *Race and Racial Identity in Psychotherapy: Toward a Racially Inclusive Model* (New York: Wiley, 1995b); Rita Chi-Ying Chung et al., "Challenges in Promoting Race Dialogues in Psychology Training: Race and Gender Perspectives," *Counseling Psychologist* 46, no. 2 (2018): 213–40, doi.org /10.1177/0011000018758262.

3. Lillian Comas-Díaz, Gordon N. Hall, and Helen A. Neville, "Racial Trauma: Theory, Research, and Healing: Introduction to the Special Issue," *American Psychologist* 74, no. 1 (2019): 1–5, dx.doi.org/10.1037/amp0000442.

4. American Psychological Association, "Guidelines for Race and Ethnicity in Psychology" (2019), https://www.apa.org/about/policy/guidelines-race-ethnicity.pdf.

5. Carter, *Race and Racial Identity in Psychotherapy*; Robert T. Carter, "Uprooting Inequity and Disparities in Counseling and Psychology: An Introduction," in *Handbook of Racial-Cultural Counseling and Psychology*, vol. 1, *Theory and Research*, ed. Robert T. Carter (New York: Wiley, 2005c), xv–xxviii.

6. Don E. Davis et al., "The Multicultural Orientation Framework: A Narrative Review," *Psychotherapy* 55, no. 1 (2018): 89, doi.org/10.1037%2Fpst0000160.

7. Janet E. Helms and Donelda A. Cook, *Using Race and Culture in Counseling and Psychotherapy: Theory and Process* (Boston: Allyn and Bacon, 1999).

8. Robert T. Carter, "The Road Less Traveled: Research on Race," in *The Handbook of Multicultural Counseling*, 4th ed., ed. J. Manuel Casas et al. (Thousand Oaks, CA: Sage, 2016), 71–80.

9. Martin Marger, *Race and Ethnic Relations: American and Global Perspectives*, 10th ed. (Stamford, CT: Cengage Learning, 2015), 15–17; Manivong J. Ratts and Paul B. Pedersen, *Counseling for Multiculturalism and Social Justice: Integration, Theory, and Application*, 4th ed. (Alexandria, VA: American Counseling Association, 2014).

10. Helms and Cook, *Using Race and Culture in Counseling and Psychotherapy*, 28–29.

11. Carrie Hemmings and Amanda M. Evans, "Identifying and Treating Race-Based Trauma in Counseling," *Journal of Multicultural Counseling and Development* 46, no. 1 (2018): 20–39, doi.org/10.1002/jmcd.12090.

12. Suman Fernando, *Cultural Diversity, Mental Health and Psychiatry: The Struggle Against Racism* (New York: Brunner-Routledge, 2004); Helms and Cook, *Using Race and Culture in Counseling and Psychotherapy*.

13. Marger, *Race and Ethnic Relations*.

14. For example, José M. Causadias, Joseph A. Vitriol, and Annabelle Lin Atkin, "Do We Overemphasize the Role of Culture in Behavior of Racial/Ethnic Minorities? Evidence of a Cultural (Mis)Attribution Bias in American Psychology," *American Psychologist* 73, no. 3 (2018): 243–55, doi.org/10.1037/amp0000099; Robert V. Guthrie, *Even the Rat Was White: A Historical View of Psychology*, 2nd ed. (Upper Saddle River, NJ: Pearson Education, 2004); J. Philippe Rushton and Elizabeth W. Rushton, "Brain Size, IQ, and Racial-Group Differences: Evidence from Musculoskeletal Traits," *Intelligence* 31, no. 2 (2003): 139–55, doi.org/10.1016/S0160-2896(02)00137-X.

15. Causadias et al., "Do We Overemphasize the Role of Culture in Behavior of Racial/Ethnic Minorities?," 243.

16. Causadias et al., "Do We Overemphasize the Role of Culture in Behavior of Racial/Ethnic Minorities?," 252.

17. Ratts and Pedersen, *Counseling for Multiculturalism and Social Justice*, 1–15; Derald Wing Sue et al., *Multicultural Counseling Competencies: Individual and Organizational Development* (Thousand Oaks, CA: Sage, 1998), 14–25.

18. Charles S. Carver and Michael F. Scheier, *Perspectives on Personality*, 8th ed. (Boston: Pearson, 2017); Helms and Cook, *Using Race and Culture in Counseling and Psychotherapy*, 7–14.

19. Audrey Smedley and Brian D. Smedley, *Race in North America: Origin and Evolution of a Worldview*, 4th ed. (Boulder, CO: Westview, 2012), 41–73.

20. Erik H. Erikson, *Identity and the Life Cycle: Selected Papers* (New York: International University Press, 1959).

21. Carter, *Race and Racial Identity in Psychotherapy*; Chalmer E. Thompson and Robert T. Carter, eds., *Racial Identity Theory: Applications to Individual, Group, and Organizational Interventions* (Mahwah, NJ: Lawrence Erlbaum, 2012 [1997]), 97–108.

22. Derald Wing Sue et al., *Counseling the Culturally Diverse: Theory and Practice*, 8th ed. (Hoboken, NJ: Wiley, 2019), 5–34.

23. Janet E. Helms, "Toward a Theoretical Explanation of the Effects of Race on Counseling: A Black and White Model," *Counseling Psychologist* 12, no. 4 (1984): 153–65, doi.org/10.1177/0011000084124013; Janet E. Helms, ed., *Black and*

White Racial Identity: Theory, Research, and Practice (Westport, CT: Greenwood, 1990).

24. Carter, "Uprooting Inequity and Disparities in Counseling and Psychology"; Carter, "The Road Less Traveled: Research on Race."

25. Carter, *Race and Racial Identity in Psychotherapy.*

26. Riana E. Anderson et al., "EMBRacing racial Stress and Trauma: Preliminary Feasibility and Coping Responses of a Racial Socialization Intervention," *Journal of Black Psychology* 44, no. 1 (2017): 25–46, doi.org/10.1177/0095798417732930.

27. Smedley and Smedley, *Race in North America.*

28. David Rollock and Edmund W. Gordon, "Racism and Mental Health into the 21st Century: Perspectives and Parameters," *American Journal of Orthopsychiatry* 70 (2000): 5–16, doi.org/10.1037/h0087703; Thompson and Carter, *Racial Identity Theory.*

29. Sue et al., *Counseling the Culturally Diverse.*

30. Carter, "The Road Less Traveled: Research on Race."

31. Thomas Byrne Edsall and Mary D. Edsall, *Chain Reaction: The Impact of Race, Rights and Taxes on American Politics* (New York: Norton and Company, 1991), 84–85.

32. Ta-Nehisi Coates, *We Were Eight Years in Power: An American Tragedy* (New York: One World, 2017).

33. E. J. Dionne Jr., Norman J. Ornstein, and Thomas E. Mann, *One Nation After Trump: A Guide for the Perplexed, the Disillusioned, the Desperate, and the Not-Yet Desperate* (New York: St. Martin's, 2017).

34. Richard Rothstein, *The Color of Law: A Forgotten History of How Our Government Segregated America* (New York: Liveright, 2017).

35. Thomas F. Pettigrew, "Social Psychological Perspectives on Trump Supporters," *Journal of Social and Political Psychology* 5, no. 1 (2017): 107–16, doi.org/10.5964/jspp.v5i1.750; Nicholas A. Valentino, Fabian Guy Neuner, and L. Matthew Vandenbroek, "The Changing Norms of Racial Political Rhetoric and the End of Racial Priming," *Journal of Politics* 80, no. 3 (2018): 757–71, doi.org/10.1086/694845.

36. Julia Azari and Marc J. Hetherington, "Back to the Future? What the Politics of the Late Nineteenth Century Can Tell Us About the 2016 Election," *ANNALS of the American Academy of Political and Social Science* 667, no. 1 (2016): 92–109, doi.org/10.1177/0002716216662604.

37. Brenda Major, Alison Blodorn, and Gregory Major Blascovich, "The Threat of Increasing Diversity: Why Many White Americans Support Trump in the 2016 Presidential Election," *Group Processes and Intergroup Relations* (October 2016), https://doi.org/10.1177/1368430216677304.

38. Joe R. Feagin and Karyn D. McKinney, *The Many Costs of Racism* (Lanham, MD: Rowman and Littlefield, 2003).

39. Isha Mackenzie-Mavinga, *The Challenge of Racism in Therapeutic Practice: Engaging with Oppression in Practice and Supervision* (New York: Palgrave, 2016).

40. Hemmings and Evans, "Identifying and Treating Race-Based Trauma in Counseling."

41. Sue et al., *Counseling the Culturally Diverse*; Robert T. Carter, ed., *Handbook of Racial-Cultural Psychology and Counseling*, vol. 2, *Training and Practice* (Hoboken, NJ: Wiley, 2005b); Carter, "The Road Less Traveled: Research on Race."

42. American Psychological Association, "Guidelines on Multicultural Education, Training, Research, Practice, and Organizational Change for Psychologists," *American Psychologist* 58, no. 5 (2003): 308.

43. Robert T. Carter, "Racism and Psychological and Emotional Injury: Recognizing and Assessing Race-Based Traumatic Stress," *Counseling Psychologist* 35, no. 1 (2007): 13–105, doi:10.1177/0011000006292033.

44. Carter, *Race and Racial Identity in Psychotherapy*; Helms and Cook, *Using Race and Culture in Counseling and Psychotherapy*.

45. Robert T. Carter et al., "The Development of Classes of Racism Measures for Frequency and Stress Reactions: Relationships to Race-Based Traumatic Symptoms," *Traumatology* 22, no. 1 (2016): 63–74; Joshua Miller and Ann Marie Garran, *Racism in the United States: Implications for the Helping Professions* (New York: Springer, 2017); David R. Williams and Selina A. Mohammed, "Racism and Health I: Pathways and Scientific Evidence," *American Behavioral Scientist* 57, no. 8 (2013): 1152–73, doi:10.1177/0002764213487340.

46. Joshua Miller and Ann Marie Garran, "The Web of Institutional Racism," *Smith College Studies in Social Work* 77, no. 1 (2007): 33–67, doi.org/10.1300/J497v77n01_03.

47. Tamara R. Buckley and Erica Gabrielle Foldy, "A Pedagogical Model for Increasing Race-Related Multicultural Counseling Competency," *Counseling Psychologist* 38, no. 5 (2010): 691–713.

48. Jeffrey M. Jones, "Six in 10 Americans Say Racism Against Blacks Is Widespread," Gallup, August 17, 2016, http://www.gallup.com/poll/194657/six—Americans-Say-Racism-Against-Blacks-Widespread.asp.

49. Pew Research Center, "The Partisan Divide on Political Values Grows Even Wider," October 5, 2017, http://www.people-press.org/2017/10/05/the-partisan-divide-on-political-values-grows-even-wider/.

50. Elizabeth Dais, John Eligon, and Richard A. Oppel Jr., "Philadelphia Starbucks Arrests Outrageous to Some, Are Everyday Life for Others," *New York Times*, April 18, 2018, https://www.nytimes.com/2018/04/17/us/starbucks-arrest-philadelphia.html.

51. For example, American Psychological Association, *Stress in America: The Impact of Discrimination: Stress in America Survey* (Washington, DC: American

Psychological Association, 2016); E. Ann Carson, *Prisoners in 2013*, U.S. Department of Justice, Office of Justice Programs, Bureau of Justice Statistics, September 2014, https://www.bjs.gov/content/pub/pdf/p13.pdf; Brian D. Smedley, Adrienne Y. Stith, and Alan R. Nelson, eds., *Unequal Treatment: Confronting Racial and Ethnic Disparities in Health Care* (Washington, DC: National Academies Press, 2003); U.S. Department of Health and Human Services (USD-HHS), *Mental Health: Culture, Race and Ethnicity: A Supplement to Mental Health: A Report of the Surgeon General* (Washington, DC: USDHHS, 2001).

52. Pew Research Center, "On Views of Race and Inequality, Blacks and Whites Are Worlds Apart," June 27, 2016, http://www.pewsocialtrends.org/2016/06/27/on -views-of-race-and-inequality-blacks-and-whites-are-worlds-apart/.

53. Lillian Comas-Díaz, "Racial Trauma Recovery: A Race Informed Therapeutic Approach to Racial Wounds," in *The Cost of Racism for People of Color: Contextualizing Experiences of Discrimination*, ed. Alvin N. Alvarez, Christopher T. H. Liang, and Helen A. Neville (Washington, DC: American Psychological Association, 2016), 249–71, doi.org/10.1037/14852-012; Comas-Díaz, Hall and Neville, "Racial Trauma: Theory, Research, and Healing"; Nia J. Heard-Garris et al., "Transmitting Trauma: A Systematic Review of Vicarious Racism and Child Health," *Social Science and Medicine* 199 (2018): 230–40, dx.doi.org /10.1016/j.socscimed.2017.04.018.

54. Anthony G. Greenwald et al., "Understanding and Using the Implicit Association Test: III. Meta-Analysis of Predictive Validity," *Journal of Personality and Social Psychology* 97, no. 1 (2009): 17–41, doi.org/10.1037/a0015575.

55. Carter, "Racism and Psychological and Emotional Injury."

56. Alex Madva, "Social Psychology, Phenomenology, and the Indeterminate Content of Unreflective Racial Bias," in *Race as Phenomena: Between Phenomenology and Philosophy of Race*, ed. E. S. Lee (Lanham, MD: Rowman & Littlefield International, 2019), 87–106; Frederick L. Oswald et al., "Predicting Ethnic and Racial Discrimination: A Meta-Analysis of IAT Criterion Studies," *Journal of Personality and Social Psychology* 105, no. 2 (2013): 171–92, doi.org/10.1037/a0032734.

57. Greenwald et al., "Understanding and Using the Implicit Association Test: III. Meta-Analysis of Predictive Validity."

58. Hart Blanton and James Jaccard, "Unconscious Racism: A Concept in Pursuit of a Measure," *Annual Review of Sociology* 34 (2008): 278, doi.org/10.1146/an-nurev.soc.33.040406.131632.

59. Oswald et al., "Predicting Ethnic and Racial Discrimination: A Meta-Analysis of IAT Criterion Studies," *Journal of Personality and Social Psychology* 105, no. 2 (2013): 183, doi.org/10.1037/a0032734.

60. German Lopez, "For Years, This Popular Test Measured Anyone's Racial Bias. But It Might Not Work After All," *Vox*, March 7, 2017, https://www.vox.com /identities/2017/3/7/14637626/implicit-association-test-racism.

61. John Sommers-Flanagan and Rita Sommers-Flanagan, *Clinical Interviewing*, 6th ed. (Hoboken, NJ: Wiley, 2016); James R. Morrison, *The First Interview* (New York: Guilford, 2014).

62. Lillian Polanco-Roman, Ashley Allison Danies, and Deidre M. Anglin, "Racial Discrimination as Race-Based Trauma, Coping Strategies and Dissociative Symptoms Among Emerging Adults," *Psychological Trauma: Theory, Research, Practice, and Policy* 8, no. 5 (2016): 609–17, doi.org/10.1037/tra0000125.

63. Robert T. Carter and Jessica M. Forsyth, "Reactions to Racial Discrimination: Emotional Stress and Help-Seeking Behaviors," *Psychological Trauma: Theory, Research, Practice, and Policy* 2, no. 3 (2010): 183–91, doi.org/10.1037/a0020102.

64. Vetta L. Sanders Thompson, Anita Bazile, and Maysa Akbar, "African Americans' Perceptions of Psychotherapy and Psychotherapists," *Professional Psychology: Research and Practice* 35, no. 1 (2004): 24, doi.org/10.1037/0735-7028.35.1.19.

65. Thompson and Carter, *Racial Identity Theory*.

66. Zinzi D. Bailey et al., "Structural Racism and Health Inequities in the USA: Evidence and Interventions," *Lancet* 389, no. 10077 (April 8, 2017): 1453.

67. Hans Oh et al., "Major Discriminatory Events and Risk for Psychotic Experiences Among Black Americans," *American Journal of Orthopsychiatry* 86, no. 3 (2016): 277–85, doi.org/10.1037/ort0000158; Hans Oh et al., "Discrimination and Suicidality Among Racial and Ethnic Minorities in the United States," *Journal of Affective Disorders* 245 (2019): 517–23; Alice P. Villatoro et al., "Perceived Need for Mental Health Care: The Intersection of Race, Ethnicity, Gender, and Socioeconomic Status," *Society and Mental Health* 8, no. 1 (2018): 1–24, doi.org /10.1177/2156869317718889; Monnica Williams et al., "Discrimination and Symptoms of Obsessive-Compulsive Disorder Among African Americans," *American Journal of Orthopsychiatry* 87, no. 6 (2017): 636–45, doi.org/10.1037/ort0000285.

68. American Psychiatric Association, *Diagnostic and Statistical Manual of Mental Disorders*, 5th ed. (Washington, DC: American Psychiatric Association, 2013).

69. Carter, "Racism and Psychological and Emotional Injury"; Robert T. Carter and Thomas D. Scheuermann, "Legal and Policy Standards for Addressing Workplace Racism: Employer Liability and Shared Responsibility for Race-Based Traumatic Stress," *University of Maryland Law Journal of Race, Religion, Gender and Class* 12, no. 1 (2012): 1–100; Robert T. Carter and Thomas D. Scheuermann, *Confronting Racism: Integrating Mental Health Research into Legal Reform* (New York: Routledge, 2020).

70. Ronald C. Kessler, "The Effects of Stressful Life Events on Depression," *Annual Review of Psychology* 48, no. 1 (1997): 191–214.

71. Lillian Comas-Díaz and Frederick M. Jacobsen, "Ethnocultural Allodynia," *Journal of Psychotherapy Practice and Research* 10, no. 4 (2001): 246–47.

72. Raymond Monsour Scurfield and David W. Mackey, "Racism, Trauma and Positive Aspects of Exposure to Race-Related Experiences: Assessment and

Treatment Implications," *Journal of Ethnic and Cultural Diversity in Social Work* 10, no. 1 (2001): 28.

73. Scurfield and Mackey, "Racism, Trauma and Positive Aspects of Exposure to Race-Related Experiences," 30.

74. Monnica T. Williams et al., "Assessing Racial Trauma Within a DSM-5 Framework: The UConn Racial/Ethnic Stress and Trauma Survey," *Practice Innovations* 3, no. 4 (2018): 242–60, doi.org/10.1037/pri0000076; Monnica T. Williams, Jonathan W. Kanter, and Terrence H. W. Ching, "Anxiety, Stress and Trauma Symptoms in African Americans: Negative Affectivity Does Not Explain the Relationship Between Microaggressions and Psychopathology," *Journal of Racial and Ethnic Health Disparities* 5, no. 5 (2018): 919–27.

75. For example, Naomi Breslau, "The Epidemiology of Posttraumatic Stress Disorder: What Is the Extent of the Problem?" *Journal of Clinical Psychiatry* 62, Suppl. 17 (2001): 16–22; Daniel W. McNeil et al., "Assessment of Culturally Related Anxiety in American Indians and Alaska Natives," *Behavior Therapy* 31, no. 2 (2000): 301–25, dx.doi.org/10.1016/S0005-7894(00)80017-9.

76. Julia L. Perilla, Fran H. Norris, and Evelyn A. Lavizzo, "Ethnicity, Culture, and Disaster Response: Identifying and Explaining Ethnic Differences in PTSD Six Months After Hurricane Andrew," *Journal of Social and Clinical Psychology* 21, no. 1 (2002): 20–45.

77. Fran H. Norris, "Epidemiology of Trauma Frequency and Impact of Different Potentially Traumatic Events on Different Demographic Groups," *Journal of Consulting and Clinical Psychology* 60, no. 3 (1992): 417.

78. Chalsa M. Loo et al., "Measuring Exposure of Racism: Development and Validation of a Race-Related Stressor Scale (RRSS) or Asian American Vietnam Veterans," *Psychological Assessment* 13 (2001): 503–20, doi.org/10.1037/1040-3590.13.4.503.

79. Robert T. Carter, Katherine Kirkinis, and Veronica Johnson, "Race-Based Traumatic Stress and General Trauma Symptoms," *Traumatology* (in press); John C. Norcross and Bruce E. Wampold, "Relationships and Responsiveness in the Psychological Treatment of Trauma: The Tragedy of the APA Clinical Practice Guideline," *Psychotherapy* (April 22, 2019), advance online publication, dx.doi.org/10.1037/pst0000228.

80. Maria P. P. Root, "Reconstructing the Impact of Trauma on Personality," in *Personality and Psychopathology: Feminist Reappraisals*, ed. Laura S. Brown and Mary Ballou (New York: Guilford, 1992), 229–65; Paul B. Perrin, "Humanistic Psychology's Social Justice Philosophy: Systemically Treating the Psychosocial and Health Effects of Racism," *Journal of Humanistic Psychology* 53, no. 1 (2013): 52–69, doi.org/10.1177/0022167812447133; Barbara C. Wallace and Robert T. Carter, eds., *Understanding and Dealing with Violence: A Multicultural Approach* (Thousand Oaks, CA: Sage), 2003.

81. Polanco-Roman et al., "Racial Discrimination as Race-Based Trauma, Coping Strategies and Dissociative Symptoms Among Emerging Adults"; Williams et al., "Discrimination and Symptoms of Obsessive-Compulsive Disorder Among African Americans"; *Merriam-Webster's Collegiate Dictionary*, 11th ed. (Springfield, MA: Merriam-Webster Inc., 2003); *Merriam-Webster's Collegiate Dictionary*, New edition (Springfield, MA.: Merriam-Webster Inc., 2016).

82. Carter and Scheuermann, *Confronting Racism: Integrating Mental Health Research into Legal Strategies and Reforms* (New York: Routledge, 2020).

83. Carter, "Racism and Psychological and Emotional Injury"; Robert T. Carter, Carrie Muchow, and Alex L. Pieterse, "Construct, Predictive Validity, and Measurement Equivalence of the Race-Based Traumatic Stress Symptom Scale for Black Americans," *Traumatology* 24, no. 1 (2018): 8–16, doi.org/10.1037/trm0000128; Robert T. Carter and Carrie Muchow, "Construct Validity of the Race-Based Traumatic Stress Symptom Scale and Tests of Measurement Equivalence," *Psychological Trauma: Theory, Research, Practice, and Policy* 9, no. 6 (2017): 688–95, doi.org/10.1037/tra0000256.

84. Eve B. Carlson, *Trauma Assessments: A Clinician's Guide* (New York: Guilford Press, 1997), 26–33.

85. Bailey et al., "Structural Racism and Health Inequities in the USA"; Anthony D. Ong, Thomas E. Fuller-Rowell, and Anthony L. Burrow, "Racial Discrimination and the Stress Process," *Journal of Personality and Social Psychology* 96, no. 6 (2009): 1259, doi.org/10.1037/a0015335.

86. Andrea K. Delgado, "On Being Black," in *Effective Psychotherapy for Low-Income and Minority Patients*, ed. Frank Xavier Acosta, Joe Yamamoto, and Leonard A. Evans (New York: Plenum, 1982), 109–16; Feagin and McKinney, *The Many Costs of Racism*; Eduardo Bonilla-Silva, *Racism Without Racists: Color-Blind Racism and the Persistence of Racial Inequality in America*, 5th ed. (Lanham, MD: Rowman and Littlefield, 2017).

87. Derald Wing Sue et al., "Racial Microaggressions in Everyday Life: Implications for Clinical Practice," *American Psychologist* 62 (2007): 271–86, doi.org/10.1037/0003-066X.62.4.271; Kevin L. Nadal, *Microaggressions and Traumatic Stress: Theory, Research, and Clinical Treatment* (Washington, DC: American Psychological Association), 2018.

88. Robert T. Carter et al., "A Meta-Analytic Review of Racial Discrimination: Relationships to Health and Culture," *Race and Social Problems* 11, no. 1 (2019): 15–32, doi.org/10.1007/s12552-018-9256-y; Amanda Geller et al., "Aggressive Policing and the Mental Health of Young Urban Men," *American Journal of Public Health* 104, no. 12 (2014): 2321–27, doi.org/10.2105/AJPH.2014.302046.

89. Carter, "Racism and Psychological and Emotional Injury."

90. Robert T. Carter and Janet E. Helms, "Racial Discrimination and Harassment: A Racially Based Trauma" (paper presented at the American College of Forensic Examiners Conference, Orlando, FL, September 2002).

91. Helms, *Black and White Racial Identity Attitudes*; Carter, *Race and Racial Identity in Psychotherapy*; Carter and Johnson, "Racial Identity Statuses"; Thompson and Carter, *Racial Identity Theory*.

92. Carter, *Race and Racial Identity in Psychotherapy*.

93. Thompson and Carter, *Racial Identity Theory*.

94. See also Helms and Cook, *Using Race and Culture in Counseling and Psychotherapy*.

95. Hugh F. Butts, "The Black Mask of Humanity: Racial/Ethnic Discrimination and Post-Traumatic Stress Disorder," *Journal of the American Academy of Psychiatry and the Law* 30, no. 3 (2002): 336–39.

96. Derrick Bell, *Race, Racism and American Law*, 5th ed. (Gaithersburg, MD: Aspen Law and Business, 2008); Carter and Scheuermann, "Legal and Policy Standards for Addressing Workplace Racism"; Carter and Scheuermann, *Confronting Racism*.

97. Carter and Scheuermann, "Legal and Policy Standards for Addressing Workplace Racism"; Carter and Scheuermann, *Confronting Racism*.

98. Robert T. Carter and Jessica M. Forsyth, "Examining Race and Culture in Psychology Journals: The Case of Forensic Psychology," *Professional Psychology: Research and Practice* 38, no. 2 (2007): 133–42, doi.org/10.1037/0735-7028.38.2.133; Robert T. Carter and Jessica M. Forsyth, "A Guide to the Forensic Assessment of Race-Based Traumatic Stress Reactions," *Journal of the American Academy of Psychiatry and the Law* 37, no. 1 (2009): 28–40.

99. For example, Thema Bryant-Davis and Carlota Ocampo, "The Trauma of Racism: Implications for Counseling, Research, and Education." *Counseling Psychologist* 33 (2005b): 574–78, doi.org/10.1177/0011000005276581; Butts, "The Black Mask of Humanity"; Comas-Díaz and Jacobsen, "Ethnocultural Allodynia"; Loo et al., "Measuring Exposure of Racism"; Scurfield and Mackey, "Racism, Trauma and Positive Aspects of Exposure to Race-Related Experiences"; Comas-Díaz, "Racial Trauma Recovery"; Comas-Díaz, Hall, and Neville, "Racial Trauma: Theory, Research, and Healing."

100. Scurfield and Mackey, "Racism, Trauma and Positive Aspects of Exposure to Race-Related Experiences," 28.

101. Bryant-Davis and Ocampo, "The Trauma of Racism."

102. Bryant-Davis and Ocampo, "The Trauma of Racism."

103. Nadal, *Microaggressions and Traumatic Stress*.

104. Susan Stefan, "The Protection Racket: Rape Trauma Syndrome, Psychiatric Labeling, and the Law," *Northwestern University Law Review* 88, no. 4 (1994): 1275.

105. Samantha C. Holmes, Vanessa C. Facemire, and Alexis M. DaFonseca, "Expanding Criterion a for Posttraumatic Stress Disorder: Considering the Deleterious Impact of Oppression," *Traumatology* 22, no. 4 (2016): 314–21.

106. Stefan, "The Protection Racket," 1275.

107. Bryant-Davis and Ocampo, "The Trauma of Racism."

108. Bryant-Davis and Ocampo, "The Trauma of Racism."

109. Calvin John Smiley and David Fakunle, "From 'Brute' to 'Thug': The Demonization and Criminalization of Unarmed Black Male Victims in America," *Journal of Human Behavior in the Social Environment* 26, no. 3–4 (2016): 350–66, dx.doi.org/10.1080/10911359.2015.1129256.

110. Donna Chrobot-Mason and Willaim K. Hepworth, "Examining Perceptions of Ambiguous and Unambiguous Threats of Racial Harassment and Managerial Response Strategies," *Journal of Applied Social Psychology* 35, no. 11 (July 2005): 2215–61, doi.org/10.1111/j.1559-1816.2005.tb02101.x.

111. Carter, "Racism and Psychological and Emotional Injury."

112. Nikole Hannan-Jones, 2019b. "The Idea of America: 1619 Project." *New York Times Magazine*, August 20, 2019, 14–26.

113. Derald Wing Sue, *Overcoming Our Racism: The Journey to Liberation* (San Francisco: Jossey-Bass, 2003), 31.

114. Scurfield and Mackey, "Racism, Trauma and Positive Aspects of Exposure to Race-Related Experiences."

115. Bryant-Davis and Ocampo, "The Trauma of Racism."

116. Carter et al., "A Meta-Analytic Review of Racial Discrimination: Relationships to Health and Culture."

117. Carter, "Racism and Psychological and Emotional Injury."

118. Angela Bermudez-Millan et al., "Behavioral Reactivity to Acute Stress Among Black and White Women with Type 2 Diabetes: The Role of Income and Racial Discrimination," *Journal of Health Psychology* 21, no. 9 (2016): 2085–97, doi.org/10.1177/1359105315571776; Lora L. Black, Rhonda Johnson, and Lisa Van-Hoose, "The Relationship Between Perceived Racism/Discrimination and Health Among Black American Women: A Review of the Literature from 2003–2013," *Journal of Racial and Ethnic Health Disparities* 2 (2015): 11–20, doi.org/10.1007/s40615-014-0043-1; Angelitta M. Britt-Spells et al., "Effects of Perceived Discrimination on Depressive Symptoms Among Black Men Residing in the United States: A Meta-Analysis," *American Journal of Men's Health* 12, no. 1 (2016): 52–63, doi.org/10.1177/1557988315624509.

119. Jessica Forsyth and Robert T. Carter, "The Influence of Racial Identity Status Attitudes and Racism-Related Coping on Mental Health Among Black Americans," *Cultural Diversity and Ethnic Minority Psychology* 18, no. 2 (2012): 128–40, doi.org/10.1037/a0027660; Jessica Forsyth and Robert T. Carter, "The Development and Preliminary Validation of the Racism-Related Coping Scale,"

Psychological Trauma: Theory, Policy, Research, and Practice 6, no. 6 (2014): 632–43, doi.org/10.1037/a0036702.

120. Robert T. Carter et al., "Race-Based Traumatic Stress, Racial Identity Status, and Psychological Functioning: An Exploratory Investigation," *Professional Psychology: Research and Practice* 48, no. 1 (2017): 20–37, doi.org/10.1037/pro0000116; Carter and Johnson, "Racial Identity Statuses."

121. Carter and Helms, "Racial Discrimination and Harassment: A Racially Based Trauma."

122. Robert T. Carter et al., "Initial Development of the Race-Based Traumatic Stress Symptom Scale: Assessing the Emotional Impact of Racism," *Psychological Trauma: Theory, Research, Practice, and Policy* 5, no.1 (2013): 1–9, doi.org/10.1037/a0025911.

6. Measuring Race-Based Traumatic Stress

1. Rahshida Atkins, "Instruments Measuring Perceived Racism/Racial Discrimination: Review and Critique of Factor Analytic Techniques," *International Journal of Health Services* 44, no. 4 (2014): 711–34; Joao Luiz Bastos et al., "Racial Discrimination and Health: A Systematic Review of Scales with a Focus on Their Psychometric Properties," *Social Science and Medicine* 70, no. 7 (2010): 1091–99; Nancy R. Kressin, Kristal L. Raymond, and Meredith Manze, "Perceptions of Race/Ethnicity-Based Discrimination: A Review of Measures and Evaluation of Their Usefulness for the Health Care Setting," *Journal of Health Care for the Poor and Underserved* 19 (2008): 697–730, doi.org/10.1353/hpu.0.0041; Shawn O. Utsey, "Assessing the Stressful Effects of Racism: A Review of Instrumentation," *Journal of Black Psychology* 24, no. 3 (1998): 269–88, doi.org/10.1177/00957984980243001.

2. Robert T. Carter et al., "Race-Based Traumatic Stress Symptom Scale and White Americans: Construct Validity," unpublished manuscript, 2018; Yin Paradies et al., "Racism as a Determinant of Health: A Systematic Review and Meta-Analysis," *PloS one* 10, no. 9 (2015): 1–48, doi:10.137/journal.pone.0138511; Alex L. Pieterse et al., "Perceived Racism and Mental Health Among Black American Adults: A Meta-Analytic Review," *Journal of Counseling Psychology* 59, no. 1 (January 2012): 1–9, doi.org/10.1037/a0026208.

3. Thema Bryant-Davis, *Thriving in the Wake of Trauma: A Multicultural Guide* (Westport, CT: Praeger, 2005); Eve B. Carlson, *Trauma Assessments: A Clinician's Guide* (New York: Guilford Press, 1997); Robert T. Carter, "Racism and Psychological and Emotional Injury: Recognizing and Assessing Race-Based Traumatic Stress," *Counseling Psychologist* 35, no. 1 (2007): 13–105, doi:10.1177/0011000006292033; Judith Lewis Herman, *Trauma and Recovery: The*

Aftermath of Violence from Domestic Abuse to Political Terror, rev. ed. (New York: Basic Books, 1997).

4. See Carter, "Racism and Psychological and Emotional Injury."

5. Robert T. Carter et al., "Racial Discrimination and Race-Based Traumatic Stress: An Exploratory Investigation," in *Handbook of Racial-Cultural Psychology and Counseling*, vol. 2, *Training and Practice*, ed. Robert T. Carter (Hoboken, NJ, Wiley, 2005), 447–76.

6. Robert T. Carter and Janet E. Helms, "Racial Discrimination and Harassment: A Race-Based Traumatic Stress," paper presented at the American College of Forensic Examiners Conference, Orlando, FL, September 2002.

7. Carter and Helms, "Racial Discrimination and Harassment," 14–16.

8. Carter et al., "Racial Discrimination and Race-Based Traumatic Stress."

9. Carter et al., "Racial Discrimination and Race-Based Traumatic Stress."

10. Carlson, *Trauma Assessments*, 20–38.

11. American Psychiatric Association, *Diagnostic and Statistical Manual of Mental Disorder*, 4th ed., text revision (Washington, DC: American Psychiatric Association, 2000).

12. Carter and Helms, "Racial Discrimination and Harassment."

13. Robert T. Carter et al., "Does Racism Predict Psychological Harm or Injury: Mental Health and Legal Implication," *Law Enforcement Executive Forum* 7, no. 5 (2007): 129–54.

14. Compare Carter et al., "Does Racism Predict Psychological Harm or Injury."

15. Elizabeth Brondolo et al., "Coping with Racism: A Selective Review of the Literature and a Theoretical and Methodological Critique," *Journal of Behavioral Medicine* 32, no. 1 (2009): 64–88, https://link.springer.com/article/10.1007%2Fs10865-008-9193-0; Robert T. Carter, Janet E. Helms, and Heather L. Juby, "The Relationship Between Racism and Racial Identity for White Americans: A Profile Analysis," *Journal of Multicultural Counseling and Development* 32, no. 1 (January 2004): 2–17, doi.org/10.1002/j.2161-1912.2004.tb00357.x; Robert M. Sellers and J. Nicole Shelton, "The Role of Racial Identity in Perceived Racial Discrimination," *Journal of Personality and Social Psychology* 84, no. 5 (2003): 1079–92, doi.org/10.1037/0022-3514.84.5.1079; Chalmer E. Thompson and Robert T. Carter, eds., *Racial Identity Theory: Applications to Individual, Group, and Organizational Interventions* (New York: Routledge, 2012 [1997]).

16. Robert T. Carter and Jessica M. Forsyth, "Reactions to Racial Discrimination: Emotional Stress and Help-Seeking Behaviors," *Psychological Trauma: Theory, Research, Practice, and Policy* 2, no. 3 (2010): 183–91, doi.org/10.1037/a0020102.

17. Shelly P. Harrell, "The Racism and Life Experiences Scale (RaLES)," unpublished manuscript, 1997.

18. Carter, "Racism and Psychological and Emotional Injury."

19. Carter et al., "Racial Discrimination and Race-Based Traumatic Stress"; Carter et al., "Does Racism Predict Psychological Harm or Injury."

20. Joseph L. Fleiss, "Measuring Nominal Scale Agreement Among Many Raters," *Psychological Bulletin* 76, no. 5 (1971): 378–82, dx.doi.org/10.1037/h0031619.

21. See Carter and Forsyth, "Reactions to Racial Discrimination," 185

22. Carter and Forsyth, "Reactions to Racial Discrimination," 187

23. Carter and Forsyth, "Reactions to Racial Discrimination," 189

24. Renee V. Dawis, "Scale Construction and Psychometric Considerations," in *Handbook of Applied Multivariate Statistics and Mathematical Modeling*, ed. H. E. A. Tinsley and S. D. Brown (San Diego, CA: Academic Press, 2000), 65–92; Jeffrey H. Kahn, "Factor Analysis in Counseling Psychology Research, Training, and Practice: Principles, Advances, and Applications," *Counseling Psychologist* 34, no. 5 (2006): 684–718, doi.org/10.1177/001100 0006286347; Roger L. Worthington and Tiffany A. Whittaker, "Scale Development Research: A Content Analysis and Recommendations for Best Practices," *Counseling Psychologist* 34, no. 6 (2006): 806–39, doi.org/10.1177/00110 00006288127.

25. See Robert T. Carter and Jessica M. Forsyth, "Examining Race and Culture in Psychology Journals: The Case of Forensic Psychology," *Professional Psychology: Research and Practice* 38, no. 2 (2007): 133–42, doi.org/10.1037/0735-7028.38.2.133; Robert T. Carter and Jessica M. Forsyth, "A Guide to the Forensic Assessment of Race-Based Traumatic Stress Reactions," *Journal of the American Academy of Psychiatry and the Law* 37, no. 1 (2009): 28–40; Elizabeth Brondolo, Linda C. Gallo, and Hector F. Myers, "Race, Racism and Health: Disparities, Mechanisms, and Interventions," *Journal of Behavioral Medicine* 32, no. 1 (2009): 1–8, doi.org/10.1007/s10865-008-9190-3.

26. Robert T. Carter et al., "Initial Development of the Race-Based Traumatic Stress Symptom Scale: Assessing the Emotional Impact of Racism," *Psychological Trauma: Theory, Research, Practice, and Policy* 5, no.1 (2013): 1–9, doi.org/10.1037/a0025911.

27. Carter et al., "Initial Development of the Race-Based Traumatic Stress Symptom Scale," 5.

28. Robert T. Carter, Veronica Johnson, and Katheryn Roberson, "John F. Kennedy Behavioral Health: Site Report for the Race-Based Traumatic Stress Scale Research Study," Teachers College, Columbia University, unpublished manuscript, 2014.

29. F. W. Weathers, "Rational and Empirical Scoring Rules for the Clinician-Administered PTSD Scale," unpublished manuscript, 1993.

30. Carter, "Racism and Psychological and Emotional Injury," 90.

31. Robert T. Carter, Sinead M. Sant-Barket, and Shawna Stotts, "The Consortium: Site Report for the Race-Based Traumatic Stress Scale Research Study,"

Teachers College, Columbia University, unpublished manuscript, 2014; David R. Williams and Selina A. Mohammed, "Racism and Health I: Pathways and Scientific Evidence," *American Behavioral Scientist* 57, no. 8 (2013): 1152–73, doi:10.1177/0002764213487340.

32. Carter, "Racism and Psychological and Emotional Injury."

33. Carter et al., "Initial Development of the Race-Based Traumatic Stress Symptom Scale."

34. John Briere and Marsha Runtz, "The Trauma Symptom Checklist (TSC-33): Early Data on a New Scale," *Journal of Interpersonal Violence* 4, no. 2 (1989): 151–63, doi.org/10.1177/088626089004002002.

35. Robert T. Carter, Katherine Kirkinis, and Veronica Johnson, "Race-Based Traumatic Stress and General Trauma Symptoms," *Traumatology* (September 9, 2019), https://doi-org.tc.idm.oclc.org/10.1037/trm0000217.

36. Robert T. Carter and Sinead Sant-Barket, "Assessment of the Impact of Racial Discrimination and Racism: How to Use the Race-Based Traumatic Stress Symptom Scale in Practice," *Traumatology* 21, no. 1 (2015): 36.

37. Carter, "Racism and Psychological and Emotional Injury."

38. Carter, "Racism and Psychological and Emotional Injury."

39. Kressin, Raymond, and Manze, "Perceptions of Race/Ethnicity-Based Discrimination."

40. For example, Carter et al., "Racial Discrimination and Race-Based Traumatic Stress."

41. Bastos et al., "Racial Discrimination and Health"; Carter et al., "Race-Based Traumatic Stress Symptom Scale and White Americans"; David R. Williams and Selina A. Mohammed, "Discrimination and Racial Disparities in Health: Evidence and Needed Research," *Journal of Behavioral Medicine* 32 (2009): 20–47, doi:10.1007/s10865-008-9185-0.

42. Carter, "Racism and Psychological and Emotional Injury."

43. See Alex L. Pieterse, "Attending to Racial Trauma in Clinical Supervision: Enhancing Client and Supervisee Outcomes," *Clinical Supervisor* 37, no. 1 (2018): 204–20, doi.org/10.1080/07325223.2018.1443304.

7. Empirical Research Evidence Associated with the Race-Based Traumatic Stress Symptom Scale

1. Robert T. Carter et al., "Initial Development of the Race-Based Traumatic Stress Symptom Scale: Assessing the Emotional Impact of Racism," *Psychological Trauma: Theory, Research, Practice, and Policy* 5, no.1 (2013): 1–9, doi.org/10.1037/a0025911.

2. Eve B. Carlson, *Trauma Assessments: A Clinician's Guide* (New York: Guilford Press, 1997), 29.

3. Robert T. Carter and Sinead Sant-Barket, "Assessment of the Impact of Racial Discrimination and Racism: How to Use the Race-Based Traumatic Stress Symptom Scale in Practice," *Traumatology* 21, no. 1 (2015): 32–39.

4. Alissa Sherry and Robin K. Henson, "Conducting and Interpreting Canonical Correlation Analysis in Personality Research: A User-Friendly Primer," *Journal of Personality Assessment* 84, no. 1 (2005): 37–48.

5. Carter and Sant-Barket, "Assessment of the Impact of Racial Discrimination and Racism," 35.

6. Carter and Sant-Barket, "Assessment of the Impact of Racial Discrimination and Racism."

7. Carter and Sant-Barket, "Assessment of the Impact of Racial Discrimination and Racism," 38.

8. Robert T. Carter, "Racism and Psychological and Emotional Injury: Recognizing and Assessing Race-Based Traumatic Stress," *Counseling Psychologist* 35, no. 1 (2007): 13–105, doi:10.1177/0011000006292033.

9. Carter and Sant-Barket, "Assessment of the Impact of Racial Discrimination and Racism," 37.

10. Fong Chan et al., "Structural Equation Modeling in Rehabilitation Counseling Research," *Rehabilitation Counseling Bulletin* 51, no. 1 (2007): 53–66, doi.org/10.1177/00343552070510010701.

11. Randall E. Schumacker and Richard G. Lomax, *A Beginner's Guide to Structural Equation Modeling*, 2nd ed. (Mahwah, NJ: Lawrence Erlbaum, 2004).

12. Rex B. Kline, *Principles and Practice of Structural Equation Modeling*, 3rd ed. (New York: Guilford Press, 2011).

13. Rebecca Weston and Paul A. Gore, "A Brief Guide to Structural Equation Modeling," *Counseling Psychologist* 34, no. 5 (2006): 719–51, doi.org/10.1177/0011000006286345.

14. Robert T. Carter and Carrie Muchow, "Construct Validity of the Race-Based Traumatic Stress Symptom Scale and Tests of Measurement Equivalence," *Psychological Trauma: Theory, Research, Practice, and Policy* 9, no. 6 (2017): 688–95, doi.org/10.1037/tra0000256.

15. Carter et al., "Initial Development of the Race-Based Traumatic Stress Symptom Scale."

16. William T. Hoyt, Rosalia E. Warbasse, and Erica Y. Chu, "Construct Validation in Counseling Psychology Research," *Counseling Psychologist* 34, no. 6 (2006): 777. doi.org/10.1177/0011000006287389.

17. Paul Barrett, "Structural Equation Modeling: Adjudging Model Fit," *Personality and Individual Differences* 42, no. 5 (2007): 815–24, doi:10.1016/j.paid.2006.09.018.

18. Li-tze Hu and Peter M. Bentler, "Cutoff Criteria for Fit Indexes in Covariance Structure Analysis: Conventional Criteria Versus New Alternatives," *Structural*

Equation Modeling: A Multidisciplinary Journal 6, no. 1 (1999): 1–55, dx.doi.org /10.1080/10705519909540118.

19. James B. Schreiber et al., "Reporting Structural Equation Modeling and Confirmatory Factor Analysis Results: A Review," *Journal of Educational Research* 99, no. 6 (2006): 323–38, doi.org/10.3200/JOER.99.6.323-338.

20. Kline, *Principles and Practice of Structural Equation Modeling*.

21. See, for example, Taciano L. Milfont and Ronald Fischer, "Testing Measurement Invariance Across Groups: Applications in Cross-Cultural Research," *International Journal of Psychological Research* 3, no. 1 (2010): 111–30.

22. Alex L. Pieterse et al., "Perceived Racism and Mental Health Among Black American Adults: A Meta-Analytic Review," *Journal of Counseling Psychology* 59, no. 1 (January 2012): 1–9, doi.org/10.1037/a0026208.

23. Robert T. Carter, Carrie Muchow, and Alex L. Pieterse, "Construct, Predictive Validity, and Measurement Equivalence of the Race-Based Traumatic Stress Symptom Scale for Black Americans," *Traumatology* 24, no. 1 (2018): 8–16, doi.org/10.1037/trm0000128.

24. Robert T. Carter et al., "Race-Based Traumatic Stress, Racial Identity Status, and Psychological Functioning: An Exploratory Investigation," *Professional Psychology: Research and Practice* 48, no. 1 (2017): 20–37, doi.org /10.1037/pro0000116.

25. Robert T. Carter, "Racism and Psychological and Emotional Injury."

26. Carter, "Racism and Psychological and Emotional Injury," 18.

27. Janet E. Helms and Robert T. Carter, "Development of the White Racial Identity Inventory," in *Black and White Racial Identity: Theory, Research, and Practice*, ed. Janet E. Helms (Westport, CT: Greenwood, 1990), 67–80.

28. Helms and Carter, "Development of the White Racial Identity Inventory."

29. David R. Williams et al., "Research on Discrimination and Health: An Exploratory Study of Unresolved Conceptual and Measurement Issues," *American Journal of Public Health* 102 (2012): 975–78, doi.org/10.2105/AJPH.2012 .300702.

30. Kelly M. Bower, Roland J. Thorpe, and Thomas A. LaVeist, "Perceived Racial Discrimination and Mental Health in Low-Income, Urban-Dwelling Whites," *International Journal of Health Services* 43, no. 2 (2013): 267–80, doi.org/10.2190/ HS.43.2.e.

31. Jennifer L. Bratter and Bridget K. Gorman, "Is Discrimination an Equal Opportunity Risk? Racial Experiences, Socioeconomic Status, and Health Status Among Black and White Adults," *Journal of Health and Social Behavior* 52, no. 3 (2011): 365–82, doi.org/10.1177/0022146511405336; Williams et al., "Research on Discrimination and Health."

32. Robert T. Carter et al., "Racial Discrimination and Race-Based Traumatic Stress: An Exploratory Investigation," in *Handbook of Racial-Cultural Psychology*

and Counseling, vol. 2, Training and Practice, ed. Robert T. Carter (Hoboken, NJ: Wiley, 2005), 447–76.

33. Janet E. Helms, ed., Black and White Racial Identity: Theory, Research, and Practice (Westport, CT: Greenwood, 1990).

34. Helms and Carter, "Development of the White Racial Identity Inventory," 68.

35. Janet E. Helms, "An Update of Helms's White and People of Color Racial Identity Models," in Handbook of Multicultural Counseling, ed. Joseph G. Ponterotto et al. (Thousand Oaks, CA: Sage, 1995), 181–98.

36. Carter et al., "Race-Based Traumatic Stress, Racial Identity Status, and Psychological Functioning"; Robert T. Carter and Veronica E. Johnson, "Racial Identity Statuses: Applications To Practice," Practice Innovations 4, no. 1 (2019): 42–58, dx.doi.org/10.1037/pri0000082.

37. Carter et al., "Race-Based Traumatic Stress Symptom Scale and White Americans," 6–11.

38. Mijke Rhemtulla, Patricia E. Brosseau-Liard, and Victoria Savalei, "When Can Categorical Variables Be Tested as Continuous? A Comparison of Robust Continuous and Categorical Sem Estimation Methods Under Suboptimal Conditions," Psychological Methods 17, no. 3 (2012): 354–73, dx.doi.org/10.1037/a0029315.

39. B. Muthén, S. H. C. du Toit, and D. Spisic, "Robust Inference Using Weighted Least Squares and Quadratic Estimating Equations in Latent Variable Modeling with Categorical and Continuous Outcomes," accepted for publication in Psychometrika, 1997.

40. Robert T. Carter, Katheryn Roberson, and Veronica E. Johnson, "Race-Based Stress in White Adults: Exploring the Role of White Racial Identity Status Attitudes and Type of Racial Events," Journal of Multicultural Counseling and Development (in press).

41. Robert T. Carter et al., "The Development of Classes of Racism Measures for Frequency and Stress Reactions: Relationships to Race-Based Traumatic Symptoms," Traumatology 22, no. 1 (2016): 63–74.

42. Carter, "Racism and Psychological and Emotional Injury," 75.

43. Carter, "Racism and Psychological and Emotional Injury."

44. Andy P. Field, Discovering Statistics Using SPSS: (and Sex, Drugs, and Rock 'n' Roll), 3rd ed. (Thousand Oaks, CA: Sage, 2009); Roger L. Worthington and Tiffany A. Whittaker, "Scale Development Research: A Content Analysis and Recommendations for Best Practices," Counseling Psychologist 34, no. 6 (2006): 806–39, doi.org/10.1177/0011000006288127.

45. Carlson, Trauma Assessments.

46. Carter, "Racism and Psychological and Emotional Injury."

8. The Short Form and the Interview Schedule of the Race-Based Traumatic Stress Symptom Scale

1. Laia Bécares, James Nazroo, and James Jackson, "Ethnic Density and Depressive Symptoms Among African Americans: Threshold and Differential Effects Across Social and Demographic Subgroups," *American Journal of Public Health* 104, no. 12 (2014): 2334–41, doi.org/10.2105/AJPH.2014.302047; Robert T. Carter et al., "A Meta-Analytic Review of Racial Discrimination: Relationships to Health and Culture," *Race and Social Problems* 11, no. 1 (March 2019): 15–32, doi.org/10.1007/s12552-018-9256-y; Que-Lam Huynh, Thierry Devos, and Robyn Goldberg, "The Role of Ethnic and National Identifications in Perceived Discrimination for Asian Americans: Toward a Better Understanding of the Buffering Effect of Group Identifications on Psychological Distress," *Asian American Journal of Psychology* 5, no. 3 (2014): 161–71; Yin Paradies et al., "Racism as a Determinant of Health: A Systematic Review and Meta-Analysis," *PloS one* 10, no. 9 (2015): 1–48, doi:10.137/journal.pone.0138511.

2. Robert T. Carter et al., "Initial Development of the Race-Based Traumatic Stress Symptom Scale: Assessing the Emotional Impact of Racism," *Psychological Trauma: Theory, Research, Practice, and Policy* 5, no.1 (2013): 1–9, doi.org/10.1037/a0025911.

3. Louis M. Rea and Richard Allen Parker, *Designing and Conducting Survey Research: A Comprehensive Guide* (San Francisco: Jossey-Bass, 2014).

4. Jeffrey M. Stanton et al., "Issues and Strategies for Reducing the Length of Self-Report Scales," *Personnel Psychology* 55, no. 1 (2002): 167–94, doi.org/10.1111/j.1744-6570.2002.tb00108.x.

5. John Bound, Charles Brown, and Nancy Mathiowetz, "Measurement Error in Survey Data," *Handbook of Econometrics* 5 (2001): 3705–843, doi.org/10.1016/S1573-4412(01)05012-7.

6. Jörg M. Müller et al., "Comparison of Eleven Short Versions of the Symptom Checklist 90-Revised (SCL-90-R) for Use in the Assessment of General Psychopathology," *Journal of Psychopathology and Behavioral Assessment* 32, no. 2 (2010): 246–54, doi.org/10.1007/s10862-009-9141-5.

7. Carter et al., "Initial Development of the Race-Based Traumatic Stress Symptom Scale."

8. Karen Larwin and Milton Harvey, "A Demonstration of a Systematic Item-Reduction Approach Using Structural Equation Modeling," *Practical Assessment, Research and Evaluation* 17, no. 8 (April 2012): 1–19; Sophie van der Sluis, Conor V. Dolan, and Reinoud D. Stoel, "A Note on Testing Perfect Correlations in SEM," *Structural Equation Modeling* 12, no. 4 (2005): 551–77, doi.org/10.1207/s15328007sem1204_3.

9. Timothy A. Brown, *Confirmatory Factor Analysis for Applied Research* (New York: Guilford Press, 2015).

10. Steven E. Gregorich, "Do Self-Report Instruments Allow Meaningful Comparisons Across Diverse Population Groups? Testing Measurement Invariance Using the Confirmatory Factor Analysis Framework," *Medical Care* 44, no. 11 (suppl. 3, 2006): S78–S94, dx.doi.org/10.1097%2Fo1.mlr.0000245454.12228.8f; Taciano L. Milfont and Ronald Fischer, "Testing Measurement Invariance Across Groups: Applications in Cross-Cultural Research," *International Journal of Psychological Research* 3, no. 1 (2010): 111–30.

11. Sehee Hong, Mary L. Malik, and Min-Kyu Lee, "Testing Configural, Metric, Scalar, and Latent Mean Invariance Across Genders in Sociotropy and Autonomy Using a Non-Western Sample," *Educational and Psychological Measurement* 63, no. 4 (2003): 636–54, doi.org/10.1177/0013164403251332.

12. L. K. Muthén and B. O. Muthén, Mplus 7.3 (software) (Los Angeles: Muthén and Muthén, 2014).

13. A. Nayena Blankson and John J. McArdle, "Measurement Invariance of Cognitive Abilities Across Ethnicity, Gender, and Time Among Older Americans," *Journals of Gerontology: Series B* 70, no. 3 (2015): 386–97, doi.org/10.1093/geronb/gbt106.

14. Dimiter M. Dimitrov, "Testing for Factorial Invariance in the Context of Construct Validation," *Measurement and Evaluation in Counseling and Development* 43, no. 2 (2010): 121–49, doi.org/10.1177/0748175610373459; Blankson and McArdle, "Measurement Invariance of Cognitive Abilities Across Ethnicity, Gender, and Time Among Older Americans."

15. Dimitrov, "Testing for Factorial Invariance in the Context of Construct Validation."

16. Dimitrov, "Testing for Factorial Invariance in the Context of Construct Validation."

17. For example, Gordon W. Cheung and Roger B. Rensvold, "Evaluating Goodness-of-Fit Indexes for Testing Measurement Invariance," *Structural Equation Modeling* 9, no. 2 (2002): 233–55, doi.org/10.1207/S15328007SEM0902_5; Hong, Malik, and Lee, "Testing Configural, Metric, Scalar, and Latent Mean Invariance Across Genders in Sociotropy and Autonomy Using a Non-Western Sample"; Jeffrey H. Kahn, "Factor Analysis in Counseling Psychology Research, Training, and Practice: Principles, Advances, and Applications," *Counseling Psychologist* 34, no. 5 (2006): 684–718, doi.org/10.1177/0011000006286347.

18. Cheung and Rensvold, "Evaluating Goodness-of-Fit Indexes for Testing Measurement Invariance."

19. Li-tze Hu and Peter M. Bentler, "Cutoff Criteria for Fit Indexes in Covariance Structure Analysis: Conventional Criteria Versus New Alternatives," *Structural Equation Modeling: A Multidisciplinary Journal* 6, no. 1 (1999): 1–55, dx.doi.org

/10.1080/10705519909540118; Rens van de Schoot, Peter Lugtig, and Joop Hox, "A Checklist for Testing Measurement Invariance," *European Journal of Developmental Psychology* 9, no. 4 (2012): 486–92, doi.org/10.1080/17405629 .2012.686740.

20. Cheung and Rensvold, "Evaluating Goodness-of-Fit Indexes for Testing Measurement Invariance"; Blankson and McArdle, "Measurement Invariance of Cognitive Abilities Across Ethnicity, Gender, and Time Among Older Americans."

21. Dimitrov, "Testing for Factorial Invariance in the Context of Construct Validation."

22. Blankson and McArdle, "Measurement Invariance of Cognitive Abilities Across Ethnicity, Gender, and Time Among Older Americans."

23. Clairice T. Veit and John E. Ware, "The Structure of Psychological Distress and Well-Being in General Populations," *Journal of Consulting and Clinical Psychology* 51, no. 5 (1983): 730–42, doi.org/10.1037/0022-006X.51.5.730.

24. Robert T. Carter, "Racism and Psychological and Emotional Injury: Recognizing and Assessing Race-Based Traumatic Stress," *Counseling Psychologist* 35, no. 1 (2007): 13–105, doi:10.1177/0011000006292033; Carter et al., "Initial Development of the Race-Based Traumatic Stress Symptom Scale," 6.

25. Robert T. Carter and Carrie Muchow, "Construct Validity of the Race-Based Traumatic Stress Symptom Scale and Tests of Measurement Equivalence," *Psychological Trauma: Theory, Research, Practice, and Policy* 9, no. 6 (2017): 688–95, doi.org/10.1037/tra0000256: 692.

26. Carter et al., "A Meta-Analytic Review of Racial Discrimination."

27. Paradies et al., "Racism as a Determinant of Health."

28. Elizabeth A. Pascoe and Laura Smart Richman, "Perceived Discrimination and Health: A Meta-Analytic Review," *Psychological Bulletin* 135, no. 4 (2009): 531–54, doi.org/10.1037%2Fa0016059: 539.

29. Nagy A. Youssef et al., "Exploration of the Influence of Childhood Trauma, Combat Exposure, and the Resilience Construct on Depression and Suicidal Ideation Among U.S. Iraq/Afghanistan–Era Military Personnel and Veterans," *Archives of Suicide Research* 17, no. 2 (2013): 106–22, doi.org/10.1080/138 11118.2013.776445.

30. Robert T. Carter et al., "The Development of Classes of Racism Measures for Frequency and Stress Reactions: Relationships to Race-Based Traumatic Symptoms," *Traumatology* 22, no. 1 (2016): 63–74.

31. John Briere and Marsha Runtz, "The Trauma Symptom Checklist (TSC-33): Early Data on a New Scale," *Journal of Interpersonal Violence* 4, no. 2 (1989): 151–63, doi.org/10.1177/088626089004002002.

32. Leonard R. Derogatis and Patricia A. Cleary, "Confirmation of the Dimensional Structure of the SCL-90: A Study on Construct Validation," *Journal of*

Clinical Psychology 33, no. 4 (October 1977): 981–89, doi.org/10.1002/1097-4679 (197710)33:4%3C981::AID-JCLP2270330412%3E3.0.CO;2-0.

33. Glenn P. Smith, "Assessment of Malingering with Self-Report Measures," in *Clinical Assessment of Malingering and Deception*, 2nd ed., ed. Richard Rogers (New York: Guilford, 1997), 351–70.

34. Robert T. Carter and Sinead Sant-Barket, "Assessment of the Impact of Racial Discrimination and Racism: How to Use the Race-Based Traumatic Stress Symptom Scale in Practice," *Traumatology* 21, no. 1 (2015): 38–39.

35. Robert T. Carter and Jessica M. Forsyth, "A Guide to the Forensic Assessment of Race-Based Traumatic Stress Reactions," *Journal of the American Academy of Psychiatry and the Law* 37, no. 1 (2009): 28–40.

9. Clinical Applications of the Race-Based Traumatic Stress Model

1. Marie C. Adams and D. Martin Kivlighan III, "When Home Is Gone: An Application of the Multicultural Orientation Framework to Enhance Clinical Practice with Refugees of Forced Migration," *Professional Psychology: Research and Practice* 50, no. 3 (2019): 176; Riana E. Anderson et al., "EMBRacing Racial Stress and Trauma: Preliminary Feasibility and Coping Responses of a Racial Socialization Intervention," *Journal of Black Psychology* 44, no. 1 (2017): 25–46, doi.org/10.1177/0095798417732930; Riana Elyse Anderson and Howard C. Stevenson, "RECASTing Racial Stress and Trauma: Theorizing the Healing Potential of Racial Socialization in Families," *American Psychologist* 74, no. 1 (2019): 63–75; Eleonora Bartoli and Aarti Pyati, "Addressing Clients' Racism and Racial Prejudice in Individual Psychotherapy: Therapeutic Considerations," *Psychotherapy: Theory, Research, Practice, Training* 46, no. 2 (2009): 145–57, doi .org/10.1037/a0016023; Carl C. Bell and Edward Dunbar, "Racism and Pathological Bias as a Co-occurring Problem in Diagnosis and Assessment," in *Oxford Handbook of Personality Disorders*, ed. Thomas A. Widiger (Oxford, UK: Oxford University Press, 2012), 694–709; Lorraine T. Benuto et al., "Training Culturally Competent Psychologists: Where Are We and Where Do Need to Go," *Training and Education in Professional Psychology*, 13 no. 1 (2019): 65–62; Thema Bryant-Davis and Carlota Ocampo, "A Therapeutic Approach to the Treatment of Racist-Incident-Based Trauma," *Journal of Emotional Abuse* 6, no. 4 (2006): 1–22, doi:10.1300/J135v06n04_01; Marie Carlson et al., "Addressing the Impact of Racism on Veterans of Color: A Race-Based Stress and Trauma Intervention," *Psychology of Violence* 8, no. 6 (2018): 748–62; Lillian Comas-Díaz, "Racial Trauma Recovery: A Race Informed Therapeutic Approach to Racial Wounds," in *The Cost of Racism for People of Color: Contextualizing Experiences of Discrimination*, ed. Alvin N. Alvarez, Christopher T. H. Liang, and Helen A. Neville (Washington, DC: American Psychological Association,

2016), 249–71, doi.org/10.1037/14852-012; Carrie Hemmings and Amanda M. Evans, "Identifying and Treating Race-Based Trauma in Counseling," *Journal of Multicultural Counseling and Development* 46, no. 1 (2018): 20–39, doi.org/10.1002/jmcd.12090; Isha McKenzie-Mavinga, *The Challenge of Racism in Therapeutic Practice: Engaging with Oppression in Practice and Supervision* (New York: Palgrave, 2016); Matthew J. Miller et al., "Practice Recommendations for Addressing Racism: A Content Analysis of the Counseling Psychology Literature," *Journal of Counseling Psychology*, 65, no. 6 (2018): 669–80.

2. American Psychological Association, "Guidelines for Providers of Psychological Services to Ethnic, Linguistic, and Culturally Diverse Populations," *American Psychologist*, 48 (1993): 45–48.

3. American Psychological Association, "Guidelines on Multicultural Education, Training, Research, Practice, and Organizational Change for Psychologists," *American Psychologist* 58, no. 5 (2003): 377–402.

4. American Psychological Association, "Multicultural Guidelines: An Ecological Approach to Context, Identity and Intersectionality," 2017c, http://www.apa.org/about/policy/multicultural-guidelines.pdf. See also American Psychological Association, *Guidelines and Principles for Accreditation of Programs in Professional Psychology (G&P)*, 2006, rev. 2013, http://www.apa.org/ed/accreditation/about/policies/guiding-principles.pdf.

5. See the 2002 and 2010 versions: American Psychological Association, "Ethical Principles of Psychologists and Code of Conduct," *American Psychologist* 57 (2002): 1060–73, www.apa.org/ethics/code; American Psychological Association, "2010 Amendments to the 2002 'Ethical Principles of Psychologists and Code of Conduct,'" *American Psychologist* 65 (2010): 493, www.apa.org/ethics/code.

6. American Psychological Association, "Ethical Principles of Psychologists and Code of Conduct," 2017a, General Principles, Principle E, www.apa.org/ethics/code.

7. American Psychological Association, "Guidelines on Race and Ethnicity in Psychology," https://www.apa.org/about/policy/guidelines-race-ethnicity.pdf.

8. See, for example, M. A. Garcia and M. Tehee, "Society of Indian Psychologists Commentary on the American Psychological Association's (APA's) Ethical Principles of Psychologists and Code of Conduct," Society of Indian Psychologists, 2014, https://www.apa.org/pi/oema/resources/communique/2014/12/indian-psychologists-ethics.

9. American Psychological Association, "Ethical Principles of Psychologists and Code of Conduct," 2017a.

10. Randy Phelps, James H. Bray, and Lisa K. Kearney, "A Quarter Century of Psychological Practice in Mental Health and Health Care: 1990–2016," *American Psychologist* 72, no. 8 (2017): 822, http://psycnet.apa.org/doi/10.1037/amp0000192.

11. Patient Protection and Affordable Care Act (ACA), H.R. 3590, 111th Cong., 2010, www.congress.gov/bill/111th-congress/house-bill/3590.

12. Phelps, Bray, and Kearney, "A Quarter Century of Psychological Practice in Mental Health and Health Care," 832.

13. Phelps, Bray, and Kearney, "A Quarter Century of Psychological Practice in Mental Health and Health Care," 825.

14. See Robert T. Carter, *The Influence of Race and Racial Identity in Psychotherapy: Toward a Racially Inclusive Model* (New York: Wiley, 1995a); Harriet A. Washington, *Medical Apartheid: The Dark History of Medical Experimentation on Black Americans from Colonial Times to the Present* (New York: Doubleday, 2006).

15. Zachary D. Cohen and Robert J. DeRubeis, "Treatment Selection in Depression," *Annual Review of Clinical Psychology* 14 (2018): 209–36, doi.org/10.1146/annurev-clinpsy-050817-084746.

16. American Psychological Association, "Clinical Practice Guidelines for the Treatment of Posttraumatic Stress Disorder (PTSD) in Adults," Guidelines Development Panel for Treatment of PTSD in Adults, adopted as APA policy February 24, 2017b, 67–68, www.apa.org/ptsd-guideline/ptsd.pdf.

17. For example, Bryant-Davis and Ocampo, "A Therapeutic Approach to the Treatment of Racist-Incident-Based Trauma"; Thema Bryant-Davis, "The Cultural Context of Trauma Recovery: Considering the Posttraumatic Stress Disorder Practice Guideline and Intersectionality," *Psychotherapy* 56, no. 3 (2019): 400–08; Comas-Díaz, "Racial Trauma Recovery"; Lillian Comas-Díaz, Gordon N. Hall, and Helen A. Neville, "Racial Trauma: Theory, Research, and Healing: Introduction to the Special Issue," *American Psychologist* 74, no. 1 (2019): 1–5, dx.doi.org/10.1037/amp0000442; Monnica T. Williams et al., "Assessing Racial Trauma Within a DSM-5 Framework: The UConn Racial/Ethnic Stress and Trauma Survey," *Practice Innovations* 3, no. 4 (2018): 242–60, doi.org/10.1037/pri0000076.

18. Samantha C. Holmes, Vanessa C. Facemire, and Alexis M. DaFonseca, "Expanding Criterion A for Posttraumatic Stress Disorder: Considering the Deleterious Impact of Oppression," *Traumatology* 22, no. 4 (2016): 314.

19. Robert T. Carter and Jessica M. Forsyth, "Reactions to Racial Discrimination: Emotional Stress and Help-Seeking Behaviors," *Psychological Trauma: Theory, Research, Practice, and Policy* 2, no. 3 (2010): 183–91, doi.org/10.1037/a0020102; Vetta L. Sanders Thompson, Anita Bazile, and Maysa Akbar, "African Americans' Perceptions of Psychotherapy and Psychotherapists," *Professional Psychology: Research and Practice* 35, no. 1 (2004): 19–26, doi.org/10.1037/0735-7028.35.1.19.

20. Nancy Downing Hansen et al., "Do We Practice What We Preach? An Exploratory Survey of Multicultural Psychotherapy Competencies," *Professional Psychology: Research and Practice* 37, no. 1 (February 2006): 66–74.

21. Thompson, Bazile, and Akbar, "African Americans' Perceptions of Psychotherapy and Psychotherapists."

22. Alice P. Villatoro et al., "Perceived Need for Mental Health Care: The Intersection of Race, Ethnicity, Gender, and Socioeconomic Status," *Society and Mental Health* 8, no. 1 (2018): 1–24, doi.org/10.1177/2156869317718889.

23. Thompson, Bazile, and Akbar, "African Americans' Perceptions of Psychotherapy and Psychotherapists," 23.

24. Thompson, Bazile, and Akbar, "African Americans' Perceptions of Psychotherapy and Psychotherapists," 23.

25. Thompson, Bazile, and Akbar, "African Americans' Perceptions of Psychotherapy and Psychotherapists," 24.

26. Hansen et al., "Do We Practice What We Preach?"

27. Hansen et al., "Do We Practice What We Preach?," 67.

28. Hansen et al. "Do We Practice What We Preach?," 68.

29. Hemmings and Evans, "Identifying and Treating Race-Based Trauma in Counseling."

30. Hemmings and Evans, "Identifying and Treating Race-Based Trauma in Counseling," 31.

31. Benuto et al., "Training Culturally Competent Psychologists: Where Are We and Where Do Need to Go."

32. Robert T. Carter, "Racism and Psychological and Emotional Injury: Recognizing and Assessing Race-Based Traumatic Stress," *Counseling Psychologist* 35, no. 1 (2007): 13–105, doi:10.1177/0011000006292033.

33. Chalmer E. Thompson and Robert T. Carter, eds., *Racial Identity Theory: Applications to Individual, Group, and Organizational Interventions* (New York: Routledge, 2012 [1997]).

34. Johanne Eliacin et al., "The Relationship Between Race, Patient Activation, and Working Alliance: Implications for Patient Engagement in Mental Health Care," *Administration and Policy in Mental Health and Mental Health Services Research* 45, no. 1 (2016): 186–92, doi.org/10.1007/s10488-016-0779-5.

35. Eliacin et al., "The Relationship Between Race, Patient Activation, and Working Alliance," 5; Villatoro et al., "Perceived Need for Mental Health Care."

36. Eliacin et al., "The Relationship Between Race, Patient Activation, and Working Alliance," 3.

37. Telsie A. Davis, Julie R. Ancis, and Jeffrey S. Ashby, "Therapist Effect, Working Alliance, and African American Women Substance Users," *Cultural Diversity and Ethnic Minority Psychology* 21, no. 3 (2015): 126–35, doi.org/10.1037/a0036944; Lisa B. Dixon, Yael Holoshitz, and Ilana Nossel, "Treatment Engagement of Individuals Experiencing Mental Illness: Review and Update," *World Psychiatry* 15, no. 1 (2016): 13–20, doi.org/10.1002/wps.20306; Eliacin et al., "The Relationship Between Race, Patient Activation, and Working Alliance."

38. Sandra Matter, "Cultural Considerations in Trauma Psychology Education, Research and Training," *Traumatology* 16, no. 4 (2010): 50, doi.org/10.1177/1534765 610388305.

39. Matter, "Cultural Considerations in Trauma Psychology Education, Research and Training," 50.

40. Krista M. Malott and Scott Schaefle, "Addressing Clients' Experiences of Racism: A Model for Clinical Practice," *Journal of Counseling and Development* 93 (2015): 362, doi.org/10.1002/jcad.12034.

41. Enrique W. Neblett, "Racism and Health: Challenges and Future Directions in Behavioral and Psychological Research," *Cultural Diversity and Ethnic Minority Psychology* 25, no. 1 (2019): 12–20.

42. Malott and Schaefle, "Addressing Clients' Experiences of Racism," 362.

43. Robert T. Carter and Veronica E. Johnson, "Racial Identity Statuses: Applications to Practice," *Practice Innovations* 4, no. 1 (2019): 44, doi.org/10.1037/pri0000082.

44. Malott and Schaefle, "Addressing Clients' Experiences of Racism," 366.

45. Matter, "Cultural Considerations in Trauma Psychology Education, Research and Training," 362.

46. Victoria E. Kress et al., "The Use of Relational-Cultural Theory in Counseling Clients Who Have Traumatic Stress Disorders," *Journal of Counseling and Development* 96, no. 1 (2018): 106–14, doi.org/10.1002/jcad.12182.

47. Malott and Schaefle, "Addressing Clients' Experiences of Racism," 363.

48. Bryant-Davis and Ocampo, "A Therapeutic Approach to the Treatment of Racist-Incident-Based Trauma"; Carter and Johnson, "Racial Identity Statuses: Applications to Practice"; Comas-Díaz, "Racial Trauma Recovery"; Comas-Díaz et al., "Racial Trauma: Theory, Research, and Healing"; Hemmings and Evans, "Identifying and Treating Race-Based Trauma in Counseling."

49. Derald Wing Sue et al., *Counseling the Culturally Diverse: Theory and Practice*, 8th ed. (Hoboken, NJ: Wiley, 2019); Shawn O. Utsey, Carol A. Gernat, and Lawrence Hammar, "Examining White Counselor Trainees' Reactions to Racial Issues in Counseling and Supervision Dyads," *Counseling Psychologist* 33, no. 4 (2005): 449–78, doi.org/10.1177/0011000004269058.

50. John Sommers-Flanagan and Rita Sommers-Flanagan, *Clinical Interviewing*, 6th ed. (Hoboken, NJ: Wiley, 2016).

51. Robert T. Carter et al., "Initial Development of the Race-Based Traumatic Stress Symptom Scale: Assessing the Emotional Impact of Racism," *Psychological Trauma: Theory, Research, Practice, and Policy* 5, no.1 (2013): 1–9, doi.org/10.1037/a0025911.

52. Robert T. Carter et al., "The Development of Classes of Racism Measures for Frequency and Stress Reactions: Relationships to Race-Based Traumatic Symptoms," *Traumatology* 22, no. 1 (2016): 63–74.

53. Jessica Forsyth and Robert T. Carter, "The Development and Preliminary Validation of the Racism-Related Coping Scale," *Psychological Trauma: Theory, Research, Practice, and Policy* 6, no. 6 (2014): 632–43, doi.org/10.1037/a0036702.

54. Rebecca Rangel Campón and Robert T. Carter, "The Appropriated Racial Oppression Scale: Development and Preliminary Validation," *Cultural Diversity and Ethnic Minority Psychology* 21, no. 4 (2015): 497–506, doi.org/10.1037/cdp0000037.

55. Carter et al., "Initial Development of the Race-Based Traumatic Stress Symptom Scale"; Carter and Johnson, "Racial Identity Statuses: Applications to Practice."

56. Carter, *The Influence of Race and Racial Identity in Psychotherapy*; Carter et al., "Initial Development of the Race-Based Traumatic Stress Symptom Scale"; Carter and Johnson, "Racial Identity Statuses: Applications to Practice"; Thompson and Carter, *Racial Identity Theory*.

57. Janet E. Helms, "Toward a Theoretical Explanation of the Effects of Race on Counseling: A Black and White Model," *Counseling Psychologist* 12, no. 4 (1984): 153–65, doi.org/10.1177/0011000084124013; Janet E. Helms, "An Update of Helms's White and People of Color Racial Identity Models," in *Handbook of Multicultural Counseling*, ed. Joseph G. Ponterotto et al. (Thousand Oaks, CA: Sage, 1995), 181–98.

58. Helms, "Toward a Theoretical Explanation of the Effects of Race on Counseling"; Helms, "An Update of Helms's White and People of Color Racial Identity Models."

59. Carter, *The Influence of Race and Racial Identity in Psychotherapy*.

60. Robert T. Carter and Janet E. Helms, "The Counseling Process Defined by Relationship Types: A Test of Helms' Interactional Model," *Journal of Multicultural Counseling and Development* 20, no. 4 (1992): 181–201, doi.org/10.1002/j.2161-1912.1992.tb00576.x; Carter and Johnson, "Racial Identity Statuses: Applications to Practice."

61. Janet E. Helms, ed., *Black and White Racial Identity: Theory, Research, and Practice* (Westport, CT: Greenwood, 1990), 141–42.

62. Carter, *The Influence of Race and Racial Identity in Psychotherapy*, 194.

63. Carter, *The Influence of Race and Racial Identity in Psychotherapy*; Carter and Johnson, "Racial Identity Statuses: Applications to Practice," 45.

64. Carter, *The Influence of Race and Racial Identity in Psychotherapy*; Thompson and Carter, *Racial Identity Theory*, 101.

65. Edward Dunbar, "Counseling Practices to Ameliorate the Effects of Discrimination and Hate Events: Toward a Systematic Approach to Assessment and Intervention," *Counseling Psychologist* 29, no. 2 (2001): 285.

66. Bryant-Davis and Ocampo, "A Therapeutic Approach to the Treatment of Racist-Incident-Based Trauma," 5.

67. Bryant-Davis and Ocampo, "A Therapeutic Approach to the Treatment of Racist-Incident-Based Trauma," 6.
68. Bryant-Davis and Ocampo, "A Therapeutic Approach to the Treatment of Racist-Incident-Based Trauma," 7.
69. For example, Comas-Díaz, "Racial Trauma Recovery"; Williams et al., "Assessing Racial Trauma Within a DSM-5 Framework."
70. Bryant-Davis and Ocampo, "A Therapeutic Approach to the Treatment of Racist-Incident-Based Trauma."
71. Holmes, Facemire, and DaFonseca, "Expanding Criterion A for Posttraumatic Stress Disorder," 315.
72. Thompson and Carter, "An Overview and elaboration of Helms's Racial Identity development theory"; *Racial Identity Theory*. 15.
73. Carter, *The Influence of Race and Racial Identity in Psychotherapy*, 231.
74. Carter and Johnson, "Racial Identity Statuses: Applications to Practice," 44.
75. Stephen E. Finn and Mary E. Tonsager, "How Therapeutic Assessment Became Humanistic," *Humanistic Psychologist* 30, no. 1–2 (2002): 10–22, doi.org/10.1080/08873267.2002.9977019.
76. Comas-Díaz, "Racial Trauma Recovery," 255.
77. Janet E. Helms, Guerda Nicolas, and Carlton E. Green, "Racism and Ethnoviolence as Trauma: Enhancing Professional Training," *Traumatology* 16, no. 4 (2010): 53–62, doi.org/10.1177/1534765610389595.
78. Sommers-Flanagan and Sommers-Flanagan, *Clinical Interviewing*.
79. Comas-Díaz, "Racial Trauma Recovery"; Dunbar, "Counseling Practices to Ameliorate the Effects of Discrimination and Hate Events."
80. Matthew J. Miller et al., "Practice Recommendations for Addressing Racism: A Content Analysis of the Counseling Psychology Literature."
81. Dunbar, "Counseling Practices to Ameliorate the Effects of Discrimination and Hate Events," 281.
82. Kellina Craig-Henderson and L. Ren Sloan, "After the Hate: Helping Psychologists Help Victims of Racist Hate Crime," *Clinical Psychology: Science and Practice* 10, no. 4 (2003): 484, doi.org/10.1093/clipsy.bpg048.
83. See Robert T. Carter and Jessica M. Forsyth, "A Guide to the Forensic Assessment of Race-Based Traumatic Stress Reactions," *Journal of the American Academy of Psychiatry and the Law* 37, no. 1 (2009): 28–40.
84. Craig-Henderson and Sloan, "After the Hate," 487–88.
85. Nancy Boyd-Franklin, "Group Therapy for Black Women: A Therapeutic Support Model," *American Journal of Orthopsychiatry* 57, no. 3 (1987): 394–401; Don Elligan and Shawn Utsey, "Utility of an African-Centered Support Group for African American Men Confronting Societal Racism and Oppression," *Cultural Diversity and Ethnic Minority Psychology* 5, no. 2 (1999): 156–65, doi.org

/10.1037/1099-9809.5.2.156; Anderson J. Franklin, "Therapy with African American Men," *Families in Society* 73, no. 6 (1992): 350–55.

86. Anderson J. Franklin and Nancy Boyd-Franklin, "Invisibility Syndrome: A Clinical Model of the Effects of Racism on African-American Males," *American Journal of Orthopsychiatry* 70, no. 1 (2000): 40.

87. Lance C. Smith and Richard Q. Shin, "Social Privilege, Social Justice, and Group Counseling: An Inquiry," *Journal for Specialists in Group Work* 33, no. 4 (2008): 351–66.

88. Ibrahim A. Kira et al., "Group Therapy for Refugees and Torture Survivors: Treatment Model Innovations," *International Journal of Group Psychotherapy* 62, no. 1 (2012): 76.

89. Robert T. Carter, "Racism and Psychological and Emotional Injury: Recognizing and Assessing Race-Based Traumatic Stress."

90. Joshua Miller and Susan Donner, "More than Just Talk: The Use of Racial Dialogues to Combat Racism," *Social Work With Groups* 23, no. 1 (2000): 31–53; Derek M. Griffith et al., "Dismantling Institutional Racism: Theory and Action," *American Journal of Community Psychology* 39, no. 3–4 (2007): 381–92.

91. Carlson et al., "Addressing the Impact of Racism on Veterans of Color," 749.

92. Carlson et al. "Addressing the Impact of Racism on Veterans of Color."

93. Phelps, Bray, and Kearney, "A Quarter Century of Psychological Practice in Mental Health and Health Care."

10. A Guide to Forensic Assessment

1. For example, Robert T. Carter et al., "Racial Discrimination and Health Outcomes Among Racial/Ethnic Minorities: A Meta-Analytic Review," *Journal of Multicultural Counseling and Development* 45, no. 4 (2017): 232–59, doi.org/10 .1002/jmcd.12076; Robert T. Carter et al., "A Meta-Analytic Review of Racial Discrimination: Relationships to Health and Culture," *Race and Social Problems* 11, no. 1 (2019): 15–32; Valerie A. Earnshaw et al., "Everyday Discrimination and Physical Health: Exploring Mental Health Processes," *Journal of Health Psychology* 21, no. 10 (2015): 2218–228, doi.org/10.1177/1359105315572456; Vickie L. Shavers, William M. P. Klein, and Pebbles Fagan, "Research on Race/ Ethnicity and Health Care Discrimination: Where We Are and Where We Need to Go," *American Journal of Public Health* 102, no. 5 (2012): 930–32, doi .org/10.2105/AJPH.2012.300708.

2. Robert T. Carter and Jessica M. Forsyth, "Examining Race and Culture in Psychology Journals: The Case of Forensic Psychology," *Professional Psychology: Research and Practice* 38, no. 2 (2007): 133–42, doi.org/10.1037/0735-7028 .38.2.133.

3. See Robert T. Carter and Thomas D. Scheuermann, *Confronting Racism: Integrating Mental Health Research into Legal Strategies and Reforms* (New York: Routledge, 2020).

4. Gary B. Melton et al., *Psychological Evaluations for the Courts: A Handbook for Mental Health Professionals and Lawyers*, 4th ed. (New York: Guilford, 2018).

5. Carter and Forsyth, "Examining Race and Culture in Psychology Journals."

6. James W. Hicks, "Ethnicity, Race and Forensic Psychiatry: Are We Color-Blind?" *Journal of American Academy of Psychiatry and the Law* 32, no. 1 (2004): 21–33.

7. Carl C. Bell and Edward Dunbar, "Racism and Pathological Bias as a Co-Occurring Problem in Diagnosis and Assessment," in *Oxford Handbook of Personality Disorders*, ed. Thomas A. Widiger (Oxford, UK: Oxford University Press, 2012), 694–709.

8. Melton et al., *Psychological Evaluations for the Courts*.

9. For example, Samantha C. Holmes, Vanessa C. Facemire, and Alexis M. DaFonseca, "Expanding Criterion A for Posttraumatic Stress Disorder: Considering the Deleterious Impact of Oppression," *Traumatology* 22, no. 4 (2016): 314–21.

10. Rebecca Rangel Campón and Robert T. Carter, "The Appropriated Racial Oppression Scale: Development and Preliminary Validation," *Cultural Diversity and Ethnic Minority Psychology* 21, no. 4 (2015): 497–506, dx.doi.org/10.1037/cdp0000037.

11. American Psychiatric Association, *Diagnostic and Statistical Manual of Mental Disorders*, 4th ed., text revision (Washington, DC: American Psychiatric Association, 2000); American Psychiatric Association, *Diagnostic and Statistical Manual of Mental Disorders*, 5th ed. (Washington, DC: American Psychiatric Association, 2013).

12. Holmes, Facemire, and DaFonseca, "Expanding Criterion A for Posttraumatic Stress Disorder," 315.

13. Robert T. Carter and Thomas D. Scheuermann, "Legal and Policy Standards for Addressing Workplace Racism: Employer Liability and Shared Responsibility for Race-Based Traumatic Stress," *University of Maryland Law Journal of Race, Religion, Gender and Class* 12, no. 1 (2012): 1–100; Carter and Scheuermann, *Confronting Racism*.

14. K. Heilburn, T. Grisso, and A. M. Goldstein, *Foundations of Forensic Mental Health Assessment* (New York: Oxford University Press, 2009), 13.

15. Melton et al., *Psychological Evaluations for the Courts*, 9.

16. Melton et al., *Psychological Evaluations for the Courts*, 10.

17. Melton et al., *Psychological Evaluations for the Courts*, 37.

18. Carter and Scheuermann, "Legal and Policy Standards for Addressing Workplace Racism," 28, 58, 64–70; Carter and Scheuermann, *Confronting Racism*. 97, 121

19. David R. Williams and Selina A. Mohammed, "Racism and Health I: Pathways and Scientific Evidence," *American Behavioral Scientist* 57, no. 8 (2013): 1152–73, doi:10.1177/0002764213487340.

20. Gary G. Bennett et al., "Perceived Racism and Affective Responses to Ambiguous Interpersonal Interactions Among African American Men," *American Behavioral Scientist* 47, no. 7 (2004): 63–76, doi.org/10.1177%2F000276420 3261070.

21. Samuel Noh, Violet Kaspar, and Kandauda A. S. Wickrama, "Overt and Subtle Racial Discrimination and Mental Health: Preliminary Findings for Korean Immigrants," *American Journal of Public Health* 97, no. 7 (2007): 1269–74, doi .org/10.2105/AJPH.2005.085316.

22. P. K. Chew and R. E. Kelly, "Unwrapping Racial Harassment Law," *Berkeley Journal of Employment Law* 49 (2006): 1–51, https://ssrn.com/abstract=1273737.

23. Carter and Scheuermann, "Legal and Policy Standards for Addressing Workplace Racism," 73; Carter and Scheuermann, *Confronting Racism*, 121.

24. Chew and Kelly, "Unwrapping Racial Harassment Law," 84.

25. Carter and Scheuermann, "Legal and Policy Standards for Addressing Workplace Racism," 62–67.

26. Renée L. Binder and Dale E. McNiel, "'He Said–She Said': The Role of the Forensic Evaluator in Determining Credibility of Plaintiffs Who Allege Sexual Exploitation and Boundary Violations," *Journal of the American Academy of Psychiatry and the Law* 35 (2007): 211–18; Robert T. Carter and Jessica M. Forsyth, "A Guide to the Forensic Assessment of Race-Based Traumatic Stress Reactions," *Journal of the American Academy of Psychiatry and the Law* 37, no. 1 (2009): 28–40.

27. Shelley E. Taylor, *Health Psychology*, 9th ed. (Boston: McGraw-Hill, 2015), 120–26. David R. Williams, "Stress and the Mental Health of Populations of Color: Advancing Our Understanding of Race-Related Stressors," *Journal of Health and Social Behavior* 59, no. 4 (2018): 469.

28. Eve B. Carlson, *Trauma Assessments: A Clinician's Guide* (New York: Guilford Press, 1997), 30.

29. Nancy R. Kressin, Kristal L. Raymond, and Meredith Manze, "Perceptions of Race/Ethnicity-Based Discrimination: A Review of Measures and Evaluation of Their Usefulness for the Health Care Setting," *Journal of Health Care for the Poor and Underserved* 19 (2008): 697–730, doi.org/10.1353/hpu.0.0041.

30. Carlson, *Trauma Assessments*, 72.

31. Thema Bryant-Davis and Carlota Ocampo, "Racist-Incident-Based Trauma," *Counseling Psychologist* 33, no. 4 (2005a): 479–500.

32. Carter and Scheuermann, "Legal and Policy Standards for Addressing Workplace Racism," 31.

33. Robert T. Carter et al., "The Development of Classes of Racism Measures for Frequency and Stress Reactions: Relationships to Race-Based Traumatic Symptoms," *Traumatology* 22, no. 1 (2016): 63–74.

34. Taylor, *Health Psychology*, 120–21.

35. Carlson, *Trauma Assessments*, 62.

36. Stuart A. Greenberg, Daniel W. Shuman, and Robert G. Meyer, "Unmasking Forensic Diagnosis," *International Journal of the Law and Psychiatry* 27, no. 1 (2004): 2, dx.doi.org/10.1016/j.ijlp.2004.01.001.

37. Robert T. Carter et al., "Race-Based Traumatic Stress, Racial Identity Status, and Psychological Functioning: An Exploratory Investigation," *Professional Psychology: Research and Practice* 48, no. 1 (2017): 20–37, doi.org/10.1037/pr000 00116.

38. Robert T. Carter and Veronica E. Johnson, "Racial Identity Statuses: Applications to Practice," *Practice Innovations* 4, no. 1 (2019): 42–58, dx.doi.org/10.1037 /pri0000082.

39. Camille A. Nelson, "Of Eggshells and Thin-Skulls: A Consideration of Racism-Related Mental Illness Impacting Black Women," *International Journal of the Law and Psychiatry* 29 (2006): 116, doi.org/10.1016/j.ijlp.2004.03.012.

40. Melton et al., *Psychological Evaluations for the Courts*, 206.

41. William J. Koch et al., *Psychological Injuries: Forensic Assessment, Treatment, and Law* (New York: Oxford University Press, 2006), 3, 4.

42. Carter and Scheuermann, "Legal and Policy Standards for Addressing Workplace Racism," 48.

43. Robert T. Carter, "Racism and Psychological and Emotional Injury: Recognizing and Assessing Race-Based Traumatic Stress," *Counseling Psychologist* 35, no. 1 (2007): 13–105, doi:10.1177/0011000006292033.

44. Carter and Forsyth, "A Guide to the Forensic Assessment of Race-Based Traumatic Stress Reactions," 36.

45. Greenberg, Shuman, and Meyer, "Unmasking Forensic Diagnosis," 13.

46. Hicks, "Ethnicity, Race and Forensic Psychiatry," 24; Holmes, Facemire, and DaFonseca, "Expanding Criterion a for Posttraumatic Stress Disorder," 319.

47. Bryant-Davis and Ocampo, "Racist-Incident-Based Trauma," 486.

48. Holmes, Facemire, and DaFonseca, "Expanding Criterion a for Posttraumatic Stress Disorder," 316.

11. Training Mental Health Professionals to Treat Racial Trauma

1. Alisha Ali and Corianna E. Sichel, "Structural Competency as a Framework for Training in Counseling Psychology," *Counseling Psychologist* 42, no. 7 (2014): 901–18, doi.org/10.1177/0011000014550320; American Psychological Association, "Guidelines on Multicultural Education, Training, Research, Prac-

tice, and Organizational Change for Psychologists," *American Psychologist* 58, no. 5 (2003): 377–402; American Psychological Association, "Multicultural Guidelines: An Ecological Approach to Context, Identity and Intersectionality," 2017c, www.apa.org/about/policy/multicultural-guidelines.pdf; Azad Athahiri Anuar and Rafidah Aga Mohd Jaladin, "Development and Evaluation of a Multicultural Counseling Competencies (MCC) Training Module for Trainee Counselors," *Journal of Asia Pacific Counseling* 6, no. 1 (2016): 41–50; Candice Presseau et al., "Trainee Social Justice Advocacy: Investigating the Roles of Training Factors and Multicultural Competence," *Counselling Psychology Quarterly*, online (May 31, 2018): 1–15, doi.org/10.1080/09515070.2018.1476837; Manivong J. Ratts and Paul B. Pedersen, *Counseling for Multiculturalism and Social Justice: Integration, Theory, and Application*, 4th ed. (Alexandria, VA: American Counseling Association, 2014); Derald Wing Sue, Patricia Arredondo, and Roderick J. McDavis, "Multicultural Counseling Competencies and Standards: A Call to the Profession," *Journal of Counseling and Development* 70, no. 4 (1992): 477–86, doi.org/10.1002/j.1556-6676.1992.tb01642.x.

2. Robert T. Carter, "The Road Less Traveled: Research on Race," in *The Handbook of Multicultural Counseling*, 4th ed., ed. J. Manuel Casas et al. (Thousand Oaks, CA: Sage, 2016), 71–80; Janet E. Helms and T. Q. Richardson, "How 'Multiculturalism' Obscures Race and Culture as Differential Aspects of Counseling Competency," in *Multicultural Counseling Competencies: Assessment, Education and Training, and Supervision*, ed. Donald B. Pope-Davis and Harden L. K. Coleman, *Multicultural Aspects of Counseling Series*, vol. 7 (Thousand Oaks, CA: Sage, 1997), 60–79; Laura Smith et al., "The Territory Ahead for Multicultural Competence: The 'Spinning' of Racism," *Professional Psychology: Research and Practice* 39, no. 3 (2008): 337–45, doi.org/10.1037/0735-7028.39.3.337.

3. Nadine J. Kaslow et al., "Facilitating the Pipeline Progress from Doctoral Degree to First Job," *American Psychologist* 73, no. 1 (2018): 47–62, dx.doi.org/10.1037/amp0000120.

4. Presseau et al., "Trainee Social Justice Advocacy: Investigating the Roles of Training Factors and Multicultural Competence."

5. American Psychological Association, "Guidelines on Multicultural Education, Training, Research, Practice, and Organizational Change for Psychologists," 2003; American Psychological Association, "Multicultural Guidelines: An Ecological Approach to Context, Identity and Intersectionality," 2017c ; Lorraine T. Benuto et al., "Training Culturally Competent Psychologists: Where Are We and Where Do Need to Go," *Training and Education in Professional Psychology* 13, no. 1 (2019): 65–62; Alex L. Pieterse et al., "Multicultural Competence and Social Justice Training in Counseling Psychology and Counselor Education: A Review and Analysis of a Sample of Multicultural Course Syllabi,"

Counseling Psychologist 37, no. 1 (2009): 93–115, doi.org/10.1177/0011000008
319986.

6. Abreu, Chung, and Atkinson, "Multicultural Counseling Training."

7. See Matthew J. Miller et al., "Practice Recommendations for Addressing Racism: A Content Analysis of the Counseling Psychology Literature," *Journal of Counseling Psychology* 65, no. 6 (2018): 669–80.

8. Teceta Thomas Tormala et al., "Developing Measurable Cultural Competence and Cultural Humility: An Application of the Cultural Formulation," *Training and Education in Professional Psychology* 12, no. 1 (2018): 54, dx.doi.org /10.1037/tep0000183.

9. Jose M. Abreu, Ruth H. Gim Chung, and Donald R. Atkinson, "Multicultural Counseling Training: Past, Present and Future Directions," *Counseling Psychologist* 28, no. 5 (September 2000): 642.

10. Pieterse et al., "Multicultural Competence and Social Justice Training in Counseling Psychology and Counselor Education," 97.

11. Leslie C. Jackson, "Ethnocultural Resistance to Multicultural Training: Students and Faculty," *Cultural Diversity and Ethnic Minority Psychology* 5, no. 1 (February 1999): 29; Alex L. Pieterse, Minsun Lee, and Alexa Fetzer, "Racial Group Membership and Multicultural Training: Examining the Experiences of Counseling and Counseling Psychology Students," *International Journal for the Advancement of Counselling* 38, no. 1 (2016): 44, doi.org/10.1007%2Fs10447-015-9254-3; Gina C. Torino, "Examining Biases and White Privilege: Classroom Teaching Strategies That Promote Cultural Competence," *Women and Therapy* 38, no. 3–4 (2015): 301, doi.org/10.1080/02703149.2015.1059213.

12. Glenn Adams et al., "Decolonizing Psychological Science: Introduction to the Special Thematic Section," *Journal of Social and Political Psychology* 3, no. 1 (2015): 213–38; Rachael D. Goodman et al., "Decolonizing Traditional Pedagogies and Practices in Counseling and Psychology Education: A Move Towards Social Justice and Action," in *Decolonizing "Multicultural" Counseling Through Social Justice*, ed. Rachael D. Goodman and Paul C. Gorski (New York: Springer, 2015), 147–64; Matthew J. Miller et al., "Practice Recommendations for Addressing Racism: A Content Analysis of the Counseling Psychology Literature."

13. Robert T. Carter, *The Influence of Race and Racial Identity in Psychotherapy: Toward a Racially Inclusive Model* (New York: Wiley, 1995a), 23.

14. Lorraine T. Benuto et al., "Training Culturally Competent Psychologists: Where Are We and Where Do Need to Go"; Kim A. Case, "Raising White Privilege Awareness and Reducing Racial Prejudice: Assessing Diversity Course Effectiveness," *Teaching of Psychology* 34, no. 4 (2007): 231–35, doi.org /10.1080/00986280701700250; Pieterse et al., "Multicultural Competence and Social Justice Training in Counseling Psychology and Counselor Education."

15. Robert T. Carter, *Handbook of Racial-Cultural Psychology and Counseling*, vol. 1, *Theory and Research* (Hoboken, NJ: Wiley, 2005a); John Sommers-Flanagan and Rita Sommers-Flanagan, *Counseling and Psychotherapy Theories in Context and Practice: Skills, Strategies and Techniques*, 3rd ed. (Hoboken, NJ: Wiley, 2018).

16. Sommers-Flanagan and Sommers-Flanagan, *Counseling and Psychotherapy Theories in Context and Practice*, 29.

17. Roy Moodley, Falak Mujtaba, and Sela Kleiman, "Critical Race Theory and Mental Health," in *Routledge International Handbook of Critical Mental Health*, ed. Bruce M. Z. Cohen (Milton, UK: Taylor and Francis, 2017).

18. Carter, *The Influence of Race and Racial Identity in Psychotherapy*; Carter, *Handbook of Racial-Cultural Psychology and Counseling*; Derald Wing Sue et al., *Counseling the Culturally Diverse: Theory and Practice*, 8th ed. (Hoboken, NJ: Wiley, 2019).

19. Zofia Kumas-Tan et al., "Measures of Cultural Competence: Examining Hidden Assumptions," *Academic Medicine* 82, no. 6 (2007): 554.

20. Brent D. Slife, Kari A. O'Grady, and Russell D. Kosits, eds., *The Hidden Worldviews of Psychology's Theory, Research, and Practice* (New York: Routledge, 2017).

21. Sue et al., *Counseling the Culturally Diverse*. 5.

22. See Derald Wing Sue et al., "The Diversification of Psychology: A Multicultural Revolution," *American Psychologist* 54, no. 12 (1999): 1063, dx.doi.org /10.1037/0003-066X.54.12.1061.

23. Don E. Davis et al., "The Multicultural Orientation Framework: A Narrative Review," *Psychotherapy* 55, no. 1 (2018): 89, doi.org/10.1037%2Fpst0000160.

24. Martin Marger, *Race and Ethnic Relations: American and Global Perspectives*, 10th. ed. (Stamford, CT: Cengage Learning, 2015), 15–18.

25. Eleonora Bartoli et al., "What Do White Counselors and Psychotherapists Need to Know About Race? White Racial Socialization in Counseling and Psychotherapy Training Programs," *Women and Therapy* 38, no. 3–4 (2015): 246–62; Robert T. Carter, "Back to the Future in Cultural Competence Training," *Counseling Psychologist* 29 (2001): 787–89, doi.org/10.1177/0011000001296001; Robert T. Carter, "Becoming Racially and Culturally Competent: The Racial-Cultural Counseling Laboratory," *Journal of Multicultural Counseling* 31, no. 1 (2003): 20–30, doi.org/10.1002/j.2161-1912.2003.tb00527.x; Alex L. Pieterse, Robert T. Carter, and Kilynda A. Ray, "The Relationship Between Perceived Racism, Stress, and Psychological Functioning Among Black Women," *Journal of Multicultural Counseling and Development* 41 (2013): 36–46, doi.org/10.1002/j.2161 -1912.2013.00025.x.

26. Noah M. Collins and Alex L. Pieterse, "Critical Incident Analysis-Based Learning: An Approach to Training for Active Racial and Cultural Awareness," *Journal*

of Counseling and Development 85, no. 1 (2007): 14–23, doi.org/10.1002/j.1556-6678.2007.tb00439.x.

27. Erica L. Campbell, "Transitioning from a Model of Cultural Competency Toward an Inclusive Pedagogy of 'Racial Competency' Using Critical Race Theory," *Journal of Social Welfare and Human Rights* 3, no. 1 (2015): 1–16, doi .org/10.15640/jswhr.v3n1a2.

28. José M. Causadias, Joseph A. Vitriol, and Annabelle Lin Atkin, "Do We Overemphasize the Role of Culture in Behavior of Racial/Ethnic Minorities? Evidence of a Cultural (Mis)Attribution Bias in American Psychology," *American Psychologist* 73, no. 3 (2018): 243, doi.org/10.1037/amp0000099.

29. Causadias et al., "Do We Overemphasize the Role of Culture in Behavior of Racial/Ethnic Minorities?," 254.

30. Causadias et al., "Do We Overemphasize the Role of Culture in Behavior of Racial/Ethnic Minorities?," 252.

31. Edward C. Stewart and Milton J. Bennett, *American Cultural Patterns: A Cross-Cultural Perspective*, 2nd ed. (London: Nicholas Brealey, 2005).

32. Marger, *Race and Ethnic Relations*, 115.

33. Hector F. Myers, "Ethnicity- and Socio-Economic Status-Related Stresses in Context: An Integrative Review and Conceptual Model," *Journal of Behavioral Medicine* 32, no. 1 (2009): 9–19, doi.org/10.1007/s10865-008-9181-4.

34. Louis M. Rea and Richard Allen Parker, *Designing and Conducting Survey Research: A Comprehensive Guide* (San Francisco: Jossey-Bass, 2014); Myers, "Ethnicity- and Socio-Economic Status-Related Stresses in Context," 12.

35. Marger, *Race and Ethnic Relations*, 116.

36. Carter, *The Influence of Race and Racial Identity in Psychotherapy*; Carter, "The Road Less Traveled," 28.

37. Robert T. Carter and Alex L. Pieterse, "Race: A Social and Psychological Analysis of the Term and Its Meaning," in *Handbook of Racial-Cultural Psychology and Counseling*: vol. 1, *Theory and Research*, ed. Robert T. Carter (Hoboken, NJ: Wiley, 2005), 41–63.

38. Carter and Pieterse, "Race: A Social and Psychological Analysis of the Term and Its Meaning."

39. Tara M. Mandalaywala et al., "The Nature and Consequences of Essentialist Beliefs About Race in Early Childhood," *Child Development* (April 2018): 1, doi .org/10.1111/cdev.13008.

40. Mandalaywala et al., "The Nature and Consequences of Essentialist Beliefs About Race in Early Childhood," 11.

41. Paul Pedersen, "The Importance of 'Cultural Psychology' Theory for Multicultural Counselors," in *Handbook of Racial-Cultural Psychology and Counseling*, vol. 1, *Theory and Research*, ed. Robert T. Carter (New York: Wiley, 2005), 3–16; Juris G. Draguns, "Cultural Psychology: Its Early Roots and Present Sta-

tus," in *Handbook of Racial-Cultural Counseling and Psychology*, vol. 1, *Theory and Research*, ed. Robert T. Carter (New York: Wiley, 2005), 163–83.

42. Graham Richards, *"Race," Racism and Psychology: Towards a Reflexive History* (New York: Routledge, 2012): 15–16Audrey Smedley and Brian D. Smedley, "Race as Biology Is Fiction, Racism as a Social Problem Is Real: Anthropological and Historical Perspectives on the Social Construction of Race," *American Psychologist* 60, no. 1 (2005): 20, doi.org/10.1037/0003-066X.60.1.16.

43. Carter, *The Influence of Race and Racial Identity in Psychotherapy*; Robert V. Guthrie, *Even the Rat Was White: A Historical View of Psychology*, 2nd ed. (Upper Saddle River, NJ: Pearson Education, 2004).

44. See Carter, *The Influence of Race and Racial Identity in Psychotherapy*, 31–32.

45. Joseph L. Graves Jr., *The Emperor's New Clothes: Biological Theories of Race at the Millennium* (New Brunswick, NJ: Rutgers University Press, 2001); James M. Jones, *Prejudice and Racism*, 2nd ed. (New York: McGraw-Hill, 1997).

46. Marger, *Race and Ethnic Relations*, 15–16.

47. Margaret T. Hicken et al., "Racial Inequalities in Health: Framing Future Research," *Social Science and Medicine* 199 (February 2018): 11.

48. Stanley J. Huey et al., "The Contribution of Cultural Competence to Evidence-Based Care for Diverse Populations," *Annual Review of Clinical Psychology* 10 (2014): 305–38, doi.org/10.1146/annurev-clinpsy-032813-153729.

49. Carter and Pieterse, "Race: A Social and Psychological Analysis of the Term and Its Meaning."

50. Suman Fernando, "Persistence of Racism Through White Power," in *Institutional Racism in Psychiatry and Clinical Psychology*, ed. Suman Fernando (Cham, Switz.: Palgrave Macmillan, 2017), 135–52; Dwight Turner, "'You Shall Not Replace Us!': White Supremacy, Psychotherapy and Decolonisation," *Journal of Critical Psychology, Counselling and Psychotherapy* 18, no. 1 (March 2018): 1–12.

51. Carter and Pieterse, "Race: A Social and Psychological Analysis of the Term and Its Meaning," 54.

52. Carter, *The Influence of Race and Racial Identity in Psychotherapy*, 82–83.

53. Carter, *The Influence of Race and Racial Identity in Psychotherapy*, 76.

54. Janet E. Helms and Donelda A. Cook, *Using Race and Culture in Counseling and Psychotherapy: Theory and Process* (Boston: Allyn and Bacon, 1999), 7–8.

55. Shelly P. Harrell, "Compassionate Confrontation and Empathic Exploration: The Integration of Race-Related Narratives in Clinical Supervision," in *Multiculturalism and Diversity in Clinical Supervision: A Competency-Based Approach*, ed. Carol Falender and Edward Shafranske (Washington DC: American Psychological Association, 2014), 83–110.

56. Carter, *The Influence of Race and Racial Identity in Psychotherapy*; Alex L. Pieterse, "Attending to Racial Trauma in Clinical Supervision: Enhancing Client

and Supervisee Outcomes," *Clinical Supervisor* 37, no. 1 (2018): 204–20, doi.org /10.1080/07325223.2018.1443304; Chalmer E. Thompson and Robert T. Carter, eds., *Racial Identity Theory: Applications to Individual, Group, and Organizational Interventions* (New York: Routledge, 2012 [1997]).

57. Diane Hughes et al., "Parents' Ethnic-Racial Socialization Practices: A Review of Research and Directions for Future Study," *Developmental Psychology* 42 (2006): 747–70, doi.org/10.1037/0012-1649.42.5.747.

58. Helen A. Neville, Roger L. Worthington, and Lisa B. Spanierman, "Race, Power, and Multicultural Counseling Psychology: Understanding White Privilege and Color-Blind Racial Attitudes," in *Handbook of Multicultural Counseling*, 2nd ed., ed. Joseph G. Ponterotto et al. (Thousand Oaks, CA: Sage, 2001), 257–88.

59. Hicken et al., "Racial Inequalities in Health"; Helena Hansen, Joel Braslow, and Robert M. Rohrbaugh, "From Cultural to Structural Competency: Training Psychiatry Residents to Act on Social Determinants of Health and Institutional Racism," *AMA Psychiatry* 75, no. 2 (2018): 117–18, doi.org/10.1001/ jamapsychiatry.2017.3894.

60. Harrell, "Compassionate Confrontation and Empathic Exploration."

61. John F. Dovidio, Samuel L. Gaertner, and Adam R. Pearson, "Aversive Racism and Contemporary Bias," in *The Cambridge Handbook of the Psychology of Prejudice*, ed. Chris G. Sibley and Fiona Kate Barlow (Cambridge, UK: Cambridge University Press, 2016), 267–91.

62. Rita Chi-Ying Chung et al., "Challenges in Promoting Race Dialogues in Psychology Training: Race and Gender Perspectives," *Counseling Psychologist* 46, no. 2 (2018): 213–40, doi.org/10.1177/0011000018758262.

63. Bartoli et al., "What Do White Counselors and Psychotherapists Need to Know About Race?"

64. Larry Ortiz and Jayshree Jani, "Critical Race Theory: A Transformational Model for Teaching Diversity," *Journal of Social Work Education* 46, no. 2 (2010): 177, doi.org/10.5175/JSWE.2010.200900070.

65. Natoya H. Haskins and Anneliese A. Singh, "Critical Race Theory and Counselor Education Pedagogy: Creating Equitable Training," *Counselor Education and Supervision* 54, no. 4 (2015): 288–301, doi.org/10.1002/ceas.12027.

66. Carter, "Becoming Racially and Culturally Competent"; Robert T. Carter, *Handbook of Racial-Cultural Psychology and Counseling*, vol. 2, *Training and Practice* (Hoboken, NJ: Wiley, 2005b).

67. Chung et al. "Challenges in Promoting Race Dialogues in Psychology Training"; Adrienne Dessel, Mary E. Rogge, and Sarah B. Garlington, "Using Intergroup Dialogue to Promote Social Justice and Change," *Social Work* 51, no. 4 (2006): 303–15, doi.org/10.1093/sw/51.4.303.

68. Bartoli et al., "What Do White Counselors and Psychotherapists Need to Know About Race?"; Collins and Pieterse, "Critical Incident Analysis-Based Learning."

69. Judith Nihill de Ricco and Daniel T. Sciarra, "The Immersion Experience in Multicultural Counselor Training: Confronting Covert Racism," *Journal of Multicultural Counseling and Development* 33, no. 1 (2005): 2–16, doi.org /10.1002/j.2161-1912.2005.tb00001.x.

70. Chalmer E. Thompson and Helen A. Neville, "Racism, Mental Health, and Mental Health Practice," *Counseling Psychologist* 27, no. 2 (1999): 207.

71. Robert T. Carter, "Becoming Racially and Culturally Competent: The Racial-Cultural Counseling Laboratory," *Journal of Multicultural Counseling* 31, no. 1 (2003): 20–30, doi.org/10.1002/j.2161-1912.2003.tb00527.x.

72. See also Joe R. Feagin, *Racist America: Roots, Current Realities, and Future Reparations*, 3rd ed. (New York: Routledge, 2014).

73. Pieterse, "Attending to Racial Trauma in Clinical Supervision."

74. Shelly P. Harrell, "A Multidimensional Conceptualization of Racism-Related Stress: Implications for the Well-Being of People of Color," *American Journal of Orthopsychiatry* 70, no. 1 (2000): 42–57, doi.org/10.1037/h0087722; Shawn O. Utsey, Mark A. Bolden, and Andraé L. Brown, "Visions of Revolution from the Spirit of Frantz Fanon: A Psychology of Liberation for Counseling African Americans Confronting Societal Racism and Oppression," in *Handbook of Multicultural Counseling*, 2nd ed., ed. Joseph G. Ponterotto et al. (Thousand Oaks, CA: Sage, 2001), 311–36.

75. Elizabeth Fast and Delphine Collin-Vézina, "Historical Trauma, Race-Based Trauma and Resilience of Indigenous Peoples: A Literature Review," *First Peoples Child and Family Review* 5, no. 1 (2010): 126–36.

76. For example, Alex L. Pieterse et al., "Multicultural Competence and Social Justice Training in Counseling Psychology and Counselor Education: A Review and Analysis of a Sample of Multicultural Course Syllabi," *Counseling Psychologist* 37, no. 1 (2009): 93–115, doi.org/10.1177/0011000008319986.

77. Joshua Miller and Ann Marie Garran, *Racism in the United States: Implications for the Helping Professions* (New York: Springer, 2017).

78. American Psychological Association, "Ethical Principles of Psychologists and Code of Conduct," *American Psychologist* 57 (2002): 1060–73, www.apa.org /ethics/code; American Psychological Association, "2010 Amendments to the 2002 'Ethical Principles of Psychologists and Code of Conduct,'" *American Psychologist* 65 (2010): 493, www.apa.org/ethics/code.

79. American School Counselors Association, "ASCA Ethical Standards for School Counselors," adopted 1984, rev. 1992, 1998, 2004, 2010, and 2016. www.school counselor.org/asca/media/asca/Ethics/EthicalStandards2016.pdf.

80. National Association of Social Workers, "Code of Ethics," 2017, www.social workers.org/about/ethics/code-of-ethics/code-of-ethics-english.

81. Pieterse et al., "Multicultural Competence and Social Justice Training in Counseling Psychology and Counselor Education."

82. See Fred Newdom, "Invitation to the School's Anti-Racism Commitment," address to incoming students, Smith College, May 31, 2015, www.smith.edu /ssw/about/anti-racism-commitment/invitation-schools-anti-racism -commitment.

83. Riana Elyse Anderson and Howard C. Stevenson, "RECASTing Racial Stress and Trauma: Theorizing the Healing Potential of Racial Socialization in Families," *American Psychologist* 74, no. 1 (2019): 63–75; Carter, *The Influence of Race and Racial Identity in Psychotherapy*; Ashley B. Evans et al., "Racial Socialization as a Mechanism for Positive Development Among African American Youth," *Child Development Perspectives* 6, no. 3 (2012): 251–57, doi.org/10.1 111/j.1750-8606.2011.00226.x.

84. Shawn O. Utsey, Carol A. Gernat, and Mark A. Bolden, "Teaching Racial Identity Development and Racism Awareness," in *Handbook of Racial and Ethnic Minority Psychology*, ed. Guillermo Bernal et al., *Racial and Ethnic Minority Psychology Series*, vol. 4 (Thousand Oaks, CA: Sage, 2003), 147–66.

85. Robert T. Carter and Veronica E. Johnson, "Racial Identity Statuses: Applications to Practice," *Practice Innovations* 4, no. 1 (2019): 42–58, dx.doi.org/10.1037 /pri0000082.

86. Kevin L. Nadal, *Microaggressions and Traumatic Stress: Theory, Research, and Clinical Treatment* (Washington, DC: American Psychological Association, 2018).

87. Frederick L. Oswald et al., "Predicting Ethnic and Racial Discrimination: A Meta-Analysis of IAT Criterion Studies," *Journal of Personality and Social Psychology* 105, no. 2 (2013): 171–92, doi.org/10.1037/a0032734.

88. Guy A. Boysen, "Integrating Implicit Bias into Counselor Education," *Counselor Education and Supervision* 49, no. 4 (2010): 210–27, doi.org/10.1002/j.1556 -6978.2010.tb00099.x.

89. Huey et al., "The Contribution of Cultural Competence to Evidence-Based Care for Diverse Populations."

90. Erica Gabrielle Foldy and Tamara R. Buckley, *The Color Bind: Talking (and Not Talking) About Race at Work* (New York: Russell Sage Foundation, 2014); Biren (Ratnesh) A. Nagda and Ximena Zuniga, "Fostering Meaningful Racial Engagement Through Intergroup Dialogues," *Group Processes and Intergroup Relations* 6, no. 1 (2003): 111–28, doi.org/10.1177/1368430203006001015.

91. Adrienne Dessel and Mary E. Rogge, "Evaluation of Intergroup Dialogue: A Review of the Empirical Literature," *Conflict Resolution Quarterly* 26, no. 2 (2008): 201, doi.org/10.1002/crq.230.

92. Brent Mallinckrodt, Joe R. Miles, and Jacob J. Levy, "The Scientist-Practitioner-Advocate Model: Addressing Contemporary Training Needs for Social Justice Advocacy," *Training and Education in Professional Psychology* 8, no. 4 (2014): 303–11, doi.org/10.1037/tep0000045.

93. Mark E. Engberg, "Improving Intergroup Relations in Higher Education: A Critical Examination of the Influence of Educational Interventions on Racial Bias," *Review of Educational Research* 74, no. 4 (2004): 473–524, doi.org/10.3102/00346543074004473.

94. Rebecca A. Willow, "Lived Experience of Interracial Dialogue on Race: Proclivity to Participate," *Journal of Multicultural Counseling and Development* 36, no. 1 (2008): 40–51, dx.doi.org/10.1002/j.2161-1912.2008.tb00068.x.

95. Anthony De Jesús et al., "Putting Racism on the Table: The Implementation and Evaluation of a Novel Racial Equity and Cultural Competency Training/Consultation Model in New York City," *Journal of Ethnic and Cultural Diversity in Social Work* 25, no. 4 (2016): 300–19, doi.org/10.1080/15313204.2016.1206497.

96. Sommers-Flanagan and Sommers-Flanagan, *Counseling and Psychotherapy Theories in Context and Practice*, 25.

97. Lillian Comas-Díaz, "Racial Trauma Recovery: A Race Informed Therapeutic Approach to Racial Wounds," in *The Cost of Racism for People of Color: Contextualizing Experiences of Discrimination*, ed. Alvin N. Alvarez, Christopher T. H. Liang, and Helen A. Neville (Washington, DC: American Psychological Association, 2016), 249–71, doi.org/10.1037/14852-012; Alex L. Pieterse, Robert T. Carter, Sarah A. Evans, and Rebecca A. Walter, "An Exploratory Examination of the Associations Among Racial and Ethnic Discrimination, Racial Climate, and Trauma-Related Symptoms in a College Student Population," *Journal of Counseling Psychology* 57, no. 3 (2010): 255–63.

98. Ibrahim Aref Kira, "Taxonomy of Trauma and Trauma Assessment," *Traumatology* 7, no. 2 (2001): 73–86, doi.org/10.1177/153476560100700202.

99. Esteban V. Cardemil and Cynthia L. Battle, "Guess Who's Coming to Therapy? Getting Comfortable with Conversations About Race and Ethnicity in Psychotherapy," *Professional Psychology: Research and Practice* 34, no. 3 (2003): 278–86, doi.org/10.1037/0735-7028.34.3.278; Dorothy Evans Holmes, "Racial Transference Reactions in Psychoanalytic Treatment: An Update," in *Race, Culture and Psychotherapy: Critical Perspectives in Multicultural Practice*, ed. Roy Moodley and Stephen Palmer (New York: Routledge, 2014), 79–91.

100. Krista M. Malott and Scott Schaefle, "Addressing Clients' Experiences of Racism: A Model for Clinical Practice," *Journal of Counseling and Development* 93 (2015): 363, doi.org/10.1002/jcad.12034.

101. Clara E. Hill, Jessica Stahl, and Melissa Roffman, "Training Novice Psychotherapists: Helping Skills and Beyond," *Psychotherapy: Theory, Research, Practice, Training* 44, no. 4 (2007): 364–70, doi.org/10.1037/0033-3204.44.4.364.

102. See Hill, Stahl, and Roffman, "Training Novice Psychotherapists."
103. Chung et al., "Challenges in Promoting Race Dialogues in Psychology Training," 214; Shawn O. Utsey, Carol A. Gernat, and Lawrence Hammar, "Examining White Counselor Trainees' Reactions to Racial Issues in Counseling and Supervision Dyads," *Counseling Psychologist* 33, no. 4 (2005): 463, doi.org /10.1177/0011000004269058.
104. Isha Mackenzie-Mavinga, *The Challenge of Racism in Therapeutic Practice: Engaging with Oppression in Practice and Supervision* (New York: Palgrave, 2016); Pieterse, "Attending to Racial Trauma in Clinical Supervision."
105. Alan W. Burkard et al., "Supervisors' Experiences of Providing Difficult Feedback in Cross-Ethnic/Racial Supervision," *Counseling Psychologist* 42, no. 3 (2014): 314–44, doi:10.1177/0011000012461157.
106. See Matthew McKay, Jeffrey C. Wood, and Jeffrey Brantley, *The Dialectical Behavior Therapy Skills Workbook: Practical DBT Exercises for Learning Mindfulness, Interpersonal Effectiveness, Emotion Regulation and Distress Tolerance* (Oakland, CA: New Harbinger Publications, 2010).
107. Nicholas Ladany, "Does Psychotherapy Training Matter? Maybe Not," *Psychotherapy: Theory, Research, Practice, Training* 44, no. 4 (2007): 392–96, doi.org /10.1037/0033-3204.44.4.392.
108. Len Jennings et al., "Bringing It All Together: A Qualitative Meta-Analysis of Seven Master Therapists' Studies from Around the World," in *Expertise in Counseling and Psychotherapy: Master Therapist Studies Around the World*, ed. Len Jennings and Thomas Skovholt (New York: Oxford University Press, 2016), 227–73, doi.org/10.1093/med:psych/9780190222505.003.0008.
109. Candice Presseau et al., "Trainee Social Justice Advocacy: Investigating the Roles of Training Factors and Multicultural Competence," *Counselling Psychology Quarterly* 32, no. 2 (2019): 260–74, doi.org/10.1080/09515070.2018 .1476837.

12. Emerging Issues in Practice and Research

1. Robert T. Carter et al., "A Meta-Analytic Review of Racial Discrimination: Relationships to Health and Culture," *Race and Social Problems* 11, no. 1 (March 2019): 15–32, doi.org/10.1007/s12552-018-9256-y; Anissa I. Vines et al., "Perceived Racial/Ethnic Discrimination and Mental Health: A Review and Future Directions for Social Epidemiology," *Current Epidemiology Reports* 4, no. 2 (2017): 156–65, doi.org/10.1007/s40471-017-0106-z.
2. Robert T. Carter and Thomas D. Scheuermann, *Confronting Racism: Integrating Mental Health Research into Legal Strategies and Reforms* (New York: Routledge, 2020).

3. Gordon Bower and Heidi Sivers, "Cognitive Impact of Traumatic Events," *Development and Psychopathology* 10, no. 4 (1998): 625–53, doi.org/10.1017/S0954579498001795.

4. Dorthie Cross et al., "Neurobiological Development in the Context of Childhood Trauma," *Clinical Psychology: Science and Practice* 24, no. 2 (June 2017): 111–24, dx.doi.org/10.1111/cpsp.12198; Christine Heim et al., "Neurobiological and Psychiatric Consequences of Child Abuse and Neglect," *Developmental Psychobiology* 52, no. 7 (2010): 671–90, doi.org/10.1002/dev.20494; Janine Oldfield and Theresa Jackson, "Childhood Abuse and Trauma: A Racial Perspective," *Children Australia* 44, no. 1 (2019): 42–48; Audrey R. Tyrka et al., "The Neurobiological Correlates of Childhood Adversity and Implications for Treatment," *Acta Psychiatrica Scandinavica* 128, no. 6 (2013): 434–47, doi.org/10.1111/acps.12143; Bessel A. Van Der Kolk, "Developmental Trauma Disorder: Toward a Rational Diagnosis for Children with Complex Trauma Histories," *Psychiatric Annals* 35, no. 5 (2017): 401–408, doi.org/10.3928/00485713-20050501-06; Bessel A. Van Der Kolk, "The Developmental Impact of Childhood Trauma," in *Understanding Trauma: Integrating Biological, Clinical, and Cultural Perspectives*, ed. Lawrence J. Kirmayer, Robert Lemelson, and Mark Barad (New York: Cambridge University Press, 2007), 224–41, doi.org/10.1017/CBO9780511500008.016.

5. Anne Murphy et al., "Adverse Childhood Experiences (ACEs) Questionnaire and Adult Attachment Interview (AAI): Implications for Parent Child Relationships," *Child Abuse and Neglect* 38, no. 2 (2014): 224–33, doi.org/10.1016/j.chiabu.2013.09.004.

6. Ioannis Angelakis et al., "Childhood Maltreatment and Adult Suicidality: A Comprehensive Systematic Review with Meta-Analysis." *Psychological Medicine* 49, no. 7 (2019): 1057–78; Clara Passmann Carr et al., "The Role of Early Life Stress in Adult Psychiatric Disorders: A Systematic Review According to Childhood Trauma Subtypes," *Journal of Nervous and Mental Disease* 201, no. 12 (2013): 1007–20, doi.org/10.1097/NMD.0000000000000049; Alicia F. Lieberman et al., "Trauma in Early Childhood: Empirical Evidence and Clinical Implications," *Development and Psychopathology* 23, no. 2 (2011): 397–410, doi.org/10.1017/S0954579411000137; Charles B. Nemeroff, "Neurobiological Consequences of Childhood Trauma," *Journal of Clinical Psychiatry* 65 (Suppl. 1, 2004): 18–28.

7. Christopher M. Layne et al., "The Core Curriculum on Childhood Trauma: A Tool for Training a Trauma-Informed Workforce," *Psychological Trauma: Theory, Research, Practice, and Policy* 3, no. 3 (2011): 243, doi.org/10.1037/a0025039.

8. Aprile Benner, "The Toll of Racial/Ethnic Discrimination on Adolescents' Adjustment," *Child Development Perspectives* 11, no. 4 (2017): 251–56, doi.org/10.1111/cdep.12241.

9. Lee M. Pachter and Cynthia Garcia Coll, "Racism and Child Health: A Review of the Literature and Future Directions," *Journal of Developmental and Behavioral Pediatrics* 30, no. 3 (2009): 255, dx.doi.org/10.1097%2FDBP.obo13e31 81a7ed5a.

10. Naomi Priest et al., "A Systematic Review of Studies Examining the Relationship Between Reported Racism and Health and Wellbeing for Children and Young People," *Social Science and Medicine* 95 (2013): 115–27, doi.org/10.1016/j.socscimed.2012.11.031.

11. Maryam M. Jernigan and Jessica Henderson Daniel, "Racial Trauma in the Lives of Black Children and Adolescents: Challenges and Clinical Implications," *Journal of Child and Adolescent Trauma* 4, no. 2 (2011): 126.

12. Alicia F. Lieberman and Kathleen Knorr, "The Impact of Trauma: A Developmental Framework for Infancy and Early Childhood," *Pediatric Annals* 36, no. 4 (2007): 209–15, doi.org/10.3928/0090-4481-20070401-10; Tamika C. B. Zapolski et al., "Collective Ethnic-Racial Identity and Health Outcomes Among African American Youth: Examination of Promotive and Protective Effects," *Cultural Diversity and Ethnic Minority Psychology* 25, no. 3 (2019): 388–96.

13. See Van Der Kolk, "Developmental Trauma Disorder."

14. Andres J. Pumariega, "The Reaction to Historical Trauma Among Minority Youth," *Journal of the American Academy of Child and Adolescent Psychiatry* 56, no. 10 (2017): S75, doi.org/10.1016/j.jaac.2017.07.297.

15. Lillian Comas-Díaz, "Racial Trauma Recovery: A Race Informed Therapeutic Approach to Racial Wounds," in *The Cost of Racism for People of Color: Contextualizing Experiences of Discrimination*, ed. Alvin N. Alvarez, Christopher T. H. Liang, and Helen A. Neville (Washington, DC: American Psychological Association, 2016), 249–71, doi.org/10.1037/14852-012.

16. Lillian Comas-Díaz, Gordon N. Hall, and Helen A. Neville, "Racial Trauma: Theory, Research, and Healing: Introduction to the Special Issue," *American Psychologist* 74, no. 1 (2019): 1–5, dx.doi.org/10.1037/amp0000442.

17. Monnica T. Williams et al., "Assessing Racial Trauma Within a DSM-5 Framework: The UConn Racial/Ethnic Stress and Trauma Survey," *Practice Innovations* 3, no. 4 (2018): 242–60, doi.org/10.1037/pri0000076.

18. Dean G. Kilpatrick et al., "National Estimates of Exposure to Traumatic Events and PTSD Prevalence Using DSM-IV and DSM-5 Criteria," *Journal of Traumatic Stress* 26, no. 5 (October 2013): 537–47; Nicholas J. Sibrava et al., "Posttraumatic Stress Disorder in African American and Latinx Adults: Clinical Course and the Role of Racial and Ethnic Discrimination." *American Psychologist* 74, no. 1 (2019): 101–16.

19. Kilpatrick et al., "National Estimates of Exposure to Traumatic Events and PTSD Prevalence Using DSM-IV and DSM-5 Criteria."

20. See Lawrence G. Calhoun and Richard G. Tedeschi, "Beyond Recovery from Trauma: Implications for Clinical Practice and Research," *Journal of Social Issues* 54, no. 2 (1998): 357–71, doi.org/10.1111/j.1540-4560.1998.tb01223.x; Kelli N. Triplett et al., "Posttraumatic Growth, Meaning in Life, and Life Satisfaction in Response to Trauma," *Psychological Trauma: Theory, Research, Practice, and Policy* 4, no. 4 (2012): 400, doi.org/10.1037/a0024204.

21. Michelle Sotero, "A Conceptual Model of Historical Trauma: Implications for Public Health Practice and Research," *Journal of Health Disparities Research and Practice* 1, no. 1 (2006): 94, 95, https://ssrn.com/abstract=1350062.

22. See Laurence J. Kirmayer, Joseph P. Gone, and Joshua Moses, "Rethinking Historical Trauma," *Transcultural Psychiatry* 51 (2014): 299–319, doi.org/10.1177 /1363461514536358.

23. Graham Danzer, "African-Americans' Historical Trauma: Manifestations In and Outside of Therapy," *Journal of Theory Construction and Testing* 16, no. 1 (2012): 16–21.

24. Donna K. Nagata, Jackie H. Kim, and Teresa U. Nguyen, "Processing Cultural Trauma: Intergenerational Effects of the Japanese American Incarceration," *Journal of Social Issues* 71, no. 2 (2015): 356–70, doi.org/10.1111/josi.12115.

25. Joseph P. Gone, "'We Never Was Happy Living Like a Whiteman': Mental Health Disparities and the Postcolonial Predicament in American Indian Communities," *American Journal of Community Psychology* 40, no. 3–4 (2007): 290–300, doi.org/10.1007/s10464-007-9136-x.

26. Michelle Alexander, *The New Jim Crow: Mass Incarceration in the Age of Colorblindness* (New York: New Press, 2012); Ron Eyerman, *Cultural Trauma: Slavery and the Formation of African American Identity* (Cambridge, UK: Cambridge University Press, 2001).

27. Monica C. Skewes and Arthur W. Blume, "Understanding the Link Between Racial Trauma and Substance Use Among American Indians," *American Psychologist* 74, no. 1 (2019): 88–100.

28. Kirmayer, Gone, and Moses, "Rethinking Historical Trauma," *Transcultural Psychiatry* 51 (2014): 299–319, doi.org/10.1177/1363461514536358.

29. Nagata, Kim, and Nguyen, "Processing Cultural Trauma."

30. Les B. Whitbeck et al., "Conceptualizing and Measuring Historical Trauma Among American Indian People," *American Journal of Community Psychology* 33, no. 3–4 (2004): 119–30, doi.org/10.1023/B:AJCP.0000027000.77357.31.

31. Joseph Gone et al., "The Impact of Historical Trauma on Health Outcomes for Indigenous Populations in the USA and Canada: A Systematic Review," *American Psychologist* 74, no. 1 (2019): 20.

32. Nagata, Kim, and Nguyen, "Processing Cultural Trauma"; Michael J. Halloran, "African American Health and Posttraumatic Slave Syndrome: A Terror Management Theory Account," *Journal of Black Studies* 50, no. 1 (2019): 45–65.

33. George W. Albee, "Preventing Psychopathology and Promoting Human Potential," *American Psychologist* 37, no. 9 (1982): 1043–50, doi.org/10.1037//0003-066X.37.9.1043; George W. Albee, "Toward a Just Society: Lessons from Observations on the Primary Prevention of Psychopathology," *American Psychologist* 41, no. 8 (1986): 891–98.

34. John L. Romano and Sally M. Hage, "Prevention and Counseling Psychology: Revitalizing Commitments for the 21st Century," *Counseling Psychologist* 28, no. 6 (2000): 733–63, doi.org/10.1177/0011000000286001.

35. Sally M. Hage et al., "Best Practice Guidelines on Prevention, Practice, Research, Training, and Social Advocacy for Psychologists," *Counseling Psychologist* 35, no. 4 (2007): 510, doi.org/10.1177%2F0011000006291411.

36. Carter et al., "A Meta-Analytic Review of Racial Discrimination"; David R. Williams and Selina A. Mohammed, "Racism and Health I: Pathways and Scientific Evidence," *American Behavioral Scientist* 57, no. 8 (2013): 1152–73, doi:10.1177/0002764213487340; David R. Williams, "Stress and the Mental Health of Populations of Color: Advancing Our Understanding of Race-Related Stressors," *Journal of Health and Social Behavior* 59, no. 4 (2018): 466–85.

37. Fran H. Norris et al., "60,000 Disaster Victims Speak: Part I. An Empirical Review of the Empirical Literature, 1981–2001," *Psychiatry* 65, no. 3 (2002): 207–39.

38. Amanuel Elias and Yin Paradies, "Estimating the Mental Health Costs of Racial Discrimination," *BMC Public Health* 16, no. 1 (2016): 1205, doi.org/10.1186/s12889-016-3868-1; Thomas A. LaVeist, Darrell Gaskin, and Patrick Richard, "Estimating the Economic Burden of Racial Health Inequalities in the United States," *International Journal of Health Services* 41, no. 2 (2011): 231–38, doi.org/10.2190/HS.41.2.c.

39. Jennifer Jee-Lyn García and Mienah Zulfacar Sharif, "Black Lives Matter: A Commentary on Racism and Public Health," *American Journal of Public Health* 105, no. 8 (2015): e27–e30.

40. Billie Castle et al., "Public Health's Approach to Systemic Racism: A Systematic Literature Review," *Journal of Racial and Ethnic Health Disparities* 6, no. 1 (2019): 27–36, doi.org/10.1007/s40615-018-0494-x.

41. James A. Johnson, James Allen Johnson III, and Cynthia B. Morrow, "Historical Developments in Public Health and the 21st Century," in *Novick and Morrow's Public Health Administration*, ed. Leiyu Shi and James A. Johnson (Burlington, MA: Jones and Bartlett Learning, 2013), 11–31.

42. Chandra L. Ford and Collins O. Airhihenbuwa, "Critical Race Theory, Race Equity, and Public Health: Toward Antiracism Praxis," *American Journal of Public Health* 100, no. S1 (April 1, 2010): S30–S35, doi.org/10.2105/AJPH.2009.171058.

43. Gilbert C. Gee, Katrina M. Walsemann, and Elizabeth Brondolo, "A Life Course Perspective on How Racism May Be Related to Health Inequities,"

American Journal of Public Health 102, no. 5 (2012): 967–74, dx.doi.org/10.2105 %2FAJPH.2012.300666.

44. Larisa Buhin and Elizabeth M. Vera, "Preventing Racism and Promoting Social Justice: Person-Centered and Environment-Centered Interventions," *Journal of Primary Prevention* 30, no. 1 (2009): 43–59, doi.org/10.1007/s10935 -008-0161-9.

45. Emory L. Cowen, "Social and Community Interventions," *Annual Review of Psychology* 24 (1973): 433, doi.org/10.1146/annurev.ps.24.020173.002231.

46. Pamela J. Sawyer et al., "Discrimination and the Stress Response: Psychological and Physiological Consequences of Anticipating Prejudice in Interethnic Interactions," *American Journal of Public Health* 102, no. 5 (2012): 1020–26, doi .org/10.2105/AJPH.2011.300620.

47. Y. Joel Wong, Ellen L. Vaughan, and Elyssa M. Klann, "The Science and Practice of Prevention from Multicultural and Social Justice Perspectives," *Cambridge Handbook of International Prevention Science*, ed. Moshe Israelashvilli and John L. Romano (New York: Cambridge University Press, 2017), 107–32.

48. Buhin and Vera, "Preventing Racism and Promoting Social Justice."

49. Arthur L. Whaley and King E. Davis, "Cultural Competence and Evidence-Based Practice in Mental Health Services: A Complementary Perspective," *American Psychologist* 62 (2007): 563–74, doi.org/10.1037/0003-066X.62.6.563.

50. Carrie Hemmings and Amanda M. Evans, "Identifying and Treating Race-Based Trauma in Counseling," *Journal of Multicultural Counseling and Development* 46, no. 1 (2018): 20–39, doi.org/10.1002/jmcd.12090.

51. Simon Corneau and Vicky Stergiopoulos, "More Than Being Against It: Anti-Racism and Anti-Oppression in Mental Health Services," *Transcultural Psychiatry* 49, no. 2 (2012): 261–82, doi.org/10.1177/1363461512441594.

52. Patricia Arredondo et al., "Operationalization of the Multicultural Counseling Competencies," *Journal of Multicultural Counseling and Development* 24, no. 1 (1996): 42–78.

53. George J. Sefa Dei, "Unmasking Racism: A Challenge for Anti-Racial Educators in the 21st Century," in *Engaging Equity: New Perspectives on Anti-Racist Education*, ed. Leeno Luke Karumanchery (Calgary, Can.: Detselig, 2005), 141.

54. Corneau and Stergiopoulos, "More Than Being Against It."

55. Suzanne L. Stewart, Roy Moodley, and Ashley Hyatt, eds., *Indigenous Cultures and Mental Health Counselling: Four Directions for Integration with Counselling Psychology* (New York: Routledge, 2016).

56. Patricia Arredondo and Daniel C. Rosen, "Applying Principles of Multicultural Competencies, Social Justice, and Leadership in Training and Supervision," in *Advancing Social Justice Through Clinical Practice*, ed. E. Aldarondo (Mahwah, NJ: Lawrence Erlbaum, 2007), 453.

57. Rebecca Rangel Campón and Robert T. Carter, "The Appropriated Racial Oppression Scale: Development and Preliminary Validation," *Cultural Diversity and Ethnic Minority Psychology* 21, no. 4 (2015): 497–506, dx.doi.org/10.1037/cdp0000037.

58. Ford and Airhihenbuwa, "Critical Race Theory, Race Equity, and Public Health: Toward Antiracism Praxis."

59. See Carter et al., "A Meta-Analytic Review of Racial Discrimination"; Carter et al., "Racial Discrimination and Health Outcomes Among Racial/Ethnic Minorities: A Meta-Analytic Review," *Journal of Multicultural Counseling and Development* 45, no. 4 (2017): 232–59, doi.org/10.1002/jmcd.12076; Yin Paradies et al., "Racism as a Determinant of Health: A Systematic Review and Meta-Analysis," *PloS one* 10, no. 9 (2015): 1–48, doi:10.137/journal.pone.0138511.

60. Lenny R. Vartanian, Marlene B. Schwartz, and Kelly D. Brownell, "Effects of Soft Drink Consumption on Nutrition and Health: A Systematic Review and Meta-Analysis," *American Journal of Public Health* 97, no. 4 (2007): 667–75, doi.org/10.2105/AJPH.2005.083782; Leonore M. de Wit et al., "Depression and Obesity: A Meta-Analysis of Community-Based Studies," *Psychiatry Research* 178, no. 2 (2010): 230–35, dx.doi.org/10.1016/j.psychres.2009.04.015.

61. David L. Katz et al., "Public Health Strategies for Preventing and Controlling Overweight and Obesity in School and Worksite Settings: A Report on Recommendations of the Task Force on Community Preventive Services," *Morbidity and Mortality Weekly Report: Recommendations and Reports* 54, no. 10 (October 7, 2005): 1–12.

62. World Health Organization, Maximizing Positive Synergies Collaborative Group, "An Assessment of Interactions Between Global Health Initiatives and Country Health Systems," *Lancet* 373, no. 9681 (2009): 2137–69, doi.org/10.1016/S0140-6736(09)60919-3.

63. Ford and Airhihenbuwa, "Critical Race Theory, Race Equity, and Public Health: Toward Antiracism Praxis."

64. Rachel R. Hardeman, Eduardo M. Medina, and Katy B. Kozhimannil, "Structural Racism and Supporting Black Lives: The Role of Health Professionals," *New England Journal of Medicine* 375, no. 22 (2016): 2114, doi.org/10.1056/NEJMp1609535.

65. See American Psychological Association, "Ethical Principles of Psychologists and Code of Conduct," 2017a, www.apa.org/ethics/code.

66. Skewes and Blume, "Understanding the Link Between Racial Trauma and Substance Use Among American Indians," *American Psychologist* 74, no. 1 (2019): 88–100.

67. Angeline S. Ferdinand, Yin Paradies, and Margaret Kelaher, "Enhancing the Use of Research in Health-Promoting, Anti-Racism Policy," *Health Research Policy and Systems* 15, no. 1 (2017): 61, doi.org/10.1186/s12961-017-0223-7.

68. Corneau and Stergiopoulos, "More Than Being Against It."

69. Jessica Forsyth and Robert T. Carter, "The Development and Preliminary Validation of the Racism-Related Coping Scale," *Psychological Trauma: Theory, Research, Practice, and Policy* 6, no. 6 (2014): 632–43, doi.org/10.1037/a0036702; Kumea Shorter-Gooden, "Multiple Resistance Strategies: How African American Women Cope with Racism and Sexism," *Journal of Black Psychology* 30, no. 3 (2004): 406–25, doi.org/10.1177/0095798404266050.

70. Roni Strier, "Anti-Oppressive Research in Social Work: A Preliminary Definition," *British Journal of Social Work* 37, no. 5 (2006): 857, doi.org/10.1093/bjsw/bcl062.

71. Brett G. Stoudt, Madeline Fox, and Michelle Fine, "Contesting Privilege with Critical Participatory Action Research," *Journal of Social Issues* 68, no. 1 (2012): 180–81, doi.org/10.1111/j.1540-4560.2011.01743.x.

72. Sigrid Herring et al., "The Intersection of Trauma, Racism, and Cultural Competence in Effective Work with Aboriginal People: Waiting for Trust," *Australian Social Work* 66, no. 1 (2013): 104–17, doi.org/10.1080/0312407X.2012.697566.

73. Don Elligan and Shawn Utsey, "Utility of an African-Centered Support Group for African American Men Confronting Societal Racism and Oppression," *Cultural Diversity and Ethnic Minority Psychology* 5, no. 2 (1999): 156–65, dx.doi.org/10.1037/1099-9809.5.2.156; Anderson J. Franklin and Nancy Boyd-Franklin, "Invisibility Syndrome: A Clinical Model of the Effects of Racism on African-American Males," *American Journal of Orthopsychiatry* 70, no. 1 (2000): 33–41.

74. Roy F. Baumeister, Kathleen D. Vohs, and David C. Funder, "Psychology as the Science of Self-Reports and Finger Movements: Whatever Happened to Actual Behavior?" *Perspectives on Psychological Science* 2, no. 4 (2007): 396–403, doi.org/10.1111/j.1745-6916.2007.00051.x.

75. Isaac Prilleltensky, "Values, Assumptions, and Practices: Assessing the Moral Implications of Psychological Discourse and Action," *American Psychologist* 52, no. 5 (1997): 517–35, psycnet.apa.org/doi/10.1037/0003-066X.52.5.517.

76. Ignacio Martín-Baró, "Public Opinion Research as a De-Ideologizing Instrument," trans. Jean Carroll and Adrianne Aron, in *Writings for a Liberation Psychology*, by Ignacio Martín-Baró, ed. Adrianne Aron (Cambridge, MA: Harvard University Press, 1996), 186–97.

77. Geraldine Moane, "Bridging the Personal and the Political: Practices for a Liberation Psychology," *American Journal of Community Psychology* 31, no. 1–2 (2003): 92, doi.org/10.1023/A:1023026704576.

78. Eduardo Duran, Judith Firehammer, and John Gonzalez, "Liberation Psychology as the Path Toward Healing Cultural Soul Wounds," *Journal of Counseling and Development* 86, no. 3 (2008): 288–95, dx.doi.org/10.1002/j.1556-6678.2008.tb00511.x; Campón and Carter, "The Appropriated Racial Oppression Scale."

79. Roderick J. Watts, M. A. Diemer, and A. M. Voight, "Critical Consciousness: Current Status and Future Directions," in *Youth Civic Development: Work at the Cutting Edge*, ed. C. A. Flanagan and B. D. Christens, *New Directions for Child and Adolescent Development Series*, no. 134 (New York: Wiley, 2011), 44.

80. Duran, Firehammer, and Gonzalez, "Liberation Psychology as the Path Toward Healing Cultural Soul Wounds"; Roderick J. Watts and Carlos P. Hipolito-Delgado, "Thinking Ourselves to Liberation? Advancing Sociopolitical Action in Critical Consciousness," *Urban Review* 47, no. 5 (2015): 847–67, doi.org /10.1007/s11256-015-0341-x.

81. Mia A. Smith Bynum, E. Thomaseo Burton, and Candace Best, "Racism Experiences and Psychological Functioning in African American College Freshmen: Is Racial Socialization a Buffer?" *Cultural Diversity and Ethnic Minority Psychology* 13, no. 1 (2007): 64–73, doi.org/10.1037/1099-9809.13.1.64; Jamila E. Reynolds and Melinda A. Gonzales-Backen, "Ethnic-Racial Socialization and the Mental Health of African Americans: A Critical Review," *Journal of Family Theory and Review* 9, no. 2 (2017): 182–200, dx.doi.org/10.1111/jftr.12192.

82. Callie H. Burt, Man Kit Lei, and Ronald L. Simons, "Racial Discrimination, Racial Socialization, and Crime: Understanding Mechanisms of Resilience," *Social Problems* 64, no. 3 (2017): 414–38, doi.org/10.1093/socpro/spw036; Linda P. Juang et al., "Reactive and Proactive Ethnic-Racial Socialization Practices of Second-Generation Asian American Parents," *Asian American Journal of Psychology* 9, no. 1 (2018): 4, doi.org/10.1037/aap0000101; Enrique W. Neblett Jr et al., "Patterns of Racial Socialization and Psychological Adjustment: Can Parental Communications About Race Reduce the Impact of Racial Discrimination?" *Journal of Research on Adolescence* 18, no. 3 (2008): 477–515, doi.org/10.1111/j.1532 -7795.2008.00568.x.

83. Alison W. Hu, Xiang Zhou, and Richard M. Lee, "Ethnic Socialization and Ethnic Identity Development Among Internationally Adopted Korean American Adolescents: A Seven-Year Follow-Up," *Developmental Psychology* 53, no. 11 (2017): 2066, doi.org/10.1037/dev0000421; Diane Hughes et al., "Parents' Ethnic-Racial Socialization Practices: A Review of Research and Directions for Future Study," *Developmental Psychology* 42 (2006): 747–70, doi.org/10.1037/0012-1649.42.5.747; Naomi Priest et al., "Understanding the Complexities of Ethnic-Racial Socialization Processes for Both Minority and Majority Groups: A 30-Year Systematic Review," *International Journal of Intercultural Relations* 43, part B (November 2014): 139–55, doi.org/10.1016/j.ijintrel.2014.08.003.

84. Julian D. Ford, "Trauma, Posttraumatic Stress Disorder, and Ethnoracial Minorities: Toward Diversity and Cultural Competence in Principles and Practices," *Clinical Psychology: Science and Practice* 15, no. 1 (March 2008): 62–67, doi .org/10.1111/j.1468-2850.2008.00110.x; Ibrahim A. Kira et al., "Measuring Cumulative Trauma Dose, Types, and Profiles Using a Development-Based Taxonomy of

Traumas," *Traumatology* 14, no. 2 (2008): 62–87, doi.org/10.1177/1534765608319324; Marinella Rodi-Risberg and J. Roger Kurtz, "Problems in Representing Trauma," in *Trauma and Literature*, ed. J. Roger Kurtz (Cambridge, UK: Cambridge University Press, 2018), 110–23.

85. Shawn O. Utsey, Mark A. Bolden, and Andraé L. Brown, "Visions of Revolution from the Spirit of Frantz Fanon: A Psychology of Liberation for Counseling African Americans Confronting Societal Racism and Oppression," in *Handbook of Multicultural Counseling*, 2nd ed., ed. Joseph G. Ponterotto et al. (Thousand Oaks, CA: Sage, 2001), 311–36.

86. Julian D. Ford, "Complex Trauma and Developmental Trauma Disorder in Adolescence," *Adolescent Psychiatry* 7, no. 4 (2017): 220–35.

87. Thema Bryant-Davis et al., "The Trauma Lens of Police Violence Against Racial and Ethnic Minorities," *Journal of Social Issues* 73, no. 4 (2017): 852–71, doi.org/10.1111/josi.12251; Thema Bryant-Davis, "The Cultural Context of Trauma Recovery: Considering the Posttraumatic Stress Disorder Practice Guideline and Intersectionality," *Psychotherapy* 56, no. 3 (2019): 400–408.

88. Fred Bemak and Rita Chi-Ying Chung, "Refugee Trauma: Culturally Responsive Counseling Interventions," *Journal of Counseling and Development* 95, no. 3 (2017): 299–308, doi.org/10.1002/jcad.12144; Maria Yellow Horse Brave Heart et al., "Historical Trauma Among Indigenous Peoples of the Americas," in *Wounds of History: Repair and Resilience in the Trans-Generational Transmission of Trauma*, ed. Jill Salberg and Sue Grand (New York: Routledge, 2016), 250–67; B. Range et al., "Mass Trauma in the African American Community: Using Multiculturalism to Build Resilient Systems," *Contemporary Family Therapy* (December 2017): 1–15, dx.doi.org/10.1007/s10591-017-9449-3; Monnica T. Williams, Adriana Peña, and Judy Mier-Chairez, "Tools for Assessing Racism-Related Stress and Trauma Among Latinos," in *Toolkit for Counseling Spanish-Speaking Clients: Enhancing Behavioral Health Services*, ed. Lorraine T. Benuto (Cham, Switz.: Springer, 2017), 71–95.

REFERENCES

Abreu, Jose M., Ruth H. Gim Chung, and Donald R. Atkinson. 2000. "Multicultural Counseling Training: Past, Present and Future Directions." *Counseling Psychologist* 28, no. 5 (September): 641–56.

Adams, Glenn, Ignacio Dobles, Luis H. Gómez, Tuğçe Kurtiş, and Ludwin E. Molina. 2015. "Decolonizing Psychological Science: Introduction to the Special Thematic Section." *Journal of Social and Political Psychology* 3, no. 1: 213–38.

Adams, Marie C., and D. Martin Kivlighan III. 2019. "When Home Is Gone: An Application of the Multicultural Orientation Framework to Enhance Clinical Practice with Refugees of Forced Migration." *Professional Psychology: Research and Practice* 50, no. 3: 176–83.

Alamilla, Saul G., Bryan S. K. Kim, and Alexandra Lam. 2010. "Acculturation, Enculturation, Perceived Racism, Minority Status Stressors, and Psychological Symptomatology Among Latino/as." *Hispanic Journal of Behavioral Sciences* 32, no. 1: 55–76. doi.org/10.1177/0739986309352770.

Alamilla, Saul G., Bryan S. K. Kim, Tamisha Walker, and Frederick Riley Sisson. 2017. "Acculturation, Enculturation, Perceived Racism and Psychological Symptoms Among Asian American College Students." *Journal of Multicultural Counseling and Development* 45, no. 1: 37–65. doi.org/10.1002/jmcd.12062.

——. 2019. "Mental Health Care Among Blacks in America: Confronting Racism and Constructing Solutions." *Health Services Research* 54, no. 2: 346–55.

Albee, George W. 1982. "Preventing Psychopathology and Promoting Human Potential." *American Psychologist* 37, no. 9: 1043–50, doi.org/10.1037//0003-066X.37.9.1043.

——. 1986. "Toward a Just Society: Lessons from Observations on the Primary Prevention of Psychopathology." *American Psychologist* 41, no. 8: 891–98.

Alexander, Michelle. 2012. *The New Jim Crow: Mass Incarceration in the Age of Colorblindness*. New York: New Press.

Ali, Alisha, and Corianna E. Sichel. 2014. "Structural Competency as a Framework for Training in Counseling Psychology." *Counseling Psychologist* 42, no. 7: 901–18. doi.org/10.1177/0011000014550320.

Allen, Jessica, Reuben Balfour, Ruth Bell, and Michael Marmot. 2014. "Social Determinants of Mental Health." *International Review of Psychiatry* 26, no. 4: 392–407.

Alvarez, Alvin N., Christopher T. H. Liang, and Helen Neville, eds. 2016. *The Cost of Racism for People of Color: Contextualizing Experiences of Discrimination.* Washington, DC: American Psychological Association.

American Psychiatric Association. 1987. *Diagnostic Criteria from DSM-III-R.* Washington, DC: American Psychiatric Association.

——. 1994. *Diagnostic and Statistical Manual of Mental Disorders,* 4th ed. Washington, DC: American Psychiatric Association.

——. 2000. *Diagnostic and Statistical Manual of Mental Disorders,* 4th ed., text revision. Washington, DC: American Psychiatric Association.

——. 2013. *Diagnostic and Statistical Manual of Mental Disorders,* 5th ed. Washington, DC: American Psychiatric Association.

American Psychological Association. 1993. "Guidelines for Providers of Psychological Services to Ethnic, Linguistic, and Culturally Diverse Populations." *American Psychologist* 48: 45–48.

——. 2002. "Ethical Principles of Psychologists and Code of Conduct." *American Psychologist* 57: 1060–73. www.apa.org/ethics/code.

——. 2003. "Guidelines on Multicultural Education, Training, Research, Practice, and Organizational Change for Psychologists." *American Psychologist* 58, no. 5: 377–402.

——. 2006. *Guidelines and Principles for Accreditation of Programs in Professional Psychology (G&P),* rev. 2013. www.apa.org/ed/accreditation/about/policies/guiding-principles.pdf.

——. 2010. "2010 Amendments to the 2002 'Ethical Principles of Psychologists and Code of Conduct.'" *American Psychologist* 65: 493. www.apa.org/ethics/code.

——. 2015. "Standards of Accreditation for Health Service Psychology." Commission on Accreditation. www.apa.org/ed/accreditation/about/policies/standards-of-accreditation.pdf.

——. 2016. *Stress in America: The Impact of Discrimination: Stress in America Survey.* Washington, DC: American Psychological Association.

——. 2017a. "Ethical Principles of Psychologists and Code of Conduct." www.apa.org/ethics/code.

——. 2017b. "Clinical Practice Guidelines for the Treatment of Posttraumatic Stress Disorder (PTSD) in Adults." Guidelines Development Panel for Treatment of PTSD in Adults, adopted as APA policy February 24. www.apa.org/ptsd-guideline/ptsd.pdf.

——. 2017c. "Multicultural Guidelines: An Ecological Approach to Context, Identity and Intersectionality." www.apa.org/about/policy/multicultural-guidelines.pdf.

——. 2019. "Guidelines for Race and Ethnicity in Psychology." https://www.apa.org/about/policy/guidelines-race-ethnicity.pdf.

American School Counselors Association. 2016. "ASCA Ethical Standards for School Counselors." Adopted 1984, rev. 1992, 1998, 2004, 2010, and 2016. www.schoolcounselor.org/asca/media/asca/Ethics/EthicalStandards2016.pdf.

Anderson, Riana E., Monique McKenny, Amari Mitchell, Lydia Koku, and Howard C. Stevenson. 2017. "EMBRacing Racial Stress and Trauma: Preliminary Feasibility and Coping Responses of a Racial Socialization Intervention." *Journal of Black Psychology* 44, no. 1: 25–46. doi.org/10.1177/0095798417732930.

Anderson, Riana Elyse, and Howard C. Stevenson. 2019. "RECASTing Racial Stress and Trauma: Theorizing the Healing Potential of Racial Socialization in Families." *American Psychologist* 74, no. 1: 63–75.

Angelakis, Ioannis, Emma Louise Gillespie, and Maria Panagioti. 2019. "Childhood Maltreatment and Adult Suicidality: A Comprehensive Systematic Review with Meta-Analysis." *Psychological Medicine* 49, no. 7: 1057–78.

Anglin, Deidre M., Michelle Greenspoon, Quenesha Lighty, and Lauren M. Ellman. 2016. "Race-Based Rejection Sensitivity Partially Accounts for the Relationship Between Racial Discrimination and Distressing Attenuated Positive Psychotic Symptoms." *Early Intervention in Psychiatry* 10, no. 5: 411–18. doi.org/10.1111/eip.12184.

Anglin, Deidre M., Quenesha Lighty, Michelle Greenspoon, and Lauren M. Ellman. 2014. "Racial Discrimination Is Associated with Distressing Subthreshold Positive Psychotic Symptoms Among US Urban Ethnic Minority Young Adults." *Social Psychiatry and Psychiatric Epidemiology* 49, no. 10: 1545–55. doi.org/10.1007/s00127-014-0870-8.

Anglin, Deidre M., F. Lui, A. Espinosa, A. Tikhonov, and L. Ellman. 2018. "Ethnic Identity, Racial Discrimination and Attenuated Psychotic Symptoms in an Urban Population of Emerging Adults." *Early Intervention in Psychiatry* 12, no. 3: 380–90.

Anuar, Azad Athahiri, and Rafidah Aga Mohd Jaladin. 2016. "Development and Evaluation of a Multicultural Counseling Competencies (MCC) Training Module for Trainee Counselors." *Journal of Asia Pacific Counseling* 6, no. 1: 41–50.

Araújo, Beverly Y., and Luisa N. Borrell. 2006. "Understanding the Link Between Discrimination, Mental Health Outcomes, and Life Chances Among Latinos." *Hispanic Journal of Behavioral Sciences* 28, no. 2 (May): 245–66. doi.org/10.1177%2F0739986305285825.

Arredondo, Patricia, and Daniel C. Rosen. 2007. "Applying Principles of Multicultural Competencies, Social Justice, and Leadership in Training and Supervision."

In *Advancing Social Justice Through Clinical Practice*, ed. E. Aldarondo, 443–58. Mahwah, NJ: Lawrence Erlbaum.

Arredondo, Patricia, Rebecca Toporek, Sherlon Pack Brown, Janet Jones, Don C. Locke, Joe Sanchez, and Holly Stadler. 1996. "Operationalization of the Multicultural Counseling Competencies." *Journal of Multicultural Counseling and Development* 24, no. (1): 42–78.

Assari, Shervin. 2018. "Educational Attainment Better Protects African American Women than African American Men Against Depressive Symptoms and Psychological Distress." *Brain Sciences* 8, no. 10: 182. doi.org/10.3390/brainsci8100182.

Assari, Shervin, Frederick X. Gibbons, and Ronald L. Simons. 2018. "Perceived Discrimination Among Black Youth: An 18-Year Longitudinal Study." *Behavioral Sciences* 8, no. 5 (April 27): 44.

Atkins, Rahshida. 2014. "Instruments Measuring Perceived Racism/Racial Discrimination: Review and Critique of Factor Analytic Techniques." *International Journal of Health Services* 44, no. 4: 711–34.

Austen, Ian. 2017. "Canada to Pay Millions in Indigenous Lawsuit Over Forced Adoptions." *New York Times*, October 6. www.nytimes.com/2017/10/06/world/canada/indigenous-forced-adoption-sixties-scoop.html.

Azari, Julia, and Marc J. Hetherington. 2016. "Back to the Future? What the Politics of the Late Nineteenth Century Can Tell Us About the 2016 Election." *ANNALS of the American Academy of Political and Social Science* 667, no. 1: 92–109. doi.org/10.1177/0002716216662604.

Bailey, Zinzi D., Nancy Krieger, Madina Agénor, Jasmine Graves, Natalia Linos, and Mary T. Bassett. 2017. "Structural Racism and Health Inequities in the USA: Evidence and Interventions." *Lancet* 389, no. 10077 (April 8): 1453–63.

Barrett, Paul. 2007. "Structural Equation Modeling: Adjudging Model Fit." *Personality and Individual Differences* 42, no. 5: 815–24. doi:10.1016/j.paid.2006.09.018.

Bartoli, Eleonora, Keisha L. Bentley-Edwards, Ana María García, Ali Michael, and Audrey Ervin. 2015. "What Do White Counselors and Psychotherapists Need to Know About Race? White Racial Socialization in Counseling and Psychotherapy Training Programs." *Women and Therapy* 38, no. 3–4: 246–62.

Bartoli, Eleonora, and Aarti Pyati. 2009. "Addressing Clients' Racism and Racial Prejudice in Individual Psychotherapy: Therapeutic Considerations." *Psychotherapy: Theory, Research, Practice, Training* 46, no. 2: 145–57. doi.org/10.1037/a0016023.

Bastos, Joao Luiz, Roger Keller Celeste, Eduardo Faerstein, and Aluisio J. D. Barros. 2010. "Racial Discrimination and Health: A Systematic Review of Scales with a Focus on Their Psychometric Properties." *Social Science and Medicine* 70, no. 7: 1091–99.

Baumeister, Roy F., Kathleen D. Vohs, and David C. Funder. 2007. "Psychology as the Science of Self-Reports and Finger Movements: Whatever Happened to

Actual Behavior?" *Perspectives on Psychological Science* 2, no. 4: 396–403. doi.org /10.1111/j.1745-6916.2007.00051.x.

BBC. 2017. "Why the Fuss Over Confederate Statues?" August 17. www.bbc.com /news/world-us-canada-40966800.

Bécares, Laia, James Nazroo, and James Jackson. 2014. "Ethnic Density and Depressive Symptoms Among African Americans: Threshold and Differential Effects Across Social and Demographic Subgroups." *American Journal of Public Health* 104, no. 12: 2334–41. doi.org/10.2105/AJPH.2014.302047.

Beck, J. Gayle, and Denise M. Sloan. 2012. *The Oxford Handbook of Traumatic Stress Disorders.* New York: Oxford University Press.

Bell, Carl C., and Edward Dunbar. 2012. "Racism and Pathological Bias as a Co-Occurring Problem in Diagnosis and Assessment." In *Oxford Handbook of Personality Disorders*, ed. Thomas A. Widiger, 694–709. Oxford, UK: Oxford University Press.

Bell, Derrick. 2008. *Race, Racism and American Law*, 5th ed. Gaithersburg, MD: Aspen Law and Business.

Bell, Kimberly A., Ihori Kobayashi, Ameenat Akeeb, Joseph Lavela, and Thomas A. Mellman. 2019. "Emotional Response to Perceived Racism and Nocturnal Heart Rate Variability in Young Adult African Americans." *Journal of Psychosomatic Research* 121: 88–92.

Bemak, Fred, and Rita Chi-Ying Chung. 2017. "Refugee Trauma: Culturally Responsive Counseling Interventions." *Journal of Counseling and Development* 95, no. 3: 299–308. doi.org/10.1002/jcad.12144.

Benkert, Ramona, and Rosalind M. Peters. 2005. "African American Women's Coping with Health Care Prejudice." *Western Journal of Nursing Research* 27, no. 7: 863–89. doi.org/10.1177/0193945905278588.

Benner, Aprile. 2017. "The Toll of Racial/Ethnic Discrimination on Adolescents' Adjustment." *Child Development Perspectives* 11, no. 4: 251–56. doi.org/10.1111/ cdep.12241.

Benner, Aprile D., Yijie Wang, Yishan Shen, Alaina E. Boyle, Richelle Polk, and Yen-Pi Cheng. 2018 "Racial/Ethnic Discrimination and Well-Being During Adolescence: A Meta-Analytic Review." *American Psychologist* 73, no. 7: 855–83.

Bennett, Gary G., Marcellus M. Merritt, Christopher L. Edwards, and John J. Sollers III. 2004. "Perceived Racism and Affective Responses to Ambiguous Interpersonal Interactions Among African American Men." *American Behavioral Scientist* 47, no. 7: 63–76. doi.org/10.1177%2F0002764203261070.

Bennett, Lerone, Jr. 1988. *Before the Mayflower: A History of Black America.* Chicago: Johnson.

Benuto, Lorraine T., Jonathan Singer, Rory T. Newlands, and Jena B. Casas. 2019. "Training Culturally Competent Psychologists: Where Are We and Where Do

We Need to Go?" *Training and Education in Professional Psychology* 13, no. 1: 56–62. doi.org/10.1037/tep0000214

Bermudez-Millan, Angela, Kristina P. Schumann, Richard Feinn, Howard Tennen, and Julie Wagner. 2016. "Behavioral Reactivity to Acute Stress Among Black and White Women with Type 2 Diabetes: The Role of Income and Racial Discrimination." *Journal of Health Psychology* 21, no. 9: 2085–97. doi.org/10.1177/1359105315571776.

Bernard, Donte, Quiera M. Lige, Henry Wills, Effua Sosoo, and Enrique Neblett. 2017. "Imposter Phenomenon and Mental Health: The Influence of Racial Discrimination and Gender." *Journal of Counseling Psychology* 64, no. 2: 155–66. doi.org/10.1037/cou0000197.

Berry, John W. 2005. "Acculturation: Living Successfully in Two Cultures." *International Journal of Intercultural Relations* 29, no. 6: 697–712. doi.org/10.1016/j.ijintrel.2005.07.013.

Berry, John W., and Feng Hou. 2017. "Acculturation, Discrimination and Wellbeing Among Second Generation of Immigrants in Canada." *International Journal of Intercultural Relations* 61: 29–39. doi.org/10.1016/j.ijintrel.2017.08.003.

Betancourt, Hector, and Steven Regeser López. 1993. "The Study of Culture, Ethnicity, and Race in American Psychology." *American Psychologist* 48, no. 6: 629–37.

Binder, Renée L., and Dale E. McNiel. 2007. "'He Said–She Said': The Role of the Forensic Evaluator in Determining Credibility of Plaintiffs Who Allege Sexual Exploitation and Boundary Violations." *Journal of the American Academy of Psychiatry and the Law* 35: 211–18.

Black, Lora L., Rhonda Johnson, and Lisa VanHoose. 2015. "The Relationship Between Perceived Racism/Discrimination and Health Among Black American Women: A Review of the Literature from 2003–2013." *Journal of Racial and Ethnic Health Disparities* 2: 11–20. doi.org/10.1007/s40615-014-0043-1.

Blackmon, Sha'Kema, Laura D. Coyle, Sheron Davenport, Archandria C. Owens, and Christopher Sparrow. 2016. "Linking Racial-Ethnic Socialization to Culture and Race-Specific Coping Among African American College Students." *Journal of Black Psychology* 42, no. 6: 549–76. doi.org/10.1177/0095798415617865.

Blankson, A. Nayena, and John J. McArdle. 2015. "Measurement Invariance of Cognitive Abilities Across Ethnicity, Gender, and Time Among Older Americans." *Journals of Gerontology: Series B* 70, no. 3: 386–97. doi.org/10.1093/geronb/gbt106.

Blanton, Hart, and James Jaccard. 2008. "Unconscious Racism: A Concept in Pursuit of a Measure." *Annual Review of Sociology* 34: 277–97. doi.org/10.1146/annurev.soc.33.040406.131632.

Bonilla-Silva, Eduardo. 1997. "Rethinking Racism: Toward a Structural Interpretation." *American Sociological Review* 62, no. 3 (July): 465–80.

———. 2017. *Racism Without Racists: Color-Blind Racism and the Persistence of Racial Inequality in America*, 5th ed. Lanham, MD: Rowman and Littlefield.

Boone, M. L., D. W. Neumeister, and C. L. Charney. 2003. "Trauma." In *Trauma and Disaster Responses and Management*, ed. Robert J. Ursano and Ann E. Norwood, 1–30. *Review of Psychiatry Series* 22, no. 1. Washington, DC: American Psychiatric Publishing.

Borrell, Luisa N., David R. Jacobs, David R. Williams, Mark J. Pletcher, Thomas K. Houston, and Catarina I. Kiefe. 2007. "Self- Reported Racial Discrimination and Substance Use in the Coronary Artery Risk Development in Adults Study." *American Journal of Epidemiology* 166, no. 9: 1068–79. doi.org/10.1093/aje/kwm180.

Bound, John, Charles Brown, and Nancy Mathiowetz. 2001. "Measurement Error in Survey Data." *Handbook of Econometrics* 5: 3705–843. doi.org/10.1016/S1573-4412(01)05012-7.

Bower, Gordon, and Heidi Sivers. 1998. "Cognitive Impact of Traumatic Events." *Development and Psychopathology* 10, no. 4: 625–53. doi.org/10.1017/S0954579498001795.

Bower, Kelly M., Roland J. Thorpe, and Thomas A. LaVeist. 2013. "Perceived Racial Discrimination and Mental Health in Low-Income, Urban-Dwelling Whites." *International Journal of Health Services* 43, no. 2: 267–80. doi.org/10.2190/HS.43.2.e.

Boyd-Franklin, Nancy. 1987. "Group Therapy for Black Women: A Therapeutic Support Model." *American Journal of Orthopsychiatry* 57, no. 3: 394–401.

Boysen, Guy A. 2010. "Integrating Implicit Bias into Counselor Education." *Counselor Education and Supervision* 49, no. 4: 210–27. doi.org/10.1002/j.1556-6978.2010.tb00099.x.

Bratter, Jenifer L., and Bridget K. Gorman. 2011. "Is Discrimination an Equal Opportunity Risk? Racial Experiences, Socioeconomic Status, and Health Status Among Black and White Adults." *Journal of Health and Social Behavior* 52, no. 3: 365–82. doi.org/10.1177/0022146511405336.

Brave Heart, Maria Yellow Horse, Josephine Chase, Jennifer Elkins, and Deborah B. Altschul. 2016. "Historical Trauma Among Indigenous Peoples of the Americas." In *Wounds of History: Repair and Resilience in the Trans-Generational Transmission of Trauma*, ed. Jill Salberg and Sue Grand, 250–67. New York: Routledge.

Breslau, Joshua, Kenneth S. Kendler, Maxwell Su, Sergio Gaxiola-Aguilar, and Ronald C. Kessler. 2005. "Lifetime Risk and Persistence of Psychiatric Disorders Across Ethnic Groups in the United States." *Psychological Medicine* 35, no. 3: 317–27.

Breslau, Naomi. 2001. "The Epidemiology of Posttraumatic Stress Disorder: What Is the Extent of the Problem?" *Journal of Clinical Psychiatry* 62 (Suppl. 17): 16–22.

Briere, John, and Marsha Runtz. 1989. "The Trauma Symptom Checklist (TSC-33): Early Data on a New Scale." *Journal of Interpersonal Violence* 4, no. 2: 151–63. doi.org/10.1177/088626089004002002.

Britt-Spells, Angelitta M., Maribeth Slebodnik, Laura P. Sands, and David Rollock. 2016. "Effects of Perceived Discrimination on Depressive Symptoms Among Black Men Residing in the United States: A Meta-Analysis." *American Journal of Men's Health* 12, no. 1: 52–63. doi.org/10.1177/1557988315624509.

Brondolo, Elizabeth, Linda C. Gallo, and Hector F. Myers. 2009. "Race, Racism and Health: Disparities, Mechanisms, and Interventions." *Journal of Behavioral Medicine* 32, no. 1: 1–8. doi.org/10.1007/s10865-008-9190-3.

Brondolo, Elizabeth, Wan Ng, Kristy-Lee J. Pierre, and Robert Lane. 2016. "Racism and Mental Health: Examining the Link Between Racism and Depression From a Social Cognitive Perspective." In *The Cost of Racism for People of Color: Contextualizing Experiences of Discrimination*, ed. Alvin N. Alvarez, Christopher T. H. Liang, and Helen A. Neville, 109–132. Washington, DC: American Psychological Association.

Brondolo, Elizabeth, Nisha Brady ver Halen, Daniel Libby, and Melissa Pencille. 2011. "Racism as a Psychosocial Stressor." In *Handbook of Stress Science: Biology, Psychology, and Health*, ed. Richard J. Contrada and Andrew Baum, 167–84. New York: Springer.

Brondolo, Elizabeth, Nisha Brady ver Halen, Michelle Pencille, Danielle Beatty, and Richard J. Contrada. 2009. "Coping with Racism: A Selective Review of the Literature and a Theoretical and Methodological Critique." *Journal of Behavioral Medicine* 32, no. 1: 64–88. link.springer.com/article/10.1007%2Fs10865-008-9193-0.

Brown, Charlotte, Karen A. Matthews, Joyce T. Bromberger, and Yuefang Chang. 2006. "The Relation Between Perceived Unfair Treatment and Blood Pressure in a Racially/Ethnically Diverse Sample of Women." *American Journal of Epidemiology* 164, no. 3: 257–62.

Brown, Timothy A. 2015. *Confirmatory Factor Analysis for Applied Research*. New York: Guilford Press.

Bryant-Davis, Thema. 2005. *Thriving in the Wake of Trauma: A Multicultural Guide*. Westport, CT: Praeger.

——. 2019. "The Cultural Context of Trauma Recovery: Considering the Posttraumatic Stress Disorder Practice Guideline and Intersectionality." *Psychotherapy* 56, no. 3: 400–408.

Bryant-Davis, Thema, Tyonna Adams, Adriana Alejandre, and Anthea A. Gray. 2017. "The Trauma Lens of Police Violence Against Racial and Ethnic Minorities." *Journal of Social Issues* 73, no. 4: 852–71. doi.org/10.1111/josi.12251.

Bryant-Davis, Thema, and Carlota Ocampo. 2005a. "Racist-Incident-Based Trauma." *Counseling Psychologist* 33, no. 4: 479–500.

——. 2005b. "The Trauma of Racism: Implications for Counseling, Research, and Education." *Counseling Psychologist* 33: 574–78. doi.org/10.1177/0011000005276581.

——. 2006. "A Therapeutic Approach to the Treatment of Racist-Incident-Based Trauma." *Journal of Emotional Abuse* 6, no. 4: 1–22. doi:10.1300/J135v06n04_01.

Buckley, Tamara R., and Erica Gabrielle Foldy. 2010. "A Pedagogical Model for Increasing Race-Related Multicultural Counseling Competency." *Counseling Psychologist* 38, no. 5: 691–713. DOI: 10.1177/0011000009360917.

Buhin, Larisa, and Elizabeth M. Vera. 2009. "Preventing Racism and Promoting Social Justice: Person-Centered and Environment-Centered Interventions." *Journal of Primary Prevention* 30, no. 1: 43–59. doi.org/10.1007/s10935-008 -0161-9.

Buka, Stephen L. 2002. "Disparities in Health Status and Substance Use: Ethnicity and Socioeconomic Factors." *Public Health Reports* 117: 118–25.

Bulhan, Hussein Abdilahi. 1985. *Frantz Fanon and the Psychology of Oppression.* New York: Plenum.

Burgess, Diana J., Joseph Grill, Siamak Noorbaloochi, Joan M. Griffin, Jennifer Ricards, Michelle Van Ryn, and Melissa R. Partin. 2009. "The Effect of Perceived Racial Discrimination on Bodily Pain Among Older African American Men." *Pain Medicine* 10, no. 8: 1341–52. doi.org/10.1111/j.1526-4637.2009.00742.x.

Burkard, Alan W., Sarah Knox, Robyn D. Clarke, David L. Phelps, and Arpana G. Inman. 2014. "Supervisors' Experiences of Providing Difficult Feedback in Cross-Ethnic/Racial Supervision." *Counseling Psychologist* 42, no. 3: 314–44. doi:10.1177 /0011000012461157.

Burt, Callie H., Man Kit Lei, and Ronald L. Simons. 2017. "Racial Discrimination, Racial Socialization, and Crime: Understanding Mechanisms of Resilience." *Social Problems* 64, no. 3: 414–38. doi.org/10.1093/socpro/spw036.

Butts, Hugh F. 2002. "The Black Mask of Humanity: Racial/Ethnic Discrimination and Post-Traumatic Stress Disorder." *Journal of the American Academy of Psychiatry and the Law* 30, no. 3: 336–39.

Bynum, Mia Smith, E. Thomaseo Burton, and Candace Best. 2007. "Racism Experiences and Psychological Functioning in African American College Freshmen: Is Racial Socialization a Buffer?" *Cultural Diversity and Ethnic Minority Psychology* 13, no. 1: 64–73. doi.org/10.1037/1099-9809.13.1.64.

Calhoun, Lawrence G., and Richard G. Tedeschi. 1998. "Beyond Recovery from Trauma: Implications for Clinical Practice and Research." *Journal of Social Issues* 54, no. 2: 357–71. doi.org/10.1111/j.1540-4560.1998.tb01223.x.

Campbell, Erica L. 2015. "Transitioning from a Model of Cultural Competency Toward an Inclusive Pedagogy of 'Racial Competency' Using Critical Race Theory." *Journal of Social Welfare and Human Rights* 3, no. 1: 1–16. doi.org/10.15640/ jswhr.v3n1a2.

Campón, Rebecca Rangel, and Robert T. Carter. 2015. "The Appropriated Racial Oppression Scale: Development and Preliminary Validation." *Cultural Diversity and Ethnic Minority Psychology* 21, no. 4: 497–506. dx.doi.org/10.1037/cdp0000037.

Cardemil, Esteban V., and Cynthia L. Battle. 2003. "Guess Who's Coming to Therapy? Getting Comfortable with Conversations About Race and Ethnicity in

Psychotherapy." *Professional Psychology: Research and Practice* 34, no. 3: 278–86. doi.org/10.1037/0735-7028.34.3.278.

Carlson, Eve B. 1997. *Trauma Assessments: A Clinician's Guide.* New York: Guilford Press.

Carlson, Eve B., and Constance J. Dalenberg. 2000. "A Conceptual Framework for the Impact of Traumatic Experiences." *Trauma, Violence, and Abuse* 1, no. 1: 4–28.

Carlson, Marie, Maurice Endlsey, Darnell Motley, Lamise N. Shawahin, and Monnica T. Williams. 2018. "Addressing the Impact of Racism on Veterans of Color: A Race-Based Stress and Trauma Intervention." *Psychology of Violence* 8, no. 6: 748–62.

Carr, Clara Passmann, Camilla Maria Martins, Ana Maria Stingel, Vera Braga Lemgruber, and Mario Francisco Juruena. 2013. "The Role of Early Life Stress in Adult Psychiatric Disorders: A Systematic Review According to Childhood Trauma Subtypes." *Journal of Nervous and Mental Disease* 201, no. 12: 1007–20. doi.org/10.1097/NMD.0000000000000049.

Carson, E. Ann. 2014. *Prisoners in 2013.* U.S. Department of Justice, Office of Justice Programs, Bureau of Justice Statistics. September. www.bjs.gov/content/pub/pdf/p13.pdf.

Carter, Robert T. 1991. "Cultural Values: A Review of Empirical Research and Implications for Counseling." *Journal of Counseling and Development* 70, no. 1 (September–October): 164–73.

——. 1995. *The Influence of Race and Racial Identity in Psychotherapy: Toward a Racially Inclusive Model.* New York: Wiley.

——. 2001. "Back to the Future in Cultural Competence Training." *Counseling Psychologist* 29: 787–89. doi.org/10.1177/0011000001296001.

——. 2003. "Becoming Racially and Culturally Competent: The Racial-Cultural Counseling Laboratory." *Journal of Multicultural Counseling* 31, no. 1: 20–30. doi.org/10.1002/j.2161-1912.2003.tb00527.x.

——, ed. 2005a. *Handbook of Racial-Cultural Psychology and Counseling, vol. 1, Theory and Research.* Hoboken, NJ: Wiley.

——, ed. 2005b. *Handbook of Racial-Cultural Psychology and Counseling, vol. 2, Training and Practice.* Hoboken, NJ: Wiley.

——. 2005c. "Uprooting Inequity and Disparities in Counseling and Psychology: An Introduction." In *Handbook of Racial-Cultural Counseling and Psychology, vol. 1, Theory and Research,* ed. Robert T. Carter, xv–xxviii. Hoboken, NJ: Wiley.

——. 2007. "Racism and Psychological and Emotional Injury: Recognizing and Assessing Race-Based Traumatic Stress." *Counseling Psychologist* 35, no. 1: 13–105. doi:10.1177/0011000006292033.

——. 2016. "The Road Less Traveled: Research on Race." In *The Handbook of Multicultural Counseling*, 4th ed., ed. J. Manuel Casas, Lisa A. Suzuki, Charlene M. Alexandria, and Margo A. Jackson, 71–80. Thousand Oaks, CA: Sage.

Carter, Robert T., and Jessica M. Forsyth. 2007. "Examining Race and Culture in Psychology Journals: The Case of Forensic Psychology." *Professional Psychology: Research and Practice* 38, no. 2: 133–42. doi.org/10.1037/0735-7028.38.2.133.

——. 2009. "A Guide to the Forensic Assessment of Race-Based Traumatic Stress Reactions." *Journal of the American Academy of Psychiatry and the Law* 37, no. 1: 28–40.

——. 2010. "Reactions to Racial Discrimination: Emotional Stress and Help-Seeking Behaviors." *Psychological Trauma: Theory, Research, Practice, and Policy* 2, no. 3: 183–91. doi.org/10.1037/a0020102.

Carter, Robert T., Jessica M. Forsyth, Silvia L. Mazzula, and Bryant Williams. 2005. "Racial Discrimination and Race-Based Traumatic Stress: An Exploratory Investigation." In *Handbook of Racial-Cultural Psychology and Counseling*, vol. 2, *Training and Practice*, ed. Robert T. Carter, 447–76. Hoboken, NJ: Wiley.

Carter, Robert T., Jessica Forsyth, Bryant Williams, and Silvia L. Mazzula. 2007. "Does Racism Predict Psychological Harm or Injury: Mental Health and Legal Implication." *Law Enforcement Executive Forum* 7, no. 5: 129–54.

Carter, Robert T., Corrine Galgay, Katherine Kirkinis, and Carrie Muchow. 2018. "Race-Based Traumatic Stress Symptom Scale and White Americans: Construct Validity." Unpublished manuscript.

Carter, Robert T., and Janet E. Helms. 1988. "The Relationship Between Racial Identity Attitudes and Social Class." *Journal of Negro Education* 37, no. 1: 22–30.

——. 1992. "The Counseling Process Defined by Relationship Types: A Test of Helms' Interactional Model." *Journal of Multicultural Counseling and Development* 20, no. 4: 181–201. doi.org/10.1002/j.2161-1912.1992.tb00576.x.

——. 2002. "Racial Discrimination and Harassment: A Racially Based Trauma." Paper presented at the American College of Forensic Examiners Conference, Orlando, FL, September.

——. 2009. "Racism and Race-Based Traumatic Stress: Toward New Legal and Clinical Standards." *Law Enforcement Executive Forum* 9, no. 5: 111–24. https://iletsbeiforumjournal.com/images/Issues/FreeIssues/ILEEF%202009-9.5.pdf.

Carter, Robert T., Janet E. Helms, and Heather L. Juby. 2004. "The Relationship Between Racism and Racial Identity for White Americans: A Profile Analysis." *Journal of Multicultural Counseling and Development* 32, no. 1 (January): 2–17. doi.org/10.1002/j.2161-1912.2004.tb00357.x.

Carter, Robert T., and Veronica E. Johnson. 2019. "Racial Identity Statuses: Applications to Practice." *Practice Innovations* 4, no. 1: 42–58. dx.doi.org/10.1037/pri0000082.

Carter, Robert T., Veronica E. Johnson, Katherine Kirkinis, Katheryn Roberson, Carrie Muchow, and Corinne Galgay. 2019. "A Meta-Analytic Review of Racial Discrimination: Relationships to Health and Culture." *Race and Social Problems* 11, no. 1 (March): 15–32. doi.org/10.1007/s12552-018-9256-y.

Carter, Robert T., Veronica E. Johnson, Carrie Muchow, Jillian Lyons, Erin Forquer, and Corrine Galgay. 2016. "The Development of Classes of Racism Measures for Frequency and Stress Reactions: Relationships to Race-Based Traumatic Symptoms." *Traumatology* 22, no. 1: 63–74.

Carter, Robert T., Veronica Johnson, and Katheryn Roberson. 2014. "John F. Kennedy Behavioral Health: Site Report for the Race-Based Traumatic Stress Scale Research Study." Teachers College, Columbia University. Unpublished manuscript.

Carter, Robert T., Veronica E. Johnson, Katheryn Roberson, Silvia M. Mazzula, Katherine Kirkinis, and Sinead Sant-Barket. 2017. "Race-Based Traumatic Stress, Racial Identity Status, and Psychological Functioning: An Exploratory Investigation." *Professional Psychology: Research and Practice* 48, no. 1: 20–37. doi.org/10.1037/pro0000116.

Carter, Robert T., Katherine Kirkinis, and Veronica Johnson. 2020. "Race-Based Traumatic Stress and General Trauma Symptoms." *Traumatology* 26, no. 1: 11–18.

Carter, Robert T., Michael Y. Lau, Veronica Johnson, and Katherine Kirkinis. 2017. "Racial Discrimination and Health Outcomes Among Racial/Ethnic Minorities: A Meta-Analytic Review." *Journal of Multicultural Counseling and Development* 45, no. 4: 232–59. doi.org/10.1002/jmcd.12076.

Carter, Robert T., Silvia L. Mazzula, Rodolfo Victoria, R. Vazquez, Schekeva Hall, Sidney Smith, Sinead Sant-Barket, Jessica Forsyth, Keisha Bazelais, and Bryant Williams. 2013. "Initial Development of the Race-Based Traumatic Stress Symptom Scale: Assessing the Emotional Impact of Racism." *Psychological Trauma: Theory, Research, Practice, and Policy* 5, no. 1: 1–9. doi.org/10.1037/a0025911.

Carter, Robert T., and Carrie Muchow. 2017. "Construct Validity of the Race-Based Traumatic Stress Symptom Scale and Tests of Measurement Equivalence." *Psychological Trauma: Theory, Research, Practice, and Policy* 9, no. 6: 688–95. doi.org/10.1037/tra0000256.

Carter, Robert T., Carrie Muchow, and Alex L. Pieterse. 2018. "Construct, Predictive Validity, and Measurement Equivalence of the Race-Based Traumatic Stress Symptom Scale for Black Americans." *Traumatology* 24, no. 1: 8–16. doi.org/10.1037/trm0000128.

Carter, Robert T., and Alex L. Pieterse. 2005. "Race: A Social and Psychological Analysis of the Term and Its Meaning." In *Handbook of Racial-Cultural Psychology and Counseling*: vol. 1, *Theory and Research*, ed. Robert T. Carter, 41–63. Hoboken, NJ: Wiley.

Carter Robert T., and Amy L. Reynolds. 2011. "Race-Related Stress, Racial Identity Statuses and Emotional Reactions of Black Americans." *Cultural Diversity and Ethnic Minority Psychology* 17, no. 2: 156–62. doi.org/10.1037/a0023358.

Carter, Robert T., Katheryn Roberson, and Veronica Johnson. In press. "Race-Based Stress in White Adults: Exploring the Role of White Racial Identity Status Attitudes and Type of Racial Events." *Journal of Multicultural Counseling and Development.*

Carter, Robert T., and Sinead Sant-Barket. 2015. "Assessment of the Impact of Racial Discrimination and Racism: How to Use the Race-Based Traumatic Stress Symptom Scale in Practice." *Traumatology* 21, no. 1: 32–39.

Carter, Robert T., Sinead M. Sant-Barket, and Shawna Stotts. 2014. "The Consortium: Site Report for the Race-Based Traumatic Stress Scale Research Study." Teachers College, Columbia University. Unpublished manuscript.

Carter, Robert T., and Thomas D. Scheuermann. 2012. "Legal and Policy Standards for Addressing Workplace Racism: Employer Liability and Shared Responsibility for Race-Based Traumatic Stress." *University of Maryland Law Journal of Race, Religion, Gender and Class* 12, no. 1: 1–100.

——. 2020. *Confronting Racism: Integrating Mental Health Research into Legal Strategies and Reforms.* New York: Routledge.

Carter, Sierra E., Mei Ling Ong, Ronald L. Simons, Frederick X.. Gibbons, Man Kit Lei, and Steven R. H. Beach. 2019. "The Effect of Early Discrimination on Accelerated Aging Among African Americans." *Health Psychology.* Advance online publication, dx.doi.org.tc.idm.oclc.org/10.1037/hea0000788

Carver, Charles S., and Michael F. Scheier. 2017. *Perspectives on Personality*, 8th ed. Boston: Pearson.

Case, Kim A. 2007. "Raising White Privilege Awareness and Reducing Racial Prejudice: Assessing Diversity Course Effectiveness." *Teaching of Psychology* 34, no. 4: 231–35. doi.org/10.1080/00986280701700250.

Castillo, Richard J. 1997. *Culture and Mental Illness: A Client-Centered Approach.* Pacific Grove, CA: Brooks/Cole.

Castle, Billie, Monica Wendel, Jelani Kerr, Derrick Brooms, and Aaron Rollins. 2019. "Public Health's Approach to Systemic Racism: A Systematic Literature Review." *Journal of Racial and Ethnic Health Disparities* 6, no. 1: 27–36. doi.org/10.1007/s40615-018-0494-x.

Castro-Schilo, Laura, Alyson Cavanaugh, Yesenia Mejia, and Richard Robins. 2019. "When Discrimination Hurts: The Longitudinal Impact of Increases in Peer Discrimination on Anxiety and Depressive Symptoms in Mexican-Origin Youth." *Journal of Youth and Adolescence* 48, no. 5: 864–75. http://search.proquest.com/docview/2191942447/.

Causadias, José M., Joseph A. Vitriol, and Annabelle Lin Atkin. 2018. "Do We Overemphasize the Role of Culture in Behavior of Racial/Ethnic Minorities? Evidence of a Cultural (Mis)Attribution Bias in American Psychology." *American Psychologist* 73, no. 3: 243–55. doi.org/10.1037/amp0000099.

Chae, David H., Amani M. Nuru-Jeter, Nancy E. Adler, Gene H. Brody, Jue Lin, Elizabeth H. Blackburn, and Elissa S. Epel. 2014. "Discrimination, Racial Bias, and Telomere Length in African-American Men." *American Journal of Preventive Medicine* 46, no. 2: 103–11.

Chae, David H., Wizdom A. Powell, Amani M. Nuru-Jeter, Mia A. Smith-Bynum, Eleanor K. Seaton, Tyrone A. Forman, Rodman Turpin, and Robert Sellers. 2017. "The Role of Racial Identity and Implicit Racial Bias in Self-Reported Racial Discrimination: Implications for Depression Among African American Men." *Journal of Black Psychology* 43, no. 8: 789–812. doi.org/10.1177/0095798417690055.

Chan, Fong, Gloria K. Lee, Eun-Jeong Lee, Coleen Kubota, and Chase A. Allen. 2007. "Structural Equation Modeling in Rehabilitation Counseling Research." *Rehabilitation Counseling Bulletin* 51, no. 1: 53–66. doi.org/10.1177/00343552070 510010701.

Chandola, Tarani, and Michael G. Marmot. 2011. "Socioeconomic Status and Stress." In *Handbook of Stress Science: Biology, Psychology and Health*, ed. Richard J. Contrada and Andrew Baum, 185–95. New York: Springer.

Chávez, Noé Rubén, and Sabine Elizabeth French. 2007. "Ethnicity-Related Stressors and Mental Health in Latino Americans: The Moderating Role of Parental Racial Socialization." *Journal of Applied Social Psychology* 37, no. 9: 1974–98. doi .org/10.1111/j.1559-1816.2007.00246.x.

Chavez-Dueñas, Nayeli Y., Hector Y. Adames, Jessica G. Perez-Chavez, and Silvia P. Salas. 2019. "Healing Ethno-Racial Trauma in Latinx Immigrant Communities: Cultivating Hope, Resistance, and Action." *American Psychologist* 74, no. 1: 49–62.

Chavous, Tabbye, Bridget Richardson, Felecia Webb, Gloryvee Fonseca-Bolorin, and Seanna Leath. 2018. "Shifting Contexts and Shifting Identities: Campus Race-Related Experiences, Racial Identity, and Academic Motivation Among Black Students During the Transition to College." *Race and Social Problems* 10, no. 1: 1–18. search.proquest.com/docview/1993643837/.

Cheng, Pei-Han, Robert T. Carter, and Donald Y. Lee. 2015. "Racial Identity Status Attitudes and Acculturation of Korean and Chinese Americans: Criterion-Related Profile Analyses." *Journal of Multicultural Counseling and Development* 43, no. 2: 97–108. doi.org/10.1002/j.2161-1912.2015.00067.x.

Cheung, Gordon W., and Roger B. Rensvold. 2002. "Evaluating Goodness-of-Fit Indexes for Testing Measurement Invariance." *Structural Equation Modeling* 9, no. 2: 233–55. doi.org/10.1207/S15328007SEM0902_5.

Chew, P. K., and R. E. Kelly. 2006. "Unwrapping Racial Harassment Law." *Berkeley Journal of Employment Law* 49: 1–51. https://ssrn.com/abstract=1273737.

Chrobot-Mason, Donna, and Willaim K. Hepworth. 2005. "Examining Perceptions of Ambiguous and Unambiguous Threats of Racial Harassment and Managerial Response Strategies." *Journal of Applied Social Psychology* 35, no. 11 (July): 2215–61. doi.org/10.1111/j.1559-1816.2005.tb02101.x.

Chung, Rita Chi-Ying, Fred Bemak, Regine Talleyrand, and Joseph M. Williams. 2018. "Challenges in Promoting Race Dialogues in Psychology Training: Race and Gender Perspectives." *Counseling Psychologist* 46, no. 2: 213–40. doi.org/10.1177/0011000018758262.

Clark, Rodney, Norman B. Anderson, Vernessa R. Clark, and David R. Williams. 1999. "Racism as a Stressor for African Americans: A Biopsychosocial Model." *American Psychologist* 54, no. 10: 805–16. doi:10.1037/0003-066X.54.10.805.

Coates, Ta-Nehisi. 2017. *We Were Eight Years in Power: An American Tragedy.* New York: One World.

Cohen, Zachary D., and Robert J. DeRubeis. 2018. "Treatment Selection in Depression." *Annual Review of Clinical Psychology* 14: 209–36. doi.org/10.1146/annurev-clinpsy-050817-084746.

Collins, James W., Richard J. David, Arden Handler, Stephen Wall, and Steven Andes. 2004. "Very Low Birthweight in African American Infants: The Roles of Maternal Exposure to Interpersonal Racial Discrimination." *American Journal of Public Health* 94, no. 12: 2132–38.

Collins, Noah M., and Alex L. Pieterse. 2007. "Critical Incident Analysis-Based Learning: An Approach to Training for Active Racial and Cultural Awareness." *Journal of Counseling and Development* 85, no. 1: 14–23. doi.org/10.1002/j.1556-6678.2007.tb00439.x.

Comas-Díaz, Lillian. 2016. "Racial Trauma Recovery: A Race Informed Therapeutic Approach to Racial Wounds." In *The Cost of Racism for People of Color: Contextualizing Experiences of Discrimination*, ed. Alvin N. Alvarez, Christopher T. H. Liang, and Helen A. Neville, 249–71. Washington, DC: American Psychological Association. doi.org/10.1037/14852-012.

Comas-Díaz, Lillian, Gordon N. Hall, and Helen A. Neville. 2019. "Racial Trauma: Theory, Research, and Healing: Introduction to the Special Issue." *American Psychologist* 74, no. 1: 1–5. dx.doi.org/10.1037/amp0000442.

Comas-Díaz, Lillian, and Frederick M. Jacobsen. 2001. "Ethnocultural Allodynia." *Journal of Psychotherapy Practice and Research* 10, no. 4: 246–52.

Combs, Dennis R., David L. Penn, Jeffrey Cassisi, Chris Michael, Terry Wood, Jill Wanner, and Scott Adams. 2006. "Perceived Racism as a Predictor of Paranoia Among African Americans." *Journal of Black Psychology* 32, no. 1 (February): 87–104. doi.org/10.1177/0095798405283175.

Concepcion, William R., Eric L. Kohatsu, and Christian J. Yeh. 2013. "Using Racial Identity and Acculturation to Analyze Experiences of Racism Among Asian Americans." *Asian American Journal of Psychology* 4, no. 2: 136–42. doi.org/10.1037/a0027985.

Cooper, Hannah L. F., Samuel R. Friedman, Barbara Tempalski, and Risa Friedman. 2007. "Residential Segregation and Injection Drug Use Prevalence Among Black Adults in US Metropolitan Areas." *American Journal of Public Health* 97, no. 2: 344–52. doi.org/10.2105/AJPH.2005.074542.

Corneau, Simon, and Vicky Stergiopoulos. 2012. "More than Being Against It: Anti-Racism and Anti-Oppression in Mental Health Services." *Transcultural Psychiatry* 49, no. 2: 261–82. doi.org/10.1177/1363461512441594.

Cowen, Emory L. 1973. "Social and Community Interventions." *Annual Review of Psychology* 24: 423–72. doi.org/10.1146/annurev.ps.24.020173.002231.

Cozier, Yvette C., Lauren A. Wise, Julie R. Palmer, and Lynn Rosenberg. 2009. "Perceived Racism in Relation to Weight Change in the Black Women's Health Study." *Annals of Epidemiology* 19, no. 6: 379–87. doi.org/10.1016/j.annepidem.2009.01.008.

Craig-Henderson, Kellina, and L. Ren Sloan. 2003. "After the Hate: Helping Psychologists Help Victims of Racist Hate Crime." *Clinical Psychology: Science and Practice* 10, no. 4: 481–90. doi.org/10.1093/clipsy.bpg048.

Cross, Dorthie, Negar Fani, Abigail Powers, and Bekh Bradley. 2017. "Neurobiological Development in the Context of Childhood Trauma." *Clinical Psychology: Science and Practice* 24, no. 2 (June): 111–24. dx.doi.org/10.1111/cpsp.12198.

Cross, William E., Jr., Eleanor Seaton, Tiffany Yip, Richard M. Lee, Deborah Rivas, Gilbert C. Gee, Wendy Roth, and Bic Ngo. 2017. "Identity Work: Enactment of Racial-Ethnic Identity in Everyday Life." *Identity* 17, no. 1: 1–12. doi.org/10.1080/15283488.2016.1268535.

Dais, Elizabeth, John Eligon, and Richard A. Oppel Jr. 2018. "Philadelphia Starbucks Arrests Outrageous to Some, Are Everyday Life for Others." *New York Times*, April 18. www.nytimes.com/2018/04/17/us/starbucks-arrest-philadelphia.html.

Daly, Alfrieda, Jeanette Jennings, Joyce O. Beckett, and Bogart R. Leashore. 1995. "Effective Coping Strategies of African Americans." *Social Work* 40, no. 2: 240–48.

Danoff-Burg, Sharon, Hazel M. Prelow, and Rebecca R. Swenson. 2004. "Hope and Life Satisfaction in Black College Students Coping with Race-Related Stress." *Journal of Black Psychology* 30: 208–28. doi.org/10.1177/0095798403260725.

Danzer, Graham. 2012. "African-Americans' Historical Trauma: Manifestations In and Outside of Therapy." *Journal of Theory Construction and Testing* 16, no. 1: 16–21.

Davis, Don E., Cirleen DeBlaere, Jesse Owen, Joshua N. Hook, David P. Rivera, Elise Choe, Dan R. Van Tongeren, Everett L. Worthington Jr., and Vanessa Pla-

REFERENCES 363

ceres. 2018. "The Multicultural Orientation Framework: A Narrative Review." *Psychotherapy* 55, no. 1: 89–100. doi.org/10.1037%2Fpst0000160.

Davis, Telsie A., Julie R. Ancis, and Jeffrey S. Ashby. 2015. "Therapist Effect, Working Alliance, and African American Women Substance Users." *Cultural Diversity and Ethnic Minority Psychology* 21, no. 3: 126–35. doi.org/10.1037/a0036944.

Dawis, R. V. 2000. "Scale Construction and Psychometric Considerations." In *Handbook of Applied Multivariate Statistics and Mathematical Modeling*, ed. H. E. A. Tinsley and S. D. Brown, 65–92. San Diego, CA: Academic Press.

Dawson, Beverly Araújo. 2009. "Discrimination, Stress, and Acculturation Among Dominican Immigrant Women." *Hispanic Journal of Behavioral Sciences* 31, no. 1: 96–111. doi.org/10.1177/0739986308327502.

de Castro, A. B., Gilbert C. Gee, and David T. Takeuchi. 2008. "Job-Related Stress and Chronic Health Conditions Among Filipino Immigrants." *Journal of Immigrant and Minority Health* 10: 551–58. doi.org/10.1007/s10903-008-9138-2.

De Jesús, Anthony, Jane Hogan, Robert Martinez, Joan Adams, and Tula Hawkins Lacy. 2016. "Putting Racism on the Table: The Implementation and Evaluation of a Novel Racial Equity and Cultural Competency Training/Consultation Model in New York City." *Journal of Ethnic and Cultural Diversity in Social Work* 25, no. 4: 300–19. doi.org/10.1080/15313204.2016.1206497.

de Wit, Leonore M., Floriana Luppino, Annemarie van Straten, B. W. Penninx, Frans G. Zitman, and Pim Cuijpers. 2010. "Depression and Obesity: A Meta-Analysis of Community-Based Studies." *Psychiatry Research* 178, no. 2: 230–35. dx.doi.org/10.1016/j.psychres.2009.04.015.

Dei, George J. Sefa. 2005. "Unmasking Racism: A Challenge for Anti-Racial Educators in the 21st Century." In *Engaging Equity: New Perspectives on Anti-Racist Education*, ed. Leeno Luke Karumanchery, 135–48. Calgary, Can.: Detselig.

Delgado, Andrea K. 1982. "On Being Black." In *Effective Psychotherapy for Low-Income and Minority Patients*, ed. Frank Xavier Acosta, Joe Yamamoto, and Leonard A. Evans, 109–16. New York: Plenum.

Delgado-Romero, Edward A., Nallely Galván, Peggy Maschino, and Marcy Rowland. 2005. "Race and Ethnicity in Empirical Counseling and Counseling Psychology Research: A 10-Year Review." *Counseling Psychologist* 33, no. 4: 419–48. doi.org/10.1177/0011000004268637.

Derogatis, Leonard R., and Patricia A. Cleary. 1977. "Confirmation of the Dimensional Structure of the SCL-90: A Study on Construct Validation." *Journal of Clinical Psychology* 33, no. 4 (October): 981–89. doi.org/10.1002/1097-4679(197710)33:4%3C981::AID-JCLP2270330412%3E3.0.CO;2-0.

Dessel, Adrienne, and Mary E. Rogge. 2008. "Evaluation of Intergroup Dialogue: A Review of the Empirical Literature." *Conflict Resolution Quarterly* 26, no. 2: 199–238. doi.org/10.1002/crq.230.

Dessel, Adrienne, Mary E. Rogge, and Sarah B. Garlington. 2006. "Using Intergroup Dialogue to Promote Social Justice and Change." *Social Work* 51, no. 4: 303–15. doi.org/10.1093/sw/51.4.303.

Diemer, Matthew A., Rashmita S. Mistry, Martha E. Wadsworth, Irene López, and Faye Reimers. 2013. "Best Practices in Conceptualizing and Measuring Social Class in Psychological Research." *Analyses of Social Issues and Public Policy* 13, no. 1: 77–113. doi.org/10.1111/asap.12001.

Dimitrov, Dimiter M. 2010. "Testing for Factorial Invariance in the Context of Construct Validation." *Measurement and Evaluation in Counseling and Development* 43, no. 2: 121–49. doi.org/10.1177/0748175610373459.

Din-Dzietham, Rebecca, Wendy N. Nembhard, Rakale Collins, and Sharon K. Davis. 2004. "Perceived Stress Following Race-Based Discrimination at Work Is Associated with Hypertension in African Americans: The Metro Atlanta Heart Disease Study." *Social Science and Medicine* 58: 449–61. doi.org/10.1016/S0277-9536(03)00211-9.

Dionne, E. J., Jr., Norman J. Ornstein, and Thomas E. Mann. 2017. *One Nation After Trump: A Guide for the Perplexed, the Disillusioned, the Desperate, and the Not-Yet Desperate.* New York: St. Martin's.

Dixon, Lisa, Lisa Green-Paden, Janine Delahanty, Alicia Lucksted, Letitia Postrado, and Jo Hall. 2001. "Variables Associated with Disparities in Treatment of Patients with Schizophrenia and Co-morbid Mood and Anxiety Disorders." *Psychiatric Services* 52, no. 9: 1216–22. doi:10.1176/appi.ps.52.9.1216.

Dixon, Lisa B., Yael Holoshitz, and Ilana Nossel. 2016. "Treatment Engagement of Individuals Experiencing Mental Illness: Review and Update." *World Psychiatry* 15, no. 1: 13–20. doi.org/10.1002/wps.20306.

Dodson, Howard. 2002. *Jubilee: The Emergence of African American Culture.* Washington, DC: National Geographic Books.

Dohrenwend, Bruce P. 2006. "Inventorying Stressful Life Events as Risk Factors for Psychopathology: Toward Resolution of the Problem of Intra-Category Variability." *Psychological Bulletin* 132, no. 3 (May): 477–95.

——. 2010. "Toward a Typology of High-Risk Major Stressful Events and Situations in Posttraumatic Stress Disorder and Related Psychopathology." *Psychological Injury and Law* 3, no. 2: 89–99.

Dolezsar, Cynthia M., Jennifer J. McGrath, Alyssa J. Herzig, and Sydney B. Miller. 2014. "Perceived Racial Discrimination and Hypertension: A Comprehensive Systematic Review." *Health Psychology* 33, no. 1: 20–34. psycnet.apa.org/doi/10.1037/a0033718.

Dominguez, Tyan Parker, Christine Dunkel-Schetter, Laura M. Glynn, Calvin J. Hobel, and Curt A. Sandman. 2008. "Racial Difference in Birth Outcomes: The Role of General, Pregnancy, and Racism Stress." *Health Psychology* 27: 194–203. doi.org/10.1037/0278-6133.27.2.194.

Dovidio, John F., and Samuel L. Gaertner. 1986. *Prejudice, Discrimination, and Racism*. San Diego, CA: Academic Press.

——. 1998. "On the Nature of Contemporary Prejudice: The Causes, Consequences and Challenges of Aversive Racism." In *Racism: The Problem and the Response*, ed. Jennifer L. Eberhardt and Susan T. Fiske, 3–32. Thousand Oaks, CA: Sage.

Dovidio, John F., Samuel L. Gaertner, and Adam R. Pearson. 2016. "Aversive Racism and Contemporary Bias." In *The Cambridge Handbook of the Psychology of Prejudice*, ed. Chris G. Sibley and Fiona Kate Barlow, 267–91. Cambridge, UK: Cambridge University Press.

Dovidio, John F., Angelika Love, Fabian M. H. Schellhaas, and Miles Hewstone. 2017. "Reducing Intergroup Bias Through Intergroup Contact: Twenty Years of Progress and Future Directions." *Group Processes and Intergroup Relations* 20, no. 5: 606–20.

Draguns, Juris G. 2005. "Cultural Psychology: Its Early Roots and Present Status." In *Handbook of Racial-Cultural Counseling and Psychology*, vol. 1, *Theory and Research*, ed. Robert T. Carter, 163–83. Hoboken, NJ: Wiley.

Dunbar, Edward. 2001. "Counseling Practices to Ameliorate the Effects of Discrimination and Hate Events: Toward a Systematic Approach to Assessment and Intervention." *Counseling Psychologist* 29, no. 2: 281–307. doi.org/10.1177/0011000001292007.

Duran, Eduardo, Judith Firehammer, and John Gonzalez. 2008. "Liberation Psychology as the Path Toward Healing Cultural Soul Wounds." *Journal of Counseling and Development* 86, no. 3: 288–95. dx.doi.org/10.1002/j.1556-6678.2008.tb00511.x.

Earnshaw, Valerie A., Lisa Rosenthal, Amy Carroll-Scott, Alycia Santilli, Kathryn Gilstad-Hayden, and Jeannette R. Ickovics. 2015. "Everyday Discrimination and Physical Health: Exploring Mental Health Processes." *Journal of Health Psychology* 21, no. 10: 2218–228. doi.org/10.1177/1359105315572456.

Edsall, Thomas Byrne, and Mary D. Edsall. 1991a. "Race." *Atlantic Monthly* 267, no. 5 (May): 53–86. www.theatlantic.com/past/docs/politics/race/edsall.htm.

——. 1991b. *Chain Reaction: The Impact of Race, Rights and Taxes on American Politics*. New York: Norton.

Eisenberger, Naomi I. 2012. "The Neural Bases of Social Pain: Evidence for Shared Representations with Physical Pain." *Psychosomatic Medicine* 74, no. 2 (February–March): 126–35. doi.org/10.1097/PSY.0b013e3182464dd1.

Eliacin, Johanne, Jessica M. Coffing, Marianne S. Matthias, Diana J. Burgess, Matthew J. Bair, and Angela L. Rollins. 2016. "The Relationship Between Race, Patient Activation, and Working Alliance: Implications for Patient Engagement in Mental Health Care." *Administration and Policy in Mental Health and Mental Health Services Research* 45, no. 1: 186–92. doi.org/10.1007/s10488-016-0779-5.

Elias, Amanuel, and Yin Paradies. 2016. "Estimating the Mental Health Costs of Racial Discrimination." *BMC Public Health* 16, no. 1: 1205. doi.org/10.1186/s12889-016-3868-1.

Elligan, Don, and Shawn Utsey. 1999. "Utility of an African-Centered Support Group for African American Men Confronting Societal Racism and Oppression." *Cultural Diversity and Ethnic Minority Psychology* 5, no. 2: 156–65. dx.doi.org/10.1037 /1099-9809.5.2.156.

Ellis, B. Heidi, Helen Z. MacDonald, Julie Klunk-Gillis, Alisa Lincoln, Lee Strunin, and Howard J. Cabral. 2010. "Discrimination and Mental Health Among Somali Refugee Adolescents: The Role of Acculturation and Gender." *American Journal of Orthopsychiatry* 80, no. 4: 564–75. doi.org/10.1111/j.1939-0025.2010.01061.x.

Engberg, Mark E. 2004. "Improving Intergroup Relations in Higher Education: A Critical Examination of the Influence of Educational Interventions on Racial Bias." *Review of Educational Research* 74, no. 4: 473–524. doi.org/10.3102/0034 6543074004473.

Erikson, Erik H. 1959. *Identity and the Life Cycle: Selected Papers*. New York: International University Press.

Evans, Ashley B., Meeta Banerjee, Rika Meyer, Adriana Aldana, Monica Foust, and Stephanie Rowley. 2012. "Racial Socialization as a Mechanism for Positive Development Among African American Youth." *Child Development Perspectives* 6, no. 3: 251–57. doi.org/10.1111/j.1750-8606.2011.00226.x.

Eyerman, Ron. 2001. *Cultural Trauma: Slavery and the Formation of African American Identity*. Cambridge, UK: Cambridge University Press.

Fast, Elizabeth, and Delphine Collin-Vézina. 2010. "Historical Trauma, Race-Based Trauma and Resilience of Indigenous Peoples: A Literature Review." *First Peoples Child and Family Review* 5, no. 1: 126–36.

Feagin, Joe R. 2006. *Systemic Racism: A Theory of Oppression*. New York: Routledge.

——. 2014. *Racist America: Roots, Current Realities, and Future Reparations*, 3rd ed. New York: Routledge.

——. 2016. *How Blacks Built America*. New York: Routledge.

Feagin, Joe R., and Karyn D. McKinney. 2003. *The Many Costs of Racism*. Lanham, MD: Rowman and Littlefield.

Ferdinand, Angeline S., Yin Paradies, and Margaret Kelaher. 2017. "Enhancing the Use of Research in Health-Promoting, Anti-Racism Policy." *Health Research Policy and Systems* 15, no. 1: 61. doi.org/10.1186/s12961-017-0223-7.

Fernando, Suman. 2004. *Cultural Diversity, Mental Health and Psychiatry: The Struggle Against Racism*. New York: Brunner-Routledge.

——. 2010. *Mental Health, Race and Culture*. New York: Palgrave Macmillan.

——. 2017. "Persistence of Racism Through White Power." In *Institutional Racism in Psychiatry and Clinical Psychology*, 135–52. Cham, Switz.: Palgrave Macmillan.

Field, Andy P. 2009. *Discovering Statistics Using SPSS (and Sex, Drugs, and Rock 'n' Roll)*, 3rd ed. Thousand Oaks, CA: Sage.

Finkelman, Paul. 2018. *Supreme Injustice: Slavery in the Nation's Highest Court*. Cambridge, MA: Harvard University Press.

Finn, Stephen E., and Mary E. Tonsager. 2002. "How Therapeutic Assessment Became Humanistic." *Humanistic Psychologist* 30, no. 1–2: 10–22. dx.doi.org /10.1080/08873267.2002.9977019.

Flaherty, Colleen. 2016. "More Faculty Diversity, Not on Tenure Track." Inside Higher Education, August 22. www.insidehighered.com/news/2016/08/22/study -finds-gains-faculty-diversity-not-tenure-track.

Fleiss, Joseph L. 1971. "Measuring Nominal Scale Agreement Among Many Raters." *Psychological Bulletin* 76, no. 5: 378–82. dx.doi.org/10.1037/h0031619.

Flores, Elena, Jeanne M. Tschann, Juanita M. Dimas, Lauri A. Pasch, and Cynthia L. de Groat. 2010. "Perceived Racial/Ethnic Discrimination, Posttraumatic Stress Symptoms, and Health Risk Behaviors Among Mexican American Adolescents." *Journal of Counseling Psychology* 57, no. 3: 264–73. doi.org/10.1037/a0020026.

Foldy, Erica Gabrielle, and Tamara R. Buckley. 2014. *The Color Bind: Talking (and Not Talking) About Race at Work*. New York: Russell Sage Foundation.

Folkman, Susan. 2013. "Stress: Appraisal and Coping." In *Encyclopedia of Behavioral Medicine*, ed. Marc D. Gellman and J. Rick Turner, 1913–15. New York: Springer.

Folkman, Susan, and Richard S. Lazarus. 1988. "The Relationship Between Coping and Emotion: Implications for Theory and Research." *Social Science and Medicine* 26, no. 3: 309–17.

Ford, Chandra L., and Collins O. Airhihenbuwa. 2010. "Critical Race Theory, Race Equity, and Public Health: Toward Antiracism Praxis." *American Journal of Public Health* 100, no. S1 (April 1): S30–S35. doi.org/10.2105/AJPH.2009.171058.

Ford, Julian D. 2008. "Trauma, Posttraumatic Stress Disorder, and Ethnoracial Minorities: Toward Diversity and Cultural Competence in Principles and Practices." *Clinical Psychology: Science and Practice* 15, no. 1 (March): 62–67. doi.org/10.1111 /j.1468-2850.2008.00110.x.

——. 2017. "Complex Trauma and Developmental Trauma Disorder in Adolescence." *Adolescent Psychiatry* 7, no. 4: 220–35.

Forsyth, Jessica, and Robert T. Carter. 2012. "The Influence of Racial Identity Status Attitudes and Racism-Related Coping on Mental Health Among Black Americans." *Cultural Diversity and Ethnic Minority Psychology* 18, no. 2: 128–40. doi .org/10.1037/a0027660.

——. 2014. "The Development and Preliminary Validation of the Racism-Related Coping Scale." *Psychological Trauma: Theory, Research, Practice, and Policy* 6, no. 6: 632–43. doi.org/10.1037/a0036702.

Forsyth, Jessica, Schekeva Hall, and Robert T. Carter. 2015. "Racial Identity Among African Americans and Black West Indian Americans." *Professional Psychology: Research and Practice* 46, no. 2: 124–31. psycnet.apa.org/doi/10.1037/a0038076.

Frankenhaeuser, Marianne. 1986. "A Psychobiological Framework for Research on Human Stress and Coping." In *Dynamics of Stress*, ed. Mortimer H. Appley and Richard A. Trumbull, 101–16. Boston: Springer.

Franklin, Anderson J. 1992. "Therapy with African American Men." *Families in Society* 73, no. 6: 350–55.

Franklin, Anderson J., and Nancy Boyd-Franklin. 2000. "Invisibility Syndrome: A Clinical Model of the Effects of Racism on African-American Males." *American Journal of Orthopsychiatry* 70, no. 1: 33–41.

Franklin-Jackson, Deidre, and Robert T. Carter. 2007. "The Relationships Between Race-Related Stress, Racial Identity, and Mental Health for Black Americans." *Journal of Black Psychology* 33, no. 1: 5–26. doi.org/10.1177/0095798406295092.

Fredrickson, George Marsh. 1988. *The Arrogance of Race: Historical Perspectives on Slavery, Racism and Social Inequity.* Middleton, CT: Wesleyan University Press.

Funke, Daniel, and Tina Susman. 2016. "From Ferguson to Baton Rouge: Deaths of Black Men and Women at the Hands of Police." *LA Times,* July 12. www.latimes.com/nation/la-na-police-deaths-20160707-snap-htmlstory.html.

García, Jennifer Jee-Lyn, and Mienah Zulfacar Sharif. 2015. "Black Lives Matter: A Commentary on Racism and Public Health." *American Journal of Public Health* 105, no. 8: e27–e30.

Garcia, M. A., and M. Tehee. 2014. "Society of Indian Psychologists Commentary on the American Psychological Association's (APA's) Ethical Principles of Psychologists and Code of Conduct." Society of Indian Psychologists. https://www.apa.org/pi/oema/resources/communique/2014/12/indian-psychologists-ethics.

Gee, Gilbert C. 2002. "A Multilevel Analysis of the Relationship Between Institutional and Individual Racial Discrimination and Health Status." *American Journal of Public Health* 92, no. 4: 615–23.

Gee, Gilbert C., Annie Ro, Salma Shariff-Marco, and David Chae. 2009. "Racial Discrimination and Health Among Asian Americans: Evidence, Assessment, and Directions for Future Research." *Epidemiologic Reviews* 31: 130–51. doi.org/10.1093%2Fepirev%2Fmxp009.

Gee, Gilbert C., Andrew Ryan, David J. Laflamme, and Jeanie Holt. 2006. "Self-Reported Discrimination and Mental Health Status Among African Descendants, Mexican Americans, and Other Latinos in the New Hampshire REACH 2010 Initiative: The Added Dimension of Immigration." *American Journal of Public Health* 96, no. 10: 1821–28.

Gee, Gilbert C., Michael S. Spencer, Juan Chen, Tiffany Yip, and David T. Takeuchi. 2007. "The Association Between Self-Reported Racial Discrimination and 12-Month DSM-IV Mental Disorders Among Asian Americans." *Social Science and Medicine* 64, no. 10: 1984–96. doi.org/10.1016/j.socscimed.2007.02.013.

Gee, Gilbert C., Katrina M. Walsemann, and Elizabeth Brondolo. 2012. "A Life Course Perspective on How Racism May Be Related to Health Inequities."

American Journal of Public Health 102, no. 5: 967–74. dx.doi.org/10.2105%2FAJ PH.2012.300666.

Geller, Amanda, Jeffrey Fagan, Tom Tyler, and Bruce G. Link. 2014. "Aggressive Policing and the Mental Health of Young Urban Men." *American Journal of Public Health* 104, no. 12: 2321–27. doi.org/10.2105/AJPH.2014.302046.

Gibbons, Frederick X., Paul E. Etcheverry, Michelle L. Stock, Meg Gerrard, Chih-Yuan Weng, Marc Kiviniemi, and Ross O'Hara. 2010. "Exploring the Link Between Racial Discrimination and Substance Use: What Mediates? What Buffers?" *Journal of Personality and Social Psychology* 99: 785–801. doi.org/10.1037%2 Fa0019880.

Gibbons, Frederick X., Meg Gerard, Michael J. Cleveland, Thomas A. Wills, and Gene Brody. 2004. "Perceived Discrimination and Substance Use in African American Parents and Their Children: A Panel Study." *Journal of Personality and Social Psychology* 86, no. 4: 517–29. doi.org/10.1037/0022-3514.86.4.517.

Gone, Joseph P. 2007. "'We Never Was Happy Living Like a Whiteman': Mental Health Disparities and the Postcolonial Predicament in American Indian Communities." *American Journal of Community Psychology* 40, no. 3–4: 290–300. doi .org/10.1007/s10464-007-9136-x.

Goodman, Rachael D., Joseph M. Williams, Rita Chi-Ying Chung, Regine M. Talleyrand, Adrienne M. Douglass, H. George McMahon, and Fred Bemak. 2015. "Decolonizing Traditional Pedagogies and Practices in Counseling and Psychology Education: A Move Towards Social Justice and Action." In *Decolonizing "Multicultural" Counseling Through Social Justice*, ed. Rachael D. Goodman and Paul C. Gorski, 147–64. New York: Springer.

Goodwill, Janelle R., Daphne C. Watkins, Natasha C. Johnson, and Julie Ober Allen. 2018. "An Exploratory Study of Stress and Coping Among Black College Men." *American Journal of Orthopsychiatry* (January), advance online publication. doi.org/10.1037/ort0000313.

Goosby, Bridget, Jacob Cheadle, and Mitchell Colter. 2018. "Stress-Related Biosocial Mechanisms of Discrimination and African American Health Inequities." *Annual Review of Sociology* 44, no. 1: 319–40.

Gould, Stephen Jay. 1984. *The Mismeasure of Man*. Harmondsworth, UK: Penguin.

Graham, David A., Adrienne Green, Cullen Murphy, and Parker Richards. 2019. "An Oral History of Trump's Bigotry." *The Atlantic*, June.

Graves, Joseph L., Jr. 2001. *The Emperor's New Clothes: Biological Theories of Race at the Millennium*. New Brunswick, NJ: Rutgers University Press.

Greenberg, Stuart A., Daniel W. Shuman, and Robert G. Meyer. 2004. "Unmasking Forensic Diagnosis." *International Journal of the Law and Psychiatry* 27, no. 1: 1–15. dx.doi.org/10.1016/j.ijlp.2004.01.001.

Greene, Melissa L., Niobe Way, and Kerstin Pahl. 2006. "Trajectories of Perceived Adult and Peer Discrimination Among Black, Latino, and Asian American

Adolescents: Patterns and Psychological Correlates." *Developmental Psychology* 42, no. 2: 218–36. doi.org/10.1037/0012-1649.42.2.218.

Greenwald, Anthony G., T. Andrew Poehlman, Eric Lewis Uhlmann, and Mahzarin R. Banaji. 2009. "Understanding and Using the Implicit Association Test: III. Meta-Analysis of Predictive Validity." *Journal of Personality and Social Psychology* 97, no. 1: 17–41. doi.org/10.1037/a0015575.

Greer, Tawanda M. 2007. "Measuring Coping Strategies Among African American Women: An Exploration of the Latent Structure of the COPE Inventory." *Journal of Black Psychology* 33, no. 3: 260–77. doi.org/10.1177/0095798407302539.

——. 2011. "Coping Strategies as Moderators of the Relationship Between Race and Gender-Based Discrimination and Psychological Symptoms for African American Women." *Journal of Black Psychology* 37, no. 1: 42–54. doi.org/10.1177 /0095798410380202.

Gregorich, Steven E. 2006. "Do Self-Report Instruments Allow Meaningful Comparisons Across Diverse Population Groups? Testing Measurement Invariance Using the Confirmatory Factor Analysis Framework." *Medical Care* 44, no. 11 (Suppl. 3): S78–S94. dx.doi.org/10.1097%2F01.mlr.0000245454.12228.8f.

Griffith, Aisha N., Noelle M. Hurd, and Saida B. Hussain. 2019. "'I Didn't Come to School for This': A Qualitative Examination of Experiences with Race-Related Stressors and Coping Responses Among Black Students Attending a Predominantly White Institution." *Journal of Adolescent Research* 34, no. 2: 115–39.

Griffith, Derek M., Mondi Mason, Michael Yonas, Eugenia Eng, Vanessa Jeffries, Suzanne Plihcik, and Barton Parks. 2007. "Dismantling Institutional Racism: Theory and Action." *American Journal of Community Psychology* 39, no. 3–4: 381–92.

Guthrie, Robert V. 2004. *Even the Rat Was White: A Historical View of Psychology*, 2nd ed. Upper Saddle River, NJ: Pearson Education.

Hage, Sally M., John L. Romano, Robert K. Conyne, Maureen Kenny, Connie Matthews, Jonathan P. Schwartz, and Michael Waldo. 2007. "Best Practice Guidelines on Prevention, Practice, Research, Training, and Social Advocacy for Psychologists." *Counseling Psychologist* 35, no. 4: 493–566. doi.org/10.1177%2 F0011000006291411.

Hall, Schekeva P., and Robert T. Carter. 2006. "The Relationship Between Racial Identity, Ethnic Identity, and Perceptions of Racial Discrimination in an Afro-Caribbean Descent Sample." *Journal of Black Psychology* 32, no. 2: 155–75. doi .org/10.1177/0095798406287071.

Hannah-Jones, Nikole. 2019. "The Idea of America: 1619 Project." *New York Times Magazine*, August 20, 14–26.

Hansen, Helena, Joel Braslow, and Robert M. Rohrbaugh. 2018. "From Cultural to Structural Competency: Training Psychiatry Residents to Act on Social Determinants of Health and Institutional Racism." *AMA Psychiatry* 75, no. 2: 117–18. doi.org/10.1001/jamapsychiatry.2017.3894.

Hansen, Nancy Downing, Katherine V. Randazzo, Arielle Schwartz, Maria Marshall, David Kalis, Royce Frazier, Christopher Burke, Kendall Kershner-Rice, and Gerda Norvig. 2006. "Do We Practice What We Preach? An Exploratory Survey of Multicultural Psychotherapy Competencies." *Professional Psychology: Research and Practice* 37, no. 1 (February): 66–74.

Hardeman, Rachel R., Eduardo M. Medina, and Katy B. Kozhimannil. 2016. "Structural Racism and Supporting Black Lives: The Role of Health Professionals." *New England Journal of Medicine* 375, no. 22: 2113–15. doi.org/10.1056/NEJMp1609535.

Harrell, Shelly P. 1997. "The Racism and Life Experiences Scale (RaLES)." Unpublished manuscript.

——. 2000. "A Multidimensional Conceptualization of Racism-Related Stress: Implications for the Well-Being of People of Color." *American Journal of Orthopsychiatry* 70, no. 1: 42–57. doi.org/10.1037/h0087722.

——. 2014. "Compassionate Confrontation and Empathic Exploration: The Integration of Race-Related Narratives in Clinical Supervision." In *Multiculturalism and Diversity in Clinical Supervision: A Competency-Based Approach*, ed. Carol Falender and Edward Shafranske, 83–110. Washington DC: American Psychological Association.

Harris, Fred R., and T. Wicker. 1988. *The Kerner Report: The 1968 Report of the National Advisory Commission on Civil Disorders*. New York: Pantheon.

Harris-Britt, April, Cecelia R. Valrie, Beth Kurtz-Costes, and Stephanie J. Rowley. 2007. "Perceived Racial Discrimination and Self-Esteem in African American Youth: Racial Socialization as a Protective Factor." *Journal of Research on Adolescence* 17: 669–82. doi.org/10.1111/j.1532-7795.2007.00540.x.

Haskins, Natoya H., and Anneliese A. Singh. 2015. "Critical Race Theory and Counselor Education Pedagogy: Creating Equitable Training." *Counselor Education and Supervision* 54, no. 4: 288–301. doi.org/10.1002/ceas.12027.

Heard-Garris, Nia J., M. Cale, Linda Camaj, M. C. Hamati, and Tyan Parker Dominguez. 2018. "Transmitting Trauma: A Systematic Review of Vicarious Racism and Child Health." *Social Science and Medicine* 199: 230–40. dx.doi.org/10.1016/j.socscimed.2017.04.018.

Heilburn, K., T. Grisso, and A. M. Goldstein. 2009. *Foundations of Forensic Mental Health Assessment*. New York: Oxford University Press.

Heim, Christine, Margaret Shugart, W. Edward Craighead, and Charles B. Nemeroff. 2010. "Neurobiological and Psychiatric Consequences of Child Abuse and Neglect." *Developmental Psychobiology* 52, no. 7: 671–90. doi.org/10.1002/dev.20494.

Helms, Janet E. 1984. "Toward a Theoretical Explanation of the Effects of Race on Counseling: A Black and White Model." *Counseling Psychologist* 12, no. 4: 153–65. doi.org/10.1177/0011000084124013.

——, ed. 1990. *Black and White Racial Identity: Theory, Research and Practice*. Westport, CT: Greenwood.

——. 1995. "An Update of Helms's White and People of Color Racial Identity Models." In *Handbook of Multicultural Counseling*, ed. Joseph G. Ponterotto, J. Manuel Casas, Lisa A. Suzuki, and Charlene M. Alexander, 181–98. Thousand Oaks, CA: Sage.

——. 2014. "A Review of White Racial Identity Theory: The Sociopolitical Implications of Studying White Racial Identity in Psychology." In *Psychology Serving Humanity: Proceedings of the 30th International Congress of Psychology*, vol. 2, *Western Psychology*, ed. Saths Cooper and Kopano Ratele, 12–27. New York: Psychology Press.

Helms, Janet E., and Robert T. Carter. 1990. "Development of the White Racial Identity Inventory." In *Black and White Racial Identity: Theory, Research, and Practice*, ed. Janet E. Helms, 67–80. Westport, CT: Greenwood.

Helms, Janet E., and Donelda A. Cook. 1999. *Using Race and Culture in Counseling and Psychotherapy: Theory and Process*. Boston: Allyn and Bacon.

Helms, Janet E., Maryam Jernigan, and Jackquelyn Mascher. 2005. "The Meaning of Race in Psychology and How to Change It: A Methodological Perspective." *American Psychologist* 60, no. 1: 27–36. doi.org/10.1037/0003-066X.60.1.27.

Helms, Janet E., Guerda Nicolas, and Carlton E. Green. 2010. "Racism and Ethnoviolence as Trauma: Enhancing Professional Training." *Traumatology* 16, no. 4: 53–62. doi.org/10.1177/1534765610389595.

Helms, Janet E., and T. Q. Richardson. 1997. "How 'Multiculturalism' Obscures Race and Culture as Differential Aspects of Counseling Competency." In *Multicultural Counseling Competencies: Assessment, Education and Training, and Supervision*, ed. Donald B. Pope-Davis and Harden L. K. Coleman, 60–79. *Multicultural Aspects of Counseling Series*, vol. 7. Thousand Oaks, CA: Sage.

Hemmings, Carrie, and Amanda M. Evans. 2018. "Identifying and Treating Race-Based Trauma in Counseling." *Journal of Multicultural Counseling and Development* 46, no. 1: 20–39. doi.org/10.1002/jmcd.12090.

Henderson, Zuleka. 2019. "In Their Own Words: How Black Teens Define Trauma." *Journal of Child and Adolescent Trauma* 12: 141–51. doi.org/10.1007/s40653-017-0168-6.

Herman, Judith Lewis. 1992. *Trauma and Recovery: The Aftermath of Violence from Domestic Abuse to Political Terror*. New York: Basic Books.

——. 1997. *Trauma and Recovery: The Aftermath of Violence from Domestic Abuse to Political Terror*, rev. ed. New York: Basic Books.

Hernández, Rafael J., and Villodas, Miguel. 2019. "Collectivistic Coping Responses to Racial Microaggressions Associated with Latina/O College Persistence Attitudes." *Journal of Latinx Psychology* 7, no. 1: 76–90.

Herring, Sigrid, Jo Spangaro, Marlene Lauw, and Lorna McNamara. 2013. "The Intersection of Trauma, Racism, and Cultural Competence in Effective Work with Aboriginal People: Waiting for Trust." *Australian Social Work* 66, no. 1: 104–17. doi.org/10.1080/0312407X.2012.697566.

Hicken, Margaret T., Nicole Kravitz-Wirtzb, Myles Durkee, and James S. Jackson. 2018. "Racial Inequalities in Health: Framing Future Research." *Social Science and Medicine* 199 (February): 11–18.

Hicks, James W. 2004. "Ethnicity, Race and Forensic Psychiatry: Are We Color-Blind?" *Journal of American Academy of Psychiatry and the Law* 32, no. 1: 21–33.

Hill, Clara E., Jessica Stahl, and Melissa Roffman. 2007. "Training Novice Psychotherapists: Helping Skills and Beyond." *Psychotherapy: Theory, Research, Practice, Training* 44, no. 4: 364–70. doi.org/10.1037/0033-3204.44.4.364.

Hoggard, Lori S., Shawn C. T. Jones, and Robert M. Sellers. 2017. "Racial Cues and Racial Identity: Implications for How African Americans Experience and Respond to Racial Discrimination." *Journal of Black Psychology* 43, no. 4: 409–32. doi.org/10.1177/0095798416651033.

Holmes, Dorothy Evans. 2014. "Racial Transference Reactions in Psychoanalytic Treatment: An Update." In *Race, Culture and Psychotherapy: Critical Perspectives in Multicultural Practice*, ed. Roy Moodley and Stephen Palmer, 79–91. New York: Routledge.

Holmes, Samantha C., Vanessa C. Facemire, and Alexis M. DaFonseca. 2016. "Expanding Criterion A for Posttraumatic Stress Disorder: Considering the Deleterious Impact of Oppression." *Traumatology* 22, no. 4: 314–21.

Hong, Sehee, Mary L. Malik, and Min-Kyu Lee. 2003. "Testing Configural, Metric, Scalar, and Latent Mean Invariance Across Genders in Sociotropy and Autonomy Using a Non-Western Sample." *Educational and Psychological Measurement* 63, no. 4: 636–54. doi.org/10.1177/0013164403251332.

Horton, James Oliver, and Lois E. Horton. 2005. *Slavery and the Making of America*. New York: Oxford University Press.

Horwitz, Sari, and Emma Brown. 2017. "Justice Department Plans a New Project to Sue Universities Over Affirmative Action Policies." *Washington Post*, August 1.

Hoyt, William T., Rosalia E. Warbasse, and Erica Y. Chu. 2006. "Construct Validation in Counseling Psychology Research." *Counseling Psychologist* 34, no. 6: 769–805. doi.org/10.1177/0011000006287389.

Hu, Alison W., Xiang Zhou, and Richard M. Lee. 2017. "Ethnic Socialization and Ethnic Identity Development Among Internationally Adopted Korean American Adolescents: A Seven-Year Follow-Up." *Developmental Psychology* 53, no. 11: 2066–77. doi.org/10.1037/dev0000421.

Hu, Li-tze, and Peter M. Bentler. 1999. "Cutoff Criteria for Fit Indexes in Covariance Structure Analysis: Conventional Criteria Versus New Alternatives." *Structural Equation Modeling: A Multidisciplinary Journal* 6, no. 1: 1–55. dx.doi.org/10.1080/10705519909540118.

Hudson-Banks, Kira, and Laura P. Kohn-Wood. 2007. "The Influence of Racial Identity Profiles on the Relationship Between Racial Discrimination and Depressive Symptoms." *Journal of Black Psychology* 33, no. 3: 331–354. doi 10.1177/0095798407302540.

Hudson, Darrell L., Harold W. Neighbors, Arline T. Geronimus, and James S. Jackson. 2016. "Racial Discriminations, John Henryism, and Depression Among African Americans." *Journal of Black Psychology* 42, no. 3: 221–43. doi.org/10 .1177/0095798414567757.

Huey, Stanley J., Jacqueline L. Tilley, Eduardo O. Jones, and Caitlin A. Smith. 2014. "The Contribution of Cultural Competence to Evidence-Based Care for Diverse Populations." *Annual Review of Clinical Psychology* 10: 305–38. doi.org/10.1146/ annurev-clinpsy-032813-153729.

Hughes, Diane, James Rodriguez, Emilie P. Smith, Deborah J. Johnson, Howard C. Stevenson, and Paul Spicer. 2006. "Parents' Ethnic-Racial Socialization Practices: A Review of Research and Directions for Future Study." *Developmental Psychology* 42: 747–70. doi.org/10.1037/0012-1649.42.5.747.

Hunte, Haslyn E., and Adam E. Barry. 2012. "Perceived Discrimination and DSM-IV–Based Alcohol and Illicit Drug Use Disorders." *American Journal of Public Health* 102, no. 12: e111–e117. doi.org/10.2105/AJPH.2012.300780.

Hunte, Haslyn E. R., and David R. Williams. 2008. "The Association Between Perceived Discrimination and Obesity in a Population-Based Multiracial and Multiethnic Adult Sample." *American Journal of Public Health* 98, no. 12: 1–8.

Huynh, Que-Lam, Thierry Devos, and Robyn Goldberg. 2014. "The Role of Ethnic and National Identifications in Perceived Discrimination for Asian Americans: Toward a Better Understanding of the Buffering Effect of Group Identifications on Psychological Distress." *Asian American Journal of Psychology* 5, no. 3: 161–71.

Hyers, Lauri L. 2007. "Resisting Prejudice Every Day: Exploring Women's Assertive Responses to Anti-Black Racism, Anti-Semitism, Heterosexism, and Sexism." *Sex Roles* 56, no. 1–2: 1–12. doi.org/10.1007/s11199-006-9142-8.

Jackson, J. S., Myriam Torres, Cleopatra Howard Caldwell, Harold W. Neighbors, Randolph M. Nesse, Robert Joseph Taylor, Steve J. Trierweiler, and David R. Williams. 2004. "The National Survey of American Life: A Study of Racial, Ethnic and Cultural Influences on Mental Disorders and Mental Health." *International Journal of Methods in Psychiatric Research* 13, no. 4: 196–207. doi.org/10.1002/mpr.177.

Jackson, Leslie C. 1999. "Ethnocultural Resistance to Multicultural Training: Students and Faculty." *Cultural Diversity and Ethnic Minority Psychology* 5, no. 1 (February): 27–36.

Jefferson, Thomas. 1784. *Notes on the State of Virginia*. Philadelphia: Prichard and Hall. Documenting the American South. docsouth.unc.edu/southlit/jefferson /jefferson.html.

Jennings, Len, Ashley Sovereign, Salina Renninger, M. Goh, T. M. Skovholt, S. Lakhan, and H. Hessel. 2016. "Bringing It All Together: A Qualitative Meta-Analysis of Seven Master Therapists' Studies from Around the World." In *Expertise in Counseling and Psychotherapy: Master Therapist Studies Around the World*, ed. Len Jennings and Thomas Skovholt, 227–73. New York: Oxford University Press. doi.org/10.1093/med:psych/9780190222505.003.0008.

Jernigan, Maryam M., and Jessica Henderson Daniel. 2011. "Racial Trauma in the Lives of Black Children and Adolescents: Challenges and Clinical Implications." *Journal of Child and Adolescent Trauma* 4, no. 2: 123–41.

Johnson, James A., James Allen Johnson III, and Cynthia B. Morrow. 2013. "Historical Developments in Public Health and the 21st Century." In *Novick and Morrow's Public Health Administration*, ed. Leiyu Shi and James A. Johnson, 11–31. Burlington, MA: Jones and Bartlett Learning.

Johnson, Veronica Elaine. 2017. "Testing a Model of Black Cultural Strength Using Structural Equation Modeling." PhD diss., Teachers College, Columbia University.

Johnson, Veronica, E., and Robert T. Carter. 2019. "Black Cultural Strengths and Psychological Well-Being: An Empirical Analysis with Black American Adults." *Journal of Black Psychology*. On-Line First, December 3, 2019.

Jones, James M. 1997. *Prejudice and Racism*, 2nd ed. New York: McGraw-Hill.

Jones, James M., and Robert T. Carter. 1996. "Racism and White Racial Identity: Merging Realities." In *Impacts of Racism on White America*, 2nd ed., ed. Raymond G. Hunt and Benjamin P. Bowser, 1–23. Thousand Oaks, CA: Sage.

Jones, Jeffrey M. 2016. "Six in 10 Americans Say Racism Against Blacks Is Widespread." Gallup. August 17. news.gallup.com/poll/194657/six-americans-say-racism-against-blacks-widespread.aspx.

Jones, Shawn C. T., Daniel B. Lee, Ashly L. Gaskin, and Enrique W. Neblett. 2014. "Emotional Response Profiles to Racial Discrimination: Does Racial Identity Predict Affective Patterns?" *Journal of Black Psychology* 40, no. 4: 334–58. doi.org/10.1177/0095798413488628.

Juang, Linda P., Irene Park, Su Yeong Kim, Richard M. Lee, Desiree Qin, Sumie Okazaki, Teresa Toguchi Swartz, and Anna Lau. 2018. "Reactive and Proactive Ethnic-Racial Socialization Practices of Second-Generation Asian American Parents." *Asian American Journal of Psychology* 9, no. 1: 4–16. doi.org/10.1037/aap0000101.

Juang, Linda P., Hyung Chol Yoo, and Annabelle Atkin. 2017. "A Critical Race Perspective on an Empirical Review of Asian American Parental Racial-Ethnic Socialization." In *Asian American Parenting: Family Process and Intervention*, ed. Yoonsun Choi and Hyeouk Hahm, 11–35. Cham, Switz.: Springer. doi.org/10.1007/978-3-319-63136-3_2.

Kahn, Jeffrey H. 2006. "Factor Analysis in Counseling Psychology Research, Training, and Practice: Principles, Advances, and Applications." *Counseling Psychologist* 34, no. 5: 684–718. doi.org/10.1177/0011000006286347.

Kaslow, Nadine J., Debra A. Bangasser, Catherine L. Grus, Stephen R. McCutcheon, and Garth A. Fowler. 2018. "Facilitating the Pipeline Progress from Doctoral Degree to First Job." *American Psychologist* 73, no. 1: 47–62. dx.doi.org/10.1037/amp0000120.

Katz, David L., Meghan O'Connell, Ming-Chin Yeh, Haq Nawaz, Valentine Njike, Laurie M. Anderson, Stella Cory, and William Dietz. 2005. "Public Health Strategies for Preventing and Controlling Overweight and Obesity in School and Worksite Settings: A Report on Recommendations of the Task Force on Community Preventive Services." *Morbidity and Mortality Weekly Report: Recommendations and Reports* 54, no. 10 (October 7): 1–12.

Kendi, Ibram X. 2016. *Stamped from the Beginning: The Definitive History of Racist Ideas in America.* New York: The Nation Press.

Kerner, Otto, Jr. 1968. *Kerner Report: The 1968 Report of the National Advisory Commission on Civil Disorders.* Washington, DC: Knopf.

Kessler, Ronald C. 1997. "The Effects of Stressful Life Events on Depression." *Annual Review of Psychology* 48, no. 1: 191–214.

Khaylis, Anna, Lynn Waelde, and Elizabeth Bruce. 2007. "The Role of Ethnic Identity in the Relationship of Race-Related Stress to PTSD Symptoms Among Young Adults." *Journal of Trauma and Dissociation* 8, no. 4: 91–105. doi.org/10.1300/J229v08n04_06.

Kilpatrick, Dean G., Heidi S. Resnick, Melissa E. Milanak, Mark W. Miller, Katherine M. Keyes, and Matthew J. Friedman. 2013. "National Estimates of Exposure to Traumatic Events and PTSD Prevalence Using DSM-IV and DSM-5 Criteria." *Journal of Traumatic Stress* 26, no. 5 (October): 537–47.

Kira, Ibrahim Aref. 2001. "Taxonomy of Trauma and Trauma Assessment." *Traumatology* 7, no. 2: 73–86. doi.org/10.1177/153476560100700202.

Kira, Ibrahim A., Asha Ahmed, Fatima Wasim, Vanessa Mahmoud, Joanna Colrain, and Dhan Rai. 2012. "Group Therapy for Refugees and Torture Survivors: Treatment Model Innovations." *International Journal of Group Psychotherapy* 62, no. 1: 69–88.

Kira, Ibrahim A., Linda Lewandowski, Thomas Templin, Vidya Ramaswamy, Bulent Ozkan, and Jamal Mohanesh. 2008. "Measuring Cumulative Trauma Dose, Types, and Profiles Using a Development-Based Taxonomy of Traumas." *Traumatology* 14, no. 2: 62–87. doi.org/10.1177/1534765608319324.

Kirkinis, Katherine, Alex L. Pieterse, Christina Martin, Alex Agiliga, and Amanda Brownell. 2018. "Racism, Racial Discrimination, and Trauma: A Systematic Review of the Social Science Literature." *Ethnicity and Health* (August): 1–21. doi.org/10.1080/13557858.2018.1514453.

Kirmayer, Laurence J., Joseph P. Gone, and Joshua Moses. 2014. "Rethinking Historical Trauma." *Transcultural Psychiatry* 51: 299–319. doi.org/10.1177/136346151
4536358.

Kline, Rex B. 2011. *Principles and Practice of Structural Equation Modeling*, 3rd ed. New York: Guilford Press.

Kluckhohn, Florence Rockwood, and Fred L. Strodtbeck. 1961. *Variations in Value Orientations*. Evanston, IL: Row, Peterson.

Koch, William J., Kevin S. Douglas, Tonia L. Nicholls, and Melanie L. O'Neill. 2006. *Psychological Injuries: Forensic Assessment, Treatment, and Law*. New York: Oxford University Press.

Kraus, Michael W., Jun Won Park, and Jacinth J. X. Tan. 2017. "Signs of Social Class: The Experience of Economic Inequality in Everyday Life." *Perspectives on Psychological Science* 12, no. 3: 422–35. doi.org/10.1177/1745691616673192.

Kress, Victoria E., Maria Haiyasoso, Chelsey A. Zoldan, Jessica A. Headley, and Heather Trepal. 2018. "The Use of Relational-Cultural Theory in Counseling Clients Who Have Traumatic Stress Disorders." *Journal of Counseling and Development* 96, no. 1: 106–14. doi.org/10.1002/jcad.12182.

Kressin, Nancy R., Kristal L. Raymond, and Meredith Manze. 2008. "Perceptions of Race/Ethnicity-Based Discrimination: A Review of Measures and Evaluation of Their Usefulness for the Health Care Setting." *Journal of Health Care for the Poor and Underserved* 19: 697–730. doi.org/10.1353/hpu.0.0041.

Krieger, Nancy. 2014. "Discrimination and Health Inequities." *International Journal of Health Services* 44: 643–710. doi.org/10.2190/HS.44.4.b.

Krieger, Nancy, Diane L. Rowley, Allen A. Herman, and Byllye Avery, and Mona T. Phillips. 1993. "Racism, Sexism, and Social Class: Implications for Studies of Health, Disease, and Well-Being." *American Journal of Preventive Medicine* 9, no. 6 (Suppl.): 82–122. doi.org/10.1016/S0749-3797(18)30666-4.

Kumas-Tan, Zofia, Brenda Beagan, Charlotte Loppie, Anna MacLeod, and Blye Frank. 2007. "Measures of Cultural Competence: Examining Hidden Assumptions." *Academic Medicine* 82, no. 6: 548–57.

Kwate, Naa Oyo A., and Melody S. Goodman. 2015a. "Cross-Sectional and Longitudinal Effects of Racism on Mental Health Among Residents of Black Neighborhoods in New York City." *American Journal of Public Health* 105, no. 4: 711–18.

——. 2015b. "Racism at the Intersections: Gender and Socioeconomic Differences in the Experience of Racism Among African Americans." *American Journal of Orthopsychiatry* 85, no. 5: 397–408. doi.org/10.1037/ort0000086.

Kwate, Naa Oyo A., Heiddis B. Valdimarsdottir, Josephine S. Guevarra, and Dana H. Bovbjerg. 2003. "Experiences of Racist Events Are Associated with Negative Health Consequences for African American Women." *Journal of the National Medical Association* 95, no. 6: 450–60.

Ladany, Nicholas. 2007. "Does Psychotherapy Training Matter? Maybe Not." *Psychotherapy: Theory, Research, Practice, Training* 44, no. 4: 392–96. doi.org/10.1037 /0033-3204.44.4.392.

Landrum-Brown, J. 1990. "Black Mental Health and Racial Oppression." In *Handbook of Mental Health and Mental Disorder Among Black Americans*, ed. Dorothy Smith-Ruiz, 113–32. New York: Greenwood.

Larwin, Karen, and Milton Harvey. 2012. "A Demonstration of a Systematic Item-Reduction Approach Using Structural Equation Modeling." *Practical Assessment, Research and Evaluation* 17, no. 8 (April): 1–19.

LaVeist, Thomas A., Darrell Gaskin, and Patrick Richard. 2011. "Estimating the Economic Burden of Racial Health Inequalities in the United States." *International Journal of Health Services* 41, no. 2: 231–38. doi.org/10.2190/HS.41.2.c.

Layne, Christopher M., Chandra G. Ippen, Virginia C. Strand, Margaret A. Stuber, Robert Abramovitz, Gilbert Reyes, Lisa Amaya-Jackson, Leslie Ross, Amy Curtis, Laura Lipscomb, and Robert Pynoos. 2011. "The Core Curriculum on Childhood Trauma: A Tool for Training a Trauma-Informed Workforce." *Psychological Trauma: Theory, Research, Practice, and Policy* 3, no. 3: 243–52. doi.org/10.1037/ a0025039.

Lazarus, Richard S. 2006. *Stress and Emotion: A New Synthesis*. New York: Springer.

Lazarus, Richard S., and Susan Folkman. 1984. *Stress, Appraisal, and Coping*. New York: Springer.

Lee, Debbiesiu L., and Soyeon Ahn. 2012. "Discrimination Against Latina/os: A Meta-Analysis of Individual-Level Resources and Outcomes." *Counseling Psychologist* 40, no. 1: 28–65. doi.org/10.1177/0011000011403326.

——. 2013. "The Relation of Racial Identity, Ethnic Identity, and Racial Socialization to Discrimination-Distress: A Meta-Analysis of Black Americans." *Journal of Counseling Psychology* 60, no. 1: 1–14. doi.org/10.1037/a0031275.

Lewis-Coles, Ma'at E. Lyris, and Madonna G. Constantine. 2006. "Racism-Related Stress, Africultural Coping, and Religious Problem-Solving Among African Americans." *Cultural Diversity and Ethnic Minority Psychology* 12, no. 3: 433–43. doi.org/10.1037/1099-9809.12.3.433.

Liang, Christopher T. H., Alvin N. Alvarez, Linda Juang, and Mandy Liang. 2007. "The Role of Coping in the Relationship Between Perceived Racism and Racism-Related Stress for Asian Americans: Gender Differences." *Journal of Counseling Psychology* 54: 132–41. doi.org/10.1037/0022-0167.54.2.132.

Liang, Christopher T. H., and Carin M. Molenaar. 2016. "Beliefs in an Unjust World: Mediating Ethnicity-Related Stressors and Psychological Functioning." *Journal of Clinical Psychology* 72, no. 6: 552–62. doi.org/10.1002/jclp.22271.

Lieberman, Alicia F., Ann Chu, Patricia Van Horn, and William W. Harris. 2011. "Trauma in Early Childhood: Empirical Evidence and Clinical Implications."

Development and Psychopathology 23, no. 2: 397–410. doi.org/10.1017/S0954579 411000137.

Lieberman, Alicia F., and Kathleen Knorr. 2007. "The Impact of Trauma: A Developmental Framework for Infancy and Early Childhood." *Pediatric Annals* 36, no. 4: 209–15. doi.org/10.3928/0090-4481-20070401-10.

Link, Tanja C., and Carrie B. Oser. 2018. "The Role of Stressful Life Events and Cultural Factors on Criminal Thinking Among African American Women Involved in the Criminal Justice System." *Criminal Justice and Behavior* 45, no. 1 (January): 8–30.

Liu, William, Rossina Z. Liu, Y. L. Garrison, Cindy Ji Young Kim, Laurence Chan, Y. C. S. Ho, and Chi W. Yeung. 2019. "Racial Trauma, Microaggressions, and Becoming Racially Innocuous: The Role of Acculturation and White Supremacist Ideology." *American Psychologist* 74, no. 1: 143–55. psycnet.apa.org/record/2019 -01033-012.

Loeb, T. B., N. T. Joseph, G. E. Wyatt, M. Zhang, D. Chin, A. Thames, and Y. Aswad. 2018. "Predictors of Somatic Symptom Severity: The Role of Cumulative History of Trauma and Adversity in a Diverse Community Sample." *Psychological Trauma: Theory, Research, Practice, and Policy* 10, no. 5: 491–98.

Loo, Chalsa M., John A. Fairbank, Raymond M. Scurfield, Libby O. Ruch, Daniel W. King, Lily J. Adams, and Claude Chemtob. 2001. "Measuring Exposure of Racism: Development and Validation of a Race-Related Stressor Scale (RRSS) or Asian American Vietnam Veterans." *Psychological Assessment* 13: 503–20. doi .org/10.1037/1040-3590.13.4.503.

Lopez, German. 2017a. "For Years, This Popular Test Measured Anyone's Racial Bias. But It Might Not Work After All." *Vox*, March 7. www.vox.com/identities/2017/3 /7/14637626/implicit-association-test-racism.

——. 2017b. "The Past Year of Research Has Made It Clear: Trump Won Because of Racial Resentment." *Vox*, December 15. www.vox.com/identities/2017/12/15 /16781222/trump-racism-economic-anxiety-study.

Lu, Darlene, Julie R. Palmer, Lynn Rosenberg, Alexandra E. Shields, Esther H. Orr, Immaculata Devivo, and Yvette C Cozier. 2019. "Perceived Racism in Relation to Telomere Length Among African American Women in the Black Women's Health Study." *Annals of Epidemiology*. doi.org/10.1016/j.annepidem.2019.06.003.

Lui, P. Priscilla, and Lucia Quezada. 2019. "Associations Between Microaggression and Adjustment Outcomes: A Meta-Analytic and Narrative Review." *Psychological Bulletin* 145, no. 1: 45–78.

Mackenzie, Kwame, and Kamaldeep Buhi. 2007. "Institutional Racism in Mental Health Care." *British Medical Journal* 334, no. 7595: 649–50. doi.org/10.1136/bmj .39163.395972.80.

Mackenzie-Mavinga, Isha. 2016. *The Challenge of Racism in Therapeutic Practice: Engaging with Oppression in Practice and Supervision.* New York: Palgrave.

Madva, Alex. 2019. "Social Psychology, Phenomenology, and the Indeterminate Content of Unreflective Racial Bias." In *Race as Phenomena: Between Phenomenology and Philosophy of Race*, ed. E. S. Lee, 87–106. Lanham, MD: Rowman & Littlefield International.

Maio, Li. 2014. "Discrimination and Psychiatric Disorder Among Asian American Immigrants: A National Analysis by Subgroups." *Journal of Immigrant and Minority Health* 16, no. 6: 1157–66. doi.org/10.1007/s10903-013-9920-7.

Major, Brenda, Alison Blodorn, and Gregory Major Blascovich. 2016. "The Threat of Increasing Diversity: Why Many White Americans Support Trump in the 2016 Presidential Election." *Group Processes and Intergroup Relations* (October 20). doi .org/10.1177/1368430216677304.

Major, Brenda, Cheryl R. Kaiser, Laurie T. O'Brien, and Shannon K. McCoy. 2007. "Perceived Discrimination as Worldview Threat or Worldview Confirmation: Implications for Self-Esteem." *Journal of Personality and Social Psychology* 92, no. 6: 1068–86. doi.org/10.1037/0022-3514.92.6.1068.

Mallinckrodt, Brent, Joe R. Miles, and Jacob J. Levy. 2014. "The Scientist-Practitioner-Advocate Model: Addressing Contemporary Training Needs for Social Justice Advocacy." *Training and Education in Professional Psychology* 8, no. 4: 303–11. doi .org/10.1037/tep0000045.

Malott, Krista M., and Scott Schaefle. 2015. "Addressing Clients' Experiences of Racism: A Model for Clinical Practice." *Journal of Counseling and Development* 93: 361–69. doi.org/10.1002/jcad.12034.

Mandalaywala, Tara M., Gabrielle Ranger-Murdock, David M. Amodio, and Marjorie Rhodes. 2018. "The Nature and Consequences of Essentialist Beliefs About Race in Early Childhood." *Child Development* (April 2018). doi.org/10.1111/cdev.13008.

Marger, Martin. 2015. *Race and Ethnic Relations: American and Global Perspectives*, 10th ed. Stamford, CT: Cengage Learning.

Markus, Hazel Rose, and Shinobu Kitayama. 2010. "Cultures and Selves: A Cycle of Mutual Constitution." *Perspectives on Psychological Science* 5, no. 4: 420–30.

Martín-Baró, Ignacio. 1996. "Public Opinion Research as a De-Ideologizing Instrument." Trans. Jean Carroll and Adrianne Aron. In *Writings for a Liberation Psychology*, by Ignacio Martín-Baró, ed. Adrianne Aron, 186–97. Cambridge, MA: Harvard University Press.

Matter, Sandra. 2010. "Cultural Considerations in Trauma Psychology Education, Research and Training." *Traumatology* 16, no. 4: 48–52. doi.org/10.1177/1534 765610388305.

McClain, Paula Denise, and Jessica D. Johnson Carew. 2018. *"Can We All Get Along": Racial and Ethnic Minorities in American Politics*, 7th ed. New York: Westview.

McConahay, J. B. 1986. "Modern Racism, Ambivalence, and the Modern Racism Scale." In *Prejudice, Discrimination and Racism*, ed. John F. Dovidio and Samuel L. Gaertner, 91–126. New York: Academic.

McKay, Matthew, Jeffrey C. Wood, and Jeffrey Brantley. 2010. *The Dialectical Behavior Therapy Skills Workbook: Practical DBT Exercises for Learning Mindfulness, Interpersonal Effectiveness, Emotion Regulation and Distress Tolerance.* Oakland, CA: New Harbinger Publications.

McKinney, Karyn D. 2013. *Being White: Stories of Race and Racism.* London: Taylor and Francis.

McNeil, Daniel W., Chebon A. Porter, Michael L. Zvolensky, John M. Chaney, and Marvin Kee. 2000. "Assessment of Culturally Related Anxiety in American Indians and Alaska Natives." *Behavior Therapy* 31, no. 2: 301–25. dx.doi.org/10.1016/S0005-7894(00)80017-9.

Mellor, David. 2004. "Responses to Racism: A Taxonomy of Coping Styles Used by Aboriginal Australians." *American Journal of Orthopsychiatry* 74, no. 1: 56–71. doi.org/10.1037/0002-9432.74.1.56.

Melton, Gary B., John Petrila, Norman Godfrey Poythress, Christopher Slobogin, Randy K. Otto, Douglas Mossman, and Lois Oberlander Condie. 2018. *Psychological Evaluations for the Courts: A Handbook for Mental Health Professionals and Lawyers*, 4th ed. New York: Guilford.

Merriam-Webster's Collegiate Dictionary. 2003. 11th ed. Springfield, MA.: Merriam-Webster Inc.

——. 2016. New edition. Springfield, MA.: Merriam-Webster Inc.

Meyer, Ilan H., Sharon Schwartz, and David M. Frost. 2008. "Social Patterning of Stress and Coping: Does Disadvantaged Social Status Confer More Stress and Fewer Coping Resources?" *Social Science and Medicine* 67, no. 3 (August): 368–79.

Milfont, Taciano L., and Ronald Fischer. 2010. "Testing Measurement Invariance Across Groups: Applications in Cross-Cultural Research." *International Journal of Psychological Research* 3, no. 1: 111–30.

Miller, Gregory E., Edith Chen, Alexandra K. Fox, Hope Walker, Alvin Lim, Erin F. Nicholls, Steve Cole, and Michael S. Kobor. 2009. "Low Early-Life Social Class Leaves a Biological Residue Manifested by Decreased Glucocorticoid and Increased Proinflammatory Signaling." PNAS *Proceedings of the National Academy of Sciences of the United States of American* 106, no. 34: 14716–721. doi:10.1073/pnas.0902971106.

Miller, Joshua, and Susan Donner 2000. "More than Just Talk: The Use of Racial Dialogues to Combat Racism." *Social Work with Groups* 23, no. 1: 31–53.

Miller, Joshua, and Ann Marie Garran. 2007. "The Web of Institutional Racism." *Smith College Studies in Social Work* 77, no. 1: 33–67. doi.org/10.1300/J497v77n01_03.

——. 2017. *Racism in the United States: Implications for the Helping Professions.* New York: Springer.

Miller, Matthew J., Brian TaeHyuk Keum, Christina J. Thai, Yun Lu, Nancy N. Truong, Gloria A. Huh, Xu Li, Jeffrey G. Yeung, and Lydia HaRim Ahn. 2018. "Practice Recommendations for Addressing Racism: A Content Analysis of the Counseling Psychology Literature." *Journal of Counseling Psychology* 65, no. 6: 669–80. doi.org/10.1037/cou0000306.

Minsky, Shula, William Vega, Theresa Miskimen, Michael Gara, and Javier Escobar. 2003. "Diagnostic Patterns in Latino, African American, and European American Psychiatric Patients." *Archive of General Psychiatry* 60, no. 6: 637–44. doi:10.1001/archpsyc.60.6.637.

Moane, Geraldine. 2003. "Bridging the Personal and the Political: Practices for a Liberation Psychology." *American Journal of Community Psychology* 31, no. 1–2: 91–101. doi.org/10.1023/A:1023026704576.

Moodley, Roy, Falak Mujtaba, and Sela Kleiman. 2017. "Critical Race Theory and Mental Health." In *Routledge International Handbook of Critical Mental Health*, ed. Bruce M. Z. Cohen. Milton, UK: Taylor and Francis.

Moore-Berg, Samantha L., and Andrew Karpinski. 2019. "An Intersectional Approach to Understanding How Race and Social Class Affect Intergroup Processes." *Social and Personality Psychology Compass* 13, no. 1: 1–14. doi.org.10.1111/spc3.12426

Moradi, Bonnie, and Cristina Risco. 2006. "Perceived Discrimination Experiences and Mental Health of Latina/o American Persons." *Journal of Counseling Psychology* 53, no. 4: 411–21.

Morrison, James R. 2014. *The First Interview.* New York: Guilford.

Moynihan, Daniel Patrick. 1966. "Employment, Income, and the Ordeal of the Negro Family." In *The Negro American*, ed. Talcott Parsons and Kenneth Bancroft Clark, 134–59. Boston: Houghton-Mifflin.

Müller, Jörg M., Christian Postert, Thomas Beyer, Tilman Furniss, and Sandra Achtergarde. 2010. "Comparison of Eleven Short Versions of the Symptom Checklist 90-Revised (SCL-90-R) for Use in the Assessment of General Psychopathology." *Journal of Psychopathology and Behavioral Assessment* 32, no. 2: 246–54. doi.org/10.1007/s10862-009-9141-5.

Murphy, Anne, Miriam Steele, Shanta Rishi Dube, Jordan Bate, Karen Bonuck, Paul Meissner, Hannah Goldman, and Howard Steele. 2014. "Adverse Childhood Experiences (ACEs) Questionnaire and Adult Attachment Interview (AAI): Implications for Parent Child Relationships." *Child Abuse and Neglect* 38, no. 2: 224–33. doi.org/10.1016/j.chiabu.2013.09.004.

Mushonga, Dawnsha R., and Henneberger, Angela K. 2019. "Protective Factors Associated with Positive Mental Health in Traditional and Nontraditional Black Students." *American Journal of Orthopsychiatry* (March 28). dx.doi.org./10/1037/ort0000409.

Mustillo, Sarah, Nancy Kreiger, Erica P. Gunderson, Stephen Sidney, Heather Mc-Creath, and Catarina I. Kiefe. 2004. "Self-Reported Experiences of Racial Discrimination and Black-White Differences in Preterm and Low-Birthweight Deliveries: The CARDIA Study." *American Journal of Public Health* 94: 2125–31. doi.org/10.2105/AJPH.94.12.2125.

Muthén, B., S. H. C. du Toit, and D. Spisic. 1997. "Robust Inference Using Weighted Least Squares and Quadratic Estimating Equations in Latent Variable Modeling with Categorical and Continuous Outcomes." Accepted for publication in *Psychometrika*.

Muthén, L. K., and B. O. Muthén. 2014. Mplus 7.3 (software). Los Angeles: Muthén and Muthén.

Myers, Hector F. 2009. "Ethnicity- and Socio-Economic Status-Related Stresses in Context: An Integrative Review and Conceptual Model." *Journal of Behavioral Medicine* 32, no. 1: 9–19. doi.org/10.1007/s10865-008-9181-4.

Nadal, Kevin L. 2018. *Microaggressions and Traumatic Stress: Theory, Research, and Clinical Treatment.* Washington, DC: American Psychological Association

Nagata, Donna K., Jackie H. Kim, and Teresa U. Nguyen. 2015. "Processing Cultural Trauma: Intergenerational Effects of the Japanese American Incarceration." *Journal of Social Issues* 71, no. 2: 356–70. doi.org/10.1111/josi.12115.

Nagata, Donna K., Jacqueline H. J. Kim, and Kaidi Wu. 2019. "The Japanese American Wartime Incarceration: Examining the Scope of Racial Trauma." *American Psychologist* 74, no. 1: 36–48.

Nagda, Biren (Ratnesh) A., and Ximena Zuniga. 2003. "Fostering Meaningful Racial Engagement Through Intergroup Dialogues." *Group Processes and Intergroup Relations* 6, no. 1: 111–28. doi.org/10.1177/1368430203006001015.

National Association of Social Workers. 2017. "Code of Ethics." www.socialworkers.org/about/ethics/code-of-ethics/code-of-ethics-english.

Neblett, Enrique W. Jr. 2019. "Racism and Health: Challenges and Future Directions in Behavioral and Psychological Research." *Cultural Diversity and Ethnic Minority Psychology* 25, no. 1: 12–20. doi.org/10.1037/cdp0000253.

Neblett, Enrique W., Jr., Donte L. Bernard, and Kira Hudson Banks. 2016. "The Moderating Roles of Gender and Socioeconomic Status in the Association Between Racial Discrimination and Psychological Adjustment." *Cognitive Behavioral Practice* 23, no. 3: 385–97. doi.org/10.1016/j.cbpra.2016.05.002.

Neblett, Enrique W., Jr., Rhonda L. White, Kahlil R. Ford, Cheri L. Philip, Hoa X. Nguyen, and Robert M. Sellers. 2008. "Patterns of Racial Socialization and Psychological Adjustment: Can Parental Communications About Race Reduce the Impact of Racial Discrimination?" *Journal of Research on Adolescence* 18, no. 3: 477–515. doi.org/10.1111/j.1532-7795.2008.00568.x.

Nelson, Camille A. 2006. "Of Eggshells and Thin-Skulls: A Consideration of Racism-Related Mental Illness Impacting Black Women." *International Journal of the Law and Psychiatry* 29:112–36. doi.org/10.1016/j.ijlp.2004.03.012.

Nemeroff, Charles B. 2004. "Neurobiological Consequences of Childhood Trauma." *Journal of Clinical Psychiatry* 65 (Suppl. 1): 18–28.

Neville, Helen A., Germaine H. Awad, James E. Brooks, Michelle P. Flores, and Jamie Bluemel. 2013. "Color-Blind Racial Ideology: Theory, Training and Measurement Implications in Psychology." *American Psychologist* 68, no. 6 (September): 455–66. doi.org/10.1037%2Fa0033282.

Neville, Helen A., Puncky Paul Heppner, and Li-fei Wang. 1997. "Relations Among Racial Identity Attitudes, Perceived Stressors, and Coping Styles in African American College Students." *Journal of Counseling and Development* 75: 303–11. doi.org/10.1002/j.1556-6676.1997.tb02345.x.

Neville, Helen A., Roger L. Worthington, and Lisa B. Spanierman. 2001. "Race, Power, and Multicultural Counseling Psychology: Understanding White Privilege and Color-Blind Racial Attitudes." In *Handbook of Multicultural Counseling*, 2nd ed., ed. Joseph G. Ponterotto et al. (Thousand Oaks, CA: Sage), 257–88.

Newdom, Fred. 2015. "Invitation to the School's Anti-Racism Commitment." Address to incoming students, Smith College. May 31. www.smith.edu/ssw/about/anti-racism-commitment/invitation-schools-anti-racism-commitment.

New York Times Editorial Board. 2015. "Ending the Cycle of Racial Isolation." *New York Times* (editorial), October 17. www.nytimes.com/2015/10/18/opinion/sunday/ending-the-cycle-of-racial-isolation.html.

Nguyen, Ann W., Linda M. Chatters, Robert Joseph Taylor, María P. Aranda, Karen D. Lincoln, and Courtney S. Thomas. 2018. "Discrimination, Serious Psychological Distress, and Church-Based Emotional Support Among African American Men Across the Life Span." *The Journals of Gerontology*, Series B, 73, no. 2: 198–207.

Noh, Samuel, Violet Kaspar, and Kandauda A. S. Wickrama. 2007. "Overt and Subtle Racial Discrimination and Mental Health: Preliminary Findings for Korean Immigrants." *American Journal of Public Health* 97, no. 7: 1269–74. doi.org/10.2105/AJPH.2005.085316.

Norcross, John. C., and Bruce E. Wampold. 2019. "Relationships and Responsiveness in the Psychological Treatment of Trauma: The Tragedy of the APA Clinical Practice Guideline." *Psychotherapy*. Advance online publication (April 22). dx.doi.org/10.1037/pst0000228

Norris, Fran H. 1992. "Epidemiology of Trauma Frequency and Impact of Different Potentially Traumatic Events on Different Demographic Groups." *Journal of Consulting and Clinical Psychology* 60, no. 3: 409–18.

Norris, Fran H., Matthew J. Friedman, Patricia J. Watson, Christopher M. Byrne, Eolia Diaz, and Krys Kaniasty. 2002. "60,000 Disaster Victims Speak: Part I. An

Empirical Review of the Empirical Literature, 1981–2001." *Psychiatry* 65, no. 3: 207–39.

Oh, Hans, Courtney D. Cogburn, Deidre Anglin, Ellen P. Lukens, and Jordan E. DeVylder. 2016. "Major Discriminatory Events and Risk for Psychotic Experiences Among Black Americans." *American Journal of Orthopsychiatry* 86, no. 3: 277–85. doi.org/10.1037/ort0000158.

Oh, Hans, Andrew Stickley, Ai Koyanagi, Rebecca Yau, and Jordan E. Devylder. 2019. "Discrimination and Suicidality Among Racial and Ethnic Minorities in the United States." *Journal of Affective Disorders* 245: 517–23.

Okazaki, Sumie. 2009. "Impact of Racism on Ethnic Minority Mental Health." *Perspectives on Psychological Science* 4, no. 1: 103–7. doi.org/10.1111/j.1745-6924.2009 .01099.x.

Oldfield, Janine, and Theresa Jackson. 2019. "Childhood Abuse or Trauma: A Racial Perspective." *Children Australia* 44, no. 1: 42–48.

Omi, Michael, and Howard Winant. 1994. *Racial Formation in the United States: From the 1960s to the 1990s*, 2nd ed. New York: Routledge.

Ong, Anthony D., Thomas E. Fuller-Rowell, and Anthony L. Burrow. 2009. "Racial Discrimination and the Stress Process." *Journal of Personality and Social Psychology* 96, no. 6: 1259–71. doi.org/10.1037/a0015335.

Ortiz, Larry, and Jayshree Jani. 2010. "Critical Race Theory: A Transformational Model for Teaching Diversity." *Journal of Social Work Education* 46, no. 2: 175–93. doi.org/10.5175/JSWE.2010.200900070.

Oswald, Frederick L., Gregory Mitchell, Hart Blanton, James Jaccard, and Philip E. Tetlock. 2013. "Predicting Ethnic and Racial Discrimination: A Meta-Analysis of IAT Criterion Studies." *Journal of Personality and Social Psychology* 105, no. 2: 171–92. doi.org/10.1037/a0032734.

Pachter, Lee M., and Cynthia Garcia Coll. 2009. "Racism and Child Health: A Review of the Literature and Future Directions." *Journal of Developmental and Behavioral Pediatrics* 30, no. 3: 255–63. dx.doi.org/10.1097%2FDBP.0b013e3181a7 ed5a.

Palatini, Paolo, and Stevo Julius. 1997. "Heart Rate and Cardiovascular Risk." *Journal of Hypertension* 15, no. 1: 3–17.

Paradies, Yin. 2006. "A Systematic Review of Empirical Research on Self-Reported Racism and Health." *International Journal of Epidemiology* 35, no. 4: 888–901.

Paradies, Yin, Jehonathan Ben, Nida Denson, Amanuel Elias, Naomi Priest, Alex Pieterse, Arpana Gupta, Margaret Kelaher, and Gilbert Gee. 2015. "Racism as a Determinant of Health: A Systematic Review and Meta-Analysis." *PloS one* 10, no. 9: 1–48. doi:10.137/journal.pone.0138511.

Park, Irene J. K., Lijuan Wang, David R. Williams, and Margarita Alegria. 2017. "Does Anger Regulation Mediate the Discrimination–Mental Health Link Among Mexican-Origin Adolescents? A Longitudinal Mediation Analysis Using

Multilevel Modeling." *Developmental Psychology* 53, no. 2: 340–52. doi.org/10.1037/devoooo235.

Pascoe, Elizabeth A., and Laura Smart Richman. 2009. "Perceived Discrimination and Health: A Meta-Analytic Review." *Psychological Bulletin* 135, no. 4: 531–54. doi.org/10.1037%2Fa0016059.

Pearl, Robert. 2015. "Why Health Care Is Different If You're Black, Latino or Poor." *Forbes*, March 5. www.forbes.com/sites/robertpearl/2015/03/05/healthcare-black-latino-poor/#152a3ffa7869.

Pedersen, Paul. 2005. "The Importance of 'Cultural Psychology' Theory for Multicultural Counselors." In *Handbook of Racial-Cultural Psychology and Counseling*, vol. 1, *Theory and Research*, ed. Robert T. Carter, 3–16. New York: Wiley.

Perilla, Julia L., Fran H. Norris, and Evelyn A. Lavizzo. 2002. "Ethnicity, Culture, and Disaster Response: Identifying and Explaining Ethnic Differences in PTSD Six Months After Hurricane Andrew." *Journal of Social and Clinical Psychology* 21, no. 1: 20–45.

Perrin, Paul B. 2013. "Humanistic Psychology's Social Justice Philosophy: Systemically Treating the Psychosocial and Health Effects of Racism." *Journal of Humanistic Psychology* 53, no. 1: 52–69. doi.org/10.1177/0022167812447133.

Peters, Rosalind M. 2004. "Racism and Hypertension Among African Americans." *Western Journal of Nursing Research* 26: 612–31. doi.org/10.1177/0193945904265816.

Pettigrew, Thomas F. 2017. "Social Psychological Perspectives on Trump Supporters." *Journal of Social and Political Psychology* 5, no. 1: 107–16. doi.org/10.5964/jspp.v5i1.750.

Pew Research Center. 2016. "On Views of Race and Inequality, Blacks and Whites Are Worlds Apart." June 27. www.pewsocialtrends.org/2016/06/27/on-views-of-race-and-inequality-blacks-and-whites-are-worlds-apart/.

——. 2017. "The Partisan Divide on Political Values Grows Even Wider." October 5. www.people-press.org/2017/10/05/the-partisan-divide-on-political-values-grows-even-wider/.

Phelps, Randy, James H. Bray, and Lisa K. Kearney. 2017. "A Quarter Century of Psychological Practice in Mental Health and Health Care: 1990–2016." *American Psychologist* 72, no. 8: 822–36. psycnet.apa.org/doi/10.1037/amp0000192.

Phinney, Jean S. 1996. "When We Talk About American Ethnic Groups, What Do We Mean?" *American Psychologist* 51, no. 9: 918–27. doi.org/10.1037/0003-066X.51.9.918.

Pieper, Suzanne, Jos F. Brosschot, Rien van der Leeden, and Julian E. Thayer. 2010. "Prolonged Cardiac Effects of Momentary Assessed Stressful Events and Worry Episodes." *Psychosomatic Medicine* 72: 570–707.

Pieterse, Alex L. 2018. "Attending to Racial Trauma in Clinical Supervision: Enhancing Client and Supervisee Outcomes." *Clinical Supervisor* 37, no. 1: 204–20. doi.org/10.1080/07325223.2018.1443304.

Pieterse, Alex L., and Robert T. Carter. 2007. "An Examination of the Relationship Between General Life Stress, Racism-Related Stress and Psychological Health Among Black Men." *Journal of Counseling Psychology* 54, no. 1: 102–9. doi:10.1037/0022-0167.54.1.101.

——. 2010. "The Role of Racial Identity in Perceived Racism and Psychological Stress Among Black American Adults: Exploring Traditional and Alternative Approaches." *Journal of Applied Social Psychology* 40, no. 5: 1028–53. doi.org/10.1111 /j.1559-1816.2010.00609.x.

Pieterse, Alex L., Robert T. Carter, Sarah A. Evans, and Rebecca A. Walter. 2010. "An Exploratory Examination of the Associations Among Racial and Ethnic Discrimination, Racial Climate, and Trauma-Related Symptoms in a College Student Population." *Journal of Counseling Psychology* 57, no. 3: 255–63.

Pieterse, Alex L., Robert T. Carter, and Kilynda A. Ray. 2013. "The Relationship Between Perceived Racism, Stress, and Psychological Functioning Among Black Women." *Journal of Multicultural Counseling and Development* 41: 36–46. doi .org/10.1002/j.2161-1912.2013.00025.x.

Pieterse, Alex L., Sarah A. Evans, Amelia Risner-Butner, Noah M. Collins, and Laura Beth Mason. 2009. "Multicultural Competence and Social Justice Training in Counseling Psychology and Counselor Education: A Review and Analysis of a Sample of Multicultural Course Syllabi." *Counseling Psychologist* 37, no. 1: 93–115. doi.org/10.1177/0011000008319986.

Pieterse, Alex L., Minsun Lee, and Alexa Fetzer. 2016. "Racial Group Membership and Multicultural Training: Examining the Experiences of Counseling and Counseling Psychology Students." *International Journal for the Advancement of Counselling* 38, no. 1: 28–47. doi.org/10.1007%2Fs10447-015-9254-3.

Pieterse, Alex L., and Shantel Powell. 2016. "A Theoretical Overview of the Impact of Racism on People of Color." In *The Cost of Racism for People of Color: Contextualizing Experiences of Discrimination*, ed. Alvin N. Alvarez, Christopher T. H. Liang, and Helen A. Neville, 11–30. Washington, DC: American Psychological Association.

Pieterse, Alex L., Nathan R. Todd, Helen A. Neville, and Robert T. Carter. 2012. "Perceived Racism and Mental Health Among Black American Adults: A Meta-Analytic Review." *Journal of Counseling Psychology* 59, no. 1 (January): 1–9. doi .org/10.1037/a0026208.

Plummer, Deborah L., and Steve Slane. 1996. "Patterns of Coping in Racially Stressful Situations." *Journal of Black Psychology* 22, no. 3: 302–15. doi.org/10.1177 /00957984960223002.

Polanco-Roman, Lillian, Ashley Allison Danies, and Deidre M. Anglin. 2016. "Racial Discrimination as Race-Based Trauma, Coping Strategies and Dissociative Symptoms Among Emerging Adults." *Psychological Trauma: Theory, Research, Practice, and Policy* 8, no. 5: 609–17. doi.org/10.1037/tra0000125.

Pole, Nnamdi, Suzanne R. Best, Thomas Metzler, and Charles R. Marmar. 2005. "Why Are Hispanics at Greater Risk for PTSD?" *Cultural Diversity and Ethnic Minority Psychology* 11, no. 2: 144–61. doi.org/10.1037/1099-9809.11.2.144.

Pole, Nnamdi, Laurie Fields, and Wendy D'Andrea. 2016. "Stress and Trauma Disorders." In APA *Handbook of Clinical Psychology*, vol. 4, *Psychopathology and Health*, ed. John C. Norcross, Gary R. VandenBos, and Donald K. Freedheim, 97–133. Washington, DC: American Psychological Association.

Presseau, Candice, Linh P. Luu, Arpana G. Inman, and Cirleen DeBlaere. 2019. "Trainee Social Justice Advocacy: Investigating the Roles of Training Factors and Multicultural Competence." *Counselling Psychology Quarterly* 32, no. 2: 260–74. doi.org/10.1080/09515070.2018.1476837.

Priest, Naomi, Yin Paradies, Brigid Trenerry, Mandy Truong, Saffron Karlsen, and Yvonne Kelly. 2013. "A Systematic Review of Studies Examining the Relationship Between Reported Racism and Health and Wellbeing for Children and Young People." *Social Science and Medicine* 95: 115–27. doi.org/10.1016/j.socscimed .2012.11.031.

Priest, Naomi, Jessica Walton, Fiona White, Emma Kowal, Alison Baker, and Yin Paradies. 2014. "Understanding the Complexities of Ethnic-Racial Socialization Processes for Both Minority and Majority Groups: A 30-Year Systematic Review." *International Journal of Intercultural Relations* 43, part B (November): 139–55. doi .org/10.1016/j.ijintrel.2014.08.003.

Prilleltensky, Isaac. 1997. "Values, Assumptions, and Practices: Assessing the Moral Implications of Psychological Discourse and Action." *American Psychologist* 52, no. 5: 517–35. psycnet.apa.org/doi/10.1037/0003-066X.52.5.517.

Pumariega, Andres J. 2016. "The Reaction to Historical Trauma Among Minority Youth." *Journal of the American Academy of Child and Adolescent Psychiatry* 55, no. 10: S48 doi.org/10.1016/j.jaac.2016.07.624.

Range, B., D. Gutierrez, C. Gamboni, N. A. Hough, and A. Wojciak. 2017. "Mass Trauma in the African American Community: Using Multiculturalism to Build Resilient Systems." *Contemporary Family Therapy* (December): 1–15. dx.doi.org /10.1007/s10591-017-9449-3.

Ratts, Manivong J., and Paul B. Pedersen. 2014. *Counseling for Multiculturalism and Social Justice: Integration, Theory, and Application*, 4th ed. Alexandria, VA: American Counseling Association.

Rea, Louis M., and Richard Allen Parker. 2014. *Designing and Conducting Survey Research: A Comprehensive Guide*. San Francisco: Jossey-Bass.

Reynolds, Jamila E., and Melinda A. Gonzales-Backen. 2017. "Ethnic-Racial Socialization and the Mental Health of African Americans: A Critical Review." *Journal of Family Theory and Review* 9, no. 2: 182–200. dx.doi.org/10.1111/jftr.12192.

Rhemtulla, Mijke, Patricia E. Brosseau-Liard, and Victoria Savalei. 2012. "When Can Categorical Variables Be Tested as Continuous? A Comparison of Robust Continuous and Categorical Sem Estimation Methods Under Suboptimal Conditions." *Psychological Methods* 17, no. 3: 354–73. dx.doi.org/10.1037/a0029315.

Ricco, Judith Nihill de, and Daniel T. Sciarra. 2005. "The Immersion Experience in Multicultural Counselor Training: Confronting Covert Racism." *Journal of Multicultural Counseling and Development* 33, no. 1: 2–16. doi.org/10.1002/j .2161-1912.2005.tb00001.x.

Richards, Graham. 2012. *"Race," Racism and Psychology: Towards a Reflexive History.* New York: Routledge.

Roberts, Andrea L., Bruce P. Dohrenwend, Allison E. Aiello, Rosalind J. Wright, Andreas Maercher, Sandro Galea, Karestan C. Koenen. 2012. "The Stressor Criterion for Posttraumatic Stress Disorder: Does It Matter?" *Journal of Clinical Psychiatry* 73: 264–70. doi:10.4088/JCP.11m07054.

Roberts, Andrea L., Stephan E. Gilman, Joshua Breslau, Naomi Breslau, and K. C. Koenen. 2011. "Race/Ethnic Differences in Exposure to Traumatic Events, Development of Post-Traumatic Stress Disorder, and Treatment-Seeking for Post-Traumatic Stress Disorder in the United States." *Psychological Medicine* 41, no. 1: 71–83.

Robinson-Perez, Ada, Miesha Marzell, and Woojae Han. 2019. "Racial Microaggressions and Psychological Distress Among Undergraduate College Students of Color: Implications for Social Work Practice." *Clinical Social Work Journal* (June 1): 1–8. http://search.proquest.com/docview/2234287302/.

Rodi-Risberg, Marinella, and J. Roger Kurtz. 2018. "Problems in Representing Trauma." In *Trauma and Literature*, ed. J. Roger Kurtz, 110–23. Cambridge, UK: Cambridge University Press.

Rollock, David, and Edmund W. Gordon. 2000. "Racism and Mental Health into the 21st Century: Perspectives and Parameters." *American Journal of Orthopsychiatry* 70: 5–16. doi.org/10.1037/h0087703.

Romano, John L., and Sally M. Hage. 2000. "Prevention and Counseling Psychology: Revitalizing Commitments for the 21st Century." *Counseling Psychologist* 28, no. 6: 733–63. doi.org/10.1177/0011000000286001.

Root, Maria P. P. 1992. "Reconstructing the Impact of Trauma on Personality." *Personality and Psychopathology: Feminist Reappraisals*, ed. Laura S. Brown and Mary Ballou, 229–65. New York: Guilford.

Rothstein, Richard. 2017. *The Color of Law: A Forgotten History of How Our Government Segregated America.* New York: Liveright.

Rushton, J. Philippe, and Elizabeth W. Rushton. 2003. "Brain Size, IQ, and Racial-Group Differences: Evidence from Musculoskeletal Traits." *Intelligence* 31, no. 2: 139–55. doi.org/10.1016/S0160-2896(02)00137-X.

Rutenberg, Jim. 2015. "A Dream Undone: Inside the 50-Year Campaign to Roll Back the Voting Rights Act." *New York Times Magazine*, July 29. www.nytimes.com/2015 /07/29/magazine/voting-rights-act-dream-undone.html.

Ryff, Carol D., Corey L. M. Keyes, and Diane L. Hughes. 2003. "Status Inequalities, Perceived Discrimination, and Eudaimonic Well-Being: Do the Challenges of Minority Life Hone Purpose and Growth?" *Journal of Health and Social Behavior* 44, no. 3: 275–91. www.jstor.org/stable/1519779.

Sanchez, Delida, Whitney N. Adams, Sarah C. Arango, and Alaina E. Flannigan. 2018. "Racial-Ethnic Microaggressions, Coping Strategies, and Mental Health in Asian American and Latinx American College Students: A Mediation Model." *Journal of Counseling Psychology* 65, no. 2: 214–25. doi.org/10.1037/cou0000249.

Sanchez, Delida, Keisha L. Bentley-Edwards, J. S. Matthews, and Teresa Granillo. 2016. "Exploring Divergent Patterns in Racial Identity Profiles Between Caribbean Black American and African American Adolescents: The Links to Perceived Discrimination and Psychological Concerns." *Journal of Multicultural Counseling and Development* 44, no. 4: 285–304. doi.org/10.1002/jmcd.12054.

Sanchez, Delida, Leann Smith, and Whitney Adams. 2018. "The Relationships Among Perceived Discrimination, Marianismo Gender Role Attitudes, Racial-Ethnic Socialization, Coping Styles, and Mental Health Outcomes in Latina College Students." *Journal of Latina/o Psychology* 6, no. 1: 1–15. doi.org/10.1037/lat0000077.

Sanchez, Diana T., Mary S. Himmelstein, Danielle M. Young, Analai F. Albuja, and Julie A. Garcia. 2016. "Confronting as Autonomy Promotion: Speaking Up Against Discrimination and Psychological Well-Being in Racial Minorities." *Journal of Health Psychology* 21, no. 9: 1999–2007. doi.org/10.1177/1359105315569619.

Sanders-Phillips, Kathy, Wendy Kliewer, Taqi Tirmazi, Von Nebbit, Takisha Carter, and Heather Key. 2014. "Perceived Racial Discriminations, Drug Use, and Psychological Distress in African American Youth: A Pathway to Child Health Disparities." *Journal of Social Issues* 70, no. 2: 279–97.

Sarafino, Edward P., and Timothy W. Smith. 2014. *Health Psychology: Biopsychosocial Interactions*, 8th ed. Hoboken, NJ: Wiley.

Sawyer, Pamela J., Brenda Major, Bettina J. Casad, Sarah S. Townsend, and Wendy Berry Mendes. 2012. "Discrimination and the Stress Response: Psychological and Physiological Consequences of Anticipating Prejudice in Interethnic Interactions." *American Journal of Public Health* 102, no. 5: 1020–26. doi.org/10.2105/AJPH.2011.300620.

Schaffner, Brian F., Matthew Macwilliams, and Tatishe Nteta. 2018. "Understanding White Polarization in the 2016 Vote for President: The Sobering Role of Racism and Sexism." *Political Science Quarterly* 133, no. 1: 9–34. doi.org/10.1002/polq.12737.

Schatell, Elena. 2017. "Challenging Multicultural Disparities in Mental Health." National Alliance on Mental Illness. July 10. www.nami.org/Blogs/NAMI-Blog/July-2017/Challenging-Multicultural-Disparities-in-Mental-He.

Schmitt, Michael Thomas, Nyla R. Branscombe, Tom Postmes, and Amber Garcia. 2014. "The Consequences of Perceived Discrimination for Psychological Well-

Being: A Meta-Analytic Review." *Psychological Bulletin* 140, no. 4: 921–48. doi .org/10.1037/a0035754.

Schreiber, James B., Amaury Nora, Frances K. Stage, Elizabeth A. Barlow, and Jamie King. 2006. "Reporting Structural Equation Modeling and Confirmatory Factor Analysis Results: A Review." *Journal of Educational Research* 99, no. 6: 323–38. doi.org/10.3200/JOER.99.6.323-338.

Schumacker, Randall E., and Richard G. Lomax. 2004. *A Beginner's Guide to Structural Equation Modeling*, 2nd ed. Mahwah, NJ: Lawrence Erlbaum.

Scott, Lionel D., Jr. 2003a. "Cultural Orientation and Coping with Perceived Discrimination Among African American Youth." *Journal of Black Psychology* 29, no. 3: 235–56. doi.org/10.1177/0095798403254213.

——. 2003b. "The Relation of Racial Identity and Racial Socialization to Coping with Discrimination Among African American Adolescents." *Journal of Black Studies* 33, no. 4: 520–38. doi.org/10.1177/0021934702250035.

Scurfield, Raymond Monsour, and David W. Mackey. 2001. "Racism, Trauma and Positive Aspects of Exposure to Race-Related Experiences: Assessment and Treatment Implications." *Journal of Ethnic and Cultural Diversity in Social Work* 10, no. 1: 23–47.

Seawell, Asani H., Carolyn E. Cutrona, and Daniel W. Russell. 2014. "The Effects of General Social Support and Social Support for Racial Discrimination on African American Women's Well-Being." *Journal of Black Psychology* 40, no. 1: 3–26. doi.org/10.1177/0095798412469227.

Segerstrom, Suzanne C., Jaime K. Hardy, Daniel R. Evans, and Natalie F. Winters. 2012. "Pause and Plan: Self-Regulation and the Heart." In *How Motivation Affects Cardiovascular Response: Mechanism and Applications*, ed. Rex A. Wright and Guido H. E. Gendolla, 181–98. New York: American Psychological Association.

Sellers, Robert M., Cleopatra Howard Caldwell, Karen H. Schmeelk-Cone, and Marc Zimmerman. 2003. "Racial Identity, Racial Discrimination, Perceived Stress, and Psychological Distress Among African American Young Adults." *Journal of Health and Social Behavior* 44, no. 3: 302–17. doi.org/10.2307/1519781.

Sellers, Robert M., and J. Nicole Shelton. 2003. "The Role of Racial Identity in Perceived Racial Discrimination." *Journal of Personality and Social Psychology* 84, no. 5: 1079–92. doi.org/10.1037/0022-3514.84.5.1079.

Sellers, Robert M., Mia A. Smith, J. Nicole Shelton, Stephanie, A. J. Rowley, and Tabbye M. Chavous. 1998. "Multidimensional Model of Racial Identity: A Reconceptualization of African American Racial Identity." *Personality and Social Psychology Review* 2, no. 1: 18–39.

Sellers, Sherrill L., Vence Bonham, Harold W. Neighbors, and James W. Amell. 2009. "Effects and Health Behaviors on Mental and Physical Health of Middle-Class African American Men." *Health Education and Behavior* 36, no. 1: 31–44. doi.org/10.1177/1090198106293526.

Shavers, Vickie L., William M. P. Klein, and Pebbles Fagan. 2012. "Research on Race/Ethnicity and Health Care Discrimination: Where We Are and Where We Need to Go." *American Journal of Public Health* 102, no. 5: 930–32. doi.org/10.2105/AJPH.2012.300708.

Sherry, Alissa, and Robin K. Henson. 2005. "Conducting and Interpreting Canonical Correlation Analysis in Personality Research: A User-Friendly Primer." *Journal of Personality Assessment* 84, no. 1: 37–48.

Shorter-Gooden, Kumea. 2004. "Multiple Resistance Strategies: How African American Women Cope with Racism and Sexism." *Journal of Black Psychology* 30, no. 3: 406–25. doi.org/10.1177/0095798404266050.

Sibrava, Nicholas J., Andri S. Bjornsson, Benítez A. Pérez, Carlos I. Moitra, Ethan Weisberg, B. Risa, and Martin B. Keller. 2019. "Posttraumatic Stress Disorder in African American and Latinx Adults: Clinical Course and the Role of Racial and Ethnic Discrimination." *American Psychologist* 74, no. 1: 101–16.

Siegel, Matthew P., and Robert T. Carter. 2014. "Emotions and White Racial Identity Status Attitudes." *Journal of Multicultural Counseling and Development* 42, no. 3: 218–31. doi.org/10.1002/j.2161-1912.2014.00056.x.

Silverstein, Jake. 2019. "Editor's Note: The 1619 Project." *New York Times Magazine*, August 20, 4–5.

Simons, Ronald L., Man-Kit Lei, Steven R. H. Beach, Ashley B. Barr, Leslie G. Simons, Frederick X. Gibbons, and Robert A. Philibert. 2018. "Discrimination, Segregation, and Chronic Inflammation: Testing the Weathering Explanation for the Poor Health of Black Americans." *Developmental Psychology* 54, no. 10: 1993–2006. search.proquest.com/docview/2155147166/.

Singletary, Gilbert. 2019. "Beyond PTSD: Black Male Fragility in the Context of Trauma." *Journal of Aggression, Maltreatment, and Trauma.* doi.org/10.1080/10926771.2019.1600091

Skewes, Monica C., and Arthur W. Blume. 2019. "Understanding the Link Between Racial Trauma and Substance Use Among American Indians." *American Psychologist* 74, no. 1: 88–100.

Slife, Brent D., Kari A. O'Grady, and Russell D. Kosits, eds. 2017. *The Hidden Worldviews of Psychology's Theory, Research, and Practice.* New York: Routledge.

Smedley, Audrey, and Brian D. Smedley. 2005. "Race as Biology Is Fiction, Racism as a Social Problem Is Real: Anthropological and Historical Perspectives on the Social Construction of Race." *American Psychologist* 60, no. 1: 16. doi.org/10.1037/0003-066X.60.1.16.

——. 2012. *Race in North America: Origin and Evolution of a Worldview*, 4th ed. Boulder, CO: Westview.

Smedley, Brian D., Adrienne Y. Stith, and Alan R. Nelson, eds. 2003. *Unequal Treatment: Confronting Racial and Ethnic Disparities in Health Care.* Washington, D.C.: National Academies Press.

Smiley, Calvin John, and David Fakunle. "From 'Brute' to 'Thug': The Demonization and Criminalization of Unarmed Black Male Victims in America." *Journal of Human Behavior in the Social Environment* 26, no. 3–4 (2016): 350–66. dx.doi .org/10.1080/10911359.2015.1129256.

Smith, Glenn P. 1997. "Assessment of Malingering with Self-Report Measures." In *Clinical Assessment of Malingering and Deception*, 2nd ed., ed. Richard Rogers, 351–70. New York: Guilford.

Smith, Lance C., and Richard Q. Shin. 2008. "Social Privilege, Social Justice, and Group Counseling: An Inquiry." *The Journal for Specialists in Group Work* 33, no. 4: 351–66.

Smith, Laura, Madonna G. Constantine, Sheila V. Graham, and Chelsea B. Dize. 2008. "The Territory Ahead for Multicultural Competence: The 'Spinning' of Racism." *Professional Psychology: Research and Practice* 39, no. 3: 337–45. doi.org /10.1037/0735-7028.39.3.337.

Smith, Veronica J., Tracie Stewart, Ashley C. Myers, and Ioana M. Latu. 2008. "Implicit Coping Responses to Racism Predict African Americans' Level of Psychological Distress." *Basic and Applied Social Psychology*, 30: 246–77. doi.org/10.1080 /01973530802375110.

Sommers-Flanagan, John, and Rita Sommers-Flanagan. 2016. *Clinical Interviewing*, 6th ed. Hoboken, NJ: Wiley.

Sommers-Flanagan, John, and Rita Sommers-Flanagan. 2018. *Counseling and Psychotherapy Theories in Context and Practice: Skills, Strategies and Techniques*, 3rd ed. Hoboken, NJ: Wiley.

Sotero, Michelle. 2006. "A Conceptual Model of Historical Trauma: Implications for Public Health Practice and Research." *Journal of Health Disparities Research and Practice* 1, no. 1: 93–108. https://ssrn.com/abstract=1350062.

Speight, Suzette L. 2007. "Internalized Racism: One More Piece of the Puzzle." *Counseling Psychologist* 35, no. 1: 126–34.

Stanton, Jeffrey M., Evan F. Sinar, William K. Balzer, and Patricia C. Smith. 2002. "Issues and Strategies for Reducing the Length of Self-Report Scales." *Personnel Psychology* 55, no. 1: 167–94. doi.org/10.1111/j.1744-6570.2002.tb00108.x.

Stefan, Susan. 1994. "The Protection Racket: Rape Trauma Syndrome, Psychiatric Labeling, and the Law." *Northwestern University Law Review* 88, no. 4: 1271–346.

Sternthal, Michelle J., Natalie Slopen, and David R. Williams. 2011. "Racial Disparities in Health: How Much Does Stress Really Matter?" *Du Bois Review* 8, no. 1: 95–113.

Stevenson, Howard Carlton, and Edith G. Arrington. 2009. "Racial/Ethnic Socialization Mediates Perceived Racism and the Racial Identity of African American Adolescents." *Cultural Diversity and Ethnic Minority Psychology* 15: 125–36. doi .org/10.1037/a0015500.

Stewart, Edward C., and Milton J. Bennett. 2005. *American Cultural Patterns: A Cross-Cultural Perspective.* 2nd ed. London: Nicholas Brealey.

Stewart, Suzanne L., Roy Moodley, and Ashley Hyatt, eds. 2016. *Indigenous Cultures and Mental Health Counselling: Four Directions for Integration with Counselling Psychology.* New York: Routledge.

Stoudt, Brett G., Madeline Fox, and Michelle Fine. 2012. "Contesting Privilege with Critical Participatory Action Research." *Journal of Social Issues* 68, no. 1: 178–93. doi.org/10.1111/j.1540-4560.2011.01743.x.

Strier, Roni. 2006. "Anti-Oppressive Research in Social Work: A Preliminary Definition." *British Journal of Social Work* 37, no. 5: 857–71. doi.org/10.1093/bjsw/bcl062.

Substance Abuse and Mental Health Services Administration (SAMHSA). 2015. *Racial/Ethnic Differences in Mental Health Service Use Among Adults.* Washington, DC: SAMHSA.

Sue, Derald Wing. 2003. *Overcoming Our Racism: The Journey to Liberation.* San Francisco: Jossey-Bass.

Sue, Derald Wing, Patricia Arredondo, and Roderick J. McDavis. 1992. "Multicultural Counseling Competencies and Standards: A Call to the Profession." *Journal of Counseling and Development* 70, no. 4: 477–86. doi.org/10.1002/j.1556-6676.1992.tb01642.x.

Sue, Derald Wing, Rosie P. Bingham, Lisa Porché-Burke, and Melba J. T. Vasquez. 1999. "The Diversification of Psychology: A Multicultural Revolution." *American Psychologist* 54, no. 12: 1061–69. dx.doi.org/10.1037/0003-066X.54.12.1061.

Sue, Derald Wing, Christina M. Capodilupo, Gina C. Torino, Jennifer M. Bucceri, Aisha Holder, Kevin L. Nadal, and Marta Esquilin. 2007. "Racial Microaggressions in Everyday Life: Implications for Clinical Practice." *American Psychologist* 62: 271–86. doi.org/10.1037/0003-066X.62.4.271.

Sue, Derald Wing, Robert T. Carter, J. Manuel Casas, Nadya A. Fouad, Allen E. Ivey, Margaret Jensen, Teresa LaFromboise, Jeanne E. Manese, Joseph G. Ponterotto, and Ena Vazquez-Nutall. 1998. *Multicultural Counseling Competencies: Individual and Organizational Development.* Thousand Oaks, CA: Sage.

Sue, Derald Wing, and David Sue. 2015. *Counseling the Culturally Diverse: Theory and Practice.* 7th ed. Hoboken, NJ: Wiley.

Sue, Derald Wing, David Sue, Helen Neville, and Laura Smith. 2019. *Counseling the Culturally Diverse: Theory and Practice,* 8th ed. Hoboken, NJ: Wiley.

Szymanski, Dawn M., and Jioni A. Lewis. 2015. "Race-Related Stress and Racial Identity as Predictors of African American Activism." *Journal of Black Psychology* 41, no. 1: 170–91. doi.org/10.1177/0095798414520707.

Taylor, Shelley E. 2010. "Mechanisms Linking Early Life Stress to Adult Health Outcomes." *Proceedings of the National Academy of Sciences* 107, no. 19: 8507–12.

——. 2015. *Health Psychology,* 9th ed. Boston: McGraw-Hill.

Taylor, Teletia R., Carla D. Williams, Kepher H. Makambi, Charles Mouton, Jules P. Harrell, Yvette Cozier, Julie R. Palmer, Lynn Rosenberg, and Lucille L. Adams-Campbell. 2007. "Racial Discrimination and Breast Cancer Incidence in US Black Women." *American Journal of Epidemiology* 166, no. 1: 46–54. doi.org /10.1093/aje/kwm056.

Thai, Christina J., Heather Z. Lyons, Matthew R. Lee, and Michiko M. Iwasaki. 2017. "Microaggressions and Self-Esteem in Emerging Asian American Adults: The Moderating Role of Racial Socialization." *Asian American Journal of Psychology* 8, no. 2: 82–93. doi.org/10.1037/aap0000079.

Thayer, Julian F., Anita L. Hansen, Evelyn Saus-Rose, and Bjorn Helge Johnsen. 2009. "Heart Rate Variability, Prefrontal Neural Function, and Cognitive Performance: The Neurovisceral Integration Perspective on Self-Regulation, Adaptation, and Health." *Annals of Behavioral Medicine* 37, no. 2 (April): 141–53. doi:10.1007/s12160-009-9101-z.

Thoits, Peggy A. 2010. "Stress and Health: Major Findings and Policy Implications." *Journal of Health and Social Behavior* 51, no. 1 (Suppl.): S41–S53.

Thompson, Anita Jones, Karen McCurtis Witherspoon, and Suzette L. Speight. 2008. "Gendered Racism, Psychological Distress, and Coping Styles of African American Women." *Cultural Diversity and Ethnic Minority Psychology* 14, no. 4: 307–14. doi.org/10.1037/1099-9809.14.4.307.

Thompson, Chalmer E., and Robert T. Carter, eds. 2012 [1997]. *Racial Identity Theory: Applications to Individual, Group, and Organizational Interventions.* New York: Routledge.

Thompson, Chalmer E., and Helen A. Neville. 1999. "Racism, Mental Health, and Mental Health Practice." *Counseling Psychologist* 27, no. 2: 155–223.

Thompson, Vetta L. Sanders. 2006. "Coping Responses and the Experience of Discrimination." *Journal of Applied Social Psychology* 36, no. 5: 1198–214. doi.org/10 .1111/j.0021-9029.2006.00038.x.

Thompson, Vetta L. Sanders, Anita Bazile, and Maysa Akbar. 2004. "African Americans' Perceptions of Psychotherapy and Psychotherapists." *Professional Psychology: Research and Practice* 35, no. 1: 19–26. doi.org/10.1037/0735-7028 .35.1.19.

Thornton, John K. 2012. A *Cultural History of the Atlantic World 1250–1820.* New York: Cambridge University Press.

Torino, Gina C. 2015. "Examining Biases and White Privilege: Classroom Teaching Strategies That Promote Cultural Competence." *Women and Therapy* 38, no. 3–4: 295–307. doi.org/10.1080/02703149.2015.1059213.

Tormala, Teceta Thomas, Sita G. Patel, Ellen E. Soukup, and Annette V. Clarke. 2018. "Developing Measurable Cultural Competence and Cultural Humility: An Application of the Cultural Formulation." *Training and Education in Professional Psychology* 12, no. 1: 54–61. dx.doi.org/10.1037/tep0000183.

Torres, Lucas, Mark W. Driscoll, and Maria Voell. 2012. "Discrimination, Acculturation, Acculturative Stress, and Latino Psychological Distress: A Moderated Mediational Model." *Cultural Diversity and Ethnic Minority Psychology* 18: 17–25.
doi.org/10.1037/a0026710.

Townsend, Sarah S., Dina Eliezer, Brenda Major, Wendy Barry Mendes. 2014. "Influencing the World Versus Adjusting to Constraints: Social Class Moderates Responses to Discrimination." *Social Psychological and Personality Science* 5, no. 2:
226–34. doi.org/10.1177/1948550613490968.

Triana, María del Carmen, Mevan Jayasinghe, and Jenna R. Pieper. 2015. "Perceived
Racial Discrimination and Its Correlates: A Meta-Analysis." *Journal of Organizational Behavior* 36: 491–513. doi.org/10.1002/job.198.

Triandis, Harry C. 2018. *Individualism and Collectivism*. Boulder, CO: Routledge.

Triplett, Kelli N., Richard G. Tedeschi, Arnie Cann, Lawrence G. Calhoun, and
Charlie L. Reeve. 2012. "Posttraumatic Growth, Meaning in Life, and Life Satisfaction in Response to Trauma." *Psychological Trauma: Theory, Research, Practice,
and Policy* 4, no. 4: 400–410. doi.org/10.1037/a0024204.

Turnbull, H. Rutherford, III, and Ann P. Turnbull. 1998. *Free Appropriate Public
Education: The Law and Children with Disabilities*, 5th ed. Denver: Love.

Turner, Dwight. 2018. "'You Shall Not Replace Us!': White Supremacy, Psychotherapy and Decolonisation." *Journal of Critical Psychology, Counselling and Psychotherapy* 18, no. 1 (March): 1–12.

Tyrka, Audrey R., Darcy E. Burgers, Noah S. Philip, Lawrence H. Price, and Linda L.
Carpenter. 2013. "The Neurobiological Correlates of Childhood Adversity and
Implications for Treatment." *Acta Psychiatrica Scandinavica* 128, no. 6: 434–47.
doi.org/10.1111/acps.12143.

U.S. Department of Health and Human Services (USDHHS). 2001. *Mental Health:
Culture, Race and Ethnicity: A Supplement to Mental Health: A Report of the Surgeon General*. Washington, DC: USDHHS.

Utsey, Shawn O. 1998. "Assessing the Stressful Effects of Racism: A Review of Instrumentation." *Journal of Black Psychology* 24, no. 3: 269–88. doi.org/10.1177/0095
79849802430001.

Utsey, Shawn O., Mark A. Bolden, and Andraé L. Brown. 2001. "Visions of Revolution from the Spirit of Frantz Fanon: A Psychology of Liberation for Counseling African Americans Confronting Societal Racism and Oppression." In
Handbook of Multicultural Counseling, 2nd ed., ed. Joseph G. Ponterotto,
J. Manuel Casas, Lisa A. Suzuki, and Charlene M. Alexander, 311–36. Thousand Oaks, CA: Sage.

Utsey, Shawn O., Mark A. Bolden, Yzette Lanier, Otis Williams III. 2007. "Examining the Role of Culture-Specific Coping as a Predictor of Resilient Outcomes in
African Americans from High Risk Urban Communities." *Journal of Black Psychology* 33, no. 1: 75–93. doi.org/10.1177/0095798406295094.

Utsey, Shawn O., Carol A. Gernat, and Mark A. Bolden. 2003. "Teaching Racial Identity Development and Racism Awareness." In *Handbook of Racial and Ethnic Minority Psychology*, ed. Guillermo Bernal, Joseph E. Trimble, A. Kathleen Burlew, and Frederick T. L. Long, *Racial and Ethnic Minority Psychology Series*, vol. 4, 147–166. Thousand Oaks, CA: Sage.

Utsey, Shawn O., Carol A. Gernat, and Lawrence Hammar. 2005. "Examining White Counselor Trainees' Reactions to Racial Issues in Counseling and Supervision Dyads." *Counseling Psychologist* 33, no. 4: 449–78. doi.org/10.1177/0011000 004269058.

Utsey, Shawn O., Norman Giesbrecht, Joshua Hook, and Pia M. Stanard. 2008. "Cultural, Sociofamilial, and Psychological Resources That Inhibit Psychological Distress in African Americans Exposed to Stressful Life Events and Race-Related Stress." *Journal of Counseling Psychology* 13, no. 1 (January): 49–62. doi:10.1037/0022 -0167.55.1.49.

Utsey, Shawn O., Joseph G. Ponterotto, Amy L. Reynolds, and Anthony A. Cancelli. 2000. "Racial Discrimination, Coping, Life Satisfaction, and Self-Esteem Among African Americans." *Journal of Counseling and Development* 78, no. 1: 72–80. doi .org/10.1002/j.1556-6676.2000.tb02562.x.

Valentino, Nicholas A., Fabian Guy Neuner, and L. Matthew Vandenbroek. 2018. "The Changing Norms of Racial Political Rhetoric and the End of Racial Priming." *Journal of Politics* 80, no. 3: 757–71. doi.org/10.1086/694845.

van de Schoot, Rens, Peter Lugtig, and Joop Hox. 2012. "A Checklist for Testing Measurement Invariance." *European Journal of Developmental Psychology* 9, no. 4: 486–92. doi.org/10.1080/17405629.2012.686740.

Van Der Kolk, Bessel A. 2007. "The Developmental Impact of Childhood Trauma." In *Understanding Trauma: Integrating Biological, Clinical, and Cultural Perspectives*, ed. Lawrence J. Kirmayer, Robert Lemelson, and Mark Barad, 224–41. New York: Cambridge University Press. doi.org/10.1017/CBO9780511500008.016.

——. 2017. "Developmental Trauma Disorder: Toward a Rational Diagnosis for Children with Complex Trauma Histories." *Psychiatric Annals* 35, no. 5: 401–408. doi.org/10.3928/00485713-20050501-06.

van der Sluis, Sophie, Conor V. Dolan, and Reinoud D. Stoel. 2005. "A Note on Testing Perfect Correlations in SEM." *Structural Equation Modeling* 12, no. 4: 551–77. doi.org/10.1207/s15328007sem1204_3.

Vandiver, Beverly J., Peony E. Fhagen-Smith, Kevin Cokley, William E. Cross, Jr., and Frank C. Worrell. 2001. "Cross's Nigrescence Model: From Theory to Scale to Theory." *Journal of Multicultural Counseling and Development* 29: 174–200.

Vartanian, Lenny R., Marlene B. Schwartz, and Kelly D. Brownell. 2007. "Effects of Soft Drink Consumption on Nutrition and Health: A Systematic Review and Meta-Analysis." *American Journal of Public Health* 97, no. 4: 667–75. doi.org /10.2105/AJPH.2005.083782.

Veit, Clairice T., and John E. Ware. 1983. "The Structure of Psychological Distress and Well-Being in General Populations." *Journal of Consulting and Clinical Psychology* 51, no. 5: 730–42. doi.org/10.1037/0022-006X.51.5.730.

Villatoro, Alice P., Vickie M. Mays, Ninez A. Ponce, and Carol S. Aneshensel. 2018. "Perceived Need for Mental Health Care: The Intersection of Race, Ethnicity, Gender, and Socioeconomic Status." *Society and Mental Health* 8, no. 1: 1–24. doi.org/10.1177/2156869317718889.

Vines, Anissa I., Julia B. Ward, Evette Cordoba, and Kristin Z. Black. 2017. "Perceived Racial/Ethnic Discrimination and Mental Health: A Review and Future Directions for Social Epidemiology." *Current Epidemiology Reports* 4, no. 2: 156–65. doi.org/10.1007/s40471-017-0106-z.

Wadsworth, Emma, Kamaldeep Dhillon, Christine Shaw, Kamaldeep Bhui, Stephen A. Stansfeld, and Andrew P. Smith. 2007. "Racial Discrimination, Ethnicity, and Work Stress." *Occupational Medicine* 57, no. 1: 18–24. doi.org/10.1093/occmed/kqi088.

Walker, Rheeda, David Francis, Gene Brody, Ronald Simons, Carolyn Cutrona, and Frederick Gibbons. 2017. "A Longitudinal Study of Racial Discrimination and Risk for Death Ideation in African American Youth." *Suicide and Life-Threatening Behavior* 47, no. 1: 86–102. doi.org/10.1111/sltb.12251.

Walker, Samuel, Cassia Spohn, and Miriam DeLone. 2012. *The Color of Justice: Race, Ethnicity, and Crime in America*. Boston: Cengage Learning.

Wallace, Barbara C., and Robert T. Carter, eds. 2003. *Understanding and Dealing with Violence: A Multicultural Approach*. Thousand Oaks, CA: Sage.

Walters, Karina L., and Jane M. Simoni. 2002. "Reconceptualizing Native Women's Health: An 'Indigenist' Stress-Coping Model." *American Journal of Public Health* 92, no. 4: 520–24. doi.org/10.2105/AJPH.92.4.520.

Washington, Harriet A. 2006. *Medical Apartheid: The Dark History of Medical Experimentation on Black Americans from Colonial Times to the Present*. New York: Doubleday.

Watters, Ethan. 2010. *Crazy like Us: The Globalization of the American Psyche*. New York: Free Press.

Watts, Roderick J. 1992. "Racial Identity and Preferences for Social Change Strategies Among African Americans." *Journal of Black Psychology* 18, no. 2: 1–18. doi.org/10.1177/00957984920182002.

Watts, Roderick J., and Robert T. Carter. 1991. "Psychological Aspects of Racism in Organizations." *Group and Organization Studies* 16: 328–44. doi.org/10.1177/105960119101600307.

Watts, Roderick J., M. A. Diemer, and A. M. Voight. 2011. "Critical Consciousness: Current Status and Future Directions." In *Youth Civic Development: Work at the Cutting Edge*, ed. C. A. Flanagan and B. D. Christens, 43–57. *New Directions for Child and Adolescent Development Series*, no. 134. New York: Wiley.

Watts, Roderick J., and Carlos P. Hipolito-Delgado. 2015. "Thinking Ourselves to Liberation? Advancing Sociopolitical Action in Critical Consciousness." *Urban Review* 47, no. 5: 847–67. doi.org/10.1007/s11256-015-0341-x.

Weathers, F. W. 1993. "Rational and Empirical Scoring Rules for the Clinician-Administered PTSD Scale." Unpublished manuscript.

Wei, Meifen, Alvin N. Alvarez, Tsun-Yao Ku, Daniel Wayne Russell, and Douglas G. Bonett. 2010. "Development and Validation of a Coping with Discrimination Scale: Factor Structure, Reliability, and Validity." *Journal of Counseling Psychology* 57, no. 3: 328. doi.org/10.1037/a0019969.

West, Lindsey M., Roxanne A. Donovan, and Lizbeth Roemer. 2010. "Coping with Racism: What Works and Doesn't Work for Black Women?" *Journal of Black Psychology* 36, no. 3: 331–49. doi.org/10.1177/0095798409353755.

Weston, Rebecca, and Paul A. Gore. 2006. "A Brief Guide to Structural Equation Modeling." *Counseling Psychologist* 34, no. 5: 719–51. doi.org/10.1177/001100 0006286345.

Whaley, Arthur L. 2001. "Cultural Mistrust: An Important Psychological Construct for Diagnosis and Treatment of African Americans." *Professional Psychology, Research, and Practice* 32, no. 6: 555–62.

Whaley, Arthur L., and King E. Davis. 2007. "Cultural Competence and Evidence-Based Practice in Mental Health Services: A Complementary Perspective." *American Psychologist* 62: 563–74. doi.org/10.1037/0003-066X.62.6.563.

Whitbeck, Les B., Gary W. Adams, Dan R. Hoyt, and Xiaojin Chen. 2004. "Conceptualizing and Measuring Historical Trauma Among American Indian People." *American Journal of Community Psychology* 33, no. 3–4: 119–30. doi.org/10.1023/B:AJCP.0000027000.77357.31.

Wilkerson, Isabel. 2015. "Our Racial Moment of Truth," *New York Times* (opinion), July 19. www.nytimes.com/2015/07/19/opinion/sunday/our-racial-moment-of-truth.html.

Williams, David R. 2018. "Stress and the Mental Health of Populations of Color: Advancing Our Understanding of Race-Related Stressors." *Journal of Health and Social Behavior* 59, no. 4: 466–85.

Williams, David R., Dolly A. John, Daphna Oyserman, John Sonnega, Selina A. Mohammed, and James S. Jackson. 2012. "Research on Discrimination and Health: An Exploratory Study of Unresolved Conceptual and Measurement Issues." *American Journal of Public Health* 102: 975–78. doi.org/10.2105/AJPH.2012 .300702.

Williams, David R., and Selina A. Mohammed. 2009. "Discrimination and Racial Disparities in Health: Evidence and Needed Research." *Journal of Behavioral Medicine* 32: 20–47. doi:10.1007/s10865-008-9185-0.

——. 2013. "Racism and Health I: Pathways and Scientific Evidence." *American Behavioral Scientist* 57, no. 8: 1152–73. doi:10.1177/0002764213487340.

Williams, David R., and Harold Neighbors. 2001. "Racism, Discrimination and Hypertension: Evidence and Needed Research." *Ethnicity and Disease* 11: 800–816.

Williams, David R., Harold W. Neighbors, and James S. Jackson. 2003. "Racial/Ethnic Discrimination and Health: Findings from Community Studies." *American Journal of Public Health* 93, no. 2: 200–208. doi.org/10.2105/AJPH.93.2.200.

Williams, David R., and Ruth Williams-Morris. 2000. "Racism and Mental Health: The African-American Experience." *Ethnicity and Health* 5, no. 3–4: 243–68.

Williams, David R., Yan Yu, James S. Jackson, and Norman B. Anderson. 1997. "Racial Differences in Physical and Mental Health: Socioeconomic Status, Stress and Discrimination." *Journal of Health Psychology* 2, no. 3: 335–51. doi .org/10.1177/135910539700200305.

Williams, Linda Faye. 2004. *Constraint of Race: Legacies of White Skin Privilege in America*. University Park: Pennsylvania State University Press.

Williams, Monnica T., Jonathan W. Kanter, and Terrence H. W. Ching. 2018. "Anxiety, Stress and Trauma Symptoms in African Americans: Negative Affectivity Does Not Explain the Relationship Between Microaggressions and Psychopathology." *Journal of Racial and Ethnic Health Disparities* 5, no. 5: 919–27.

Williams, Monnica T., Isha W. Metzger, Chris Leins, and Celenia DeLapp. 2018. "Assessing Racial Trauma Within a DSM-5 Framework: The UConn Racial/Ethnic Stress and Trauma Survey." *Practice Innovations* 3, no. 4: 242–60. doi.org/10 .1037/pri0000076.

Williams, Monnica T., Adriana Peña, and Judy Mier-Chairez. 2017. "Tools for Assessing Racism-Related Stress and Trauma Among Latinos." In *Toolkit for Counseling Spanish-Speaking Clients: Enhancing Behavioral Health Services*, ed. Lorraine T. Benuto, 71–95. Cham, Switz.: Springer.

Williams, Monnica T., Robert Joseph Taylor, Dawne M. Mouzon, Linda A. Oshin, Joseph A. Himle, and Linda M. Chatters. 2017. "Discrimination and Symptoms of Obsessive-Compulsive Disorder Among African Americans." *American Journal of Orthopsychiatry* 87, no. 6: 636–45. doi.org/10.1037/ort0000285.

Williamson, Vanessa, and Isabella Gelfand. 2019. "Trump and Racism: What Do the Data Say?" Brookings Institution. August 14. brookings.edu/blog/fixgov/2019 /08/14/trump-and-racism-what-do-the-data-say/.

Willis, Henry A., and Enrique W. Neblett. 2018. "OC Symptoms in African American Young Adults: The Associations Between Racial Discrimination, Racial Identity, and Obsessive-Compulsive Symptoms." *Journal of Obsessive-Compulsive and Related Disorders* 19: 105–15.

Willow, Rebecca A. 2008. "Lived Experience of Interracial Dialogue on Race: Proclivity to Participate." *Journal of Multicultural Counseling and Development* 36, no. 1: 40–51. dx.doi.org/10.1002/j.2161-1912.2008.tb00068.x.

Wilson, John P., and Terence Martin Keane. 2004. *Assessing Psychological Trauma and PTSD*, 2nd ed. New York: Guilford.

Wong, Y. Joel, Ellen L. Vaughan, and Elyssa M. Klann. 2017. "The Science and Practice of Prevention from Multicultural and Social Justice Perspectives." *Cambridge Handbook of International Prevention Science*, ed. Moshe Israelashvilli and John L. Romano, 107–32. New York: Cambridge University Press.

Woo, Bongki, Wen Fan, Thanh V. Tran, and David T. Takeuchi. 2019. "The Role of Racial/Ethnic Identity in the Association Between Racial Discrimination and Psychiatric Disorders: A Buffer or Exacerbator?" *SSM—Population Health* 7: 100378.

Worrell, Frank, C., William E. Cross Jr., and Beverly J. Vandiver. 2001. "Nigrescence Theory: Current Status and Challenges for the Future." *Journal of Multicultural Counseling and Development* 29: 201–13.

World Health Organization. 2014. "Mental Health: A State of Well-Being." www.who.int/features/factfiles/mental_health/en/.

World Health Organization, Maximizing Positive Synergies Collaborative Group. 2009. "An Assessment of Interactions Between Global Health Initiatives and Country Health Systems." *Lancet* 373, no. 9681: 2137–69. doi.org/10.1016/S0140-6736(09)60919-3.

Worthington, Roger L., and Tiffany A. Whittaker. 2006. "Scale Development Research: A Content Analysis and Recommendations for Best Practices." *Counseling Psychologist* 34, no. 6: 806–39. doi.org/10.1177/0011000006288127.

Yang, Tse-Chuan, and Danhong Chen. 2018. "A Multi-Group Path Analysis of the Relationship Between Perceived Racial Discrimination and Self-Rated Stress: How Does It Vary Across Racial/Ethnic Groups?" *Ethnicity and Health* 23, no. 3: 249–75.

Yeh, Christine J., and Carla D. Hunter. 2005. "The Socialization of Self: Understanding Shifting and Multiple Selves Across Cultures." In *Handbook of Racial-Cultural Psychology and Counseling*, vol. 1, *Theory and Research*, ed. Robert T. Carter, 78–93. New York: Wiley.

Yip, Tiffany. 2018. "Ethnic/Racial Identity—A Double-Edged Sword? Associations with Discrimination and Psychological Outcomes." *Current Directions in Psychological Science* (May). doi.org/10.1177/0963721417739348.

Yip, Tiffany, Gilbert C. Gee, and David T. Takeuchi. 2008. "Racial Discrimination and Psychological Distress: The Impact of Ethnic Identity and Age Among Immigrant and United States–Born Asian Adults." *Developmental Psychology* 44, no. 3: 787–800. doi.org/10.1037/0012-1649.44.3.787.

Yoo, Hyung Chol, and Richard M. Lee. 2008. "Does Ethnic Identity Buffer or Exacerbate the Effects of Frequent Racial Discrimination on Situational Well-Being of Asian Americans?" *Journal of Counseling Psychology* 55, no. 1: 63–75. doi.org/10.1037/1948-1985.S.1.70.

Youssef, Nagy A., Kimberly T. Green, Eric A. Dedert, Jeffrey S. Hertzberg, Patrick S. Calhoun, Michelle F. Dennis, Mid-Atlantic Mental Illness Research Education and Clinical Center Workgroup, and Jean C. Beckham. 2013. "Exploration of the Influence of Childhood Trauma, Combat Exposure, and the Resilience Construct on Depression and Suicidal Ideation Among U.S. Iraq/Afghanistan–Era Military Personnel and Veterans." *Archives of Suicide Research* 17, no. 2: 106–22. doi.org/10.1080/13811118.2013.776445.

Zapolski, Tamika C. B., Marcy R. Beutlich, Sycarah Fisher, and Jessica Barnes-Najor. 2019. "Collective Ethnic–Racial Identity and Health Outcomes Among African American Youth: Examination of Promotive and Protective Effects." *Cultural Diversity and Ethnic Minority Psychology* 25, no. 3: 388–96.

Zweigenhaft, Richard L. 2013. "Diversity Among CEOs and Corporate Directors: Has the Heyday Come and Gone?" Who Rules America? website. August 21. https://whorulesamerica.ucsc.edu/power/diversity_among_ceos.html.

INDEX

Note: page numbers followed by *t* refer to tables.

CPSIA information can be obtained
at www.ICGtesting.com
Printed in the USA
LVHW032119070821
694084LV00001B/3